THE WEB STARTUP
SUCCESS GUIDE

Bob Walsh

Apress®

The Web Startup Success Guide

Copyright © 2009 by Bob Walsh

ISBN-13 (pbk): 978-1-4302-1985-9

ISBN-13 (electronic): 978-1-4302-1986-6

Printed and bound in the United States of America 9 8 7 6 5 4 3 2 1

Lead Editor: Jonathan Hassell
Technical Reviewer: Thomas Rushton
Editorial Board: Clay Andres, Steve Anglin, Mark Beckner, Ewan Buckingham, Tony Campbell, Gary Cornell, Jonathan Gennick, Michelle Lowman, Matthew Moodie, Jeffrey Pepper, Frank Pohlmann, Ben Renow-Clarke, Dominic Shakeshaft, Matt Wade, Tom Welsh
Senior Project Manager: Sofia Marchant
Copy Editor: Elliot Simon
Associate Production Director: Kari Brooks-Copony
Senior Production Editor: Laura Cheu
Compositor: Susan Glinert Stevens
Proofreader: Greg Teague
Indexer: BIM Indexing & Proofreading Services
Artist: April Milne
Cover Designer: Kurt Krames
Manufacturing Director: Tom Debolski

Distributed to the book trade worldwide by Springer-Verlag New York, Inc., 233 Spring Street, 6th Floor, New York, NY 10013. Phone 1-800-SPRINGER, fax 201-348-4505, e-mail orders-ny@springer-sbm.com, or visit http://www.springeronline.com.

For information on translations, please contact Apress directly at 2855 Telegraph Avenue, Suite 600, Berkeley, CA 94705. Phone 510-549-5930, fax 510-549-5939, e-mail info@apress.com, or visit http://www.apress.com.

Apress and friends of ED books may be purchased in bulk for academic, corporate, or promotional use. eBook versions and licenses are also available for most titles. For more information, reference our Special Bulk Sales–eBook Licensing web page at http://www.apress.com/info/bulksales.

This one is for Sake, who for nearly 23 years was a very good boy.

Contents at a Glance

Contents

Foreword

Last summer, Paul Graham invited me to stop by his place in Cambridge, Massachusetts, for an intimate dinner. Just him, his wife, and the founders of three dozen extremely young startups in the Y Combinator program, a boot camp/incubator/angel investment thingy.

"Would you be willing to speak to these founders about, I don't know, maybe pricing?" Paul asked me.

"Sure!" I said, and he whistled loudly to get everyone to quiet down.

I didn't really have a speech prepared. There was no PowerPoint outline I could use as a crutch. The room was jam-packed. All eyes were on me. I didn't know what I was going to say.

I thought I'd try a gambit.

"So . . ." I said. "Any questions?" Ten hands shot up. "Go ahead," I said, pointing to a kid in the front row who, I imagine, had just gotten his braces off the week before.

And for almost two hours straight, these poor kids asked me the most basic questions imaginable about the business of startups. Pricing. Features. Marketing. Invoicing. They had so many questions.

I gave them as good a brain dump as I could on each topic. They sat raptly and asked intelligent follow-up questions.

These were smart kids, mind you: usually top computer science graduates and plenty of experienced programmers. But for all their coding skills, they didn't really know the first thing about making a business successful.

Which is OK. They'll learn. It's not that hard. The hardest part is realizing that even though you're making an Internet company, writing the code and getting it to work is only a small part of the effort, and not necessarily the most critical one. The business side is just as crucial.

There's a lot you're going to need to learn to make your startup awesome. And this book that you hold in your hands, this very book, is a splendid introduction to the topic. Heck, I've been running Fog Creek for nine years now; I think I know a thing or two about a thing or two, and I learned something new on every page.

Every single page.

Yes, even that page with the interview of me.

This book is a fantastic resource for anyone doing a web startup or a software startup. Bob Walsh will teach you how to make your startup successful. Buy it, read it, put it under your pillow. Then buy copies for your cofounders. And go out there and nail it with a killer startup that makes the world a better place.

Joel Spolsky
CEO, Fog Creek Software

About the Author

 My name is Bob Walsh (bob.walsh@47hats.com), and I believe that startups and microISVs (one-person software companies) represent the future of the global software industry and of the billion-person Internet to which we are all now connected. I believe this so strongly that this is my fifth book on the subject. My previous books are *Micro-ISV: From Vision to Reality* (Apress, 2006), *Clear Blogging* (Apress, 2007), *MicroISV Sites That Sell!* (ebook, 2008), and *The Twitter Survival Guide*, with Kristen Nicole (ebook, 2008).

In addition, I do a podcast with cohost Pat Foley (The Startup Success Podcast, at http://startuppodcast.wordpress.com) and write a blog (47 Hats, at http://47hats.com). I also comoderate Joel Spolsky's Business of Software forum (http://discuss.joelonsoftware.com/default.asp?biz).

My day job is consulting with startups and microISVs on how to increase their sales by better explaining their software on their web sites. But my real job since 2007 has been to recreate myself from a Windows desktop developer into a Rails web developer so that I can build and launch a faster way for startups to succeed: StartupToDo (http://startuptodo.com).

Before I got into all of the foregoing activities, I was a custom software developer for 20-plus years, and before that a reporter. I like what I'm doing now a lot more than either of those past careers!

About the Technical Reviewer

Thomas Rushton has been programming since he got his first computer, a Sinclair ZX80. He has progressed through creating complex workflow and document management systems for financial and legal organizations. He has a BSc in computer science from Durham University and spent some research time in the field of software quality before moving into the more financially rewarding IT career roles of programmer, DBA, and consultant. He will soon be putting some of Bob Walsh's techniques into practice by creating his own microISV.

When not slaving away over a hot keyboard, he enjoys spending time with his wife, Sarah, their young son, William, and his double bass.

Acknowledgments

Writing a book—especially the way I do it, which is to ask a lot of knowledgeable people a lot of pesky questions—means you have a lot of people to thank for making it possible.

First among equals has to be Joel Spolsky, who in 2005 helped open the door for me at Apress and who was kind enough to write the Foreword to this book and to give me a long interview.

Next I wish to thank Pam Slim, Lou Carbone, Dharmesh Shah, Eric Sink, David Allen, and Guy Kawasaki for sharing first with me and now with you their time, knowledge, and insight.

But wait, there's more! For all their help I also offer hearty thanks to the following: Neil Davidson, Don Dodge, Wally Wallington, Paul Tyma, Shawn Anderson, Shane Corellain, Corey Maass, Steve Grundell, Stephen Fewer, Simon Shutter, Cedrik Savarese, Rick Chapman, Dave Westwood, Pat Foley, Andrey Butov, Gavin Bowman, Eric Chu, Jeff Haynie, Peldi Guilizzoni, Scott Morrison, Gwen Hilyard, Richard White, Rob Walling, Gene Landy, Alvin Tse, especially Shaherose Charania, Joanne Yates, Brandon Zeuner, Rebecca Lynn, Jo Anne Miller, Cindy Padnos, Stephanie Hanbury-Brown, Mairtini Ni Dhomhnaill, Alain Raynaud, Amy Hoy, Dave Collins, Matthew Bleicher, Ian Landsman, Andy Wibbels, Mike Gunderloy, Marshall Kirkpatrick, Rafe Needleman, Al Harberg, Leslie Suzukamo, Luke Armour, Ginevra Whalen, Mat Johnston, Veronica Jorden, Maria Sipka, Aaron Patzer, Tony Wright, Matt Cornell, and Tim Haughton.

In addition, I'd like to thank Thomas Rushton for again doing a great job on technical review, Sofia Marchant for managing this project, Jonathan Hassell for prodding me when I needed prodding, Elliot Simon for copyediting my prose into something readable, and Laura Cheu for managing the book's production.

Finally, as always, I give deep thanks to Tina Marie Rossi for her support and love.

Introduction

All I was doing back in 2005 was looking for a book on Amazon, honest! I'd just finished writing MasterList Professional, a Windows personal task manager, of which I planned to sell a million copies so that I could retire forever from my contract programming job. Only one problem: I couldn't find a book on Amazon that explained how to sell those million copies. After 20+ years of dealing with clients and corporations, specs and custom apps, I knew zip about marketing, branding, positioning, software downloads, credit card processing, small business legalities, and the like. I needed that book. I didn't find it.

So I wrote *Micro-ISV: From Vision to Reality* (Apress, 2006). It did well. I started spending more and more time talking with the kind of people I liked, comoderating a forum on the business of software, conducting interviews for a podcast, and then working for actual money with startups and microISVs (self-funded startups). Then I wrote another book (on blogging), followed by two e-books, and then created a new podcast (this time my own, The Startup Success Podcast, with the able help of my cohost, Pat Foley).

I like startups. Startup founders have a dream, a passion, a desire to make something happen, not just to do what others have done. But by mid-2007 I had come to realize three things. First, there had to be a better way to bootstrap a software business than either to hire someone expensive like myself or to flail at it week after week. From this realization was born the idea of StartupToDo.

Second, I realized that to create StartupToDo I'd have to go from being a Windows desktop programmer to being a Ruby on Rails developer conversant in JavaScript, Linux server admin, CSS—all the things I'd avoided up until then. I thought it would take six months for this—ha! Two years later, and with the help of a lot of people, I'm just about to launch.

Third, I realized that MasterList Professional, though a great program, was never going to sell those million copies and no longer occupied center stage in my life. It was time to move on from it, from Windows, and from desktop programming.

Thus I wrote this book. *The Web Startup Success Guide* is kind of the *Kill Bill Vol. II* of what it takes to create a successful startup. I have written it for all those developers who are ready to step up and create more than just an alternative to programming for money for someone else. There's a whole other story now to be explored and told, one being written by tens of thousands of developers on the Web, on mobile and social platforms, even on desktops. Right now it's a story unfolding in front of a backdrop of global economic disruption, which paradoxically makes it a great time for startups—disruption creates opportunity, engenders new needs, and changes old ideas.

I think this book turned out very well, thanks to the several hundred people who were kind enough to answer my questions, correct my assumptions, and share their experience. I hope you learn as much reading it as I did writing it, and I look forward to hearing about your startup's successes in the days ahead.

Introduction: What Was Is Not What Is

Please Insert Chip into Brain

"Welcome to your startup," the small grey chip intones. "Before inserting this EasyBrain™ Start-Your-Own-Startup™ Module in the USB 5.0 or greater slot at the base of your skull, the manufacturer has instructed me to acquaint you with some of the safety features, key differentiators, and software requirements for your new 21st century startup."

We're not there yet, but in this chapter I would like to provide you with some much-needed *Future Shock*[1] treatment about realities and the (mostly online) world your startup is going to face. Understanding and exploiting the way things work now instead of getting caught up in how things used to work will make a huge difference in whether creating and growing your startup turns out to be the dream of your life or a very bad nightmare.

When I wrote *Micro-ISV: From Vision to Reality* in 2005, the big news was how to build a one- or two-person self-funded startup selling software directly to customers via the Internet. This new economic reality superseded the days of *shareware* and *donationware*. Google, sites such as Download.com, and shareware[2] payment processors meant you could sell desktop software directly to customers without spending millions of dollars

---

[1] *Throughout this book you're going to find veiled and unveiled references to futurist Alvin Toffler's books, starting with* Future Shock *(1970) through* Revolutionary Wealth *(2006) but especially* The Third Wave *(1980). Why? Because, in my opinion, Toffler has consistently done a better job than anyone else publishing at publically predicting what our society is going to look like. The better handle you have on the future, the better you'll be able to live and thrive there.*

[2] *Shareware: Pre-Google 20th century software revenue model for maverick desktop programmers. Relied on propagating trial, time-limited/crippled/nagging copies via pre-Web forums called BBSs and, later, portal sites such as* Tucows.com *and* Download.com. *If you liked the app, you bought it.*

to put cardboard boxes with diskettes or CDs on the shelves of computer stores such as CompUSA.

What's Changed Since Micro-iSV: From Vision to Reality

Some of you reading this book may have read my book *Micro-ISV: From Vision to Reality* (Apress 2006) and be wondering what's changed. It's not so much what's changed—just about every section and every link in my first book is still valid. It's just that there's now a whole new layer of opportunity, tools, and expectations that have taken off: Call it Web 2.0 (or 3.0). Or call it the Online World, as I do.

What's changed is that web-based software, including web-centric desktop, social, and mobile clients, have come into their own. The days of doing it Microsoft's way or the highway are long over; so too are the days you could copy David Heinemeier Hansson's 10-minute Rails demo, slap some Google AdWords on it, and sit back and count your money.

The old ways still work—to a lesser degree. But it's the new ways that startups can define, deliver, and market their Internet and community-centric value that are the New Big Thing and what this book explores. You don't believe me? Here are a few terms/apps that had not gained the importance they now have—or didn't exist—when I wrote my first book.

Adobe AIR	Microsoft Silverlight
Amazon Web Services	Salesforce.com
Apple iPhone	StackOverflow.com
Drupal	Twitter.com
Facebook	Wikipedia.org
Joomla	WordPress
Micro VC's	

As I said, things have changed in the software startup world—and those changes are what we're going to be covering in this book.

Well, CompUSA's hundreds of computer stores with boxed software on shelves are gone; and so too are the days of easy VC money for any four people with a business plan with the words *Web 2.0* or *social media* in it.

The New Online Economic Reality and Your Startup

Things in the world outside IT have changed as well, to put it mildly, as the global economy, currently officially in recession, lurches through financial crisis after crisis and the buying habits and attitudes of people and companies in the developed world are forced to change.[3]

We are not going to talk about a lot about the woes and tribulations of the Offline Economy in this book. First, as Neil Davidson rightly points out later in this chapter, there's not much you can do about it. Second, because if you focus on the things you can do something about, your odds improve.

If you're going to win this game called Build a Successful Startup, you are going to need to get deep into it: live it, breathe it, obsess about it, suck up every bit of knowledge that can help, Google every question you have.

That means knowing some history about the industry you plan to take by storm. I know, not as much fun as the latest Rails Envy[4] podcast, but this is stuff you need to know.

A Ridiculously Short History of Software Startups

For those of you who haven't been in the industry since day 1, here's a very short history of software startups, to provide some perspective on how we got to where we are. It's a story of how an industry that got started by accident, grew to change the world, and continues to evolve today.

In the beginning (pre-1976), software wasn't something that was sold. As small communities of computer scientists huddled around dumb terminals waiting for their punch cards to read and their paper tapes to spool, software was just another kind of information to be shared in the academic/scientific world. Software was sold—but as part of the package of services, documentation, and, most of all, hardware from IBM and a few other companies.

---

[3] *"A horrific holiday season for retailers. . . . Holiday sales fell from 2% to 4% compared to a year ago, according to SpendingPulse, a division of MasterCard Advisors. Excluding gas and car sales, they dropped between 5.5% and 8% from Nov. 1 through Dec. 24, as key categories from luxury to electronics posted double-digit declines. Sales of electronics and appliances fell almost 27%."—from "Bankruptcy looms for many retail stores" (AP, January 5, 2009). "Meanwhile, online, while sales were down for some vendors, 2008 was their best holiday season yet. Amazon lead the way with selling 6.3 million items in one day that were delivered to 210 countries"—from "Amazon.com's 14th Holiday Season Is Best Ever."*

[4] `http://www.railsenvy.com/`

The 1970s saw computers shrink from the size of rooms to the size of refrigerators to something you could put on a desk without breaking the desk, as electronic hobbyists (a kind of DIY person) assembled micro-computer kits and wrote their own software that they swapped in clubs while the established mainframe computer vendors clued into the idea of actually selling their software instead of giving it away.

These computer kits could have gone the way of Heathkit FM radio kits, except for one thing—with software, they could actually do things like calculate payroll taxes. Where was the software to come from? Although the real story is a lot messier, our story comes to a fork in the road. On the high road is Richard Stallman and others who believed that software should be free—free to modify, free to own, free to do what you want with. Call this the road that led to Open Source.

Then there was the other road—the people on the first road would call the low road. It started with an open letter from a pissed-off developer who discovered his software had been pirated. "Who can afford to do professional work for nothing? What hobbyist can put three man-years into programming, finding all bugs, documenting his product and distribute for free?" The pissed-off developer was 22-year-old Bill Gates, who was struggling to make his startup's Altair BASIC a paying proposition.

Yes, that Bill Gates. While some developers can do little but grind their teeth at software pirates, not Bill—his Albuquerque, New Mexico, startup got a better name, he moved back to his folks' house in Redmond, Washington, and, oh yes, built the software colossus known as Microsoft, with 90,000 employees and global annual revenue of $60.42 billion in 2008.

The 1980s, '90s, and through to June 27, 2008, when he finally quit his day job, was The Age of Bill, during which he took PCs from being hobby kits to running the world. It was the age first of DOS, then of Windows, Windows, Windows as Developers, Developers, Developers[5] created tens of thousands of startups selling software in computer stores.

The Age of Bill was also the Age of Steve—Steve Jobs, who built Apple from a startup selling 50 personal computer kits to a local store to a 32,000-employee, $32.48 billion sales corporation, the most admired company in 2008.[6] Steve's company was always the cooler, hipper, more with it of the two, which was okay with Bill, since his company owned more than 90% of the market, through to this day. But the ads[7] hurt (Figure 1.1).

---

[5] Steve Ballmer, Bill Gates' friend from Harvard before he dropped out and, more importantly, the hard-driving CEO of Microsoft, is famous for his "Developers! Developers! Developers!" chants at various Microsoft events. See http://www.youtube.com/watch?v=8To-6VIJZRE and http://www.youtube.com/watch?v=wvsboPUjrGc&feature=related

[6] Wikipedia's Apple article, original source Fortune magazine, http://money.cnn.com/galleries/2008/fortune/0802/gallery.mostadmired_top20.fortune/index.html

Figure 1-1. PC and Mac

Since this is a ridiculously short history, I'm leaving out a great deal, such as Steve Wozniak, the U.S. Department of Justice antitrust suit against Microsoft, various business practices, good and bad, by both companies, and a lot more. The main thing is that Bill and Steve built a world of stand-alone micro-computers that are found on desks throughout most of the world, and if you wanted to start your own software company, you were most likely going to write a Windows or Mac desktop application.

Then along came the Internet, the World Wide Web, and Marc Andreessen. Andreessen cowrote the first popular web browser, Mosaic, in 1993, while in college, and then hooked up with a Silicon Valley entrepreneur named Jim Clark to found the startup Netscape Communications to popularize the World Wide Web created by Tim Berners-Lee in 1989. Over the next six years the upstart Netscape battled Microsoft, ultimately losing. During this time, the Web went from a tiny plaything you could summarize on one Netscape What's New page to at least 63 billion pages and 1.4 billion people

---

[7] Apple's *Get a Mac* ad campaign was a hit from day 1 in 2006 because the ads captured so well the personalities of Windows (suit and tie, unhip) and Mac (casual clothes, laid back).

in 2008[8] selling and buying hundreds of billions of dollars worth of goods, services, and software in the United State alone.[9]

What Andreessen and Clark started in October 1994 culminated with the dot-com boom in the closing days of the last century. It was a time of initial public offerings, Internet millionaires racing down Silicon Valley's Highway 280, sock puppets dominating Super Bowl commercials, and dot-com startups blasting into the popular culture and onto the mainstream economy's center stage.

While all the media attention was on the Web 1.0 VC-funded Silicon Valley/Alley/Fen/Forest startups, a whole bunch of the little guys who wrote software and sold it themselves in Bill and Steve's world began to cut out the software distributors and retail stores and sell directly to people and companies. Shareware and donationware was growing up from its church rummage sale–like days of being sold in plastic baggies over electronic bulletin board systems. Now, one-person firms, such as Elfring Fonts in Chicago and Nova-Mind in Queensland, Australia, could connect with a global market online.

Then dot-com boom went bust. You'd come back Thursday to a South-of-Market San Francisco dot-com startup that Wednesday had had 30 people franticly running around, phones ringing everywhere, and walk into an office with no people, no power, no phones—just a mass of Herman Miller Aeron Chairs against a wall next to a stack of PCs and CRT monitors.

For startups and VCs the game of fund it, flip it, IPO it, and become an Internet bazillionaire ended in March 2000. According to one report, the dot-com crash wiped out $5 trillion in market value of technology companies between March 2000 and October 2002.[10] With a few notable exceptions—eBay, Amazon, Google—mainstream media wrote the obituary for startups large and small.

But as with a lot of newspaper stories—back in the day when newspapers weren't writing their own obituaries—there was more to this story. While talking heads on television intoned about The End of It All as the NASDAQ tanked, three things were happening: Google—specifically Google AdWords — was making it easier and easier for software companies to find customers. The cost of creating software, of creating a startup, were dropping as distributed companies (no big office to lease), virtualization (no huge server farms), and

---

[8] http://www.worldwidewebsize.com/ and http://www.internetworldstats.com/stats.htm.

[9] http://www.shop.org/c/journal_articles/view_article_content?groupId=1&articleId=702&version=1.0

[10] http://www.qctimes.com/articles/2006/07/17/news/business/doc44bb0a1ab97ce159604273.txt

better and better Open Source tools (no large licensing outlays) chopped the cost of doing software online down to well under one-tenth of what it had cost a few short years previously.

Third, and most of all, the Web grew and grew. And it continues to grow—and to change the world—to this day.

These small, self-funded startups finally got a name and a voice when Eric Sink, the founder of one such startup wrote *Exploring Micro-ISVs* back in September 2004. The reality that made it possible for single developers to create mostly desktop, mostly consumer-orientated software began to coalesce into a set of business practices and shared knowledge and attitudes. Forums such as Joel on Software's Business of Software, books, and blog posts spread this knowledge around the global developer community while the venture capitalists were licking their dot-com-bust wounds on Sand Hill Road in Palo Alto.

If there was one single event that signaled the start of the current era of software startups, I'd point to the founding of seed-stage funding firm and startup factory Y Combinator in 2005. Paul Graham, one of those Internet millionaires, convinced that the cost of successfully launching startups had dropped to the point that it was now more about ideas and support than multimillion-dollar private equity funding, launched Y Combinator—an ongoing series of three-month-long boot camps providing access to industry insiders and funding in the range of $5000 to $20,000—betting it could transform 20-something developers into software companies.

Y Combinator graduates were only a small sliver of the wave of startups that have shaken up the established order, but they are a representative sampling of what the current wave of startups are all about, as opposed to the software companies that came before them. They are about doing things online: everything from sharing documents to making payments, to networking with online friends, to all sorts of business activities that have to do with online content and online concerns.

The three most striking attributes that distinguish startups today—and something we get to play with for the rest of this book—are the "onlineness" of these startups, how little money compared to the past is needed to launch, and how many of these startups are focused on problems and opportunities that did not exist 24 months or 12 months or 6 months or sometimes only 1 month ago. For someone interested in building a startup, it's a great time to be doing so.

So, What's a Startup? And Why Would I Want to Be One?

Let's begin with what a startup is not: It's not a business that writes code for other companies, whether that's you as a consultant, a contract programmer, a freelancer, or a custom programmer. Nor is it a small IT consulting company that has a codebase—proprietary or Open Source—that it customizes extensively for each of its clients. Nor is it a department, division, or team spun out from a corporation and told to go act like a startup and build something cool.

For the purposes of this book, a startup comprises one to about eight people, mostly developers, who've banded together to create a codebase whose benefits they will offer to the world, especially the online world. That codebase often can be accessed via the Web, but it can also become an executable on a Windows PC or Mac, run when downloaded to a game console such as Microsoft Xbox or live in a smartphone such as an Apple iPhone.

They may initially be entirely self-funded, but they're more than likely at some point early on to seek funding from either family and friends or angel investors or venture capitalists or a progression of all three. The distinction between startups and microISVs—given as much distinction as there is—revolves around funding and size. A sole developer funding the building of their software and company? That's a microISV. Three developers and a web designer who raise $200,000 to build a web app from family, friends, and an angel investor network? That's definitely a startup.

So why leave the relatively safe harbors of corporate life or consulting to venture into the global market and launch a startup? Specific motivations are as varied as the people who have them—and people in the startup world tend to be anything but homogeneous.

A startup can be about making money—and we will be focusing on that part of building a successful startup a great deal in this book—but not always so. Given how low the costs of web apps have fallen in recent years, you may decide that making money is not one of the reasons you want to build a startup. You might be motivated by simple love of coding and a desire to share something you built with others who may have the same problem you've solved.

But if I had to guess your motivation, I'd bet that the chance to make some serious, life-changing money was at the top of the list, with a close second the keen desire not to be told what to do and how to do by people who couldn't code/design their way out of a paper bag.

Good for you! That's where I'm coming from and what motivates to a lesser or greater degree nearly all of the people in this industry since it became an industry. And while some may sniff that money can't buy you happiness, not having money guarantees you unhappiness.

Now comes the first key question in this book: What kind of startup makes sense for you?

Startup Flavors—Take Your Pick

Before you decide, here's a quick rundown of what I see as the five kinds of startups that exist today.

Traditional

Directions: This tried-and-true kind of startup has been around since Silicon Valley was more orchards than office buildings. Take one serial entrepreneur/CEO, a mix of seasoned executives, and a few über-programmer gurus, sprinkle well with connections to VCs inside and out of the Valley, add $8 million in Series A VC funding. Hire a PR firm to get you mentioned in *TechCrunch*, coders (preferably offshore) to do most of the actual coding, and a customer-focus consulting company to tell you what your customers want. Preferably place everything in an office building in Palo Alto, Mountain View, or Sunnyvale, and bake. Do not worry about revenue or profit for the first few months, sometimes years, after you launch. Change the world, get bought, go public, or disappear without a trace in 18 months.

Key ingredients: An entrepreneur CEO who's done this before (hopefully successfully), a team of respected industry executives that can actually execute the mad visions of the CEO, and, most of all, VC money and lots of it.

Pros: This is more or less how every major player in this game got built—eBay, Amazon, PayPal, Google, YouTube, Skype—to name a few wildly successful examples.

Cons: This is also the model that AltaVista, Boo.com,[11] Freeinternet. com, Inktomi, and others used. Where are those companies now? Acquired for pennies on the dollar or simply gone.

Bottom line: Worked then, works now—if you're the right person (and if you are, you probably don't need to read this book). The VC-centric startup was the only way to go during the 1980s and '90s. Fortunately, we now have alternatives.

MicroISV

Directions: Take one or perhaps two experienced developers tired of working for somebody else, an unmet business or more likely consumer need, and add nights, weekends, and missed family events as you struggle to bootstrap your business while consulting or holding down a day job. Don't add outside funding. Most likely you'll deploy to Windows, Mac, or, now, the iPhone.

Key ingredients: Solid technical expertise with some basic graphic skills so that people won't point and laugh when your web site launches. Be prepared to wear many hats in your business—developer, sysadmin, marketing VP, blogger, salesman, you name it.

Pros: You can build a microISV that makes, say, three to five times as much as you can make programming for someone else. You might even be able to sell it or, if you work very, very hard, grow to be a very successful software vendor, for example, Joel Spolsky and Michael Pryor of Fog Creek Software.[12]

Cons: Bootstrapping—building your MicroISV while making a living doing something else is damned hard—too hard for most sane people. If you picked the right idea, if you can execute it, if you can then change from Doctor Programmer into Mister Marketer, if you work at your marketing day in and day out, if you keep improving your application and answer 5,000 e-mails from customers who want to ask you just one 500-word question, you may be successful. But the lack of capital,

---

[11] Boo.com went through $188 million in just six months before going bust in May 2000 attempting to build a global online fashion store. That takes style! http://query.nytimes.com/gst/fullpage.html?res=9F05E4DB103CF931A35755C0A9669C8B63

[12] http://www.fogcreek.com/About.html

the to-do list that never gets smaller, and, frankly, the loneliness may trap you in a situation where you're putting in 60-hour weeks and making about what you did working for somebody else—or less.

Bottom line: I was a microISV, bootstrapping MasterList Professional into existence, only to realize that I knew squat about everything else I had to do and that I had to write a book to learn all of that non-developer stuff.[13] Late in 2008 I sold my microISV to a sharp developer who wanted to become a microISV and I launched a web app, StartupToDo, that I hope will attract angel funding and the right partners to be a full-fledged startup.

If you check the blogs, forums such Joel on Software's Business of Software, and the Association of Shareware Professionals or attend conferences such as the Software Industry Conference in the United States or the European Software Conference, you'll find microISVs that are living the dream of successful self-employment. If you look closer, you'll find companies, such as Fog Creek Software, Brisworks, and IDV Solutions, who've successfully grown out of the microISV stage and now employee dozens, sometimes hundreds, of people. It's not easy, it's not for everyone, but it can work.

Side Project

Directions: Start with a small but persistent pain. It could be a gap between you and some existing program or web app, a feature no one seems to realize is needed, or just a desire to see what you can code. Add a programmer with some spare time but not a desire (or at least the skill sets needed) to make his or her side project a full-fledged startup.

Key ingredients: Build out the tool, library, or site, stick it up on a server, let people use it, move on.

Pros: Side projects are great résumé builders, differentiating you from other programmers and developers who haven't something cool they can show off. They can also be the starting point for any one of the other kinds of startups. Think of it as a proto-startup.

---

[13] *Trust me: you don't write a book unless circumstances or inner demons hold burning coals to the soles of your feet.*

Take, for example, Blog Action Day (http://blogactionday.org/), started by Australian web designer Collis Ta'eed in 2007 as a way of focusing bloggers worldwide on one important topic on a given day. On October 15, 2008, *12,800* bloggers—17 of the top 100 blogs—posted about poverty—with an estimated readership of 13.4 million people. "Blog Action Day is organised as a non-profit activity by a group of volunteer bloggers and the staff of Envato who donate their time and resources. It started as a 'what would happen if' question and simply took on a life of its own."

Cons: Not many. The price of a decent VPS—virtual private server—is heading south day by day, and one such server can host as many side projects as you have bandwidth and time for. But is your side project truly a side project, or is it a startup missing most of the pieces—usually those marketing, branding, nontechnical pieces?

Bottom line: Side projects are a great way to build your programming reputation, make new toys to play with, and get your feet wet in all those other things you have to do to put something out that people can actually use, besides looking good on the résumé. What's missing is both the pain of having to do right all the things you don't naturally like to do and the reward (money) that comes when you align all the pieces so that people are prepared to buy what you've created.

Open Source Project

Directions: Start as the last gasp of a software company beaten into the ground by a rival, or as a business looking to make money around instead of with a core product, or as a part-time contractor working for Chicago-based web design house who unlocks the power of an obscure Japanese programming language, or as someone who has solved a problem and wants to give back to the community of programmers who helped his or her: Open Source projects—software platforms, languages, applications, and libraries with freely available and modifiable source code—have remade the software business.

The first three examples just mentioned—Mozilla Foundation and Firefox, MySQL AB (later Sun Microsystems and now Oracle) and MySQL, and David Heinemeier Hansson and Ruby on Rails—are just the beginning of a long list of Open Source projects that have profoundly influenced software development and the values of many software developers.

Key ingredients: Rock star programmers, dozens, sometimes hundreds, of other highly skilled programmers with commit rights and, most of all, needs not being met adequately by proprietary software.

Pros: Open Source projects in an Online World where costs have plummeted to predominantly the development time can make commercial sense. MySQL AB sold to Sun for about $1 billion. And some Open Source projects, such as ExtJS (http://extjs.com), can become the starting point for successful commercial startups.

Cons: Like side projects, for every Firefox there are 5,000 Open Source projects that never ignite the imagination of enough programmers to matter much. Although many, if not most, startups use Open Source to write their code, run their servers, serve their apps, or all three, an Open Source startup is a rare bird in the wild.

Bottom line: New software companies who have at their core an Open Source project are rare, but their numbers are growing. The underlying tension between "Software should be Free!" and "We Want to Make Money!" is hard to reconcile in the pressure cooker of starting a new business as well. The most likely path of success is to build a great Open Source project, and the money will come—something most funding sources have a hard time buying.

Modern Online Software Startup

Directions: You and one to three people you know, like, and trust want to build a profitable software business on the Web. The application will most likely be a web app, but it could also be for the Apple iPhone, some other mobile device, or even a desktop app. You've not done this before, and you've never (successfully) asked your family or friends to put tens of thousands of dollars into one of your ideas, let alone hundreds of thousands of dollars from strangers.

Key ingredients: A really good original idea of how to meet a need that a lot of people have (whether they know it now is secondary), a solid, innovative, easy-to-use application that solves that need attractively and robustly (notice that I put *attractively* first), a clear and compelling unique selling proposition that you position in the marketplace via social media and standard marketing, a strong willingness and ability to learn the pieces of this particular puzzle that you don't know and may not care about, and a really stupendous amount of hard work.

Pros: The cost of software development and deployment have never been lower. The same is true for the cost of connecting to and getting sales from your market.

Meanwhile, in the offline economy, buffeted as it is by recession, globalization, and change, there has not been so much demand for new ideas and new ways of solving problems since the end of World War II. And in the online economy, which has in the last few years thrown off its dependence on the offline economy, the demand for solutions to problems and needs that didn't exist years or even months ago grows at Internet speed.

Cons: The odds are, at best, problematical (although hopefully reading this book will move them in your favor!). You could fail—spectacularly— and everyone from your parents, from whom you borrowed money, to your ex-coworkers to the modern-day gossip columnist known as *ValleyWag*[14] will let you know that you failed.

Bottom line: You wouldn't be reading this book if a major part of you didn't want to go for it and build your own startup. It will not be easy, but if you work your strengths, understand and compensate for your weaknesses, and keep moving toward the day your startup becomes a reality, it will become a reality.

When Is the Right Time to Jump?

Finally, here's one question you might be asking yourself: Is this the right time to launch a startup? There's no simple, binary answer to this. But I do think that, at least from 2009 to 2014, the answer to the opposite question—Is this the wrong time to launch a startup?—is a resounding no.

Here's the short version of why: the only sure bet you can make about this period is that economic disruption and ever-accelerating change are the rule of the day.

For a longer, more detailed answer, I called on two people who know a lot about this IT world, Neil Davidson, who runs a hundred-plus-person software company in the U.K., and Don Dodge, who seeks out startups for Microsoft to acquire to get their opinions.

---

[14] http://valleywag.com/

Neil Davidson, Business of Software Conference

Figure 1-2. Neil Davidson, Co-CEO of Red Gate Software

From starting Cambridge-based Red Gate Software in 1999, Neil Davidson (Figure 1-2) and Simon Galbraith have grown it into a 135-person company, ranked by *The Times of London* as 39th of the best 100 companies to work for in the entire United Kingdom in 2008. In addition to co-running Red Gate, Neil has teamed up with Joel Spolsky of Fog Creek Software to produce the annual Business of Software Conference, a gathering of both startups and established companies.

We'll get into the details of the Business of Software Conference in Chapter 4, but for now I wanted to tap Neil's experience and insight as to whether now is the right time to launch a startup.

Bob: We all devoutly hope this year is not going to be as bad as the last year. What do you see as the future for startups?

Neil: I think the future is pretty good for startups. I'm not sure I'd go as far as saying it's better than ever, however. I don't think the outlook in 2009 is significantly different from the outlook of 2008 or the outlook in 2007.

And the reason I said that is because I've looked into this in some detail and I've talked to quite a few professors about this. That factors that determine whether a startup succeeds or fails can broadly be split into two categories. They've got what they call of the *exogenous* factors and the *endogenous* factors, which is kind of a posh way of saying factors out of your control.

So, whether the startup succeeds or fails depends in part on the economy and depends in part on the industry that you're in. So, if you pick a dumb industry or a really dumb market niche to be in, then it's going to be hard for you to succeed.

But the other stuff, which is really important, is the internal stuff. So, it's things like motivation. So, if you are a microISV, for example, one of the key factors to determine the success of the business is how dedicated you are to your startup. So, how much time you put into it and how much effort you put into it. And if you don't put in that time, you just can't do it. I mean there's no way you can build a successful business if you're doing something else as a full-time job.

It's something you should put your heart into. It's something you going to work all day. And then you're going to go home and then you get to work another four hours. And then when you sleep, you're going to think about it a lot. And that's not something that you can do if you're not into something full time.

The other internal factor is do you really care about your product? Are you doing this product to get rich, or you're doing this product because you really, really care about what you do? This is a product that you should care so much about that you'll work incredible hours and put incredible energy in it to make it a success. Or is it a product that you're sort of doing because you think it's a cool way to make some money?

And although there are external factors like the economy and the industry and you can't affect those, and that fact is pretty core to them. The internal factors are still the same. So, whether you do your startup in 2010 or whether you did it in 2009, there's still a whole bunch of stuff that is really important, and that's not going to change.

Bob: So, really, what you're saying is the key factors to a startup's success are the internal factors that you can control mainly, your level of dedication, commitment, perseverance, and probably, most of all, work.

Neil: Yes.

Bob: And that's what really matters. The external factors are going to be the external factors, but it's those internal factors that you need to think about and do what you can to improve. Hence a good reason to go to places like the Business Software Conference.

Neil: [Laughter] Exactly! Of course, the execution is about is about the plan. So, if you pick a market that's crap or you can pick an industry that's going down it's not going to help. That's going to be the case whether in 2009 or 2008.

So, if you pick a product that isn't going to have a market, that's probably not going to have a market in either year. Obviously you don't sell a product which depends on the banking industry to succeed because that's just going to take a lot of luck.

2009 and on are going to be interesting because there's a lot of change happening, so a lot of things are changing. When stuff changes, then the status quo gets disrupted. And when the status quo gets disrupted, then there are opportunities to do things.

The other example is: When do you think it's a better time to start a startup, at the peak of a bubble or the trough of the bust? So, if you had started up a company in 2000, for example, or at the end of 1999, you pretty much had more of a chance of failing, even though that was in the kind of a peak in the middle of the bubble. But if you start a company at the trough of the bust, you pretty much have more of a chance of succeeding.

If you were setting up a company in 2000, for example, you'd probably set up a company that would do something like deliver coffee beans online, sort of do pet food online or deliver books online or whatever and you live on hope. So, the whole industry will pop. And all these venture capitalists wanted their money back and banks called their loans and it went pop.

So, you'd have a high chance of failure. But if you set up that company in 2009, for start you're not going to do a stupid idea, which has a low chance of success in a recession, because you're just not going to be that stupid. If you're going to be that stupid, then you're not going to get money for a start. So, if the quality of the ideas that you have or the quality of the ideas that are going to fly are going to be better in a recession or at the beginning of the recession, they are going to be during a boom. That's what I think, anyway.

Does that make sense or not?

Bob: I think it does. Think of it as evolution in action. If you can survive the harsh economic climates that we're looking at right now, well, everything from there goes up.
Neil: Yes.
Bob: Okay, one last question. Any advice that you would give to a developer who is thinking about getting a couple of his mates together to form a startup today?
Neil: I'd say, think about it a lot and plan it and save up the money and then just kind of do it, because it's one of the things you kind of theorize a lot, but until you actually do it, you're never going to know if it works or not.

Don Dodge, Director, Business Development at Microsoft

Figure 1-3. Don Dodge, Director of Business Development for Microsoft's Emerging Business Team

Don Dodge (Figure 1-3) is a veteran of five startups, including Forte Software, AltaVista, Napster, Bowstreet, and Groove Networks. Don is currently Director of Business Development for Microsoft's Emerging Business Team, which means his day job consists of finding startups Microsoft should either acquire, invest in, or help connect to a VC.

Bob: So, let's start with maybe just a little bit of bio. How did you end up working for Microsoft, and what have you done with your life?

Don: Well, I have been a startup guy. I did five startups. Some of them you'll know and some of them are obscure tools and database companies. But the first one was Forte Software. That was back in the late '80s, early '90s. And the company went public in the early '90s and was acquired by Sun Microsystems soon thereafter. The next one was AltaVista.

Bob: Oh, yeah.

Don: I was the director of engineering at AltaVista, and of course we were the first search engine on the Web and I started out doing that. And then later I put together a group that developed the first multimedia search, searching for pictures and video and music, which seems pretty simple now, but 10 or 12 years ago it was impossible. So, it was kind of a new thing. And after that, I joined this tiny little startup with six or eight people called Napster, which of course everybody knows about now, but at that time it was a tiny little company that nobody knew about, and that was to bring music sharing and file sharing to the Web.

And after Napster, I did another startup called Bowstreet, which was a web services application development company and back when web services was a very new thing. So, that is one of the first application servers and tools to build web service–based applications.

And the last one was Grove Networks. Grove Networks was a peer-to-peer collaboration company, and Ray Ozzie was the founder and leader of that company. And since then Microsoft acquired Grove Networks and Ray Ozzie took over for Bill Gates. I am working at Microsoft helping startups and building partnerships with Microsoft. So, there it is, 20 years.

Bob: There you go. Now, here is a question for you: What's changed and what hasn't in those 20 years between then and now?

Don: Wow, a lot! For one thing, it is much easier to start a company now than it ever has been. The first startup I did, Forte Software, we raised $32 million, and that was considered a gigantic amount of money to start a company, a software company, back then. Going forward from there, I worked at two startups that raised $150 million of venture capital to do a software startup. So, it was just incredibly expensive to start a company. Today, with web services and cloud infrastructure and free development tools, just everything is easier, less expensive, so it is just so much easier to start a company now than it ever was before.

Bob: That's one that's a big change. How about something that has stayed constant?

Don: Well, the constant I think is that, yes, it is easier to start a company today, but it still takes a lot of time and money to scale it to millions and millions of customers. So, that has stayed the same, and that is why venture capital is still a vital component of building a large company. Yes, you can start a company for almost nothing and you can get it out to the market with the Web and you can target initial users and get some traction, but if you really want to take it to the next level where you have millions and millions of users and tens of millions of dollars in revenue, it takes money to do that.

The second thing is, because it is so easy to start a company today, there are thousands and thousands of them. And the challenge is to rise above the noise and to get noticed. There are a variety of approaches you can take to do that. Some of them are free, some of them cost money, but you still have to do it.

And in some ways, it is more difficult now to be noticed just because there are so many companies out there, where in the past, the hurdle, the amount of money needed to rise and the hurdles to starting a business were larger, so there were a fewer of them.

Bob: So less money, but more noise.

Don: Exactly.

Bob: Let's talk about now and, since I am writing a book here rather than a blog, now sort of 2009, 2010, 2011: What do you see as the outlook for—I guess I will ask it two ways, startups and startups getting money from venture capital?

Don: Right. As I said earlier, it has never been easier to start a company. And in some ways, during a downturn or a recession like we are in now, it is almost easier to start a company, for several reasons. First one is, the key to starting a successful company is finding great people to work with you. And in the boom times, when everything is going great and companies are growing and new projects are being built, all the good people are busy. They are working on fun projects, and it is very difficult for a startup to lure them away from what they are doing to take on a risky startup in the boom times.

In the bad times, people are laid off, exciting new projects are cancelled, companies retrench and focus on the core competencies, so some of the exciting stuff isn't getting done. So, in these times it is easier to recruit great people to come work on the next big thing. So, that is the advantage of starting a company in difficult times. That's one. Another is that in tough times like these, only the good companies get funded. So, in some respects, it is easier to get funding because you are not competing with hundreds and hundreds of marginal ideas that would have been funded in the good days but that won't get funding in difficult times. So, if you have a really great idea that's got some initial traction, you are able to get it off the ground and get some initial traction; in some ways it is easier to get funding for that type of company today than it was four or five years ago.

Bob: Let's turn to Microsoft for a moment here. Let's start with, what does Microsoft think of all these web-app startups that are flourishing all over the place?

Don: Well, Microsoft loves startups. As you know, my job at Microsoft is working with startups and helping them get started, making introductions, introducing them to angels and venture capitalists, introducing them to people at Microsoft, getting them software, that sort of thing. We have a great new program called BizSpark.

Bob: I actually know it well, and the reason I know it well is that I am the number 1 BizSpark Partner in the world as of about a week ago.

Don: You are right, 47 Hats. I saw a report that said 47 Hats and saw all the startups that you signed up, I mean, Wow, who is this guy? You are number 1.

Bob: BizSpark is a very cool program. I mean, it does completely level the financial playing field between Microsoft, which is proprietary, and Open Source, which isn't. But that's a part of the component, that's a part of the equation. It used to be that the plan for a lot of startups was to get bought by GYM: Google, Yahoo, Microsoft. Well, that doesn't seem to be happening as much anymore. Does Microsoft still look at startups as sort of their—not to be nasty about it—but as sort of their outsourced R&D?

Don: I don't know if I'd put it that way, but we certainly look at startups as a source of innovation and disruptive ideas and leading-edge technology, for sure. Microsoft has acquired on average about 20 companies a year, and we have been acquiring 20 companies a year for the past five years. Yahoo and Google to a lesser extent, but they acquire 10 to 15 companies a year too. But, put them all together, Google, Yahoo, and Microsoft are acquiring maybe 50 companies a year. So, it never was . . . If you are putting all your eggs in that basket, it's a small basket.

Bob: It is a really small basket.

Don: Yeah. Well, about 5,000 startups start every year. So, out of those 5,000, if 50 of them are going to be acquired by Google, Yahoo, or Microsoft, that is pretty slim odds. So, I wouldn't be starting a company in order to flip it to one of the big guys. It happens, but I certainly wouldn't have that as my sole exit opportunity.

Bob: Well, it used to be the exit opportunity of choice was the IPO, and that sort of went out of style around March 2000 when the dot-com boom turned into a bust. And then it was the idea of, well, let's get acquired by GYM or other people. But GYM was always the crown jewels of acquisition. So, what is the early exit, or is there an early exit? You may start up a company, but you may plan to be there for a while.

Don: Well, the reality is that M&A has been the exit opportunity of choice for the past five years and that there have been thousands of companies acquired over the past five years. But they are acquired by some of the lesser-known names, still very good exits and good business. So, you need to look beyond just the high-profile acquisitions that you read about in *TechCrunch* or other places. There are lots of great business opportunities with smaller companies and acquisitions in that space. But I think, coupled with the idea that it takes a lot less money to start a company today, that also means that your exits can be much smaller and still be very, very lucrative. So, in the old days, when it cost $30 million or $50 million to start a company, you needed an exit of $300 million to $500 million for the VCs to make their money and the startup founders to make their money.

But, if today you are starting a company and you can bootstrap it and maybe bring in a few friends and family for couple hundred thousand dollars, if you have an exit for couple million dollars or $10 million, that's a tremendous exit. You are making really good money. So, it doesn't have to be a huge acquisition by one of the big guys to be a successful story.

Bob: So, it costs less to start and looks a lot less like winning the lottery?
Don: Right.
Bob: Okay.
Don: And I think, again, the point is start a company for as little money as possible, bootstrap it if you can, get to revenue as quickly as possible, get to cash flow break-even. And as Paul Graham says, once you are on a cash flow breakeven basis, you have infinite runway, infinite amounts of money because you can go forever. You don't need to worry about raising the next round of cash because you are cash flow positive. And from there, you can just grow organically and grow as your cash flow allows and grow a very nice business. And at some point, it might make sense to sell it, but you have options, because you are cash flow positive.
Bob: That makes sense.
Don: I think that is the key. Get your product or service on the market as quickly as possible, start collecting revenue as quickly as possible, keep your expenses low, and get the cash flow breakeven, and then you are home free.
Bob: Let's turn for a second to the private equity world and, if you can, put on your—or get in front of your crystal ball here for a bit. What do you think is happening, because I keep noticing this term *micro-VC* popping up. That is part 1. And part 2, what are these people looking for, given that we are in a global recession?
Don: Well, that's a big question, lots of things going on there. The first thing I'd say is that most venture capitalists are funding the companies that they already have. So, they are reserving more money to put into their existing investments, whereas when they made their initial investment, they thought that they would only have to put in maybe two times their initial investment and then be out of it in five to seven years.

Now they are thinking, they are going to have to put in three or four times their initial investment and going to have to carry the company for seven to ten years. So, they are focused on making sure that their existing investments have enough capital and enough runway to make it. That's their first priority.

Bob: Okay.

Don: And then if there is money left over, then they are looking at new ideas, but the bar for investing in new ideas is pretty high. They aren't making investments in the marginal ideas anymore; it is just the really, really good ones.

Bob: Let's turn back to Microsoft for a second. You mentioned that one of the things you do is you connect VCs and angel investors to startups that you work with. Why do you do that? I mean, it seems counterintuitive that you would find funding for other software companies.

Don: No, our goal is to encourage startups to build their applications on the Microsoft platforms, on Windows or SQL Server or SharePoint or Dynamics or Office or any of the many platforms that we have. Because we know that the value of our products, our platforms, is enhanced by the number of companies building applications on top of them. So, that is job 1. It is to help startups and companies build great applications on top of our platforms. So, we do a variety of things. We have partner programs and consulting programs and all kinds of things to help startups build their applications.

Bob: Which we will be covering in the book in detail. When you say as job 1, that doesn't leave much room for equivocation. Does Microsoft really want a whole lot of startups competing with it?

Don: Well, we don't view it as competition. Microsoft is a platform company, Windows is a platform, SQL Server, SharePoint, Office, Dynamics, all these platforms. And Microsoft, by and large, doesn't get into building end user applications, with rare exceptions. So, we view startups that are building applications as partners who are helping to add value to our platform. So we don't view them as competitors; we view them as partners. And we want as many of them as possible. So, that's job 1. Get partners using our development tools and our platforms to build their applications, and then provide programs for them to help them do that. Now, the other side of it and the side where I spend a lot of my time is with venture capitalists and angels. And you might ask, well, why do we do that?

Bob: OK. Why do you do that?

Don: Well, because they are the source, the funding source for all these great startups. And I get out there and see as many of them as I can. But the fact is there are hundreds and hundreds of venture capitalists and angel investors out there who are seeing more startups than I am. So, I want to help them in any way I can and open a dialog with them, so that they tell me about the great startups that they are seeing and that might be adding value to Microsoft. So then I can switch into business development mode, go see those startups and help them out, form partnerships and help them in any way we can.

So, it is a symbiotic relationship between Microsoft and the VCs. They tell us about the great companies that they have. They tell us about companies they think we ought to acquire. Microsoft acquires some of those companies, but we also are out there seeing great startups that are looking for funding. And VCs want to know about those, so we will tell the VCs about some startups that we have seen that are doing interesting things, that we like a lot, and refer them to them for funding. So, it works both ways.

Bob: This sounds an awful lot like hard work rather than marketing hype to me. And I just want to say that everything I have seen in the years that I have known you as we have gone through a couple of books and podcasts and few other things, I keep saying over and over again that Microsoft is absolutely serious about helping startups succeed. And they really would like to do it on their platform, which is understandable from where they are coming from. But that is not the only criterion that seems to be in play. It comes down to the more startups, the more the industry as a whole succeeds.

Don: Absolutely. Yeah, we are serious about this. When you look at Dan Levin's emerging business team, they are about a dozen of us and all of us came from startups. So, we are startup people. That's our nature. We love to work with startups and help them. And it is just important to Microsoft to have as many startups as possible out there, pushing the envelope, doing disruptive things. We also work with startups, by the way, that compete with us and that are doing really disruptive, innovative things, because we need to pay attention to those sorts of trends and innovations and make sure that we know what is going on, what is going to be hot and make sure that we are able to work with them. So, it is a full-time job and we are serious about it. And it is not a six-months program or a year program; we are in it for the long term.

Recap

As we've discussed in this chapter, startups have been around for a good 40 years. But while what worked for people in the last century may kind of work today, the underlying economic realities are different. We will be digging into these fundamental differences in detail throughout this book, but let me preview for you the five I think are most important.

- Startup costs to get to your first sale are now often self-fundable.

- The roles and strategies of equity funding sources have evolved, and you need to know what door to knock on if your startup requires major capital.

- Social media are rewriting the "We push, you listen" marketing contract. The new rules are to be remarkable, to talk with, not at, customers, and to keep a close eye on what is going on in the social world that can affect your company's reputation and standing.

- The startup culture of Silicon Valley has picked up and gone both global and online.

- And, most of all, now is a great time to jump in and launch your startup.

Value Is the Core of Your Startup

> *"The only difference between a problem and a solution*
> *is that people understand the solution."*
> —Charles Kettering (American inventor)

> *"Problems cannot be solved at the same level of awareness that created them."*
> —Albert Einstein (German-born American physicist)

Value and Problems, Problems and Value

If any chapter in this book is more important than any other for creating a successful startup, this is it. Much of this book deals with getting your startup where you want to go; this chapter is about deciding what your software will do to get you there.

In this chapter we focus on what your startup is going to be about and on how to decide what value your startup delivers to your customers so that they will give you money, attention, and support.

Beginning at the Beginning Is Just a Beginning

Ask most people in this industry how to decide what your startup should build, and more than likely you'll get some variation on "Find a problem people will pay to have solved and solve it."

I asked one of the more intelligent, thoughtful, and experienced people I know in the business, Microsoft's Don Dodge (whom we met in Chapter 1), where to find a really great idea. He replied, "I like to say, is your product a vitamin or a painkiller? Vitamins are nice to have, but pain killers, you got to have it, right? So, the nice-to-haves in bad times, the nice-to-haves just don't cut it, because people aren't going to spend time or money on things that are nice to have. They are going to focus on real pain points and just spend time and money on things that solve a problem that they have."

"There is another set of ideas that don't really solve a problem at all, and they are not a vitamin or a pain killer—they are more like a happy pill."

Happy pills? What's that got to do with startups?

Don replied, "Happy pills are things like YouTube or Facebook—they don't solve any particular problem, they just make you feel good. Or games, online gaming, that kind of stuff—it doesn't solve a problem, it is just fun and entertaining. One of them is solve a pain point and bring a service that solves that pain. Another is bring services that save money, that can save time or money.

"A third way is what I broadly call *entertainment*—things that make you feel good, social networks, games, online gaming, dating; online dating is probably one of the biggest businesses on the Web that is legal, other than porn or gambling. So, there are huge opportunities in those areas. You just have to do something that's unique and different, easier, faster, cheaper, something."

Now, these are good answers—and they beat the answer to build a startup like the one you read about this morning in *TechCrunch*. But they are just the beginning of getting a clear view of this stuff. "Solve a problem" doesn't tell you how big or small that problem should be (AIDS in Africa vs. a code library that makes it easy to interface with PayPal from Rails). It doesn't tell you what kinds of problems make sense for you to tackle, and it doesn't give you a theory that let's you reasonably say, If I want to do this, I'll need to do this and this to succeed. And it does nothing to help you define the value that will be the core of your startup.

Value? *Value* is one of those words with multiple meanings. In this context, we're talking mostly an economic definition: the market worth of a commodity, service, asset, or work. Put another way, it's what makes an Apple iPod worth more than a Microsoft Zune, why you'll pay dearly to live in one location rather than another, and why investors will fund and people will buy what your startup is providing.

But before we get into how to how this value thing works, we need to take a slight detour to see how a theory might simplify the job of finding a startup idea. What we need is a highly concrete example, something as solid as a rock, of how a theory can make a huge difference in what results you and your startup will achieve. And for that we need to talk to Wally.

Wally's Startup Law

Wally Wallington is a retired carpenter in Lapeer, Michigan, with 35 years' experience building things. Wally is also a guy who, using nothing more than wooden tools, figured out how to move a 1-ton concrete block by himself, then a wooden barn, and then 2- and 10-ton concrete blocks into a replica of Stonehenge (Figure 2-1)—by himself, without wheels, rollers, ropes, hoist, or power equipment or anyone else's manual labor.

Figure 2-1. Superman? Nope. That's Wally.[1]

How the hell does a single man move a 10-ton concrete block? He starts by knowing a few laws of physics, and he thinks about it for a bit. "The simple laws of physics are most helpful in moving large objects, inertia creates stability, momentum keeps things working, and kinetic energy slows things down so they can be controlled. By creating conditions, using some engineering skills, and math for weight and balance," said Wally.

📌 **NOTE** There is nothing more practical than a good theory. Information is good; information that gives you a handle on some aspect of how the future is going to play out is much, much better. Regardless of what kind of startup you're building, knowing certain theories that have some empirical evidence going for them, such as Chris Anderson's *The Long Tail*, Alvin Toffler's *Third Wave*, and *the cluetrain manifesto* is a Good Thing.

---

[1] For more on Wally, see this YouTube video: `http://www.youtube.com/watch?v=1RRDzFROMxO`. And have a look at Wally's site (`http://www.theforgottentechnology.com`).

In honor of Wally, over the next few pages we're going to talk about a way of thinking about what value your startup is going to bring to the table—not because Wally's a startup (he's not) or because building startups obeys the laws of physics at the macro level (it doesn't). But there's a set of rules that make sense at play here. What's more, understanding those rules and relationships is going to give you a big head start to applying them to your startup, instead of cargo-culting what others do.[2]

Let's start with the components of this Startup Law, the first one being *the problem* (Figure 2-2).

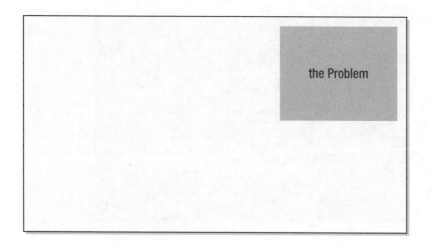

Figure 2-2. Start with a problem.

The Problem

To state the obvious, here are a few things we know about problems.

- They have *attributes*: these can be anywhere from simple to mind numbingly complex, as large as climate change to as small as getting the drop shadow right on an image in a blog.

- They have *duration*: a problem can be as old as history (meeting a mate) to as new as last week (protecting Twitter accounts from being hacked).

---

[2] *In programmer circles, cargo-culting means using code libraries and projects when you haven't a clue as to how they actually work, although they do. "Famous examples of cargo-cult activity include the setting up of mock airstrips, airports, offices, and dining rooms as well as the fetishization and attempted construction of Western goods, such as radios made of coconuts and straw"—from Wikipedia.*

- For some people—maybe everybody, maybe Japanese teenagers, maybe one guy who happens to be in charge of a piece of machinery that makes a specific kind of auto upholstery that goes into the side door panels of Mini Coopers—this thing is a thorn in their side, a rock in their show, an itch that needs scratching.

Hang in there, this is where it starts to get interesting, mainly how your startup is going to make money.

Your Startup's Value

How much your software can solve that problem, fix it, improve it, lessen it, or make it go away defines the *value* of your startup (Figure 2-3). Whether the problem is that personal financial record keeping is a pain (*Mint.com*) or that you can't manage time if you don't log it (*RescueTime. com*), to name a couple of examples from Chapter 7, to the degree these startups solve the problem, they create value, and that creates at least the opportunity to generate revenue.

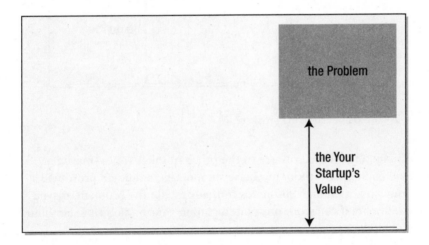

Figure 2-3. Your startup's value

All too often, developers will solve a technical problem so obscure that few people really care about it (see the later sidebar "Ten Startup Ideas Not to Do, and Why"). Those problems just don't have enough potential customers to make them significant as the basis for a startup.

It's all about moving that problem. Fine. But how do you solve that problem? That's where the next part of our theory comes in.

Your Resources

You solve a problem with *resources* (Figure 2-4). For startups, that means everything from you and your other founders' technical expertise, to the money people invest in your company, to your knowledge and understanding of the problem, to the marketing you do to find and connect to the people who care about this particular problem. These are the building blocks of your software solution to the problem, that thing you're going to build so that people want to pay you to make the problem go away or at least to get smaller.

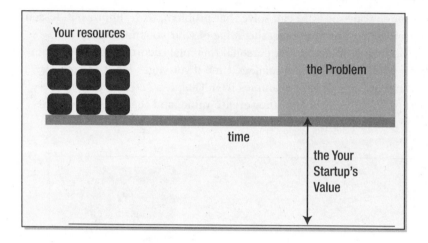

Figure 2-4. Resources solve the problem.

Connecting your resources to the problem takes time—maybe a weekend coding marathon, maybe seven months building a prototype so that you can get enough resources to really tackle the problem, maybe years and years if you work on your startup in your nonjob time, an hour here, a half-day there.

But resources are only half of what it's going to take to move that problem and create something of value. Let's now introduce the last piece of this particular puzzle.

Your Fulcrum

Just as with Wally's 10-ton concrete blocks, you need a *fulcrum* to make things happen for your startup (Figure 2-5). Joel Spolsky calls it the *secret sauce*. It's that surprising, remarkable, innovative "something" that differentiates your product from all of the other solutions to a given problem. Here are a few kinds of the components that build a good fulcrum.

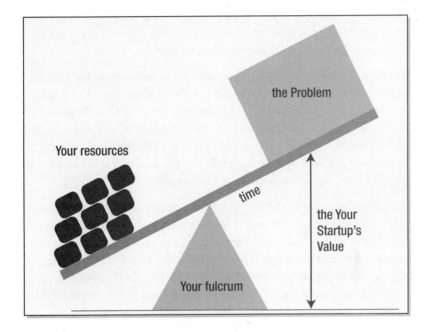

Figure 2-5. Archimedes was right.

- **Disruptive technology.** The problem? Not enough servers—be it to run a growing online business or to host a thousand such businesses. Servers and their cost were a big problem for startups and others back during the dot-com era. Then along comes virtualization, the rules change, and the problem is, if not solved, then taken down a few notches.

- **Originality/creativity/innovation.** Call it what you will, it's the spark of genius that makes the difference between a solution that solves the problem the same old, tired way and one that changes what people thought was the solution to the problem.

- **Deeper understanding of the problem.** Just about every programmer can code a basic content management system (CMS). But do you understand your intended market—be it a vertical market such as car repair garages, solo-practice podiatrists, or sports-mad soccer fans—so well, so deeply that you know exactly what that market wants and yearns for?

- **Design.** The world is full of ugly software. I know because I've written my share of it. Awkward workflows, unpleasant screens, and the like can be overlooked when there's no other choice for getting the job done; your app could be that choice. This goes deeper than attractive web design—it gets into building an app that works better to solve a given problem than its competitors.

- **Disruptive business model.** Sometimes the innovation isn't in the software; it's in the infrastructure around the product. For Apple, the secret sauce wasn't the MP3 player; it was the free iTunes app and being able to browse and buy music easily online for a reasonable price, song by song. For *Mint.com* (see Chapter 7), the secret sauce was the idea of getting credit card companies and the like to pay for your online personal finance program.

- **Combining unlikely things.** Take the accelerometer from your car's airbag system and add it to your game console, and you have the Nintendo Wii and a runaway success. Take the power of an online application and combine it with the brevity of a Short Message Service (SMS) message and you have Twitter. As the world gets more complicated, surprising, and sometimes wildly successful, solutions can be created by combining unlikely things.

- **A new platform**. As we saw with the Apple iPhone and then Google Android, new platforms create leverage for relatively old ideas. We'll have a lot more to say about this in Chapter 3.

There's one more element of Wally's Startup Law: the *lever*. In the preceding figures, I labeled it *time*: the time it takes to build a product, to find and connect and build a market, the time before others come up with their own take on the problem.

It can also be thought of as how long you as the founder are prepared to make slow and steady progress, how long your angels/VCs are prepared to fund you before cutting off your oxygen, how long before the problem changes, becomes irrelevant, or dwindles in importance.

Wally's Startup Law is not a real law: don't look for a bevy of neat equations or well-designed algorithms here. What the last few pages do is give you a reasonable theory to explain and predict how this particular dynamic works and therefore some idea of how things work for actual startups.

Implications of Wally's Startup Law

Let's look at a few of the implications of this theory we've just slogged through, especially how those implications work in reality and constrain or liberate your startup.

- *Big problems need lots of resources; not so much small problems.* If you're going to move a big problem, such as letting people talk to each other via the Internet (VoIP), you are going to need resources, and lots of them. Consider Skype: founded by Niklas Zennström and Janus Friis using the proceeds from selling the peer-to-peer file-sharing network KaZaA, it went through another $37.4 million of VC money as it grew from a few thousand users to a whopping *405 million* user accounts as of Q4 2008.[3] Oh, and along the way (September 2005), Niklas and Janus sold Skype to eBay for $2.6 billion.

- Niklas and Janus started with a very large resource base of money in the bank and the fulcrum of extremely deep knowledge of how to build a peer-to-peer Internet transmission network. Given this nearly unique starting point, they could tackle a huge problem experienced by hundreds of millions of people all over the world.

- *The bigger, smarter, and better your fulcrum of ideas, the fewer resources you will need to move the problem you are tackling.* Take the case of RescueTime, which we look at in depth in Chapter 7. Tony Wright and his two cofounders created a large and powerful fulcrum for their time management startup by realizing, even before the software was built, that the information RescueTime collected for its users and aggregated anonymously provided jaw-dropping surprises, surprises that got RescueTime press (*TechCrunch*, *New York Times*, BBC, *BusinessWeek*, etc.) other companies would happily kill for. RescueTime started as a self-funded startup, soon got $20,000 as seed money from Y Combinator, and, in September 2008, got $900,000 in Series A funding.

---

[3] *"Skype fast facts Q4 2008," Skype.*

- *You need a fulcrum.* Without some sort of fulcrum advantage—a deep understanding of the problem you are trying to solve, a remarkable approach to the problem, a disruptive technical advantage, or all three—it's going to be hard to move the problem and create value, regardless of how much time, effort, and money is committed to the other end of the lever. This antipattern (see the later sidebar "Ten Startups Not to Do, and Why") has been repeated time and time again, most recently with online video, white-box social networks, and micro-blogging platforms. In each of these cases the first startup in that space (YouTube, Ning, or Twitter) had a huge fulcrum comprising new social needs and disruptive functionality relative to what existed up to that point. Their competitors, when compared to these "first movers," don't enjoy the same kind of leverage or customer base.

- *The more specific the problem, the fewer resources are needed to move it.* Consider 37Signals. Begun as a Chicago-based web design shop, its first web app grew out of a need for just enough online project management to get the job done. That product—Basecamp—in turn became a giant fulcrum as the part-time contractor hired to work up Basecamp extracted as an Open Source project an elegant and robust framework (Ruby on Rails) that has become a major foundation for web application development.

Wally's Checklist for Your Startup Idea

One good use of a theory such as Wally's Startup Law is to see how what you want to do measures up. Here's a short checklist of questions to help you evaluate ideas around which to build your startup.

1. **Is the problem too big for the resources you can apply to it?** If so, how are you going to change the equation to be more in your favor? Reduce the scope of the problem? Improve your fulcrum of unique/disruptive/innovative ideas and insights into the problem? Get more resources—more time, more partners, more funding?

2. **Is the problem too small, given the resources and insights you have?** Sometimes you can overkill a small problem while leaving it's larger (and more profitable) relative in the wild.

3. **Is your fulcrum large enough to move the problem and thereby create real value?** This is another way of asking if your idea is remarkable enough to gain the attention you want. Or will bloggers,

investors, and, ultimately, customers find it wanting? Better to have this heart-to-heart meeting with yourself or your partners than to face it after putting 5,000 hours of work into it.

4. **What components do you have, what are you missing to make this proposition work, and how will you secure what you need?** For some startups, it's nailing down just how you and your partners are going to commit to the time needed to build 1.0; for others it's where to find someone who can sell your enterprise software to Fortune 500–size companies. Given what the problem is, who has it? And how do they decide what to buy? Do you have what you need, or can you get it?

5. **Is there going to be enough value in this startup to get the resources you'll need?** If you're going to need equity funding to get this idea off the ground, is there enough value to enough customers to give your angel investors 3 to 10 times their money back in, say, three years, and return 10-to-the-sky's-the-limit return on investment for VCs? The money guys are going to want real evidence here. Do you have it?

6. **Is the lever going to work?** Here's a subtle gotcha: You're all fired up to build a startup to take advantages of and sell to the users of a brand new platform. So you find funding and spend 18 hours a day in hand-to-hand combat with that new platform, only to emerge with your beta to discover that the million-unit first-year estimate cheerfully predicted by the platform vendor is looking like 30,000, most of those returns. Oops! And before you say it could never happen to you, I must tell you that it happened to me when Apple brought out the incredibly cool, hip, sleek . . . Apple Newton.

Sometimes it pays to look before you leap onto the latest and greatest platform.

This is a starter list of questions. Use it to grill—like the popular BBC show *The Dragon's Den*[4]—your prospective ideas before they get your time and money, let alone anyone one else's.

---

[4] `http://www.bbc.co.uk/dragonsden/`—In addition to the UK show, there are now versions of the show in Afghanistan, Australia, Canada, Finland, Israel, Japan, the Middle East, the Netherlands, New Zealand, Nigeria, and Russia and shows pending in Ireland, Sweden, and the United States (see `http://en.wikipedia.org/wiki/Dragons%27_Den`). I guess startups are getting pretty popular!

Have a Great Startup Idea? Hmm. Maybe Not.

Paul Tyma is a writer, speaker and serial entrepreneur in the software industry. He is a founder of Preemptive Solutions, Inc., a software security firm, and is currently founder/CTO of Home-Account, Inc., a web-based system out to rethink the mortgage industry. As the saying goes, he's been there, done that and has the tee shirts to prove it. His advice presented here is reprinted with his kind permission from his blog Technical Revenue at *http://paultyma.blogspot.com*.

Over the years I've started a small handful of Internet/software projects/companies. Examples include Mailinator, Preemptive Solutions, Inc., and Classhat. Actually, I've started a large handful but no one knows about most of them because they were (in no particular order): dumb ideas, unsuccessful, too hard for me to complete. Given that I now rate any new idea I get according to a set of rules that helps me filter out good ideas from bad. At least, whatever I consider bad. Keep in mind these rules are for the canonical one- or two-person pre-startup—if you have 8 million in VC, there's a lot of other magic you can do.

Here they are:

1. **If there is no business model, its a hobby, not an idea.** I love compiler optimizations. I wrote a Java optimizer soon after Java came out. I spent months trying to figure out how to turn it into a business. But guess what, people don't pay for optimizers, or compilers, or even runtimes. At least not without a strong sales team telling they need that. By and large most ideas I get are about things that I'd love to work on but have no real business model (my Classhat project took several years and is, absolutely, a hobby). There's nothing wrong with hobbies, as long as you know what they are.

2. **The best ideas make your customers money.** If your idea can say, "If a customer uses our product, they will make X% more money" (where X is a positive number, even if quite small)," you have won the game. Importantly—I did not say the customer will save X% more money. I said they'll make it. That's a big difference. Saving money is great, but you are then faced with the mission of convincing your customer that if they spend $100k on your product now, it will pay itself back in 8 months. It's way, way, way easier to say, "Use our product and you make 2% more money (of which we get a cut). Don't use it, and don't." Who wouldn't buy that?

3. **The best place to be that I know of is B2B2C.** That is, you want to be a business that serves businesses that serve consumers. If you're B2C, then welcome to some important challenges. One is to get people to pay for your stuff, which in this Internet world, we're not all that happy about doing. Secondly, welcome to support hell. Its very hard to provide consumer support (and you see many complaints across the net). It takes a lot of support people and a lot of money to do it right, which is why it rarely is. If your idea plans to charge consumers, I'd definitely think twice unless you can ramp up a support system fast. Thirdly, you'll need a powerful infrastructure (apart from support) just to handle large numbers of small transactions. Its harder to sell 1,000 $10 widgets than 10 $1,000 ones.

   On the other hand, if you're simply B2B, life isn't so bad. Big ticket sales but encompassing the market is harder. Sales cycles are long. Again, you might need a faster ramp-up of a sales and marketing infrastructure (which you are going to need eventually anyway), but you're probably okay if the idea is generally good.

4. **If you're going B2C, look for revenue models that don't come right from the consumer.** Given the last point you're probably thinking I'm crazy, given things like YouTube or MySpace or Facebook or Google. I'm not (at least I don't think I am). All those places dodged the problems of providing support and tracking sales by giving away their services for free and making money on the backside (whatever that is). Often that's advertising revenue. Often its partnership deals. Simply put there absolutely is an Eyeball Business Model. If you can get the eyeballs, you can sell them. Just try to do that instead of charging them directly. They'll be ornery about it and demand support.

5. **Revisit every bad idea every once in a while.** Why is AJAX hot? Because its enabling things technically that weren't enabled before. Are any of these mash-ups really novel ideas? Not usually. Old ideas become new again by new technology, faster computers, etc.

   When the computer game Doom came out, it included very little novel technology. All the 3D math and graphics tech had existed for years. The guys at ID were just the first ones to realize that personal computers (as opposed to graphics workstations) at the time had finally gotten powerful enough to do it all in real time.

   Every time bandwidth gets faster or cheaper, previously bad old ideas become new and shiny (e.g., video over the Internet). Mobile phones seem really ripe. Apps and usability currently sort of sucks. That's really hampering a ton of uses. With every new advancement, however, it's going to open up new doors.

6. **Do your best to create a system of recurring revenue.** Advertising on web sites and such is easy. But things like packaged software is hard. Why does Microsoft change the doc format every time it releases a new Microsoft Word. Surely it probably includes new features, but why can't old versions just ignore those and load the file (which is really text, right?) anyway? Because they don't want it to. They want you to buy a new version of Word to get all the new features (even if you just write letters to your Aunt Edna and would never use them). They want recurring revenue.

Doing that with packaged software is harder and often somewhat transparently greedy. Heard of "software as a service"? That is of course, really, "software that we can just keep charging for." Bottom line is if tires, light bulbs, or razors never wore out, the economics of those businesses would be radically different. Getting more money from your customers (hopefully while providing value to justify it) is a good way to go.

If have an idea that follows #2 above (making your customer money), do your best to simply take a small cut. Small cuts add up and the customer has no risk in trying your product.

7. **Let ideas gestate.** Every new idea seems to be the greatest idea I ever had. Usually it goes something like:

Time 0: get new idea

1 minute later: (some details)

2 minutes later: start thinking about suit I'll wear when I get to ring closing bell when we IPO

After getting way too excited about way too many ideas, I set myself a rule. Think through an idea for three days before I tell a soul. My excitement is usually killing me the first day or so, but by the third day it's rather died down. Or, if it isn't, I get a better sense of whether I'm really onto something. Simply put, ideas always look better the fresher they are. You're looking for ones that look good even when not fresh.

8. **Consider the size of your market.** If you read Guy Kawasaki's blog you'll see him mention quite often how new companies pitch to him about the immense size of their new market. Guy often chides them for their optimism, but even he knows you better believe you do have a big market (and maybe even puff the number in conversations) or you can forget it. Numbers in the hundreds of millions or billions are good—you're really only realistically hoping to glean a smidgen of that.

Consumer markets can be drastically immense. If you're one guy in your basement with an idea that will capture you a $40 billion market, that's dandy. Hopefully you have no misconceptions that you'll just own the market yourself (where there's money, there's competitors, and they'll steal plenty, if not most of it, before you can penetrate it all); but the bigger the market, the easier it is to find customers.

Niche markets like hardware stores, developers, and/or mailmen don't suck—so long as you can effectively penetrate most of it—and fast. Simple rule: bigger is better. If big enough (and your idea does actually penetrate it), you'll capture the attention of someone big who will want it for themselves. That either means buying you or chasing you—where the actual outcome happens in the execution (not the idea).

9. **"Building a business around a new developer tool" is wrong on so many levels.** Some markets are not only niche—they live in the land of the free. And I don't mean the USA—I mean a market where people are used to getting everything for free.

   The software developer inside me keeps coming up with ideas for software development tools. Occupational hazard, I suppose. I understand the domain space and understand how to solve the problem. However, development tools are, in general, a really bad place to find good business ideas. Consider that things like Netbeans and Eclipse that took thousands of person-hours to create are given away FREE. Therein lies the rub: developers have created their own culture of giving away tools for free. There is certainly nothing wrong with that, unless of course you think you're going to make a business out of it.

   Even then there are niches inside dev tools that are worse than others. Two dollars and an idea for the greatest Java software dev tool ever will buy you a cup of coffee. Java developers are especially used to getting tools for free. In contrast, Microsoft has created a nice culture of getting .NET and windows developers used to paying for stuff. In other words, if you "must" create a developer tool that you intend to sell, stick with Microsoft or some other market segment where paying is an accepted idea.

10. **Ideas really aren't worth all you think they are.** Yes, I know you're smart. Yes, you're amazingly, super-duper wonderfully creative. But in reality, very few ideas are truly novel.

   What happens is that two independent technology evolutions (say, the Internet and mobile phones) eventually progress to a point where it takes a simple idea to act as a bridge and converge the two. And a product is born. The farther ahead you see that convergence, the more "brilliant" your idea is.

But with every passing day, the distance between the two technologies lessens and your brilliant idea becomes ever so slightly more obvious. In other words, if someone else hasn't thought of it, they will soon. And as more people realize it, the odds of it hitting someone who's looking to start a company increase.

Basically, the winner will be the company that gets things to market fast, creates a marketing and sales infrastructure, and actually makes sales. Don't rely solely on an idea to make it all the way. It has to be supported. If it isn't—at a minimum—it will be stolen (at least in a market sense). You can definitely create a world-class company on a good idea and a great infrastructure. Vice versa is nowhere near as easy.

And, as an aside, once the technology progressions converge by themselves (apart from your idea)—your idea will probably be made irrelevant (hopefully you cashed out long before then).

11. **Competition is good.** If you don't have competition, you don't have an idea. Competition tells you and investors that your idea isn't wacky. If you work three years on a product with no challengers, maybe they know something about the day you're going to release and try to make sales that you don't.

Don't be afraid to chase an existing idea if you have what you consider a subidea that makes a key difference. Both AltaVista and Google did search. AltaVista was doing it long before Google started and probably laughed when they heard some challenger Google was going to take them on. I hate to say it but the concept of "stealing ideas" in business is very hard to define. Patents tried to enforce this notion, but it's so broken (although you still need them of course) that it hardly matters.

Every idea you have is already an extension of some existing idea. (Every web 2.0 idea "assumes" the Internet "exists." Every "mash-up" not only assumes, but steals functionality from two or more existing web services.) How close your new idea is to old ideas defines how many people will say you stole it. And there will *always* be people saying that.

As a concrete example: I created Mailinator in July 2003. It was the first disposable e-mail service that allowed incoming e-mails to create an inbox as they arrived. There are now a half-dozen copycat sites (some even stole my FAQ questions and license!). Does this matter? Could I do anything about it if it did? Should I try to squash them?

A better tactic is simply to outmarket them and introduce new features. Protecting an idea is nearly impossible; working to continually better serve your customers isn't. (And, by the way, the idea for Mailinator wasn't mine. It was Jack's.)

Where Do You Find Problems?

For most developers interested in building a startup around solving a given problem, that problem is very near at hand. When I talked to Tony Wright, the founder of RescueTime, the problem came from his and his cofounder's frustration with how the time management problem had been solved up until then.

"It was born out of our personal inability to understand how we spend our time," Tony said. "Every day we had a scrum agile meeting. We're a bunch of software geeks. Everyone's job was to say what they'd accomplished in the last 24 hours and what they were going to do in the next 24. We found that people's ability to articulate what they'd done, literally, just in the last work day, was terrible. People would say, well, I felt busy but I can't really articulate what I did.

"We wanted to understand that, but we recognize that despite all these time management books that say keep a log of how you spend your time, that's incredibly impractical for a technology worker who's shifting between applications and web sites, sometimes in 10-, 20- second blocks. We want something that was totally passive that would answer those questions for us and for our business without actually requiring data entry, which is no fun."

For two of the four founders of Brisworks (a client of mine)—which makes and sells Admin Arsenal, a Windows system administration tool—the problem was the frustrations they were experiencing as system administrators: "After years of seeing the bleeding, we decided to make the bandage. Upshot: We know from firsthand experience what sysadmins need," said Shawn Anderson. "We knew how expensive and overly complex most systems management solutions were. We saw a market for a simple, yet powerful solution," added Shane Corellain.

"I'm more evidence that the best products come from simple need," said Corey Maass. "My main product, *dubfiler.com*, is still in development, but has received a lot of good attention from the right people. Meaning the people I made it for—other producers, DJs, and musicians. We all share files constantly, but were tired of file-sharing sites. I said, 'Why not make the perfect one?'."

Sometimes you can spot the problem just by looking at an existing situation from a different point of view. "I was outside having a smoke break, looked into the offices at the computer screens displaying the default Windows logo screensaver, and thought, 'You'd think they'd have their own logo on there,'" added Steve Grundell, whose Any Logo Screensaver Creator at *http://www.anylogoscreensaver.com* brings in a tidy profit each and every quarter.

Often, defining the problem comes from doing something for someone not so technically orientated and thinking there's got to be a better/easier/cheaper way for nonprogrammers to do this. "I got the idea last year [for his startup, *http://www.artists-portfolio-creator.com*—see Figure 2-6] after years of helping my mum (who is an artist) make presentation CDs for when she wanted to make gallery submissions," Stephen Fewer told me.

"I have been self-employed in an unrelated area of computers for nearly two years and have always wanted to run a microISV and hopefully get another revenue stream coming in, so I had a 'light bulb moment' one day that their was a gap in the market and I could write a great piece of software to do what I had been manually hacking together previously. I thought if I could make it easy to use with great features, every artist who exhibits could want it :).

Figure 2-6. Artists Portfolio Creator

The idea for your startup might walk up to you at your day job, as it did for Simon Shutter. "The idea originated when I was hired by an engineering consulting company to review commercial calendar/scheduling software. The basic requirement was to be able to see at a glance the calendars of several team members six weeks to two months into the future. They liked how they could view multiple calendars in Outlook but didn't like how information in Outlook disappeared into the calendar grid when more than a few calendars were displayed.

"At the end of the contract I gave them my opinions on a range of commercial products and also presented a concept that was more in line with their requirements. They liked the concept the most and so I turned it into a microISV app (Schemax Calendar, at *http://calendar.schemax.com/ default.aspx*).

Or you might get your startup idea when you realize you're not the only person facing a problem. "That was four years ago, while filling out my state taxes online. Realized that even a pro couldn't make a web form right," said Cedric Savarese about his startup, FormAssembly (*http:// formassembly.com*).

"I find that to have good ideas I need to be working on some problem," said Y Combinator founder Paul Graham in a 2005 blog post. "You can't start with randomness. You have to start with a problem, then let your mind wander just far enough for new ideas to form." Paul is a very smart guy who's put a great deal of thought, time, and energy into what it takes for a startup to succeed.

Ten Startups Not to Do, and Why

Just as there are trusted patterns of software design, such as Model-View-Controller, that have proven themselves to work over time, there are anti-patterns of startup design that time after time disappointed would-be founders, angels, and investors. Now, if your startup fits into one of these antipatterns, maybe you're the exception that's going to break the rule; but you'd better know *why* you're the exception. Hope is not a plan.

- **The Me-Too! startup.** Twitter client startups are being written up in *TechCrunch* and elsewhere as their founders get funding, go to great parties, and start eyeing expensive cars. Therefore, we will do a Twitter client. For Twitter client, substitute "social media web app," "crowd-sourced video site," "enterprise CMS," "semantic web," "iPhone ad network," and so forth. Nothing wrong with these kinds of apps, but code monkey-see, code monkey-do works for most primates and some VCs—it's a lousy way to pick a business to be in for the next three to five years at least, if you succeed.

- **The Designed-by-Committee startup.** It's easy to spot this kind of startup: it's got the latest hot social media, crowd-sourced, Long Tail features for the early adopters and training wheel wizards for the late adopters. It's the triumph of configuration options because the designers didn't want to say no to anything or anyone. In short, it's an app—web, desktop, mobile—that tries too hard to be all things to all people.

- **The Port startup.** This is most often seen among desktop startups, but it's also fashionable among iPhone startups. The formula is simple: pick a program on one platform that's successful (it may be your company's or another's) and port it to a different platform—Mac to Windows, Windows to Mac, whatever. Do the port in such a way as completely to ignore the sensibilities and expectations of the market you are porting to. This is how web apps that mimic, say, Microsoft PowerPoint (except they're slower) come into being.

- **The PR-First startup.** Every so often a startup bursts on the scene, trumpeted by amazing claims that should have the giants in the industry quaking in their shoes. Well, no. Some startups are able to generate publicity in far greater amounts than their apps warrant. Sometimes it's the "Microsoft Outlook Killer" Chandler Project[5] (six years in the making, no big deal) (Figure 2-7) and the "Google Killer" Cuil[6] ("Anybody who thought [Cuil] was this Google killer can really see now that, no, that's not going to happen today—and the likelihood is that's not going to happen a year from now," says Danny Sullivan, Internet search guru and editor-in-chief of SearchEngineLand).

- **The Outsourced startup.** This is a startup that outsources not just the functions secondary to its core product, such as accounting, PR, and tech support, but then outsources the core development and coding of their application because either that's what large corporations do or that's what Angel Investor X or VC guy Z says they'd better do if they want funding. First off, while developers and development shops in India, eastern Europe, and elsewhere can code every bit as well as programmers in the United States and Europe, they (except the ones busy launching startups) are set up to implement code, have not come up with the vision in your head. Second, if they can somehow turn your hand-waving mockup into a real application, why do the money guys need you?

---

[5] "Chandler: What went wrong," by Bob Walsh, CNET Webware: http://news.cnet.com/8301-17939_109-10016837-2.html?tag=mncol and

[6] "Why Cuil Is No Threat to Google," Time.com, http://www.time.com/time/business/article/0,8599,1827331,00.html

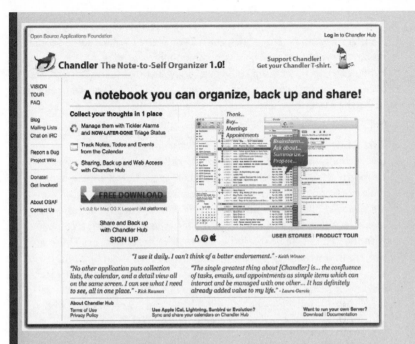

Figure 2-7. The Chandler Project: six years and $18 million later

- **The By-the-Bootstraps startup.** Try this experiment: Put on a pair of boots and find a stairway heading up. At the foot of the stairs grab the back of each boot with a hand; then in that position, jump to the first step. If you make it, jump to the next step, still holding your bootstraps. It can be done, but it's very hard, awkward, and prone to failure. *Bootstrapping*—building a startup while working full time—can be done: that's how I built *StartupToDo.com*[7] and how many others have built their startups. But it ranks on the Pain scale somewhere between getting a tooth pulled and getting your fingernails pulled off one by one.

- **The Only-a-Genius-Could-Love-It startup.** Take one incredibly smart computer science/Zen philosophy graduate who rattles off a dozen world-shaking ideas when asked if she wants milk in her coffee and go let her play. When you come back, your partner has created a software app of incredible complexity using algorithms and logic you need to study for three months just to understand how to print. One successful example of this is Stephen Wolfram's *Mathematica* computational software program, which is incredibly powerful and robust but appeals to a very, very small market.

---

[7] *That's why I built StartupToDo.com too—traditional bootstrapping was too damn hard!*

- **The Only-a-Few-Programmers-Need-It startup.** You're a programmer with an itch to scratch and a keen desire to make some serious money. So you code up a library, a component, a control, a framework. While there are successful companies doing just that (Infragistics comes to mind), you first have to compete with all the Open Source projects doing the same thing and then find enough developers to squeeze out a living better than a day job.

- **The Built-to-Flip startup.** This is a variation of the Me-Too! startup, but with a twist. You see that startup X just got acquired by Big Company Y, so you reverse-engineer their app and, more importantly, their marketing and come out with acquisition bait for Big Company Y's rivals. While there's nothing wrong with looking for an early exit (see Chapter 5 for a translation from VC-speak), building a company with that as its sole goal seldom works, for three reasons: There are too many startups trying to win that lottery. For example, Microsoft acquires about 20 companies a year. And that's it. Second, if your market of companies that might buy you out is exactly one, you're at their mercy—and they will know it. Finally, during recessions, M & A activity slows way down as big companies hunker down.

- **The We-Can-Do-it-Better-Than-Microsoft startup.** Or Google or Adobe or whatever large software company you yearn to be better than. Specifically, in this antipattern you bring out a word processor, spreadsheet, or graphics editing program just as good as and maybe a bit better than the Big Guy on their native platform. Assuming you get funding (you won't), you're going to be locked in a cage with an enraged elephant who is going to outspend, outhire, outmarket, out-PR you to a very early death. That's not to say that Microsoft or any other company is anointed to always win, but that's the way to bet. This is not the same as finding a way to build a horizontal app tailored to a different platform that delivers things that Microsoft can't or won't (Zoho.com comes to mind) or as building an app that appeals to a sliver of the horizontal market, like, say, Scrivener on the Mac (*http://www.literatureandlatte.com/scrivener.html*).

The bottom line for these antipatterns is that they share one overwhelmingly bad commonality: they're unremarkable. And that's the kiss of death in the Online World.

Recap

There are as many different ideas behind startups as there are stars in the sky. But after looking at, reading about, and talking to several hundred startups, I see some commonalities emerging.

- Most startups don't go looking for the idea that will (supposedly) make them the most money; they go looking for a solution to a problem they care passionately about.

- A problem is a starting point, not an end-all. How you see the problem, what technical, business and human insights you bring to how to state the problem, and your solution make the difference between a ho-hum me-too startup and one that can gather attention, funding, and customers.

- Resources cost; ideas multiply the effectiveness of resources. Programming takes time, funding costs equity, and marketing takes money. How effective these resources will be depend in large part on what I call the fulcrum: the approach you take to solving the problem. The bigger and more robust that fulcrum can be constructed using the sheer brain sweat of your startup's founders in order to understand the problem more fully, to see new ways of solving it, and to understand how the problem is affecting people today, not five or ten years ago, the better.

There's no shortage of problems or things people would want to do if they only could, and there's no magic or secret formula that will work for all startups everywhere. But there is a natural relationship between the size and shape of a problem you want to solve or an opportunity you want to seize, the resources you can ante up, and how you're going to see, solve, and connect to the problem that when done right can create exciting and profitable value no matter the size of the problem or the resources you have to start with.

Next we're going to turn to a major development that's changed dramatically how startups succeed from the days when commercial apps ran on either PCs or Macs: the rise of the platforms. Web apps, hybrids, Facebook apps, SaaS platforms, mobile, and more: Which platform is your startup going to call home?

So Many Platforms, So Many Options

"Life is the sum of all your choices."
—Albert Camus (French writer and philosopher)

"Choose your rut carefully; you'll be in it for the next ten miles."
—Road sign in upstate New York

Then and Now

It used to be so simple, in the age of Bill and Steve.[1] If you wanted to develop and sell software, you had a choice of two platforms: Windows and Mac. Sure, game developers could write for a given console, or you could write an app for a minicomputer such as the IBM AS400, but those were the exceptions. Starting with the IBM XT in March 1983 and the Apple Macintosh 128k seven months later, if you wanted to write commercial desktop software, they and their successors and offspring were the only game in town.

How things have changed. Now if you get together with a bunch of startups at, say, a Startup 2 Startup event (see Chapter 4), you start by talking to a founder working on a micropayment system for Facebook and then to a VP for a startup doing cross-platform virtual desktops that follow you from workplace to home like an obedient puppy, and then two developers—a Rails guy and .NET/Silverlight guy—will join in. And, of course, at least three Apple iPhone developers are within 20 feet of your little group.

Today, one of the most important decisions a startup's founder or founders have to make is what platform—or combination of platforms—will

---

[1] See Chapter 1.

be the world in which they live and, hopefully, sell. Make the right decision, and funding, attention, and revenue will flow your way; make the wrong decision, and you're left with an app no one wants.

This chapter will introduce you to the buffet of platform choices you have as a startup, how you decide what platforms are right for you, and understanding the trade-offs and opportunities each provides. Along the way we'll talk with several startups about their choice of platform, what they like and dislike about their chosen platform, and their advice to the new person on the block: you.

But first, what's a platform?

Everybody Wants to Be in the Platform Business

Here is the short answer to the question of what a platform is: A *platform* is anything on which you can write and sell a software app that will make money for you—and for whoever owns the platform. The long answer is considerably more complicated, since it's the story of the messy, sometimes-contradictory, always heady mix of marketing hyperbole and genuine breakthroughs of our industry.[2]

To bring some sanity to this buffet of platforms, I've grouped them into six categories: SaaS, PaaS, social, mobile, desktop, and hybrid.

- **SaaS (pronounced "sass")**. This is *software as a service*, such as an app written in ASP.NET, Rails, PHP, or the like, that you run from your server and either charge customers to use or monetize via advertising or some other means. Think Web 2.0 and you're thinking SaaS.

- **PaaS (pronounced "pass")**. *Platform as a service* is a different beast: you've written a web app, but it plays in someone else's sandbox/ online ecology. What come to mind are Force.com (from SalesForce), the Apple iPhone,[3] Google AppEngine, Bungee Connect, various CMS apps, such as Joomla, and Microsoft SharePoint, among others. So do enterprise-level PaaS's such as NetSuite, Oracle OPN, and others. And so too do Amazon's almost-a-PaaS weave of Web Services, Google's not-quite-an-operating system of tools and services, and Microsoft's we-finally-have-cloud operating system Azure.

---

[2] *Yes, our software industry—welcome to your new position!*

[3] *Why do I count iPhone apps as on a PaaS? Because, except for the tiny sliver of jail-broken iPhones, if you want to do a commercial iPhone app, you're going to be paying Apple 30% of your revenue.*

- **Social.** Social networks such as Facebook, Twitter, MySpace, Bebo, Hi5, Orkut, and SecondLife are platforms, but their structure, economics, and opportunities set them apart from SaaS and PaaS.

- **Mobile.** This gets its own category, for the simple reason that it's exploded as a platform: Apple iPhone,[4] Google's Android platform (gPhones), RIM BlackBerry, and Windows smartphones, to name the major and minor players.

- **Hybrid.** It's not a web app, because you launch it from your desktop; it's not a desktop app, because it uses the net and runs on PCs, Mac, and Linux boxes; it's something different. Adobe Flex/AIR and Microsoft Silverlight are the two major platforms battling for the hearts, minds, and codebases of startups here.

- **Open Source CMS.** Open Source doesn't necessarily mean you should leave your credit card behind, as major Open Source projects such as WordPress, Joomla, and Drupal demonstrate.

- **Desktop.** They may not get the respect, press, or funding they once did, but desktop apps created by startups for Windows and Macs are still very much a part of the platform mix.

There you have it: our roundup of all the usual suspects. Before we interrogate them, let's have a look at our questions for them.

NOTE **Not making a decision is a decision.** Now, you may be saying to yourself, "I'm an X developer; of course my startup is going to build software using X." That might be true. But picking the default without at least understanding what's going on in those other platform worlds is like changing lanes without looking: a bad idea. And spending a little time with those other platforms might spark the Killer Secret Sauce Idea for your startup.

Evaluating platforms: A checklist

As we get familiar with most of the platforms out there for building a startup, here's a set of questions you and your other founders might find useful in selecting which platform(s) and languages to build on.

---

[4] *Yes, the iPhone counts twice—once as a PaaS, again under mobile—because entirely different apps now make sense on a GPS-enabled, motion-sensitive handheld communication device, and startups are jumping into this pool. This has absolutely nothing to do with the iPhone glued to my body, honest.*

1. **Appropriateness to your targeted market.** That's right; it's not which language you prefer to program in. What matters here is what your targeted market (see Chapter 4) prefers. Consider Mint.com: a SaaS aimed at people in their 20s and 30s. Founder Aaron Patzer could have written a hybrid, PaaS, mobile, or even desktop app, but instead he chose a platform that allowed him to reach the maximum number of his targeted market segment.

2. **Your (team's) skill set.** Obviously, the skills, languages, and platforms you already know and use will heavily influence your platform choice—but there's a couple of catches here, which we will come to next. For now, preparing yourself and your team for this critical decision includes doing a skills inventory—nothing too complex, just who knows what and how well, and how long ago they wrote code in each particular platform and language.

3. **Is the Platform/language evolving, mature, or declining?** Keep in mind that hooking up with a platform is anything but a one-night stand—you will need to support, evolve, and innovate your startup's app for two to five years, given most post-startup scenarios. Where do you think the platform will be in that timeframe? Also, if your platform is closed source rather than Open Source, you have to factor in as best you can what the owners of your platform want. For example, more than a few companies in the 1990s brought to market software apps based on the Apple HyperCard program, only to see development stall and ultimately be abandoned by Apple in 2000 and finally withdrawn from the market in 2004. Over in Bill's world, both Active Server Page (ASP) and Visual Basic 6 were left for dead as Microsoft moved to its .NET lineup.

4. **What's the health of the ecosystem around the platform/ language?** Programmers are a somewhat fickle lot: What's hot today may be crap tomorrow. The larger and more robust the community of Open Source projects, freelancers for hire, commercial vendors, book authors, blogs, forums, and IRC channels, the better it is for your startup.

5. **Is your platform consistent with your post-startup strategy?** You don't tug on Superman's cape, and you don't sell Ruby on Rails startups to Microsoft. Are you hoping for a major player in your industry to buy you out? You'd better not develop a .NET app if your three potential suitors all are Open Source to the core. Startups are a beginning, not an end onto themselves. If your post-startup strategy is all about being acquired, you'd better know how compatible your platform is with what those other companies are committed to.

> 6. **Love the Platform, love the language, or don't go there.** Most professional programmers can write code in a number of languages for a set of platforms. That's good and fine, but if you don't have a serious emotional relationship with your platform to be, you and your team will not enjoy spending untold hours, not just coding in and for it, but tracking and learning new developments, techniques, "best practices," and all the rest.
>
> If the foregoing list causes you to slow down and not jump quite as quickly on the platform and language you had hardly thought about because they were the obvious, immediate choice for you—good. Picking a platform is serious stuff. It is the most upstream technology choice you will make for your startup over much of your life for the next several years. A little consideration applied here could make or break your startup.

Software As a Service

Overview

Start with rounded corners, add a black background and warm, fuzzy text, and label it Web 2.0. That's what SaaS is, right? Not exactly. There's a great confabulation of meaning and usage when you pack the terms *Web 2.0*, *SaaS*, and *apps in the sky*.

Part of this is historical—we've been down this road before and the ending wasn't very happy. Remember Application Service Provider (ASP) startups? Those were the brave and brash Internet pioneers during the dot-com boom that absorbed billions in VC money before people started to notice that it's a wee bit hard doing computing in the cloud using dialup modems. Let's call software that uses the net anything but ASP.

Before we get to the distinguishing markings of an SaaS app, let's examine two huge differences between the world then and the world now as far as startups are concerned. First off, the battle of broadband vs. dialup is well and truly over, and we have won. Consider the statistics from UK-based research firm Point Topic, Ltd., shown in Figure 3-1.

The stats compiled by Point Topic show dialup fading away and broadband becoming ubiquitous, worldwide. This might sound like old news, but it's anything but when you're building a SaaS startup.

I think the second major development that has contributed to the phenomenal growth of SaaS-SMRMs (software as a service startups making real money) is that there's a whole new generation of e-commerce companies geared toward the subscription model. We will be covering several of them in detail in Chapter 5, but for now the point is that these e-commerce companies further reduce the cost of entry for SaaS startups, and that, too, is a good thing.

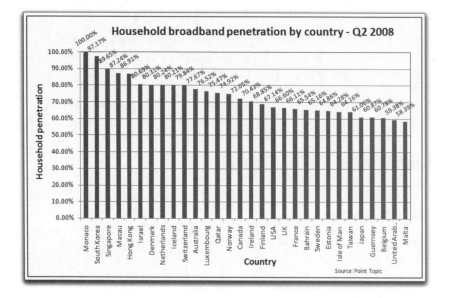

Figure 3-1. Broadband penetration, by country[5]

Main Characteristics from a Startup's Point of View

Legally, you're not licensing an application; you're providing a service. This puts you in a parallel legal universe from the EULA-centric platforms.

Technically, it's all about servers (actual, virtual, or elastic), the joys of cross-browser HTML/CSS/JavaScript compatibility, and performance. In terms of money, subscription-revenue models predominate, especially for business-related SaaS apps, with small startups eking out a living via Google AdSense, and a few out-of-the-box-thinking startups such as Mint. com that are tapping noncustomer revenue streams.

---

[5] *Point Topic,* http://point-topic.com *by way of* http://www.websiteoptimization. com/bw/0809. *Reprinted by permission.*

Advantages

If you've ever sold a desktop app or worked for a company that did, then you know that breaking free of the torture wheel of software piracy, software installers, endless updates, and configuration issues is a beautiful thing. A humble example: Fully 50% of the time I spent supporting my first commercial Windows desktop application revolved around operating system configuration issues, with another 30% devoted to providing new registration keys to users.

Breaking free of the confines of desktop software reality means that a huge percentage of your startup's resources can go into the actual service. It also means that you're out of the tawdry game of forever hounding your customers to buy upgrade after upgrade.

Disadvantages

Like every other platform in this chapter, there are trade-offs when basing your startup on the SaaS model. First and foremost are the performance and functionality constraints to which an application chained to a web browser must be reconciled. These constraints, which some would argue are a good thing and lead to software elegance and simplicity, are still constraints. Bottom line: web apps fall short of the speed, functional power, and sheer complexity of which an app running on the desktop is capable.

Here's the next thing that gives SaaS founders sleepless nights: what the Web giveth, the Web taketh away. Even the arguably most robust SaaS application on the net—Google Gmail—falls down with some regularity and goes boom.[6] Your mileage will probably be worse. From denial-of-service attacks to marauding backhoes, let alone good old developer/ sysadmin errors: all of these can make your startup blink out of existence.

Here's another issue: you're one subscription period away from ruin. If some other startup's SaaS app wins the hearts, minds, and attention of early adopters, trade press, bloggers, and your customer base, your revenue can crater overnight. Brand loyalty is so 20th century, and attempting to

---

[6] *So What Really Caused That Gmail Failure? (of Feb. 24, 2009),* `http://news.digitaltrends.com/news-article/19362/so-what-really-caused-that-gmail-failure`. *It was the first global failure of Gmail since August, and led Nelson Mattos, vice president of engineering, to say: "We're not perfect, we make mistakes."*

lock in customers by shackling their data only makes them want to leave that much sooner.

Comments

There's no denying that SaaS is an attractive platform for startups: near-zero cost of entry thanks to server virtualization combined with the sheer power to reach the global market for your application directly is a powerful combination.

Saas enterprise reality check: Rick Chapman, Softletter

While consumer-facing SaaS is booming, one nagging question keeps businesses—especially enterprise—SaaS startups—awake at night: **Will they buy?** Are large organizations, government agencies, and the like prepared to cede control of their mission-critical line of business applications to some third party that they don't own and that might—probably will!—be working for their competitors? After years of focusing on ways to protect corporate data and integrate all enterprise data into data marts, will IT departments let their companies adopt SaaS apps?

Everyone has an opinion, but one man has the data. Rick Chapman is the managing editor of *Softletter* (http://www.softletter.com), a twice-a-month subscription-based newsletter for software developers and publishers. *Softletter* tracks new marketing and distribution tactics, company operations, finance, pricing models, product management, and emerging technologies in the desktop, enterprise, Open Source, and software as a service (SAAS) market segments.

Rick was kind enough to share a few insights on the SaaS world, gleaned from his wide-ranging industry surveys, special reports, and seminars. Hopefully, Rick's answers will let a few more SaaS startups reading this book sleep a little better tonight—or get hopping! Thanks, Rick!

Bob: Rick, what's the overall acceptance rate of SaaS software in the various market segments you track (small, midsize, enterprise, public)?

Rick: SaaS acceptance is very high in all of these markets. One of the interesting things our research showed us in 2007[7] was that adoption of SaaS at the "enterprise" level was higher than conventional wisdom's assumptions. Then, the median size of a sale for an on premise/client server product was $50k; for SaaS, it was $25k, much higher than the $10k to $15k we'd projected.

---

[7] *The 2009 Softletter SaaS Report came out just as I was wrapping this chapter (http://www.softletter.com/pages/SaaS_report.shtml). The trends Rick describes here continue.*

That higher number came from corporations buying enough seats to push that median to that level. We're currently running that survey as I write this and we think that SaaS median will show continued growth.

Bob: Are these rates plateauing, growing, or shrinking?

Rick: Rapidly growing. While the economy is in a recession, SaaS isn't. In the B2C markets, there are no segments and niches in which SaaS alternatives to traditional software are not appearing.

Bob: Is SaaS penetration into small groups within organizations here and there, or is it enterprise-wide?

Rick: Within corporations, the scope and type of penetration differs based on what you're selling. Most SaaS applications are *not* broad horizontals such as word processing or spreadsheets. Everyone uses a word processor and many people use a spreadsheet.

However, how many people within a company need to use a sales incentive and compensation management product? Or a CRM system? Or a document manager? Or a marketing automation system? Or a SaaS-based litigation support system?

SaaS *is* much more of a "sell and grow" proposition. In a larger company, the typical scenario is that a division or operating unit will test the product (this happens rapidly because, in most cases, a test project can be implemented without much or any IT involvement). If the group is happy, they sign up, and the SaaS system begins to spread through the company as the word gets out. However, we are seeing a growing number of cases where the SaaS vendor convinces a company to purchase the new system for all units that need it.

Bob: Is there a "sweet spot" in pricing SaaS apps to each of these markets, or do they range in price?

Rick: Our 2009 *Softletter* SaaS Report sliced and diced this question up in several different ways.

First, we asked respondents what their primary means of pricing their product was. Here are the numbers:

- Concurrent seats (up to *X* number of users can access the system at any one time): 17%

- Named users (only registered individuals can use the system): 29%

- Per transaction or based on usage (for example, a library management system that charges based on the number of library books tracked and managed): 29%

- Projects: 6%

- Bandwidth used: 1%

- Storage: 0%

- Other: 18% (when analyzed, most of the others were variants of the top three)

When you break named users down by pricing segments, here's what you get:

- $1 to $25 per month: 39%

- $26 to $50 per month: 12%

- $51 to $75 per month: 10%

- $76 to $100 per month: 17%

- $101 to $250 per month: 7%

- $251 to $500 per month: 7%

- $501+ per month: 5%

- Other, please specify: 2%

As you can see, there *is* a pricing range. But if you aggregate the numbers, you also see 41% of the respondents are pricing between $26 and $100 per month. Of course, competition and the market in which you compete will also drive pricing.

One thing we strongly recommend SaaS companies do is look closely at the per-transaction model, as this often allows you to align your pricing with a customer's own business processes. I also strongly suggest they purchase our SaaS report because, as you can see, we've captured a lot of the numbers and data points a SaaS company needs to research when building their business.

Bob: What are the top three concerns companies have when dealing with a SaaS app? Do these concerns differ by market segment?

Rick: The top three concerns are data security and privacy, data integration, and the SaaS vendor's viability. Privacy/security concern becomes of increasing importance as the revenue size of your customers increases and is also determined by type of company. Financial services firms and banks are particularly sensitive to this issue. Don't even attempt to sell any serious SaaS application to, say, Wells Fargo unless you're SAS 70 certified. JP Morgan *will not* allow their data to be comingled with anyone's.

One of the weaknesses of SaaS is that it naturally creates data silos; this is one of the siren calls of the platform players. Many SaaS firms need to be prepared to handle developing web-based services and deploying them to facilitate integration.

Vendor viability is tricky in SaaS. With licensed products, if a vendor dies, the code doesn't. And code escrow arrangements have been around for decades in the software business. But when a SaaS vendor face-plants, an entire environment dies with them. Code escrow is not necessarily of much use. In the 2009 report, we asked companies if they were offering complete fall-over protection; in other words, a third party will maintain and provision the SaaS system in the event the SaaS vendor goes out of business. A surprisingly high 21% of respondents said yes.

Bob: Are companies more likely to be comfortable with a PaaS offering from, say, `Force.com` than standalone SaaS or not?

Rick: We asked SaaS companies if they were developing to platforms such as Force in 2007 and 2008. Year to year, only about 13% were doing so. The platform developers have a lot of work to do in terms of convincing SaaS companies to put their eggs into any particular platform basket.

From the standpoint of IT purchasers, we don't see huge concerns over platform support. Obviously, companies such as `Salesforce.com` would like to change this, but none can claim to be the next Microsoft (yet).

The death of Coghead[8] highlights the PaaS and viability issues.

Bob: What do you see from the data you've been collecting as the trend for SaaS and PaaS?

Rick: SaaS is exploding; PaaS is not. SaaS companies are worried about vendor lock-in, vendors going away and leaving them without an underlying infrastructure, and competition from the platform providers. In 2007 I wrote in an article in *Softletter* that the platform wars of the '90s, which saw Windows triumph over OS/2 and Novell, were breaking out again as platform providers fought for SaaS dominance. And don't forget Microsoft; the .Net Nuke platform (CMS) is a fascinating example of how Microsoft technology can be adapted to create a compelling SaaS system.

Platform As a Service

Overview

Why not have all the advantages of SaaS without all those nasty headaches? That's the pitch to startups of a growing legion of both large and small software companies providing a core of services but who want other companies to move in.

---

[8] `http://www.techcrunch.com/2009/02/18/coghead-grinds-to-a-halt-heads-to-the-deadpool`

At least three different species of PaaS vendors are wooing startups out there.

- **GYMAZ.** This stands for Google, Yahoo, Microsoft, Apple, and Amazon. Each, for its own reasons, revenue model, company history, corporate culture, and internal politics, offers one or more platforms as a service. Among the most prominent as of this writing were Amazon Web Services, Google App Engine (see the upcoming sidebar "Loving Google App Engine"), and the Apple iTunes Store/iPhone/iTouch infrastructure.

- **Multitenant applications.** They provide the plumbing and, sometimes, the customer base for your startup. Salesforce.com's Force. com is the most visible of this kind of PaaS (see Figure 3-2), with other startups, such as AppJet and Heroku, hoping to make it big.

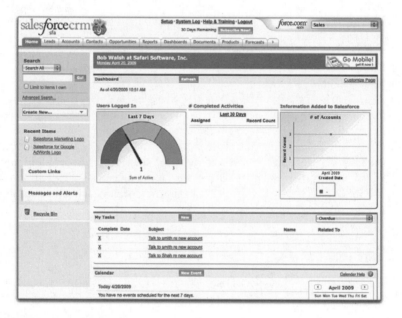

Figure 3-2. *Force.com*

- **Social platforms**. Facebook in particular provides PaaS features.

Main Characteristics from a Startup's Point of View

The good news is you don't have to get into the scaling business; the bad news is you have a landlord—who may be kind, benevolent, and helpful, but a landlord nevertheless.

One thing about landlords—they want their rent. Whether it's Apple's 30% off the top of each and every iPhone app sold or the arrangements Salesforce.com has with it's 800+ third-party apps at Force.com's AppExchange or Google App Engine's billing quota model, you are going to be paying that landlord each and every month.

Advantages

First and foremost, PaaS vendors are in the business of removing the startup heartbreak of scaling from your startup's life.

Next, PaaS vendors drastically reduce or altogether eliminate up-front infrastructure costs. It's a pay-as-you-make-money proposition, and that changes everything from how hard it is to launch a startup that takes advantage of one or more PaaS vendors to how much of your startup you'll actually still own in, say, three years.

Disadvantages

There's a certain suspension of disbelief issue here. What if one fine day Amazon CEO Jeff Bezos decides this whole Web Services thing just isn't cutting it? Or Apple decides it really wants 40% of your revenue, not 30%? Or what if you've tied your fate to a PaaS that just doesn't make it, such as Coghead (see the earlier sidebar "SaaS Enterprise Reality Check")?

Comments

The bottom line for many startups is the more PaaS, the better. Whether it means you don't need $40 million for a server farm of your very own, or it's the opportunity to sell to customers who want more from the primary vendor and you're in the right place at the right time, PaaS makes sense.

What doesn't make sense is treating a PaaS like a safe given; it's not. The startups that gain the most—and weather the worst—that PaaS platforms have to offer are the startups prepared to invest significant time, effort, and attention building as many human connections with the engineers, marketing people, and executives who run the show.

Loving Google App Engine

Dave Westwood is a cofounder of BuddyPoke (see Figure 3-3), a 3D avatar-poking app available on a variety OpenSocial networking sites,[9] and to say he's head over heels in love with Google App Engine is an understatement. Dave made this YouTube video (*Buddypoke on Google App Engine*) and bent my ear when I met him at one of Dave McCure's Startup 2 Startup dinners (see Chapter 4).

Figure 3-3. BuddyPoke

---

[9] *If you have no idea what an avatar-poking Open Social network app is, see the later section "Social Networks as Platforms."*

When I asked David via e-mail about Google App Engine, here's what he had to say.

Reasons we love App Engine:

1. *Scaling that "just works."* Many other web services provide a means to scale, but do not handle all of the scaling for you. With App Engine it just works, allowing us to concentrate on innovation and features for BuddyPoke, rather than the problems of scaling, backing up databases, etc.

2. *Scaling quickly.* OpenSocial, the iPhone, Android devices, Facebook, etc., give developers access to over 800 million users around the world. These days, more so than in the past, if an app goes viral, traffic can increase by orders of magnitude beyond what you may have hoped for. On one day BuddyPoke experienced an eightfold increase in traffic, doing 260k new users in a single day. There's simply no way we could have planned for that kind of rapid growth. With App Engine we didn't have to.

3. *Quality and global reach of Google's infrastructure.* Ninety-five percent of BuddyPoke users live outside of the United States. Google, more than any other company, has created an infrastructure that can deliver apps to users on a global scale, with minimal latency.

4. *Pay-as-we-go model.* Many social apps never take off. Many have instant overnight success and then fade away. Others have slower growth but manage to sustain a high active user count. It's difficult to predict usage for any social apps. So the pay-as-you-go model is perfect for us.

5. *Cost-effective.* We have a very good idea of what our hosting on App Engine will cost us, and it's very fairly priced. The way I think about it is I just hired some of the most talented engineers in the world **for free**, and now I'm just paying them for the bandwidth and CPU usage.

A few years back one of the most popular phrases any startup would say is "We've solved scalability!" Quite frankly it's a problem we don't want to have to solve. We're two guys with a background in 3D. The last thing we want to learn is how to scale. We're in the business of making social apps. We're happy to let Google take care of the scaling for us.

Google has been incredibly helpful in making sure we had enough App Engine quota to grow while App Engine was still in preview. And I've met many engineers from the Google OpenSocial and App Engine teams at local meetups, hackathons, etc. Google is really reaching out to developers even more so than in the past, with new developer relations groups, opening up their code labs, etc. They're trying to make themselves accessible for support and help developers succeed. For example, we just had a "weekend apps" hackathon at Google two weekends ago. Google hosted the event and had some hands-on expertise from the OpenSocial and App Engine teams. So we did receive firsthand support, but I think that support is also available to anyone that asks.

I asked Dave my standard "Any advice for startups?" question: **"I think my response is much like any other startup before us,"** Dave replied. "Just never give up. We released a product in 2007 and it was a failure. We learned from our mistakes, adapted, and tried again. Most entrepreneurs that have succeeded have looked failure in the eye at least once. Learn from it."

Microsoft's Azure Services and Mesh Platforms

For years, as Google and Amazon defined what *cloud platform* meant for developers, Microsoft's critics and developers wondered whether the desktop giant could in effect compete with itself. After all, it was the dynamic duo of Microsoft Windows and Microsoft Office preinstalled by OEM PC vendors that led to the Age of Bill. Could Microsoft offer developers who had forsaken the desktop an alternative to itself?

The short answer is yes—if someone is going to unseat Windows as the platform of choice for developers, it was going to be Microsoft, no matter how much the cash cow side of the business bellowed.

To get an understanding of just what Microsoft cloud platform is offering developers, I turned to my partner in podcasting, Patrick Foley (Figure 3-4). Pat is a Microsoft ISV evangelist based in Michigan. His job is to convince people like you that the Microsoft stack is where you should place your startup bet and then to help startups and what Microsoft calls *ISVs* (*independent software vendors*) get everything they need from the company.

Figure 3-4. Microsoft ISV evangelist Patrick Foley

Although Pat bleeds Microsoft red, as the saying goes, he's not a marketing suit. He's a former startup founder, an accomplished developer, and a guy who tells it like it is and won't blow marketing hype in your ear.

I asked Pat to give us the lowdown on Azure and Mesh and Microsoft's vision of a cloud platform for startups.

Bob: So what does Microsoft Azure and Microsoft Mesh offer startups looking for a platform on which to build?

Patrick: Cloud computing in general is a game-changer for startups. It allows startups to compete with large, established software companies without having to invest in hosting infrastructure.

The magic ingredient is scalability. You can always buy a server and host it with a reliable provider, but what happens when you need to handle an enormous amount of peak traffic, perhaps for a one-day event that's three weeks away or perhaps in response to the viral success of your application? Before the cloud, you'd have to create your own infrastructure to handle this peak load, so startups had to either invest heavily or limit themselves to solving problems that didn't require much scale.

Now with the concept of the cloud, or "utility computing," you can provision just the capabilities you need for only as long as you need them. The capacity that you can provision is enormous and nearly instantaneous. This allows for new business models and technical approaches that simply weren't possible before.

For an example, see BrowserMob [http://browsermob.com]; it uses a "brute force" approach to load testing by firing up thousands of browsers on thousands of VMs [virtual machines]. They have one full-time employee and are cash-flow positive and profitable. Their approach wasn't possible before the cloud.

What Windows Azure brings to this space is a consistent development experience for .NET developers. If you know how to program for the Windows client or ASP.NET, it's going to be pretty seamless to program for Windows Azure. That's a huge advantage. The same high-productivity development experience works with Windows Azure, traditional Windows Server, Windows client, ASP.NET, AJAX, Silverlight, Windows Mobile, embedded, and more.

So now you can focus on building assets that can be hosted in the cloud on Windows Azure or on-premise with Windows Server and get a significant amount of overlap between the two platforms. According to Steven Martin, Senior Director for Developer Platform Product Management, "The innovation in Azure and future versions of Windows Server will be shared, and that codebase will continue to cross-pollinate. The corporate data center at some point in time will look like a minicloud, partitioned by application workload."

(http://www.computerworld.com/action/article.do?command=
viewArticleBasic&articleId=9129156&intsrc=news_ts_head).

So the reach of our platforms and the choice this provides software companies and their customers are key benefits of Windows Azure and Mesh.
Startups need high productivity, reliability, reach, and value—that's what
they're going to get with all of our offerings.

Bob: How do Azure and Mesh compare to the other "in the cloud" platforms
out there, like AWS and Google App Engine?

Patrick: I was happy to see Ray Ozzie tip his hat to Amazon Web Services
when Azure was announced. Amazon has a solid production offering, and
they are currently the leader in the space. Since they now offer Windows
hosting, they also provide a viable option for Windows developers looking
to create a solution in the cloud. That said, Azure has some intriguing advantages—to understand them, we have to look at a broader view first.

There are two basic approaches to cloud computing, the virtual machine
model and the sandbox model. Amazon uses the virtual machine model with
their EC2 offering. Google and Microsoft are more focused on the sandbox
model.

There are trade-offs to each approach. The advantage of the virtual machine
model is that it is familiar to developers and you can generally get legacy
applications to work on it. The advantage of the sandbox model is that it
hides even more of the complexity of scaling from the developer and provides
greater economies of scale for the cloud provider.

In the virtual machine model, the deployable "component" is a virtual machine,
typically a stateless web stack. It has to be stateless in order to enable the
scaling magic—if you want to fire up 100 virtual machines interacting to
solve a problem, they can't each be responsible for their own state; Amazon
provides various ways of dealing with that, but developers have to understand scalable system partitioning and be disciplined if they want their apps
to scale.

By contrast, with Google App Engine [GAE] the deployable component is a
chunk of Python code, and with Windows Azure it's a .NET assembly. These
are much more granular components, and they consume far fewer resources
than virtual machines when they aren't being heavily used. That chunk of
Python or .NET code can't just be allowed to do anything, though—it has to
be "sandboxed" to prevent the developer from seeing the underlying cloud
infrastructure. You don't get to write straight to the file system, for example;
instead, you have to use storage services.

There is one enormous advantage to the sandbox model for startups—
a lower entry price point. Running virtual machines consumes precious
resources, and cloud providers have to charge for them. So it's going to cost

you around $75–$100/month to get started with the minimum infrastructure needed to host a simple web application 24/7 on Amazon's EC2, compared to $10/month or less for commodity shared hosting. That means a startup or MicroISV who is trying to scrape by on a shoestring would have to make a choice between betting on a true cloud infrastructure and investing 5–10 times more per month and starting with commodity hosting and switching to AWS once "successful."

Pricing for Windows Azure hasn't been announced yet, but Google's has . . . and it's extremely compelling for startups. Google offers a "free until you're successful" pricing model, and the only reason they can is because of the sandbox model. If you love the way Google apps work and you happen to be a Python fan, then GAE is obviously a compelling option to consider.

Again, Azure's pricing hasn't been announced yet (and I am in fact not privy to it), but my hope is that it will allow startups and microISVs to start with a true cloud infrastructure at the outset and grow seamlessly as they succeed. And because it's the same great development experience they're already used to, it's a slam-dunk for .NET developers.

Mesh is in a category all its own. The point of mesh is to allow developers to create user experiences that bring together all your devices, from Windows and Mac PCs to mobile phones to browsers. It's still quite early in its evolution, but the bits that are out there today are already remarkably useful.

I use Mesh to store my most important documents so that they automatically sync to each of the PCs I use and so that I can get to them from a browser when I need to. I use it to automatically sync shared documents with coworkers and family. It works great for this. But the true potential is as an application delivery platform—the coolest example is delivering a Silverlight application where the application and its data automatically sync across your devices. This makes for an incredibly rich implementation of the occasionally connected scenario.

It's worth noting that Mesh is implemented on Windows Azure . . . it demonstrates the kind of innovation that can be delivered on Windows Azure and the degree to which it can scale.

Bob: It's still the very early days for Azure/Mesh, but just how serious is Microsoft about becoming a "cloud provider"?

Patrick: Incredibly serious. We're investing heavily to build out data centers around the world. Initial feedback is incredibly positive and excited—this is what customers want. They also have been clear that they want the flexibility to run software in the cloud or on-premise—they want us to make it easy for them to choose and to balance on-premise with cloud resources.

Bob: What about the "old Microsoft" of Windows and Office? Doesn't Azure/Mesh in effect threaten the core of Microsoft?

Patrick: Innovate or die . . . new problems and new realities require new solutions.

That said, Windows Server and the Windows desktop obviously aren't going away anytime soon, and we're continuing to invest heavily in those areas. Customers are incredibly excited about Windows 7 and Windows Server 2008 R2.

You could argue that the proliferation of web applications in the enterprise threatened Microsoft 5 or 10 years ago, but we responded by making the best web stack out there. Now users expect more richness from those web-based applications, so we responded with Silverlight, the best RIA [rich Internet application] platform out there. If you want the absolute richest user experience, you're going to want to build a Windows Presentation Foundation [WPF] application that runs on the Windows client. The fact that Silverlight delivers so many of the capabilities of WPF with reach to Mac and Linux browsers (via Moonlight) just gives customers more choice—maybe we'll lose some Windows applications to Silverlight/Mesh because it's so good, but I think we'll win some Cocoa and Air developers over as well, so it will balance out.

The cloud is the next great frontier in our industry, and I think Windows Azure will prove itself to be the best cloud offering out there. It's still early, of course.

Competition is a wonderful thing, because it drives innovation. But there is no other company that can deliver the range and quality of platforms we do with the consistency and quality of developer experience that we do. This is our biggest advantage; when Steve Ballmer shouts that "developers are the air we breathe," I think this is what he is referring to—we provide the best overall platform for developers and startups to innovate on, and we must continue to do so as our industry evolves.

We haven't even talked about Office or MOSS or Dynamics today . . . the opportunities to innovate on our platform and to partner with Microsoft are astounding.

Bob: What kinds of apps could startups do with Azure/Mesh? I know it's (as of May 2009) very early, but speculate.

Patrick: The possibilities are endless. First of all, I think many basic web applications that are hosted with commodity shared hosting today will fit very well with Azure. Viral applications that might need to scale quickly—such as Facebook applications—are perfectly suited.

I think we'll see combination applications emerge where data is stored in the cloud but the UI [user interface] is delivered as a WPF client (or Silverlight Mesh client).

I think we'll see utility services spring up by microISVs that were not realistic to build when you had to make your own infrastructure. I have one of these in mind to build myself, in fact. I think I have a good idea, and it would be fairly easy for me to implement. What held me back in the past was the possibility of success! If I really am right that it's a good idea, then it will need to scale very quickly. Before Azure, I just didn't have the bandwidth to manage that problem. With Azure, I don't have to manage the scalability problem. Like any other microISV, now I just need to find the time and guts to do it!

We'll see more and more software companies that previously only offered on-premise versions of their software offer cloud-based versions as well. Customers want the flexibility to choose either on-premise or hosted solutions, and Azure provides the infrastructure to give software companies the ability to provide that choice to their customers.

Finally, I think we'll see some "Why didn't I think of that?" applications that were simply not possible before the cloud existed. It's a great time to create a startup.

Social Networks As Platforms

Overview

In the second half of the first decade of the 21st century, something very different started happening, not just in the tiny bubble developers and startups inhabit, but to the world at large.

Up until about 2005, if you wanted to get a really big number of people talking about the same thing, expressing the same ideas and values, and sharing a common experience and view point, you needed to found either a religion, a country, or a political ideology. Now we have MySpace, Facebook, Bebo, Twitter, and hundreds of other social networks.

Please don't think this is just a case of TWH—tired writer hyperbole. Remember all those "soft" departments you'd walk past as you headed toward the Computer Science Department? Their meat and potatoes is trying to understand how large groups of people interact—economically, socially, psychologically, historically, politically.

As of early 2009, MySpace had 76 million active users, Hi5 60 million, Xing 6.5 million, Twitter a mere 4.5 million, and Facebook a staggering 150 million.[10] Incidentally, those numbers match the populations of,

---

[10] *http://www.web-strategist.com/blog/2009/01/11/a-collection-of-soical-network-stats-for-2009*

respectively, Egypt, Italy, El Salvador, Ireland, and Russia, give or take a few million people.[11] And, unlike countries, these social networks and thousands of others are growing at Internet speeds; for example, Twitter grew by 752% or so in 2008.[12]

Whether you buy my argument that social networks are akin to countries, one thing is for sure—there's money to be made by startups on the social platform.

Main Characteristics from a Startup's Point of View

Unlike the economies of countries, social networks are nearly only about advertising. Next to that Facebook wall or MySpace page you're going to find ads, ads, and more ads. It's all about eyeballs, as the old dot.com saying used to go, and social platform startups—including the companies behind these networks—tend to be all about managing, monetizing, targeting, triangulating, and displaying ads.

But advertising was and is the low-hanging fruit of the social platform. The real power, innovation, and excitement are happening around applications that connect segments of all those users in even deeper ways.

Advantages

The real big advantage of social networks is users—and big, giant, ridiculously large numbers of them. For example, as of this writing, Causes—a Facebook app that lets you start and join causes you care about and make donations to them—had 25,892,339 monthly active users (Figure 3-5). Not bad for a little Berkeley, California, startup.

---

[11] http://en.wikipedia.org/wiki/List_of_countries_by_population

[12] http://www.web-strategist.com/blog/2009/01/11/a-collection-of-social-network-stats-for-2009

Figure 3-5. How would you like 25.8 million users?

Disadvantages

Facebook the social network is Facebook the PaaS platform—you play by our rules or we cut off your oxygen faster than you can say *Scrabulous*.[13] And it's not big, meany Facebook deciding which startups on their platform live or die; *every* social platform's terms of service jealously guard the company's right to zap you in an instant.

If you want access to our users, the social platform refrain goes, you'd better be prepared to play by our rules, including the ones we haven't made up yet.

---

[13] *Scrabulous scrapped on Facebook—http://www.msnbc.msn.com/id/25914209.*

Comments

There's a lot more to be said about social platforms and startups—like all of Chapter 6.

Mobile

Overview

What a difference a single product can make! A few years ago, while cell phone growth was blasting ever higher each quarter, *smartphones*—mobiles that could be used as platforms by aspiring startups—were a languishing minor part of the overall story. For example, Microsoft had its mobile platform's first offering in 1996, for all that most people in or out of this industry cared.

Then along came the Apple iPhone (Figure 3-6). Between June 29, 2007, when it first went on sale, to September 2008, Apple and its mobile service provider partners worldwide sold some 13 million units.[14] From July 2008 to January 2009, the number of third-party apps available for the iPhone went from zero to 15,000 applications downloaded 500 million times.[15] Then from January 2009 to April 23, 2009, another 500 downloads of more than 25,000 apps[16] brought the total to a cool 1 billion in nine months. Let's see: 25,000 apps and 1 billion downloads in nine months—**ka-ching!**[17]

---

[14] http://en.wikipedia.org/wiki/Apple_iphone

[15] http://mashable.com/2009/01/16/apple-500-million-iphone-apps-downloaded

[16] http://blogs.zdnet.com/cell-phones/?p=851

[17] http://www.apple.com/itunes/billion-app-countdown

Figure 3-6. The Apple iPhone platform

Main Characteristics from a Startup's Point of View

Back in the dot.com days, mainstream media loved profiling "dot.com millionaires" with multi-hundred-million-dollar stock options and incredibly expensive sports cars. This time around, bloggers and traditional media are writing up "iPhone millionaires"[18] as startups rack up huge monthly sales—except some of these potential iPhone millionaires are too young to drive (Figure 3-7).[19]

---

[18] http://news.bbc.co.uk/newsbeat/hi/technology/newsid_7926000/7926506.stm

[19] "Nine-year-old whiz kid writes iPhone application"—http://www.reuters.com/article/technologyNews/idUSTRE5140FI20090205?rpc=64 and http://news.bbc.co.uk/2/hi/technology/7874291.stm and http://virtualgs.larwe.com/Virtual_GS/Lim_Ding_Wen.html

Figure 3-7. A 9-year-old works on the Apple iPhone platform

Although Apple has very quickly grabbed a huge market share of the mobile platform, Apple's isn't the only mobile story. While Apple was building a proprietary high-end mobile platform, Google was taking the exact opposite approach to untangling the mess of incompatible Linux-based mobile operating systems and bringing Google Android to the party.

On the one hand Android is a complete mobile stack for cell phone providers, with the companies part of Google's Open Handset Alliance being first at the table. On the other hand, it gives developers and startups one software development kit (SDK) to absorb. On the third hand

(Androids aren't necessarily limited), Android developers have the advantage of watching what works on the iPhone and what doesn't. And on the fourth hand, 13 million iPhones may sound like a lot until you realize there are approximately 3.3 billion cell phones on the planet and that the percentage of those phones sold today that are smartphones is about 13% and accelerating fast.[20]

Although right now it's still the very early days for Android, more and more cell phone makers are going Android. And, yes, there's a Google Android app store (Figure 3-8).

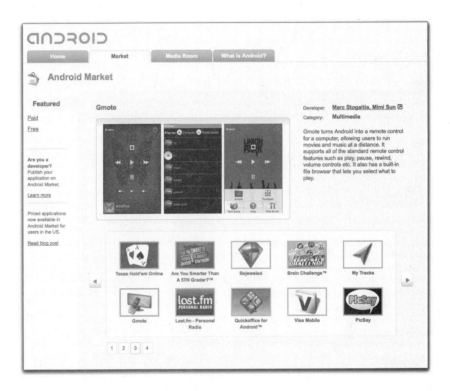

Figure 3-8. The Google Android U.S. store

---

[20] *"Our Cells, Ourselves," Washington Post* (http://www.washingtonpost.com/wp-dyn/content/article/2008/02/22/AR2008022202283.html) *and "Global smart phone shipments rise 28%,"* http://www.canalys.com/pr/2008/r2008112.htm.

Advantages

As Andrey Butov says about his concept of platform arbitrage in the upcoming sidebar, mobile means money. Fewer competitors, no established market leaders, and a public eager to spend money adding new digital bling to their new best friend is a compelling scenario for startups and investors alike.

There's a second level of chewy goodness when it comes to mobile— a platform beyond the idea of desktop computers, where GPS (Global Positioning System) and SMS mean brand new kinds of applications are possible.

Disadvantages

Although the feature set of iPhones and Android phones may at first glance appear similar, the business environment is anything but. For the iPhone, you get to do what Apple says you get to do, period. For Android, there's the danger that cell phone makers and service providers will yet again screw up a common Linux standard.

Comments

Recently I was having lunch in a popular eatery in San Francisco's tony Marina district. Out of the 50-odd patrons I counted 3 MacBooks, 1 PC, and 13 iPhones in use. I don't know of a consumer technology that has changed the daily habits of so many so fast as the iPhone—and the iPhone may prove to be the warm-up act for the Google Android.

Andrey Butov, Antair Corporation

Way back when in 2005, I interviewed Andrey Butov for my first book, just after he released his first commercial product as a microISV, a .NET developer tool. Four years later, Audrey's no-longer-micro startup sells applications (http://www.antair.com) and games (http://www.antairgames.com) for Macs and Windows. And BlackBerries. And iPhones. Here's how Andrey tells the story.

"Platform arbitrage is our approach of applying the same principles as one does in selection of the type of product to sell, to presentation of one product across multiple select platforms. While there are underdeveloped product niches which would work with an introduction of a better/cheaper product option, there are also many underdeveloped and underrepresented platforms which lack sufficient product choice.

"A few years ago, this was the Mac desktop. In recent years, it's the various mobile platforms. For Antair, we can leverage much higher yearly revenues by leveraging our products against the BlackBerry and iPhone platforms as compared with competing on a more common platform. But platform arbitrage needs to be approached with the same careful analysis as product selection. For example, we will not port any of our current products to the Android platform, as it stands, although we have had requests to do so. This may change in the future, however.

"I've always run Antair as a no-niche software company; preferring to keep out product line diverse, both in terms of the type of product sold, as well as with regard to platforms on which the product was available. We believe that "platform arbitrage," as I've come to think of it, is a wise strategy when designing a new product offering with the hopes of exposing it to as wide a market as possible."

Antair's first iPhone game, Sneezies (Figure 3-9), was a coproduction with Gavin Bowman, the founder of V4 Solutions and another microISV I had interviewed in 2005. It was something of a leap of faith for both developers. Could a cross-Atlantic development effort work?

Figure 3-9. Antair Games

"The idea for Sneezies came from my wife," Andrey e-mailed me. "She tends to play a lot of casual titles that are addictive, easy to get into, and fun to play, so we wanted to come up with something along those lines. A game that has lots of polish, offers long-lasting playability, but isn't complicated to get into. We've had some experience before with designing proper mobile titles (Asteroid Jane for the BlackBerry), so we kind of knew what to expect from the technical side, and we were familiar with what would be required from our artists.

"We thought the game was fun even in the early stages, but what Gavin delivered in the end simply blew everyone away. Sneezies was so polished, and was balanced so perfectly, that everyone from our guys at the Antair offices, to our publishers, to the players consistently commenting that they love the game and can't put it down. After shipping the game, Gavin put in a lot of marketing effort, and, as word of the game spread, Antair was hit with an avalanche of positive feedback and reviews from players around the world."

"I still wake up in the mornings and run my day as a self-employed microISV," Gavin told me as I was putting together this chapter. "Antair Games runs for the most part as an autonomous, self-sufficient entity. So I have most of the same concerns and priorities I had when I was running V4 Solutions, so I don't feel like that chapter is closed.

"The relationship with Antair has allowed me to retire a few of my "hats," as you would say, but I don't miss any of them, most notably the financials and accounting stuff. I always had a partner in V4, so there's nothing new there. But that was a largely silent arrangement; I communicate and confer with Andrey constantly. I'm also in constant contact with Craig Sharpe, our artist. He deserves as much credit for the work we do at Antair Games these days as me. He's in yet another corner of the world—we're a well-distributed team!

"As Andrey mentioned in his e-mail, our relationship is an oddity. It's very difficult to give advice or to recommend anyone follow our example, because the role trust has played in the development of that relationship is huge. However, it has worked perfectly for us. We've been able to focus entirely on making good software and getting a lot done from day 1, instead of getting bogged down in technicalities."

One of the things Andrey in New York City and Gavin in Cumbria in the "cold, dark north" of the U.K. illustrate is that whatever commonalities startups share, it is how they come into existence and who the people are that make each a unique solution to the general business problem of bringing software to life.

Eric Chu, Google Mobile Platforms Program Manager

Eric Chu has the huge task of making one of the most anticipated mobile phone platform releases live up to high expectations. I was able to ask him via e-mail a few questions about what Android as a platform offers startups.

Bob: For a startup, what are the big advantages in picking Android as their platform?

Eric: Our goal is to create a platform and content distribution system to make it easier for developers to create and distribute compelling mobile applications. Our decision to build Android from the ground up allowed us to leverage the latest technologies available to build a truly modern mobile platform.

Our Open Source model with Android makes it extremely attractive for different handset manufacturers and carriers to adopt and deploy Android-based handsets. We believe this is the best approach to drive up volume. Our investment in Android Market provides a simple "one-stop" distribution mechanism to deliver apps to many Android devices around the world. We believe the combination of a powerful platform on many different devices from a wide range of device manufacturers, coupled with a global content distribution system, makes Android an extremely attractive platform for startups to monetize on.

Bob: How would you compare Android as a platform for building a startup vs. iPhone or BlackBerry?

Eric: It is extremely hard to compare specific devices with a platform, such as Android, that will be available from many different handset makers. The Android platform offers developers the opportunity to create innovative experiences via features such as multitasking, mobile mashup, and access to hardware and system-level functions.

We also believe Android Market's open model has proven to be attractive to developers and users alike. However, it is also important to point out that approximately 1 billion handsets are sold every year. It probably makes sense for developers to make their products available on more than one platform or device.

Bob: Is there an Android developer program, above and beyond `http://code.google.com/android` and `http://developer.android.com`?

Eric: No. However, developers should also sign up with Android Market. `http://developer.android.com` is the new site for developers. We're now updating content on `http://code.google.com/android`. Developers should also visit `http://market.android.com/publish/signup` and sign up to distribute their applications through Android Market.

Bob: What advice would you give a startup mulling their platform choices?

> **Eric:** Conventional wisdom is to target volume. However, it is even more important to target the right "volume." Developers should pay close attention to the volume that equates to actual usage. While there might be billions of mobile devices out there, for each of the device types and platforms, are users really using the data services? In addition, as this market opens up, the friction that will prevent users from finding apps will continue to lower. That means users will gravitate toward great apps in larger and larger volume. It will become increasingly more important for developers to have an awesome product to guarantee success rather than distribution advantages.

Hybrid

Overview

Okay, this kind of platform should be called *cross-platform*, but reading about a cross-platform platform gives my copyeditor a headache and lacks the coolness, panache, and shininess of *hybrid*. Think of it: no more quasi-religious flame post wars over which is the best platform, no more endless debates on whether which is "better"—desktop or web.

The two big players in the hybrid platform space are Adobe Flex/AIR (Figure 3-10) and Microsoft Silverlight. For Adobe, Flex turns the ubiquitous Flash browser plug-in into the runtime for a user interface layer that delivers performance and usability not seen in standard web apps, with the very real advantage of being able to live on the Windows and Mac desktops

Microsoft Silverlight—as of this writing and I'll bet not for much longer[21]—lacks the ability to run as solely a desktop app. But what it does have is a pared-down .NET framework that lets programmers develop in Microsoft Visual Studio not only in C# and VB, but in dynamic languages such as Ruby and PHP. Furthermore, Silverlight is an extension of Microsoft's partner ecology, including a growing number of commercial .NET control vendors.

---

[21] *Silverlight 3 Beta, released March 18, 2009, added both out-of-browser and offline capabilities.*

Figure 3-10. TweetDeck—an Adobe AIR app

While the Flex platform continues to grow and evolve and make head-way behind the enterprise firewall, according to Adobe technical evangelist James Ward, Silverlight got a global-sized win when NBC used it as its online platform for the 2008 Summer Olympics and lets .NET developers be .NET developers, says Josh Holmes, Microsoft UX architect evangelist.[22]

Main Characteristics from a Startup's Point of View

Remember a few years back when desktop apps were (again) declared officially dead and the future belonged to Web 2.0? Ha! Turns out most

---

[22] *The Startup Success Podcast: Show #15: James Ward, Adobe Technical Evangelist (http://startuppodcast.wordpress.com/2009/02/15/show-15-james-ward-adobe-technical-evangelist) and Show #17: Josh Holmes, Microsoft UX Architect Evangelist (http://startup-podcast.wordpress.com/2009/03/01/show-17-josh-holmes-microsoft-ux-architect-evangelist).*

people, when given a list of the benefits of web apps and a list of the advantages of desktop apps, answer, "Both. Right now."

Cross-platform apps—especially those that can run disconnected from the net—give you as the startup founder the largest possible pool of potential customers, and that's a very nice thing to have.

Advantages

First and foremost, it's breaking the iron chains of HTML. Since the first Common Gateway Interface (CGI) form on a Netscape browser, developers working on web apps have had to use a text markup language to code. Everything at the end of the JavaScript day goes into HTML and has to come out of HTML. And don't even get me started on CSS, browser idiosyncrasies, or the joys of catering to Internet Explorer 6's perverse set of DOM "features."

The second big advantage of hybrid platforms accrues to all those desktop developers who were left behind to rot, doing maintenance years ago, by the Web App Rapture. For desktop programmers locked out of the Web 2.0 game, both Flex/AIR and Silverlight are a way to go forward with real development platforms, whether the customer uses a Mac or a Windows box, HTML be damned.

Disadvantages

Welcome to the cutting edge of technology. (Please don't bleed on this book until you've bought it.) Whether it's Flex or Silverlight, you're talking about software platforms with plenty of open manhole covers—everything is fine until you drop through the hole. In both cases platform development is out of your hands, and the feature that you absolutely have to have to build your startup's app that was sure to be in the next version real soon now may or may not be there.

A cool, snazzy 10-minute demo at a conference or in a book is one thing; a platform stable and robust enough to pour thousands of sweat equity hours and millions of equity-financed dollars into is something else again. As of this writing (May 2009), whereas there are plenty of demo apps, enterprise apps, and showoff apps for both Flex and Silverlight, there's only a handful of commercial apps.

Comments

The problem for hybrid-based apps is that startups are businesses first, places to play with cool technology second. Apple and Google, each in its own way, made sure there were real apps for sale for their respective platforms; Adobe and Microsoft, for their own reasons, haven't seen the world in that particular light, at least not yet.

For what it's worth, I think the best thing Adobe or Microsoft can do for the latest and greatest technologies is pick 25 developers, hand them each $25,000 for a nominal 5% equity stake to keep the bean counters happy, and get some real startups offering real products out there. Until something like that happens, angel investors and VCs will not be lining up to fund hybrid startups the way they have iPhone and Android startups.

Jeff Haynie, CEO, Appcelerator

In addition to Adobe and Microsoft, others out there are looking to provide a hybrid web/desktop platform for developers. One of the most interesting is Jeff Haynie and Appcelerator (http://titaniumapp.com). Building off a $4.1 million Series A funding in December 2008, Appcelerator is an early-stage startup going for the big prize by offering web-skilled JavaScript developers a way to build products that run on Windows, Mac OS X, and Linux.

What's more, Appcelerator and its development tool, Appcelerator Titanium (see Figure 3-11), are Open Source—building a tool and a community around that tool and tapping the enthusiasm of that community are the first steps in Appcelerator's long-term strategy. Earlier this decade that $4.1 million would be burned through in a matter of weeks. Today, Jeff is confident that Appcelerator's financial runway is long enough for him and his 12 employees to achieve takeoff.

Bob: What's it like being a platform startup going up against the likes of Adobe and Microsoft?

Jeff: We're excited! There's plenty of room in the industry for multiple solutions, and the industry deserves (and desperately needs) a viable open web platform that's developed in an Open Source model. It's about giving people more choice and flexibility, and we believe our platform allows for that.

Bob: What do you see as the future of bringing web technology down to the desktop?

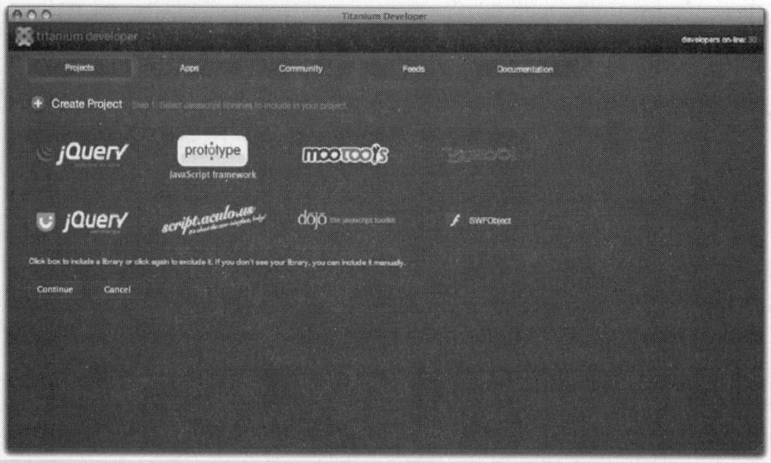

Figure 3-11. Appcelerator's Titanium developer

Jeff: I believe the convergence of cloud computing combined with the need to have access to applications across a variety of mediums (desktop, mobile, phone) provides a great opportunity for applications and application platforms to move back to the desktop—but not in a way that we are used to. Tomorrow's desktop applications will be much more web-native while still leveraging the capabilities and functionality of the desktop environment.

Bob: What's Titanium and the Appcelerator SDK's big advantage? What do you tell startups to woo them to you?

Jeff: Titanium is an open architecture, Open Source runtime for building cross–operating system, cross-technology applications for the desktop using web technologies. Our message is simple: as an application developer you can build very compelling applications that leverage your existing web tooling, web skill sets, and web infrastructure—today. And you can seamlessly run those applications across all major operating systems, completely unchanged.

Bob: Your platform is Open Source. How will you make money? And how do your investors expect to make the kind of money they are looking for?

Jeff: Our platform and tools are Open Source and will remain Open Source. Our plan is to introduce some additional, complementary cloud-services capabilities that add value by helping you reduce cost and burden in your application life cycle. However, right now we're focused on building out the best technology platform and working with application developers from around the world to deploy those applications—that's our primary focus.

Bob: Given the depth of technical expertise you have, you certainly could have brought to market one or more applications. Why focus on building a platform?

Jeff: We think that our job is to enable many other developers, worldwide, to build what they believe is creative, passionate, and interesting to them—something that scales well. We're already seeing applications being developed with our products that we never could have even dreamed of when we envisioned the uses of the platform initially. What's great about being an open architecture is that people can build on what we've done and extend the vision and capabilities to many others. We view Titanium similar to what's happened to Linux—it originally started out as an alternative to Unix but now powers everything from desktops and servers to cars and cell phones.

Bob: What's your advice to startups who are mulling over their platform choices?

Jeff: The best platforms are ones that don't require you to reinvest in new skills and new infrastructure and that ultimately give you the power to control your own destiny. That's what we believe makes a good open web platform.

Bob: Any other advice for startups?

Jeff: This is a very exciting and difficult time for startups and entrepreneurs—particularly given the world economic crisis. I think it can be summed up by two quotes: "Longevity is credibility" (Jason Calacanis) and "Sales solves everything" (Mark Cuban).

Here are some general startup thoughts I wrote a few months ago that are more relevant than ever: `http://blog.jeffhaynie.us/the-economic-downturn-and-your-startup.html`.

Peldi Guilizzoni, Balsamiq Studios

Giacomo "Peldi" Guilizzoni is a great example of how a self-funded startup can, by doing the right things in the right way, rapidly build momentum, staff, and revenue without resorting to equity financing. Peldi, an Italian, came over to the United States to work for Macromedia (now part of Adobe) as programmer in the Flash group, working on Flash Media Server and Breeze (now Adobe Connect). After years of gaining knowledge about and contributing to Adobe's effort to expand Flash to something more than a way to play video in web browsers, he returned to Bologna, Italy, focused single-mindedly on building Balsamiq Mockups (`http://www.balsamiq.com`) (Figure 3-12), an Adobe AIR tool for programmers, experienced designers, and product managers and launched.

Peldi's strategy was threefold: (1) build a great app that made mocking up web and desktop apps extremely easy, (2) get to know IT bloggers and offer them licenses and support while using his blog to share his passion and build credibility, and (3) tap Twitter as a way of connecting to even more people, especially developers checking their social networks for recommendations for prototyping, wireframing, and mockup tools.

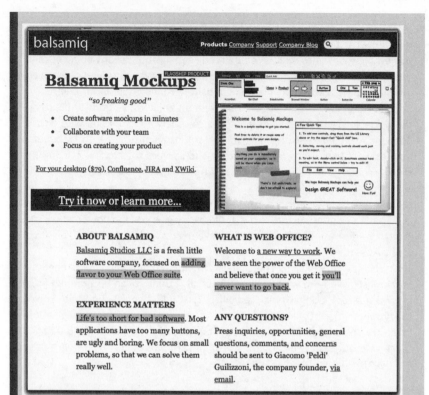

Figure 3-12. Balsamiq Mockups

Within eight months, Peldi had brought his wife into the business to help with support, hired his first full-time employee, and cleared $300,000 in revenue.

I've interviewed Peldi before, for the Startup Success Podcast. In an industry where egos inflate to blimp size after three paragraphs in *TechCrunch*, I found refreshing his combination of passion for his product, his willingness to help other startups, and his down-to-earth, get-the-job-done attitude.

Bob: What's it like dealing with two very different kinds of users—Mac and Windows—plus pure web-centric users?

Peldi: Let's not forget Linux users as well! :)

Lucky for developers, the recent advent of browser-based web apps has lowered everyone's expectations, with every web app behaving differently than the next, and very few of them having the polish of a desktop app. So you can get away with more. That said, this is an opportunity to delight your users by giving them applications that, while cross-platform and online/offline, feel native as much as possible.

In general, I have learned that people are passionate about these little differences, so you should respect them and try to fulfill them as much as possible, even if you might personally not care as much about them. That's why we use the system's window chrome instead of drawing our own, or why we offer an option to hide the app with Apple+H on the Mac, for instance.

As always, it's about providing an experience users are familiar with: "Don't make them think" (Steve Krug, http://www.sensible.com), especially about how to move, resize, and minimize a window . . . please!

Bob: What do you see as the advantages of developing a platform-independent app?

Peldi: Having grown up professionally at Macromedia, where cross-platform compatibility was considered a competitive advantage, I don't really see any other option. Building an application for a single platform feels so limiting to me, especially now that it's relatively easy to build a cross-platform one. More and more people are buying Macs these days, and Ubuntu is user-friendly enough to make it a viable consumer-level OS. Plus there's the web, of course, and mobile. I think any modern app should be able to run on all of those platforms, or it will lose out to others that can.

Bob: What about disadvantages?

Peldi: Adobe AIR takes care of most of the hassles for me: they offer APIs which abstract out most OS-specific differences nicely, and they provide a smooth installation and upgrade experience with virtually no effort on my part.

That said, there will always be platform-specific bugs to work around, so you have to be fluent in all modern operating systems, a required skill to run a microISV anyways.

I run Parallels on my laptop so that I can test features and bugs on OS X, Windows XP, and Ubuntu all on the same machine. I have resisted buying a Vista license, but I might be forced to since some of my customers are reporting a number of issues that only happen on Vista . . . not a great reason to buy an OS license is it? ;)

Bob: You're also part of the XWiki wiki "ecosystem," which is Open Source, with XWiki SAS, the creators of XWiki, selling support for it. How do you convince people to pay for a plug-in that works in an Open Source app?

Peldi: It's not an easy task, and I haven't been doing a great job at it so far. First of all, you have to find an open-source platform which will legally let you extend it commercially: XWiki uses LGPL [Lesser General Public License], but many others use GPL [General Public License], which forbids commercial extensions (or, rather, it's a gray area that I like to stay out of).

One business model that seems to work is the "free software, paid support" one, but it's not one that I'm a big fan of. Ideally, software should be easy and solid enough to require no support, right?

I would suggest looking at http://robertogaloppini.net. Roberto is a specialist in commercial Open Source software, consulting on marketing and business strategy, and his blog has a host of tips on this subject.

Bob: Balsamiq Mockups is an Adobe Flex/AIR app. What's that been like to develop?

Peldi: It's been great fun! The Flex framework is powerful, mature, and fast enough to build any sort of application that I like to build (simple ones which don't try to boil the ocean but, rather, try solve a small problem really well). Like any framework it has a bit of a learning curve. There's a huge community of developers to help you and loads of online resources to get started.

Once you have a web app built in Flex, adapting it to run on AIR takes literally a couple of hours. Adobe AIR is a fairly young platform (it's at version 1.5 at the time of writing), but it's already mature, cross-platform from the ground up, and has the mighty power of Adobe behind it. Adobe is deeply committed to the AIR and offers great support for it to its developers—via forums, mailing lists, and a very good prerelease program. They release new updates fairly often (perhaps two or three a year), so bugs get squashed fairly quickly.

The development environment (Flex Builder) is also good: it's based on Eclipse, and it offers everything a modern IDE [integrated development environment] should offer (integrated debugger, profiler, etc.). Development is really fast and allows for quick iteration easily.

There's still a lot that Air could do of course, but so far I've been really happy with it. I think senior developers out there should try to forget their old preconceptions about Flash applications and take a second look at Flex/AIR. It really has come a long way.

Bob: If your startup decided today to do another app, would you stick with Adobe?

Peldi: I'd say so, yes. For cross-platform applications that run both on the Web and offline, in my mind the choice is between either Flex/AIR or HTML+JS plus a a browser wrapper. Anything else just doesn't have the market penetration or maturity necessary to be a contender.

The choice between these depends on the nature of the application. HTML+JS has better accessibility story (better text handling, focus support, etc.), but, IMHO, nothing beats Flash for rich, highly graphical interactive experiences (like an image editor, for instance).

People get religious about these things, but I like to take a more pragmatic approach. In the end the opinion of the developer matters little relative to the overall user experience for the customer.

Bob: You also recently hired your first employee. How did you decide on who to hire when?

Peldi: Yes! His first week just ended yesterday, and already I couldn't be happier. My goal with Balsamiq has been to grow it to a four- to five-person company from the start, slowly and organically. When I started up I told myself that I would hire someone as soon as I noticed the level of customer service I was providing to my customers and prospects starting to be less than spectacular. A couple of months ago I started having over 150 new customers per week, which I could still manage (barely), but it took all of my time, leaving no time for coding new features. I started only coding on the weekends for a while, but that's not sustainable, nor is it really enough for what I want to do with the product. Since I already had enough in the bank to cover for a programmer's first year of salary, the decision to hire someone became self-evident at the end of a particularly rough day.

As for who to hire, I knew I wanted a generalist as employee #1. Marco fits the bill beautifully. He is mostly going to focus on programming at first, but he can wear all of the 47 hats (Bob Walsh, http://www.47hats.com) required for a microISV. I have interviewed many candidates in my career, and once in a blue moon someone comes in that's clearly a cut above the rest, someone who is "'done, and gets things smart" (Steve Yegge, http://steve-yegge.blogspot.com/2008/06/done-and-gets-things-smart.html). Marco is that kind of person, I got really lucky.

Bob: Any advice for startups who want to succeed?
Peldi: Ah, the million-dollar question. I think success is a combination of a number of factors: first and foremost, passion and hard, hard work. Solving a real problem which saves people money and "makes meaning" (Guy Kawasaki, http://blog.guykawasaki.com/2006/01/the_venture_cap.html, and see Chapter 9) is the most important thing. I also think company values are important (Zappos, http://about.zappos.com/our-unique-culture/zappos-core-values). We are trying to build a company that's passionate about customer service, provides outstanding user experiences, and is human, inclusive, respectful, transparent, generous, socially conscious, and green. Wouldn't you like to do business with a company like that? :)

Open Source/CMS

Overview

Ever since the first days of commercial software, there's been the phenomenon of startups springing up to complement some larger software application. For example, surrounding Microsoft Excel are literally hundreds of specialized commercial add-ins; these add-ins are an important, externalized, value that buttresses Excel market dominance.

That trend continues to this day, although it has morphed into two variants: add-ins and supplemental products for proprietary applications such as Microsoft SharePoint and Lotus Notes and plug-ins, modules, and templates for Open Source projects such as WordPress, Joomla, and Drupal.

Main Characteristics from a Startup's Point of View

If you're a [fill in the blank] developer who sees an unmet need people will pay good money to fill, creating a microISV to bring that solution to market is a natural-enough evolution.

Each of these broadly speaking content management systems is a horizontal platform just waiting for vertical solutions for industries, markets, and individuals with very specific needs.

Advantages

The good news for developers who want to go down this particular startup road is that if you have solid knowledge of the larger system you are plugging into and you execute decently, then your market is going to find you more than you need to find them. That's because they're desperate.

The common failing of any general software app is that it's too general; and the bigger the pool of users, the more needs around the edges go unmet.

Disadvantages

The bad news for developers of add-ins comes in a choice of flavors: proprietary and Open Source.

For proprietary systems such as Microsoft SharePoint, the main issue is that you're the mouse locked in the same cage as the elephant—you can get stepped on in their next release and squished flat. Assuming you don't get squished, there's another serious issue—the small size of your prospective market. The more specialized your add-in, the smaller the market and the fewer new potential customers you can sell to each year.

For those aspiring to add value to Open Source projects in a financially rewarding way, you have two major hurdles: the Open Source legal framework (for example, the GPL license), which means your app needs to be GPL with source code freely available, and the pitchforks-and-burning-torches ire most commercialized Open Source ventures get from The Community.

Comments

If you get the sense that this is my least recommended startup platform, you're right. On the one hand, as much effort and toil can go into a good add-in as into a stand-alone app. On the other, you're stuck being a very small frog in a very small pond that in the course of proprietary software evolution can dry up overnight. The cautionary tale of dozens and dozens of VB6 control makers comes to mind.

As for commercial startups orbiting Open Source projects, you might be happily acquired by a larger company (such as the case of antispam comment startup Defensio's acquisition by publically traded online security giant Websense[23]), if you happen to be one of those fortunate people on a first-name basis with Luck.

Mac Desktop and Windows Desktop

Overview

As we wrap up our tour of potential platforms for your startup, we're back to the future: the desktop. It's easy to forget in this business so dominated by all things online just where the vast bulk of applications, companies, and revenue is—on the desktop. For example, Gartner, Inc., estimated that worldwide 2008 SaaS enterprise revenue had grown 27% to $6.4 billion.[24] Compare that to the worldwide packaged software industry for all platforms, estimated by International Data Corp. at $179 billion in 2004, according to the Software & Information Industry Association.

Main Characteristics from a Startup's Point of View

Simply put, its users. For most practical purposes, everyone your startup might sell to uses a computer running either Microsoft's or Apple's operating system, with the split being 88.41% Windows, 9.61% Mac and Linux, and all the rest the balance as of March 8, 2009, according to Market Share.[25]

---

[23] *http://www.techcrunch.com/2009/01/27/websense-acquires-spam-blocker-defensio/*

[24] *http://www.gartner.com/it/page.jsp?id=783212*

[25] *http://marketshare.hitslink.com/operating-system-market-share.aspx?qprid=8*

Advantages

"Quantity has a quality all its own," whether you're referring to tank production during World War II or the number of people out there who can buy your software. Add to that mature operating systems, robust development platforms, well-defined categories, and all the rest, and it adds up to still the single biggest game in town for startups.

Also, there's desktop software and there's desktop software. How many thousands, if not tens of thousands, of software applications out there are as functional today as the day 1.0 hit the streets but no longer rise to what customers and businesses expect in the Internet Age?

If everything was perfect about desktop computing, we'd still be in the Age of Bill and Steve. But it's not. Desktop software, compared to all the other platforms, tends to look quaint, unsexy, and maybe, just maybe, one foot in the grave.

Disadvantages

The biggest problem for startups when it comes to desktop platforms is their maturity. Most of the big battles over which vendor would dominate a given market have been fought and decided years ago. The number of startups trying to take on market leaders on their own desktop turf are few, far between, and dwindling.

Comments

Online media aside, desktop software is going to be with us for a long, long time, and there's still plenty of money to be made and startups to be developed for both Windows and Mac boxes. If your passion takes you toward the desktop, more power to you and your customers.

Scott Morrison, Founder, Indev

Scott Morrison's InDev (http://www.indev.ca) sells two add-in applications for Apple Mail on the Mac: Mail Act On and Mail Tags. I asked him what's it like being a Mac desktop software company these days.

Bob: What do you see as the current advantages of developing commercial applications for the Mac?

Scott:

1. *Fabulous development environment and frameworks.* Xcode has really matured since OS X 10.0 days, when it was called Project Builder. Now it is a free but first-rate programming IDE built upon widely used and supported tools such as GCC and GDB. The application framework (Cocoa) that is the core of application development has evolved significantly as well—given programmers a well-designed and documented toolbox for creating apps.

   Many things that would take a significant effort a short time ago or on other platforms, such as UI animation, are given to you so that you spend less time worrying about details and reinventing the wheel and more time focused on building the solution/application you want. In short, it makes it much easier to develop high-quality applications.

2. *A high standard of quality.* Macs are noted for their high standard of quality—and this is not due to just the hardware and the OS. Indeed, part of the "quality equation" of the Mac are high-quality applications produced by companies other than Apple. This give developers many fantastic models for what can be done and what is the expectation of quality. However, just because the bar is often set high, it doesn't mean that it is unattainable. In fact, some of the best software available for the Mac is done by companies that number under five people, and many great apps are by one-person operations. This gives the startup developer a lot of encouragement that such quality is reasonably attainable.

3. *Very healthy platform.* Over the last five years, the Mac has become a very healthy platform. Some could say this is part of the iPod halo effect. But in reality, if the platform wasn't solid, there could be no Mac consequence of Apple's having an exploding iPod market. The iPod didn't make the Mac great. The Mac was great and the easy accessibility of the iPod to a broad audience brought more exposure to Mac so that more people could appreciate the OS X platform more.

   Consequently, the Mac is a strong market, and, more importantly, it is a market where quality of experience, rather than price, is the main selling proposition. And when you are looking at people who purchase on the basis of quality, you have a better market: those who will are looking for more than "good enough" and are willing to pay a bit more to get it. You get a marketplace that is more willing to open its wallet when it sees what it likes.

4. *Expansion of applications into sectors such as iPhone.* With the advent of the iPhone, there is a surge of interest in development in one of Apple's core technologies—Objective-C and Cocoa. With these technologies on both platforms now, a Mac developer is that much more versatile. Toss in 280North work on Objective-J and Cappuccino, and you can add web app development into the mix. While these frameworks are not 100% transferable, they subscribe to a similar philosophy and approach to application development, and most skills and understandings can be transferable. On that vein, last year at WWDC [Worldwide Developers Conference] there was a session "iPhone development for Mac developers." This year there is a session "Mac development for iPhone developers." It is an exciting time to be a developer looking at Objective C and Cocoa because it opens doors to three different and very dynamic platforms and markets.

5. *A friendly and vibrant developer community.* I just returned from NSConference 2009 in the UK, and it was perhaps the best conference I attended. There is a tremendous amount of collegiality and openness among those who are working on the Objective–C/Cocoa platform. It is very easy to get assistance and advice from others, who are often in (or were recently in) the same position as a developer trying to get their first product together. This advice is also not just about coding—but will cover a wide range of pertinent topics, such as running a microISV company, building a store or an interface or a web site, etc.

Bob: How about disadvantages?

Scott: Thinking hard about this question, one has to separate the downsides about being a microISV from being a Mac microISV. I think there are two that are specific to being a Mac microISV: First, you are not ostensibly dealing with as large a market share as Windows. That said, I think this is somewhat overestimated, particularly with respect to microISVs. While by some reckoning the Windows market is nine time the Mac market, once you deal with the number of machines in the hands of individual users or small businesses/organization, where purchasing decisions are not made by a CTO, there is not as much disproportion in market share.

Large organizations routinely don't purchase the kinds of software that most microISVs make, and there is greater push from those markets toward web-based solutions. Where microISVs make their bread and butter is with individuals and small organizations and businesses. It is a more level playing field when you consider platforms at this level. Furthermore, it is my experience and estimation that Mac users spend more on microISV products than do Windows users. In all I think it more or less balances out, and some people have said that market share difference is often negligible and that sometimes Mac products will sell better than their Windows counterparts, despite perceptions of market share.

The other disadvantage is finding community of developers in specific locals. I am based in Montreal and it is tough finding other Cocoa programmers here. Different areas have larger communities, but I think here is one area where market share has a perceivable impact. Mind you, this will change with time, and there are some great opportunities, such as NSConference in the UK and C4 in Chicago, where a short flight is all it takes to have two to three days of Cocoa discussion bliss and to build those contacts that sustain continuing online discussions.

Bob: What would you say to other developers who think, "Desktop apps are obsolete"?

Scott: Not at all. Or more specifically, this may be more true for Windows applications than for OS X applications. Because of what the OS X application experience is, many OS-X users are less satisfied by web apps than are Windows users. One example: I have watched Windows users work with Windows applications and with web applications—and quite frankly the experience is essentially the same: open files by navigating through open dialog boxes, copying and pasting text, pictures, etc., dealing with lots of modal and semimodal interfaces. When watching Mac users work with desktop apps—it is a different experience. People use drag-and-drop, SpotLight, QuickLook, Expose, the Dock to a much greater extent. And when they start using a web application, they are stymied and have to "downgrade" their experience to a less dynamic one.

Mind you, web apps are improving, and there are certain advantages, such as ease of sharing of data with others, that web apps will always have over desktop apps, for user and developer alike. But I think that there are still many applications that, because of the experience, will generally feel better on the computer than on the Web. The other thing to reflect on for OS X developers is that with the development of tools such as Objective-J and Cappuccino, web apps can leverage existing programming experience and technologies to a great extent.

Bob: Any advice for those developers who want to create a Mac-centric startup?

Scott: Become passionate about programming and the environment first—find a way to monetize that passion. There was a discussion at the NSConference where I made an observation that there are a large number of developers hitting the iPhone SDK because they see a gold rush.

As a result, we sometimes see a race for the bottom—underpricing and undervaluing of applications because there isn't always a bar of quality that is being met. The sense is that developers are wanting to cash in on a phenomenon and not really grasping the essence of what that phenomenon is about. But I also am starting to see a bit of a pushback from passionate developers and the push that better apps are ones that demand a little better price because they are meeting higher estimations of standards.

Take Tweetie [http://www.atebits.com/tweetie-mac], for example. Here is an application that came first to the iPhone, where, at $2.99, it was more expensive than many other Twitter clients. But because it was designed and developed with a better sense of the user experience, it has succeeded more than others. A couple days ago it was released for the Mac—and it is a beautifully executed, well-designed application that is a pleasure and fun to use. There are dozens of Twitter applications, some cocoa based, others based on frameworks such as Air. But Tweetie got my nod. Why? Because more than having the right mix of features, the app captured, better than others, that passion of what it is to be a Mac application.

To me, this is a company that is passionate about the platform environment and the experience and that has developed a product that monetizes this passion and that will in the long run be more sustainable than a company that is concerned with making a buck.

Gwen Hilyard, Cofounder, Brisworks

Gwen Hilyard is one of four cofounders of Brisworks (http://brisworks.com), a distributed company that makes and sells a Windows Active Directory–centric network management application: Admin Arsenal. I asked Gwen what's it like building a desktop software company when seemingly all the press and adulation goes elsewhere.

Bob: Admin Arsenal is a Windows system administration tool. What's it like being a Windows app in an age when seemingly everyone touts the Web?

Gwen: There is a certain faddishness to web-based applications. They have their place, certainly, but it seems too many applications are shoehorned into the space. From a systems administrator perspective, it gets a bit annoying when an application requires installation in IIS [Internet Information Services], even though it doesn't really need it (because such installations can be a real headache). While many web apps are getting there, we have discovered that some system administration tasks just perform better from an installed application. We don't really think very many would look down on a desktop application, since there is so much out there that doesn't go the web route. Users will run what works; they don't really care about the difference.

Bob: You and your three cofounders have a huge amount of sys admin experience among you. Why did you decide to do a desktop app?

Gwen: Browser-based applications still lag behind their GUI [graphical user interface] counterparts in richness and interactivity. Ajax is closing the gap, but it's still got quite a ways to go. Also, not requiring a server of any kind (web server or database server) makes our deployment much simpler. Some of Admin Arsenal's predecessors were web based, but they were internally developed applications where we had full control of all server and security functionality.

Our main reason for going with a desktop app was to get away from server infrastructure and all the installation and configuration headaches. A selling point of Admin Arsenal is the minimal time it takes from download to usability, and a server would get in the way of that.

Bob: What do you see as the best reasons today for doing a Windows desktop app?

Gwen: It depends on the application, really. Rich client functionality is drop-dead simple on the desktop, relative to Ajax, even with powerful frameworks. Web-based applications work best with occasional users who may be on different operating systems. There's a trade-off for that kind of ubiquity.

Bob: What do you and your cofounders like the most—and the least—about being part of the Microsoft world?

Gwen: There is a huge market, great development tools, and a gap in the native systems administration functionality.

Bob: What do you see about developing for Windows that recommends itself to a new startup?

Gwen: Startups need to base platform decisions on the needs of their apps and markets. It's usually quite clear which way to go, when it comes time to decide. You need to be unafraid of going with solid, "unsexy" options if it serves your market. To paraphrase an old quote, "It's the users, stupid." Though we will say that one advantage of Windows, specifically, is Microsoft Visual Studio. It gets pooh-poohed out on the Interwebs, but it's a marvel of engineering and a joy to use.

Recap

At the beginning of this chapter we talked again about the Age of Bill (Gates) and Steve (Jobs) and bipolar platform choices open to startups through the last two decades of the previous century. But that was then and this is now, and that means that if you're going to build a startup, perhaps the single most important decision you are going to make is what platform or platforms you will build on.

Whether it is SaaS, PaaS, social, mobile, hybrid, Open Source/CMS, desktop, or something else, each platform affords certain advantages and takes away potential opportunities. There is no one right platform, better platform, or best platform for your startup. The only wrong platform choice is the one you make without thought as to whether the startup into which you want to breathe life can prosper there. Just because you're a web developer or a desktop developer, love all things social networky, or sleep with your iPhone does not mean that that particular platform is the automatic right business/technical choice for you as you commit yourself.

Hopefully this drive-by tour of platforms has you thinking about the one or more platforms that give the startup you want to create, or the startup you have created, the best shot at the big gold ring.

Just as you're the beneficiary of where the software industry has evolved to, you're also in line to be able to take advantage of a whole slew of technologies, services, and tools that will make your life as a startup developer easier. Next stop, the *startup development zone* (cue the *Twilight Zone* theme)!

Tools and Groups for Startups

"A successful tool is one that was used to do something undreamt of by its author."

—Stephen C. Johnson (programmer who wrote the Portable C compiler)

"Never doubt that a small group of thoughtful people could change the world. Indeed, it's the only thing that ever has."

—Margaret Mead (American cultural anthropologist)

Back in the Day . . .

In this chapter we're going to stock up your startup toolkit with a few power tools to get the job done faster and more easily and have a look at startup groups, gatherings, and events, online and off.

Now, this is not a book about programming tools—given the number of platforms we just covered in Chapter 3; that would be a six-volume set. Instead, by tools for startups I mean the services, sites, and programs that exist today to make it easier for you to start a small software company. Some of these items are on offer from large IT companies who want you to build on what they've done; some are from startups themselves who are solving problems whose solutions you need. A few have been around for over a decade, helping developers become founders; several are so new (fair warning—including one of my own) that the paint is barely dry.

Open Source libraries and tools are something we as developers use in one fashion or another every workday, but the rules change when you start talking about incorporating Open Source code in your startup's DNA. We'll talk with someone who really understands the ins and outs of this: Gene Landy, author of *IT/Digital Legal Companion,* about some of the do's and don'ts of using Open Source code.

Having loaded up with tools and services that help your startup, it's time to get you out from behind your monitors and out mingling, meeting, learning from, and even having fun with people who are facing many of the same challenges you are—the Startup Community, both in the analog world and online. I think you'll be surprised as to just how many people share and want to share entrepreneurism and the startup mindset with you.

Finally, we'll swing back to take a look at two big IT evangelism companies that have programs that merit your serious consideration: Microsoft BizSpark and Sun Startup Essentials.

One interesting thing about the tools and applications mentioned in this chapter is that few of them existed two or three years ago. The tools and services and, above all, the social groups of and by startups you'll find here are part of the explosive growth of what I like to call the Startup Community. Only a few years ago, being a startup was much more of a lonely calling.

Tools for Startups

One of the nice things about doing a startup today as opposed to, say three years ago is the number of other startups and small software vendors who offer great tools you can buy or subscribe to instead of build. In this section, we'll take a look at 16 of them, starting with three tools for keeping your most valuable startup asset—your codebase—safe and secure.

Version Control for Your Startup

Solid, offsite, robust code version control is a must-have for a startup. Whether or not you know and love what version control can do for you, this is simply something that needs to be done right.

GitHub

What it is: A combination Git-centric version control system for both Open Source and proprietary projects and a growing social network for programmers (80,000 as of May 2009).

URL: http://github.com (Figure 4-1)

What it costs: Free to $200/month; the Small ($12/month) and Medium ($22/month) plans should fit the needs of most startups in terms of private repositories (10 or 20) and private collaborators (5 or 10).

Figure 4-1. GitHub

Special mojo/shiny goodness: Since its launch in July 2008, GitHub has rapidly become the preferred repo site for the Ruby on Rails community. Git, a distributed version control system written largely by Linux creator Linus Torvalds in 2005 because he was dissatisfied with other Open Source options such as Subversion and BitKeeper, has been winning over developers, especially from the more obtuse Subversion system.

GitHub is now the home of a growing list of major Ruby and non-Ruby Open Source projects, including Capistrano, Haml, JUnit, MooTools, Prototype, YUI, and Perl.

Why you should know about it: If your startup is using Ruby on Rails or Perl, you probably already know about GitHub as a source for Open Source code. GitHub makes Open Source's fork-and-extend legal capability a practical reality. Over and over at GitHub you'll find forks of useful Open Source projects that add value while maintaining a clean connection to their original project.

The other kind of repositories—private, SSL-secure repositories—are something you really want to be using day to day; with GitHub, that's as easy as typing **Git push origin master**.

But how secure is your private code? After all, your codebase is the core of your business. Here's an illuminating exchange between Chris Wanstrath, one of GitHub's cofounders, and a startup about the startup's concerns: "As a startup, what assurances would we have that hosting our code (which is also our IP and represents almost our entire company value) as a private repo on GitHub will work for us?" wrote Bradley Wright in the GitHub Google Group.[1] "Do GitHub employees have access to private repos, for example? What kind of security is in place for private repos?"

Wanstrath replied, "We only access your repositories to help with support issues. Both GitHub and Engine Yard are very serious about security. It's something we worry about and constantly try to improve. We even have a security expert on retainer who has helped us out with issues in the past. I consider this one of the benefits of choosing GitHub over self-hosting—is security as high a priority on your internal network?"

Overall, I think the advantages of having a secure, offsite private code repository with a company outweigh the benefits of and is more secure than diverting time to a DIY system.

Unfuddle

What it is: Subversion and Git repository plus project management.

URL: http://unfuddle.com (Figure 4-2)

What it costs: Free to $99/month, with either the Micro ($9/month) or Compact ($24/month) plan looking good for a startup.

Special mojo/shiny goodness: I had originally planned to include Unfuddle because it seems to be a good offsite Subversion service for developers who still prefer Subversion; then they added Git, making it a good alternative for those who don't want to go with GitHub. But Unfuddle is more than an offsite repo—it provides a solid, if basic, set of project management tools, including messaging between developers within a project, creating bug/feature tickets, setting milestones, and more—all nicely arranged/accessible in a project dashboard.

Why you should know about it: If you're using Subversion (or Git) and you also want a core set of software project management functionality, Unfuddle is my recommendation.

---

[1] http://groups.google.com/group/github/browse_thread/thread/a434ef8706d98c03

Figure 4-2. Unfuddle

SourceGear Vault

What it is: Proprietary version control system primarily for Microsoft-centric codebases.

URL: http://www.sourcegear.com/vault (Figure 4-3)

What it costs: Free for a single developer, $249 per developer, $299 with product maintenance. If your startup has more than one developer, you'll need a paid-for license for *each* developer.

Special mojo/shiny goodness: Vault has become the de facto version control system for .NET developers. Microsoft's version control system, SourceSafe, wandered off the development field years ago and has not been heard from since. Vault integrates into Visual Studio (and Eclipse and Dreamweaver too) and has proven rock solid, and SourceGear provides excellent support for Vault and its other products.

Figure 4-3. SourceGear Vault

Why you should know about it: If you are beginning to wonder whether I am obsessed with version control systems and protecting your codebase, you're right. I know of at least three instances—including my first microISV product—that either were put out of business or came within a hair of that fate because they mismanaged their codebase. If you want to be taken seriously as a startup, you need to protect your code.

Customer/Beta Tester Feedback

Our next five tools for startups get at what people online think about your product or service. If you wander down the halls of any major company, you'll hear terms such as *focus group* and *consumer research* and *customer survey*. That's because these businesses understand how important it is to know what their customers and prospective customers are thinking about. For startups, it's not important—it's vital.

Feedback from your beta testers and, later, your customers is the lifeblood of your startup. Without it, you have no real idea of whether your product or service is on target, what your next release should focus on, what customers are saying—or want to say—about your app.

In the online marketplace, conversing with your customers is increasingly a necessity rather than an option as company after company wises up that markets are conversations, not monologues. Here's a small selection of tools to help you reach out and connect to your customers and beta testers.

SurveyMonkey.com

What it is: Free to low-cost online survey design, implementation, and analysis.

URL: `http://www.surveymonkey.com` (Figure 4-4)

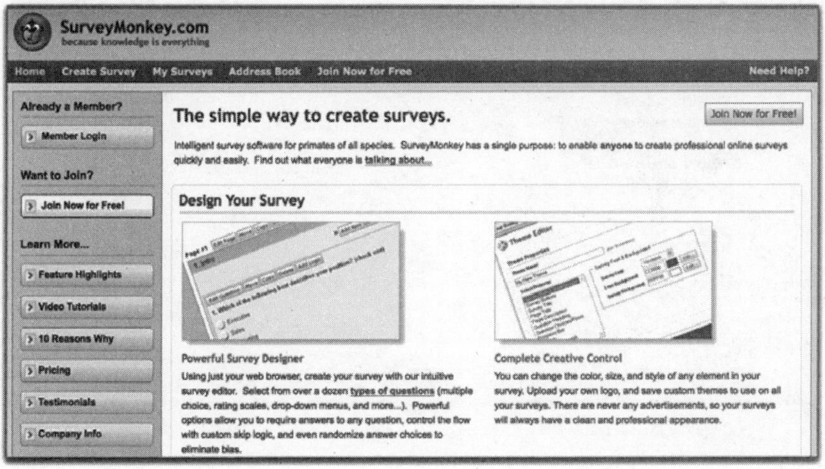

Figure 4-4. *SurveyMonkey.com*

What it costs: Free for up to 10 questions in a survey and 100 responses; Monthly Pro (19.95/month) plan allows 1,000 responses per month, while the Annual Pro ($200/year) is unlimited.

Special mojo/shiny goodness: SurveyMonkey is a well-thought-out, well-designed service that guides you though designing a survey—20 different question types you can drop in any one of 50 themed survey templates. All you need to do to get the survey to your desired audience is to provide them with the custom SurveyMonkey link; or, if you feel you must, you can present a survey as a pop-up on your site.

The analytical features do more than get the job done; you can browse individual responses, publish results, filter and cross-tab responses, or download raw data or nicely arranged PDF summaries.

Why you should know about it: Whether it's sending a quick survey to your beta testers that they will actually complete, asking recent customers what brought them to your doorstep, or finding out what people really think of the customer support you're providing, SurveyMonkey.com makes getting this kind of feedback quick and easy—and therefore something your startup is more likely to do.

PollDaddy

What it is: Create quick, targeted polls.

URL: http://www.polldaddy.com (Figure 4-5)

Figure 4-5. A PollDaddy poll in the wild

What it costs: Free, if you don't mind a built-in link back to PollDaddy; $200/year to remove the link.

Special mojo/shiny goodness: Surveys are good when you have an existing connection to those being surveyed, who therefore they will take the time to answer it. But what if you don't? Another way to go is to embed a quick snap poll—one question, a set of answers for the respondent to pick from—right where you need it in your site or blog. Although PollDaddy now offers surveys, it's these quick embeddable polls I like.

Since PollDaddy is owned by Automattic, the creators of WordPress, integration with WordPress-hosted and stand-alone blogs is extremely easy. For example, Figure 4-5 shows a poll I created in under 5 minutes for the Startup Success Podcast.[2] Here's the entire HTML content of that post: [polldaddy poll="1462723"]. Now that's easy!

---

[2] *http://startuppodcast.wordpress.com;on iTunes, just search the iTunes Store for "startup."*

Why you should know about it: Getting feedback from your community is not a one-shot deal: the more times and ways you ask them, the better, and the better the quality and quantity of information. PollDaddy works especially well for communicating with readers of your startup's blog.

CrazyEgg

What it is: Site analytics that really work.

URL: http://crazyegg.com (Figure 4-6)

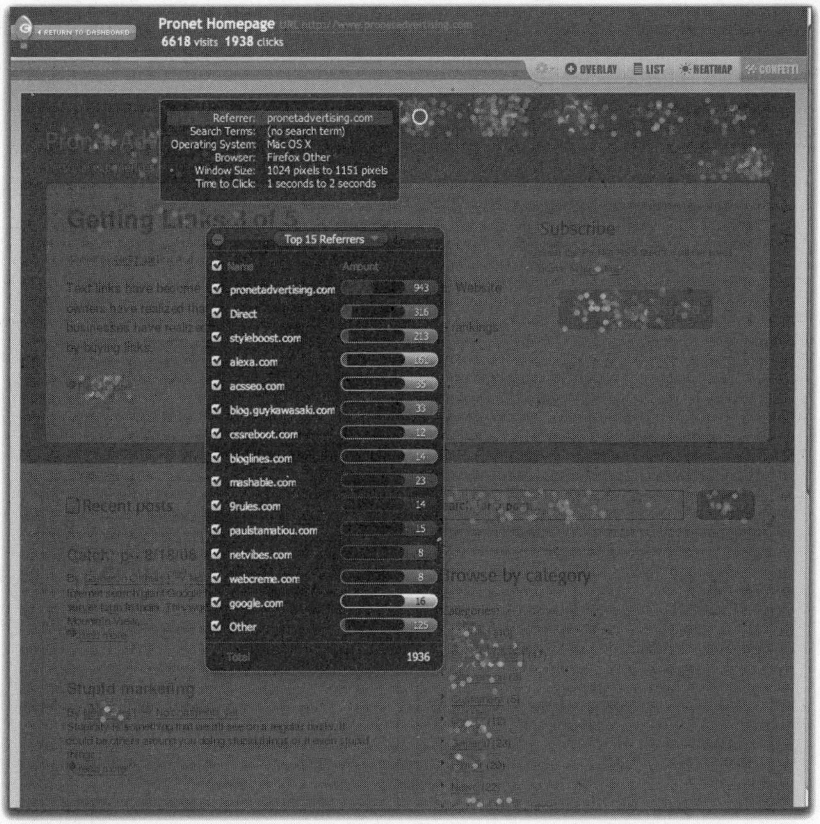

Figure 4-6. CrazyEgg's Confetti view

What it costs: From $9/month to track 10,000 visits to your site and 10 pages up to $99/month to track 250,000 visits/100 pages. The Standard ($19/month—25,000 visits on 20 pages) would seem a good fit.

Special mojo/shiny goodness: Unlike, say, Google Analytics, the beauty of CrazyEgg is that it shows you visually exactly where people are clicking on a given page, by overlaying on the page for you either a heat map or aggregated click counts or actual clicks that can each display more information. Stats are one thing—and CrazyEgg does that as well—but, at least for me, being able to see the page and to see where people are clicking makes it easier to comprehend what's working and what's not.

Why you should know about it: CrazyEgg is a very cool way to find out what's working on your site and what's not—quickly. You can invest untold hours into analyzing your server logs and you won't get the same actionable knowledge that a single glance at a CrazyEgg-monitored page will show you.

UserVoice

What it is: In-site customer feedback.

URL: http://uservoice.com (Figure 4-7)

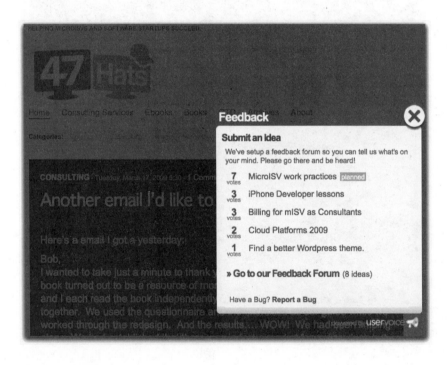

Figure 4-7. UserVoice at work

What it costs: From free for a single site recording up to 500 votes (see below) up to $589/month for unlimited sites and 25,000 votes.

Special mojo/shiny goodness: UserVoice is all about giving your site's visitors a dirt easy means to provide you feedback on your site or service, and giving you a structured process for marshalling that feedback, muffling too-vocal users and focusing that feedback into useful channels.

On a UserVoice-enabled site, such as http://47hats.com, visitors see a small tab on the right or left margin. When they click this tab, they see a JavaScript widget with the five top vote-receiving ideas at your UserVoice Feedback Forum, as shown in Figure 4-7.

The fun begins when they click on one of the ideas or go to Feedback Forum, where they can "spend" their 10 votes voting up various ideas. For ideas, substitute possible product or service enhancements, features to be added to you startup's iPhone app, or whatever you need structured feedback for in the form of votes and comments.

Why you should know about it: UserVoice is by turns instant market research tool, future feature prioritizer, bug reporter, and suggestions and comments tool. By separating bug reports from voting on ideas for your software, you make for a much more manageable flow of information from customers. Since each person is limited to 10 votes, you're less likely to have your feature priority list set by "loud" customers and more likely to spot ideas for your product or service that have broad appeal. And because you can set the status of each idea and each comment on it, you can fine-tune your customers' expectations.

I interviewed Richard White, the founder of UserVoice.com, for the Startup Success Podcast. To understand more behind Richard's extremely well-thought-out Web 2.0 approach to feedback, give it a listen.[3]

Get Satisfaction

What it is: Web 2.0/social network customer support.

URL: http://getsatisfaction.com (Figure 4-8)

What it costs: The free account is good for up to a thousand visitors per month; above that the Basic account (ad-free, with support for up to 10 moderators from your startup) costs $149 a month. They also have a Starter Package that makes sense for a startup: 1 moderator and 1,000 visitors a month.[4]

---

[3] http://startuppodcast.wordpress.com/2009/01/22/show-12-richard-white

[4] http://www.getsatisfaction.com/companies/new

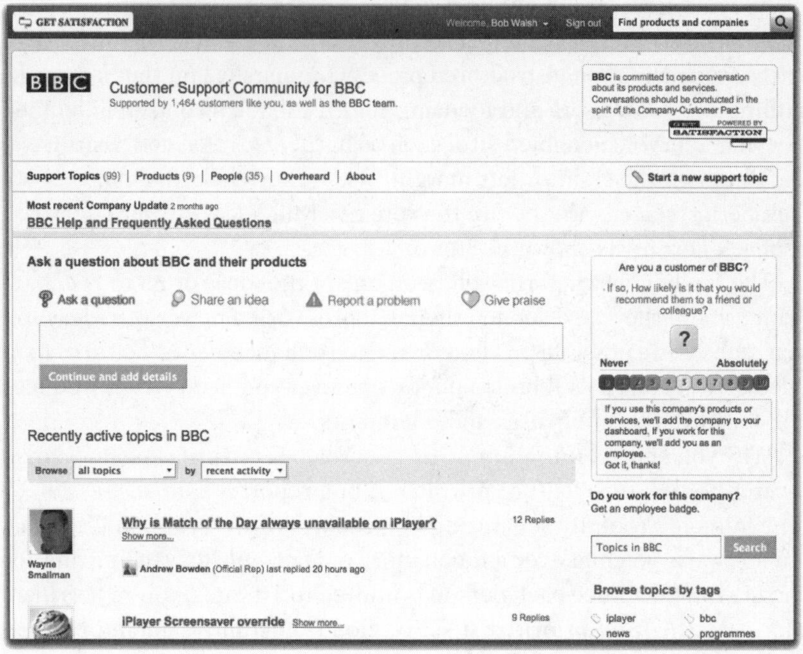

Figure 4-8. Get Satisfaction

Special mojo/shiny goodness: Get Satisfaction is all about disrupting the old approach to customer support that we all know and hate: either calling the company and getting connected to someone who can provide only scripted answers to stock questions or, worse, being directed to an "Advanced Web Forum," where you are invited to waste the rest of your life reading through unanswered posts. "We realized that if you could reimagine customer support as a community conversation between users and the company," Lane Becker, one of the founders of Get Satisfaction, told Apple,[5] "rather than as an overloaded and understaffed call center, all sorts of good things will happen."

Get Satisfaction is crowd-driven support—you can set up a forum about a company whether or not that company wants to participate. Given that, it makes sense, once you release, to get into this particular conversation by claiming your forum and having one or more people in your startup moderate it.

---

[5] *http://www.apple.com/business/profiles/getsatisfaction*

Why you should know about it: Nothing is perfect in this world—including your startup. You are going to need to provide customer support—and, if done right, it can improve your startup's online reputation. By turning customer support into online conversation you get happier customers, better feedback, and crowd-donated technical support.

Looking Good/Going Video

Next we have two graphic-related tools you should know about, because, let's face it, most software developers suck at graphic art and web site visual "stuff."

As developers, we tend to underestimate, even denigrate, how important good visual presentation is to most people. Simply put, for most people *ugly* equals *avoid*. A good logo is the start of your visual presentation. It shapes the visual architecture, even the culture of your company.

As for video, this is a medium you'll want to tap as you explain and present the value of your software, the kind of experience people are in for. Screencasts[6] are a very effective way to make your case. But more than that, video is now, for some purposes, the best way to communicate online.

99designs

What it is: Crowd-sourced logo design.

URL: http://99designs.com (Figure 4-9)

What it costs: This costs $39 for the contest process and then whatever amount you set, generally between $100 and $600.

Special mojo/shiny goodness: 99designs works thusly: You describe what your logo should be and post it at site—that's where the $39 goes. When you post, you set what you will pay for the winning logo entry. Then graphic designers get to work. Lots of graphic designers—over 30,000 designers are 99designs members, any number of whom can decide to try their hand at your logo. For example, one of the most popular design contests at the site today had 365 entries. That's a lot of custom logos to choose from. And all of it is public, so you can get further ideas for your branding.

---

[6] *You might want to listen to Show #21 ("The Art and Science of Screencasts") at the Startup Success Podcast. Pat Foley and I got a detailed crash course in doing screencasts right from Ian Ozsvald of ProCasts (http://startuppodcast.wordpress.com/2009/04/04/show-21-the-art-and-science-of-screencasts).*

Figure 4-9. 99designs

Why you should know about it: You're not a real startup until you have a real logo, something that doesn't look like it crawled out of Microsoft Word's clip art folder. But good graphic designs can take weeks and thousands of dollars. What you need is something good enough, fast, and relatively cheap. 99designs fills the bill. And because you pick the winning design from dozens of entries, you get a logo you like, or at least one you can live with until your Series A funding arrives.

Jing

What it is: Screenshot and video capture for Windows and Macs.
URL: http://www.jingproject.com/ (Figure 4-10)

Figure 4-10. Jing

What it costs: Free, or for $14.95 a year you can acquire Pro, which handles MPEG-4, one-button YouTube upload and brand-free videos.

Special mojo/shiny goodness: Jing makes easy the capturing to video of what's on your screen and sharing it with another developer, a customer needing support, or the world. Sometimes a minute-long video will calm a customer, explain a programming problem, or entice an investor when words simply would not get the job done. Although other tools, notably Jing's "big brother," Camtasia Studio, have editing capabilities you'll need to create more formal videos, such as product screencasts, Jing—with its abilities to capture both video and what you have to say, to automatically upload it to TechSmith's Screencast.com, and to stick a URL on your clipboard—is a tool you will not want to be without.

Why you should know about it: Jing adds to your problem-solving arsenal instant video screen capture with audio. That's a powerful tool in all sorts of situations when you want to communicate with one or many other people quickly, informally, and simply. I've found Jing to be a far better way to provide tech support to users of my various apps than dreary multistep instructions. And it's faster.

Testing Your Site and Your Software

How are you going to test your site, especially if you're startup is offering a web-based service? Are you going to dodge doing this because you are afraid that your site will turn to mush in Internet Explorer or crumble under the load of a real bunch of customers?

And what about usability—the novel concept that unless people understand your web app they are not going to buy it? Here are three tools whose value far outweighs their costs—especially the cost of not doing the testing you should be doing in the first place.

Browsershots

What it is: Takes screenshots of how your site renders in different browsers—lots of browsers.

URL: http://browsershots.org or http://browsershots.org/ priority (Figure 4-11)

What it costs: Free, if you can handle the ads and the wait; $29.95/ month for ad-free and fast.[7]

Special mojo/shiny goodness: Sure, your web app might look great in the latest Firefox on your dev machine. But how about IE 5.5, Opera 9. 62, Google Chrome 2.0, or Safari 3.2? Feed Browsershots a URL, decide if you want it with or without JavaScript, Flash, or other goodies, and pick as many browser/versions as you want.

Now, the free version will take its own sweet time rendering and then saving in jpeg format what your designated page looks like in each browser. But the paid-for version is a fast 30 to 50 screenshots within 2 to 5 minutes, and they don't get publically displayed.

Why you should know about it: This is a classic example of a something far cheaper to buy than to build, with the added goodness that you

---

[7] http://browsershots.org/priority

don't have to keep track of new browser versions on other platforms (you've got enough on your plate).

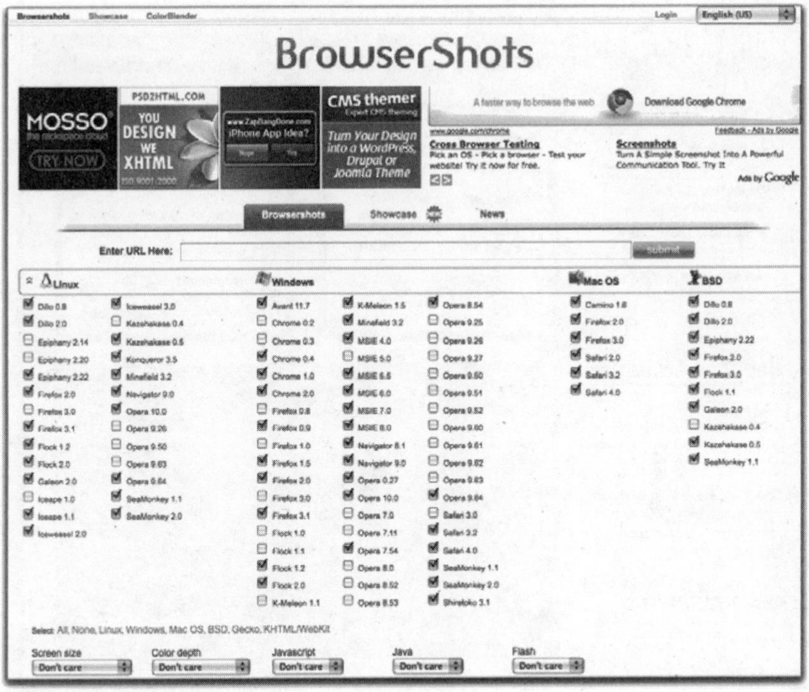

Figure 4-11. Browsershots

BrowserMob

What it is: On-demand, low-cost load testing with real browsers.

URL: http://browsermob.com/load-testing (Figure 4-12)

What it costs: BrowserMob offers two kinds of testing: Simulated HTTP traffic for $.20 hour per virtual user, and web traffic generated by what BrowserMob calls Real Browser Users for $2 per browser per hour—actual Firefox browsers running on E2C Amazon Web Services virtual servers.

Special mojo/shiny goodness: BrowserMob lets you set up Selenium test scripts to record the interactions you want to scale out—and they can be as simple or as complex as you wish to make them. Traditional load-testing tools aren't up to the task of dealing with a typical Web 2.0 Ajax-enabled web app without a great deal of work, work that's hard to modify if your site changes and you need to modify your tests.

Figure 4-12. BrowserMob

Why you should know about it: Would you rather find out now that your web app can't handle 3,000 users without crumbling or wait until after you launch and have 3,000 users? How about that new build with all the new functionality? What happens to your customers when it starts seeing significant traffic? BrowserMob is much better than simple http traffic testing, and it's much cheaper than non-AWS-powered testing services.

If you want to know more about BrowserMob, check out show #18 of the *Startup Success Podcast*.[8]

---

[8] http://startuppodcast.wordpress.com/2009/03/10/show-18-patrick-lightbody-browsermobcom

UserTesting.com

What it is: Structured usability testing at dirt-cheap prices.

URL: http://www.usertesting.com (Figure 4-13)

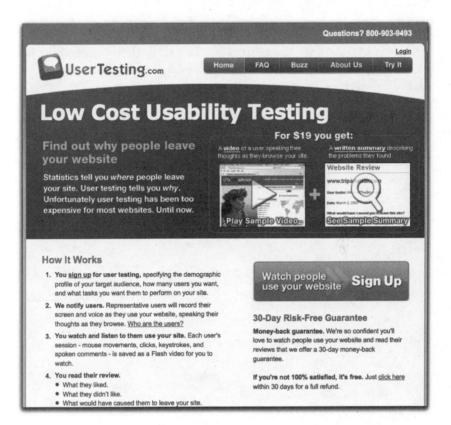

Figure 4-13. *UserTesting.com*

What it costs: $19 per usability test.

Special mojo/shiny goodness: User testing is the acid test for apps. That's where someone who's never seen your pride and joy, let alone written it, uses your application. Traditional user testing, complete with video camera mounted behind one-way mirrors, runs hundreds of dollars per test. With UserTesting, you fill in a form with your URL, indicate what tasks you want them to perform, such as sign up with your service and create a user profile, select how many testers you want, choose what, if any, demographic (gender, age, annual household income, computer/web expertise), and pay your money, and you'll get back both a Flash movie of exactly what each user did on your site (with commentary) for about a 15-minute period and a written report.

Why you should know about it: There is simply no substitute for seeing how a first-time user of your site or service reacts. You can't do it yourself—you know too much, you've already internalized the model of reality your software uses. You can get friends, buddies, people off the street—but how are you going to record and study their interaction with your app? UserTesting's crowd-sourced approach makes user testing a reality for startups.

uTest

What it is: Crowd-sourced functional testing.

URL: http://www.uTest.com (Figure 4-14)

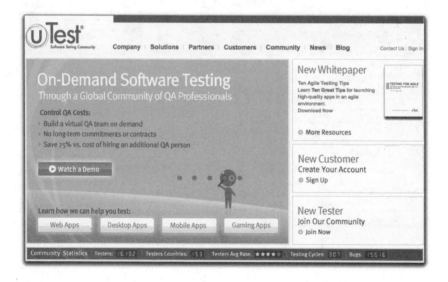

Figure 4-14. *uTest.com*

What it costs: Variable, but $1,500 or so is a good rough estimate.

Special mojo/shiny goodness: Which would you as a CEO rather do: hire a couple of testers who will be idle a good deal of the time and quickly become stale from looking at the same screens over and over, or put your app in front of over 15,000 testers who will race to find new and clever ways to be first to break your build? *Hint*: the latter.

That's what uTest is all about: a paid-for-performance online community of software testers who make money and have fun scouring your software. You have a lot of control over who tests what at uTest—this is not offshored functional testing.

Why you should know about it: Structuring functional testing as uTest has means lower cost for you per detected bug and a constant new mix of people available to test with fresh eyes and speed—you can start a test cycle late Friday and have it done by Monday.[9]

Subscription Startup Communities

Next up are two subscription-based communities expressly for developers who want to start their own software companies and are looking for "one-stop shops" (other than this book) for the knowledge they need. Warning! One of these is my startup, StartupToDo.com. Obviously I'm nothing like objective about it. On the other hand, a lot of startup founders have used it to save countless hours by not having to reinvent the wheels their startups need.

The Six Figure Software Micropreneur Academy

What it is: Online training for developers who want to become "Micropreneurs"—one-person software companies

  URL: http://www.sixfiguresoftware.com

  What it costs: $97 a month.

  Special mojo/shiny goodness: Rob Walling—the founder of The Six Figure Software Micropreneur Academy—is a successful microISV and blogger who's passionate about helping other developers launch their own software businesses. Within The Micropreneur Academy, Rob has created a set of seven instruction modules (see the upcoming sidebar for a sample) that provide highly practical information on creating a solo software company.

  "I realized there's a small amount of real information on the subject of one-person companies, and even less is focused on things that matter to us as software developers/entrepreneurs," Rob told me. "The problem is that nearly every entrepreneurial book or blog is aimed at starting either a retail store, a consulting firm, or a high-growth startup. And many of the resources that address one-person entrepreneurship (what I call *Micropreneurship*) are heavy on theory and light on practical steps."

---

[9] *Another Startup Success Podcast worth listening to is that of Matt Johnston, uTest VP of Marketing and Community:* http://startuppodcast.wordpress.com/2009/04/15/show-22-crowd-sourced-bug-detection-with-utest

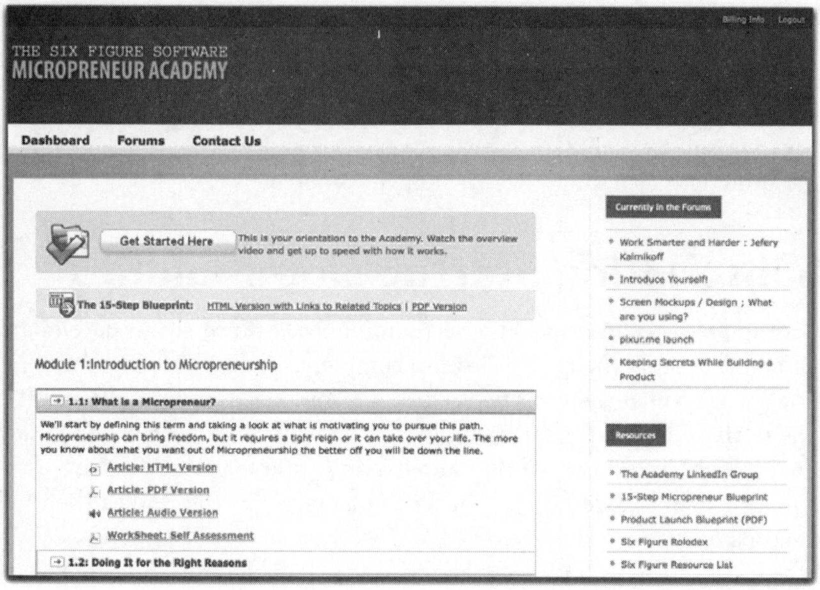

Figure 4-15. The Micropreneur Academy

Why a paid site? "Since the Academy is a membership site, it allows for high-quality, detailed information presented in multiple formats, with the positive side effect of a private community of committed Micropreneurs," Rob added.

Why you should know about it: Resources for creating a solo software company are few and far between; you'll find more info out there about starting a dry cleaner. While I obviously think this book and the next tool are very helpful, The Micropreneur Academy is a valuable resource, will suit some people better, and adds to your ammo for starting a microISV.

Rob Walling, The Micropreneur Academy

With Rob's kind permission, I've reprinted here one of the topics from Module 1: Introduction to Micropreneurship—Changing Your Time Mindset.

Lesson 1.4—Changing Your Time Mindset

It's a big leap moving from employee to Micropreneur. One of the biggest adjustments is accepting that time is your most precious commodity.

Dollarizing

The phrase *dollarize* is used in sales to describe the approach of showing your prospect how your price is less expensive than your competition due to the amount of money they will save in the long run.

For example, you can dollarize a screw by showing how your deliveries are always on time, your defect rate is half that of your competitors, and your screws can withstand an additional 500 lb of stress, each resulting in time saved in material handling and warranty calls.

If you take it a step further and you possess the appropriate data, you can approximate how much money your screws will save your prospect in a given year based on the number of times your competitors deliver late and how many defects they will avoid by using your screws.

It's a powerful technique and a way to turn an otherwise commodity purchase into a bottom-line savings.

Dollarizing Your Time

In the same vein, dollarizing your time is the idea of putting a theoretical dollar amount on each hour you work. If you value your time at $100 per hour, it makes certain decisions, such as outsourcing work to a $6/hour virtual assistant, a no-brainer.

Putting a value on your time is a foundational step in becoming a Micropreneur, and it's a step many entrepreneurs never take. Skipping this step can result in late nights performing menial tasks you should be outsourcing. It's one of the reasons most MicroISV owners earn less than $25/hour.

It never seems like a good idea to pay someone out of your own pocket for something you can do yourself . . . until you realize the economics of the situation.

Approaches to Dollarizing Your Time

There are two approaches to dollarizing your time. Choose the one that makes the most sense for your situation.

Approach #1: Freelance Rates

If you are a freelance developer or consultant, you probably have an hourly rate. This is a good way to begin dollarizing your time. If you bill clients $60/hour, then an hour of your time is worth $60.

If you don't perform freelance work, do a search on Craigslist or Guru for freelancers *in your local area* with similar skills. As a developer with a few years of experience you'll likely see rates in the $40 and up range. Frankly, if you have no other information, $50/hour is a good number to start with.

Approach #2: Salary

If you don't perform freelance work or have difficulty finding comparative freelancers online, another approach is to divide your current salary + benefits by 2,000 (the approximate number of hours worked in a year), rounded up to the nearest $5 increment.

It varies widely, but a typical benefits package, including 401k matching, disability insurance, health care, and time off, can range from 20% to 45% of your salary. You can come close to determining the real dollar amount using your pay stub and a bit of math, but if you just want to take a swing at it use 30%.

So if your salary is $60,000 per year, 30% of that is an additional $18,000, making your effective salary $78,000. $78,000 divided by 2,000 gives you an hourly rate of approximately $39/hour, or $40/hour when rounded.

Be aware that freelance rates are nearly always higher than salaried rates because freelancers spend a portion of their time on nonbillable tasks such as invoicing, marketing, sales, etc., so they have to increase their billable rate to make up for these nonbillable hours.

Ultimately it's up to you, but I would tend toward using the higher freelance rate for your time, especially since it's closer to what you would receive on the open market if you chose to pursue freelance work.

Keep in Mind: Desired Earnings

Realizing your time is worth $50/hour is the first step; the next step is actually generating $50 for every hour you work, and the third step is figuring out how to make your time worth $75 or $100/hour. If you continue to think your time is worth $50/hour, it will to stay at $50/hour.

$100/hour is a good long-term goal to shoot for. If you've done your research on one-person software companies, the reality for most tends to be closer to $25/hour.

If you are making $25/hour as a Micropreneur, you are doing something wrong. Improve your marketing, grow your sales, find a new niche, outsource, and automate. $25/hour is not, in my opinion, an acceptable dollarized rate for a successful Micropreneur.

While you won't be earning anywhere near $50/hour when you begin building your product, once you launch you should aim to hit that number within six months. In the early stages your dollarized rate is a mental state, but you want to make it a reality as soon as possible and increase it from there.

Realizations

Several realizations stem from dollarizing your time.

Realization #1: Outsourcing Is a Bargain

Once you've established you're worth $50/hour, paying someone $6/hour to handle administrative tasks or $15/hour to write code seems like a trip to the dollar store.

Outsourcing some aspects of your business is the single most powerful approach I've seen to increasing your true hourly rate as a Micropreneur. If I didn't outsource my administrative tasks, my true hourly rate would plummet.

Instead, outsourcing provides me with 20–60 additional hours each month that I can use to market a new product, improve marketing campaigns on existing products, or spend with my family.

The first two will bring more revenue in future months; the latter is invaluable to my lifestyle.

Realization #2: Keep Work and Play Separate

Wasting time is bad. Boring movies, bad TV, and pointless web surfing are expensive propositions. If you aren't enjoying something, stop doing it.

Last night, in fact, a group of friends came over to watch a movie and about 30 minutes in I fell asleep. I woke up after a while and, realizing I wasn't enjoying the film, retired to my room and went to sleep. It occurred to me that watching the film was less important than being alert and productive the next day.

These are the judgment calls you have to make every time you start a movie, book, or TV show.

I need to reiterate here: I'm not saying you should never relax, have fun, watch movies, play with your kids, watch TV, or surf the Web. I'm saying that you should be deliberate about your work and your free time and get the maximum benefit from both. In other words,

Work hard and play hard, but never do both at once.

Numerous times throughout the day I ask myself:

At this very moment am I making progress toward crossing off a to-do, or am I relaxing and reenergizing?

If I'm doing neither, I evaluate the situation and change it.

If you aren't enjoying a movie, walk out.

If you're playing with your kids and working on your iPhone, you're not really working or playing—you're doing both poorly. Put the iPhone away and focus on your kids; it will shock you how much more fun you have and how, after making this choice, you'll feel energized and ready to dive back into work.

The same goes for multitasking work in front of the TV. This used to be my standard mode of operation, but about a year ago I realized my productivity level is around 50% when I'm trying to do both, and once the evening is done I feel as if I worked the whole night (but didn't get much done).

In other words, I don't receive the benefit of being productive or feeling relaxed. It's the worst of both worlds and something I've curtailed almost entirely.

Realization #3: Waiting Is Bad

If your time is worth, say, $75/hour, standing in line at the bank is painful. Sitting in traffic is another money waster—every nonproductive, nonleisure minute you spend is another $1.25 down the drain.

Since it's not practical to assume you will never wait in line again, the best counterattack I've found is having a notebook and pen handy at all times and using this time for high-level thinking, something I have a hard time doing in front of a computer.

It's amazing that most of us think we can remember our important thoughts. Due to the amount of information and chaos you consume each day, a thought stays in your head for a few seconds before it disappears. Perhaps you will think of it again, perhaps not. Writing down important ideas is critical to building a list of ways to improve your business.

I've had some amazing insights while in line at the post office.

For years I've carried a notebook everywhere I go, for this exact purpose. I use it to capture keyword ideas, product ideas, niche ideas, to-do's, and any other valuable information that surfaces.

The best system I've found to manage it is to maintain three discrete lists:

- Personal to-dos

- Long-term work to-dos

- Short-term work to-dos (things to be done this week)

This allows me to think both short- and long-term and to easily capture big-picture ideas without cluttering my day-to-day to-do list with things I won't be able to implement for six months.

Again, I'm not saying you should be working all the time—if you want to bring a magazine to read in line, by all means do it. If your mind needs to rest when you're running errands, then use this as a time to reenergize so you can hit your work harder when you return to it.

The real statement here is that you should never find yourself *killing time*— this is as close to a sin as it comes for a Micropreneur.

Realization #4: Information Consumption Is Only Good When It Produces Something

The following discussion excludes consumption for pleasure (reading a novel, watching John Stewart, catching a movie).

Consuming and synthesizing are very different things; it's easy to consume in mass quantity. It's much more difficult to synthesize information.

Have you ever read through an entire magazine only to realize you can't remember anything specific about what you just read?

As someone who enjoys consuming in large quantities, at some point I realized I was wasting an enormous amount of time. So I put the following into place:

When I'm reading blogs or books or listening to podcasts or audio books, I take action notes.

Action notes are short- or long-term to-do items that apply directly to my businesses.

For example, I listen to several SEO podcasts. If they mention an interesting web site, I make a note to check it out the next time I'm able.

As they mention a new SEO technique, I create a specific to-do to try that approach on one of my web sites. I make the action note specific so I can act on it quickly the next time I have a few spare minutes. If I were to write something general like "Google Webmaster Tools," it doesn't help me. But if I write "Create Google Webmaster Tools Account for DotNetInvoice," I can act on this quickly and cross it off my list without having to do much real thinking.

Action notes have allowed me to quickly determine which resources provide real value and which are fluff.

Since implementing action notes I've canceled two magazine subscriptions, removed 40+ blogs from my RSS reader, and have become choosy about the audio books I buy.

This approach provides me with real-time feedback on the value of any consumable. A $4.99 audio book is actually a cost if it chews up four hours of your time and provides no actionable items.

Your Assignment

1. Using one of the approaches described here, dollarize your time. Write that hourly rate on a Post-it, and stick it to your desk as a reminder.

2. Purchase a half-size notebook (Moleskines are pricey but durable) and a nice pen. Start your idea notebook the next time you feel like you're killing time.

3. Make a list of day-to-day tasks you should outsource. You may not be able to offload everything at once, but start with the tasks that are easiest and cheapest to outsource and work your way up the list.

Begin taking action notes when you consume books, magazines, blogs, podcasts, and audio books. Start eliminating resources that don't generate actionable items.

StartupToDo.com

What it is: Productivity app/social network for startups.

URL: http://startuptodo.com

What it costs: As of this writing, $30 a month per founder, less if you subscribe by the quarter, half-year, or year.

Special mojo/shiny goodness: StartupToDo.com is a startup productivity/training application with hundreds of projects *already* defined for you and improved by a community of your peers. Instead of constantly figuring out what you need to do next to build your successful startup or microISV, you can pick and choose from well-researched and community-commented projects to complete.

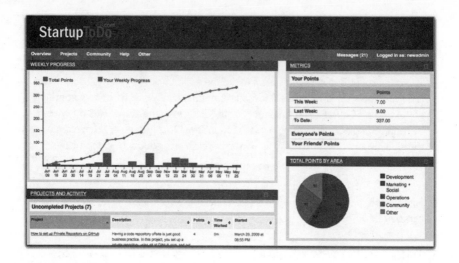

Figure 4-16. *StartupToDo.com*

Here's a typical scenario. You have three hours right now to work on your startup. What are you going to do? Without StartupToDo.com, you're likely to spend those three hours just Googling information, tips, and recommendations on, for example, how to set up your startup blog, and you will probably have nothing to show for your time. With StartupToDo.com, you can browse to the "Creating a self-hosted Startup Blog" Project, work through the 14 steps already defined (with eight comments from other startup founders), and have another part of the puzzle up and running.

Projects come with points, so you can measure your progress week to week and against other members, and there's a quick and easy way to get confidential feedback on your site or web app from the StartupToDo.com community and other features designed to help you succeed faster.

Why you should know about it: Bootstrapping—building a startup while holding down a day job—is quite simply murder. Too much time gets wasted figuring out what to do; too little time is left for the actual doing. StartupToDo.com saves you huge amounts of time you'd otherwise spend figuring out what you need to do and finding information, tips, and recommendations online. Especially for startups with one or a few founders, StartupToDo's point system, peer comments, and groups feature mean you get the support, quality information, and metrics that you hunger for.

I hope you won't mind the foregoing bit of shameless self-promotion: I've tried to treat my startup just as I have the other tools and services I've described in this chapter.

As a change of pace before we get into startup organizations, here's an interview with one of the sharpest legal minds in the startup world.

Gene Landy, IT/Digital Legal Companion Author and Attorney

Just exactly how can a startup incorporate Open Source into its product legally? You can spend the next three hours on the Web and hope that the people you read know what they are talking about, or you can read what Gene Landy, author of *IT/Digital Legal Companion* (Syngress, 2008) and respected startup attorney, has to say.

Keep in mind that, as with all legal advice, Gene's answers deal with the general case. You should get good legal advice about the specifics of your startup's use of Open Source code. But at least this should give you a solid grounding in the subject, and it won't cost you $450 an hour. Thanks Gene!

Bob: Maybe the place to start is about Open Source and use thereof in startups.
Gene: OK. Well, the key to Open Source is to read the license. There is some subtlety in it, but basically there are just two broad varieties of licenses: those that allow you to do wherever you want as long as you give attribution.
Bob: For instance, MIT (Massachusetts Institute of Technology)?
Gene: Yeah, MIT license is a pretty good example of that kind of license. BSD (Berkeley Software Distribution) license would be a good example for that kind of license. And they are very simple, and they basically say you give us copyright attribution and you repeat our licensure, you can do whatever you want, up to and including putting the software in your app and running the license you want.
Bob: OK.
Gene: Those licenses are pretty mild. They don't really interfere with you. They do require some disclosure, but otherwise they don't really crimp your style very much. And there is an enormous amount of software that's under that kind of license.
Bob: Now, does that apply to Open Source that you incorporate in a desktop commercial product or a web-based commercial product, or it doesn't make a difference?
Gene: Well, it doesn't make a difference. I mean if you take a product and you have a third of the code that is under the MIT license or the BSD license and other kind of non-copyleft kind of license, there is no reason why you can't distribute it like any other piece of software. You are required to disclose and document the limitation, usually on disk, that these license codes are there. But you are not required to license the products, you are not required to make copies available, you are not required to disclose the source code. It is pretty user-friendly.
Bob: OK. Well, under what circumstance would using Open Source code open your proprietary source code or give people that possibility?
Gene: Well, the places where that happens is where you have what is called a *copyleft license,* and the classic copyleft license is the GNU General Public License or the GPL or the LGPL. Those are the ones that have these copyleft aspects that require you to use license and only that and require you to make source code available.

So those licenses create a problem, because if you license that code and then you distribute that code inconsistently with that, you don't have a proper license for the code that is in the product. It is not true that, although it is common misperception, if you didn't know that kind of copyleft code and you include it in your product and distribute under a normal license, you sometimes are automatically required to disclose the source. That's not really the problem. The problem is that you just don't have a proper license because you have the code under a license that you didn't comply with.

Bob: I see. So it doesn't necessarily open up your code, but you have a problem because you haven't got a proper license.

Gene: That's right. You got a perfectly good license, but it requires you to do things that you haven't done, so therefore you haven't met the conditions in the license, so you don't have a valid right to distribute it, so you give it to your customer, customer has got unlicensed code. Now, very often, quite frankly, most copyright owners in Open Source code don't generally sue, even if their code is improperly distributed. Sometimes they do and sometimes they threaten to. It is not very common. So misuse of copyleft-type code can expose you to enforcement actions by a copyright owner because you are distributing code in violation of the copyright and you don't have a good license to do it.

Bob: What type of documentation should a startup keep on where it is getting its code? I mean is it just basically a list of the pieces of code with licenses?

Gene: Yeah, I mean I think the reality is—I guess that's one problem that startups have is that you basically have to be able to show where every piece of your product came from. And you may not have to do that for your customers; they might not care, although you will probably sign an agreement that says you have all rights.

And if you haven't tracked where the software comes from, you may not know. But where it really comes into play is when you want to raise money and the investor does some due diligence or you want to sell the company and the buyer does due diligence as the buyer finds out your code. Then they will point and say, you don't really own your software and I am not giving you any funding.

Startup Organizations and Groups Online and Off

It used to be that if you wanted to find another person who was actually interested in starting his or her own software company and you didn't live between San Francisco and San Jose, California, you were out of luck. The odds were just not in your favor of finding other, like-minded people.

That was then (prior to this century), this is now, and now there are literally hundreds of organizations, events, associations, and conferences by, for, and of startups, all over the world as well as online. In this section, we're going to take a quick tour of just some of them. No matter how comfortable you are working alone, networking professionally and socially with people who understand and share your values and passions is a very cool thing and well worth getting away from your computer on occasion. Moreover, getting connected to—and perhaps funding from—angel investors and VCs is very much a face-to-face, offline social networking thing: it behooves you to get out, get known, make acquaintances, and friends in the greater Startup World.

College Entrepreneurial Groups

First off, if you're still in college (and you don't want to waste a decade or more as some of us have before answering our inner entrepreneurial imperative), check out whether your school has something like Stanford University's BASES—Business Association of Stanford Entrepreneurial Students.

BASES (http://bases.stanford.edu/) is one of the largest student-run entrepreneurship organizations in the United States, with over 5,000 active/alumni members. It's all about the entrepreneurial approach to business, and, being at Stanford in the heart of Silicon Valley,[10] it has a strong IT bent.

Besides workshops and seminars sprinkled throughout the school year, one of BASES biggest activities is the E-Challenge, where teams create and present business plans for both cash prizes ($50,000 is in the pot) and face-to-face time with VCs who just might fund them.

I happened to bump into Alvin Tse, the current vice president of E-Challenge, at another startup event (see Startup2Startup at http://Startup2Startup.com) and he clued me in on what this—and similar student-led groups at schools such as Wharton and Harvard—are all about today. "I think BASES provides them some fundamentals frameworks of starting up as BASES organize a lot of panels and workshops throughout the year. Also, joining BASES allows you to mix with like-minded entrepreneurial students."

What's it like to be in BASES? "Being in BASES means different things to different people," Alvin replied. "For general members, being in

---

[10] *Some would say Stanford is the heart of Silicon Valley, given how many companies (notably Google) draw their DNA from it.*

BASES means signing up on mailing lists, going to the workshops. But for us executive members, being in BASES means being leaders in the entrepreneurial community at Stanford and educating students who have interests in doing startups."

Colleges are all about passing along and exploring ideas—and one idea that has caught fire and planted roots is that going startup can be a lot more lucrative and fulfilling than going to work for existing companies.

Startup Groups

But what if you're out of college and still want to mingle with fellow would-be founders? Then there's various startup-centric groups out there such as **Startup2Startup** and **Women 2.0**.

Each month, Startup2Startup (Figure 4-17) hosts a dinner meeting for startups and VCs. Each dinner has a speaker who talks on a subject in which startups are interested—for example, in January 2009 when I attended, Amy Jo Kim, the cofounder/CEO at ShuffleBrain, a startup building games for social networks and an internationally recognized expert on online community architecture and game mechanics, spoke on how nongame startups can tap these techniques to improve their software and get more customers. Interesting stuff indeed!

However, the real action is the interaction between representatives of some of the leading VC firms in Silicon Valley and founders looking to make that first key contact with the money people. The organizers of Startup2Startup—Dave McClure, who's been by turns developer, startup, and angel investor and who now runs a seed-stage investment program for Founders Fund, a VC group run by several of the founders of PayPal—and Leonard Speiser, entrepreneur-in-residence at the VC firm Trinity Ventures—have the star power in Silicon Valley to ensure that each dinner table of eight has at least one VC who is ready, willing, and talking to the assembled hopefuls.

Another startup organization that's building a positive reputation for itself is Women 2.0 (Figure 4-18). Their About page explains the mission of the group: "As young women with world-changing aspirations, we recognize entrepreneurship as the means to fulfill our life goals. After attending numerous local networking events for entrepreneurs in the Silicon Valley, we asked 'Where are all the women in the Silicon Valley?'"

Women 2.0 puts on an impressive number of events: from Girl Geek Dinners to Women 2.0 Startup Competition to workshops with successful women executives, VCs, and entrepreneurs.

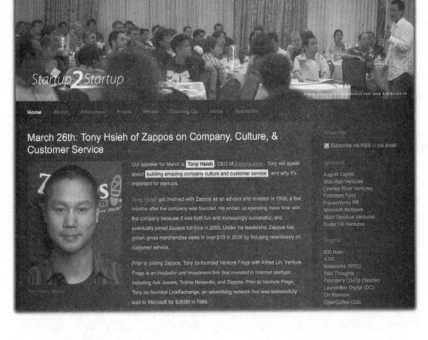

Figure 4-17. *Startup2Startup.com*

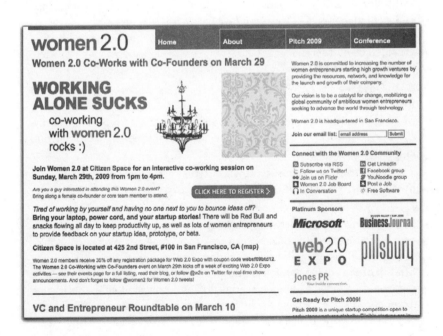

Figure 4-18. Women 2.0

Shaherose Charania, a founder of Women 2.0 and its general manager, shared with me why Women 2.0 is needed and her perspective from inside the Startup Culture.

Shaherose Charania, Women 2.0

Working days as product manager at the entertainment startup Talenthouse and nights at both Women 2.0–sponsored events and other startup events in Silicon Valley, Shaherose is both a Silicon Valley insider and a person striving passionately to open up and diversify "the Valley" and the IT industry. For more information on Women 2.0's many activities, check their website at http://women2.org.

Bob: What is Women 2.0, and why is it needed?

Shaherose: Women 2.0 is committed to increasing the number of women entrepreneurs starting high-growth ventures by providing the resources, network, and knowledge for the launch and growth of their company.

Our vision is to be a catalyst for change, mobilizing a global community of ambitious women entrepreneurs seeking to advance the world through technology.

We host networking events, workshops, VC Roundtables, and an annual startup competition to support entrepreneurs in the idea stage as well as entrepreneurs in early stage of launch—beta stage.

Why Women 2.0? There are less than 5% of women in technology startups at the cofounder or CxO level, and we believe there is no reason for this to be so low. With education, role models, and inspiration, women who are meant to be entrepreneurs should embrace this life path, and we hope to support them in the journey to succeed.

Bob: Does the startup economy offer more or less opportunity for women to succeed?

Shaherose: Startups offer a set of opportunities that a corporate environment or small business does not offer—not just for women, but for anyone in the startup economy.

This is an article we wrote about why startups are a great place to work: http://www.oreillynet.com/pub/a/womenintech/2007/09/20/tech-startups-a-safe-bet.html

Bob: Silicon Valley for decades has had its "old boys network" of entrepreneurs/VCs and others. Should women seek to become part of that, or should they create their own network or something else entirely?

Shaherose: Women 2.0 doesn't believe in building anything exclusive but, rather, adding to the existing entrepreneurial environment. Our events include experienced entrepreneurs and investors, male and female. If we build an exclusive network, it limits the value that can be shared and created. We envision a day when the Silicon Valley network comprises a near-equal number of males and females through our networking events, startup competition, and educational programs.

Bob: Has Silicon Valley and the startup economy (not necessarily the same thing) become more diverse/distributed?

Shaherose: Yes—Silicon Valley is no longer the only hub of innovation. The following trends contribute to the distribution of the startup economy beyond silicon valley:

1. *Reverse migration*: In 2005, 52% of Silicon Valley startups were immigrant founded, but now more and more skilled immigrant workers are returning home as immigration to the United States becomes more difficult and their home countries offer opportunities to innovate.

2. *New startup hubs*: We find new hubs for startups, such as Colorado, Seattle, Bangalore, Hyderabad, Boston—all offer a pool of technical talent, government support, and infrastructure and some access to funding.

Bob: As someone who knows a lot of startups, what do you see as the key factors for a startup's success?

Shaherose: *The people*: What skills do they offer to the venture/idea?

The relationships: Do the founders of the company have an open, trusting, synergistic relationship? How the founders work together at the time of launch determines future success.

Alignment: Are the founders aligned on their goals and expectations of the venture/idea?

Execution: Once the team is in place, can they execute as Planned.

The idea is only half the battle; it's the people, how they work together, and their quality of output that determines success. These factors allow a team to face adversity with strength and quickly to adjust course in the face of required change.

Bob: Are they're more, fewer, or about the same number of startups today as, say, three years ago? Are more of them successful?

Shaherose: As the economy contracts, the number of startups is decreasing, but the quality of the remaining startups is increasing and they are better positioned to succeed.

Startup Groups Near You—Offline and On

Both Startup2Startup and Women 2.0 are parts of the actual Silicon Valley culture in northern California. What if you hail from Austin, Texas? Where and how do you find other, like-minded people with whom to spend some rewarding face-to-face time?

Try **Meetup** and **Eventbrite**. They are two of those "something huge happening on the Internet while no one was watching" things. The ethos and values of "startupism" have spread far and wide, thanks to how easy it is to connect people who share a given interest, not just online but in actuality.

For example, recently I went rummaging for entrepreneur events at Meetup.com (Figure 4-19). Check out those stats: 271,343 entrepreneur Meetup Group members (plus another 47,137 interested people) have had 19,209 meetups in 761 cities in 36 countries. You are most definitely not alone.

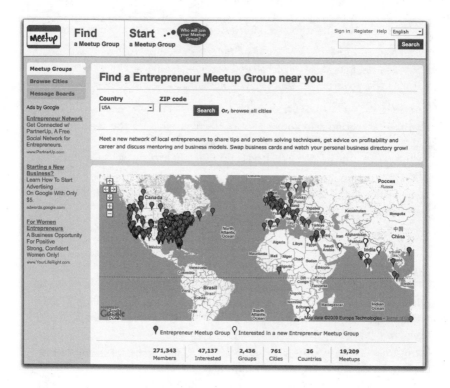

Figure 4-19. Startups on *Meetup.com*

So what kinds of meetups are out there for startups? Here's a small sampling that caught my eye from Atlanta, Georgia, and London, England.

- **Atlanta's Entrepreneurial Think Tank**—AETT is a professional networking group for strong-minded entrepreneurs who either have their own businesses or would like to go into business for themselves. (563 members)

- **Atlanta Web Entrepreneurs**—EMPOWERING ATLANTA ENTREPRENEURS! Atlanta Web Entrepreneurs is a business-focused membership organization dedicated to developing a robust ecosystem supporting entrepreneurs in the greater metropolitan Atlanta area. (1,310 members)

- **AWSome Atlanta (cloud computing user's group)**—Cloud technology in Atlanta. A technology meetup to discuss Amazon's new cloud offerings, EC2 and S3. However, all cloud technologies are fair game for discussion. (180 members)

- **The London Entrepreneur Meetup Group**—Meet a new network of local entrepreneurs to share tips and problem-solving techniques, get advice on profitability and career, and discuss mentoring and business models. Swap business cards and watch your personal business directory grow! (644 members)

- **London Creative Entrepreneurs**—Anyone running or setting up a creative business who wants to meet other creative entrepreneurs, swap ideas, tips, and gossip, get remotivated, have a coffee or a drink somewhere stylish, go to art exhibitions, workshops, and seminars on developing your business skills while nurturing your creative talents. (392 members)

- **Geektails**—After-work drinks in central London each month, for those who love Internet startups to meet and share ideas socially. Open to Internet entrepreneurs, CEOs, developers, VCs, angel investors, and just general geeks! (252 members)

Meetup.com is not the only way to find other startup founders offline: at **Eventbrite** (http://www.eventbrite.com/find-events?) I found 76 events ranging from startup weekends (see next paragraph) to Lunch 2.0 to Executing the Exit workshops.

And meetups and events are not the only way to get in the same room with other startup-minded people. Begun in 2007 by Andrew Hyde, each **Startup Weekend** (25 as of March 2009 in the United States and Europe) brings together developers, business managers, startup enthusiasts, graphic artists, and more for an intense 54-hour experience: build the code and business beginnings of a startup.

Here's how it works: Having signed up in Eventbrite for $40 to cover meals, the meeting facility, and a tee-shirt, about 100 people gather at a given location Friday night to share and vote on scores of ideas for startups. The list gets winnowed down to eight or nine projects and then people get to intense work for the rest of the weekend.

The combination of coding and business building like mad, plus drop-in special guests such as local VCs and angle investors, plus working face to face with a team of programmer/business types/graphic artists with a shared goal to launch—or at least prototype—a startup by weekend's end is the type of extraordinary experience that gets results (Figure 4-20).

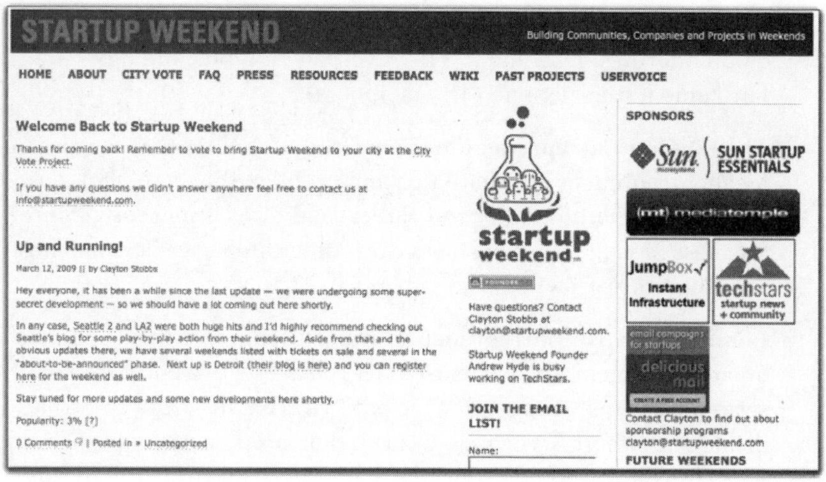

Figure 4-20. Startup Weekend

Now, this approach may not be what you want for your startup, and a good many of these efforts end up in the dead pool.[11] But like most things, practice makes perfect and getting to know other people with the same burning ambitions as you have is a great first step to connecting with future cofounders.

One more place worth checking if you're looking for a startup group to join: **YouNoodle** (at `http://younoodle.com`). YouNoodle is fast becoming a major node in the startup world: you can profile your startup there to attract investor and team members, find startup events, browse other people looking for startups to join, and find and create entrepreneurial groups. YouNoodle also has something called its Startup Predictor: feed it data about your startup and it will, based on a database of past startups, predict your likelihood of success.

Although I am more than a little skeptical that startup success can be reduced to a database filtering exercise, it's worth a look, and the rest of YouNoodle is really valuable.

---

[11] http://startupweekend.com/past-weekend-status-i

Online Forums

So where can you go for recommendations on whether you need business insurance for your startup, dealing with companies who want you to invoice them, finding a code repository, and other questions about running your startup business? I'd recommend the **Joel on Software Business of Software forum** (BOS, see Figure 4-21).[12]

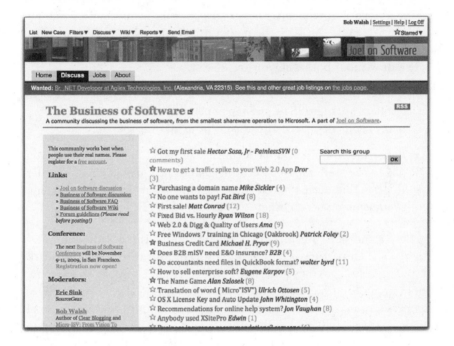

Figure 4-21. Business of Software Forum

I first wandered into BOS when I was searching for help on how to sell my first commercial product, back in 2004. I was amazed to find a spam-free, troll-free online community of successful and aspiring software vendors who'd share what they found works in their business.

That search lead to my first book,[13] and the book led to Joel Spolsky's asking me to join Eric Sink and, as of 2009, Andy Brice and Patrick McKenzie in moderating BOS. Several things are unique about BOS that aren't the case at your run-of-the-mill phpBB forum.

---

[12] http://discuss.joelonsoftware.com/default.asp?biz
[13] *Micro-ISV: From Vision to Reality* (Apress, 2006)

- *Spam*. Since BOS runs on FogBugz's forum software (see Chapter 8), nearly all spam never sees the light of day, and the few spammy posts quickly get zapped by one of the moderators.

- *Trolls, flame-war baiters, and abusive people check in but fade away fast*. One problem every online forum contends with is that small percentage of humanity who look to pick fights online or for people to belittle or who just go into Online Road Rage Mode over the slightest disagreement. These types poison the information well for everyone else. At BOS, the moderators spray them with a magical disinfectant that lets them have the satisfaction of a good abusive rant without bothering anyone else ☺.

- *A wide range of software industry participants*. Though a lot of BOS regulars are microISVs, a range of people regularly contribute from many segments of the IT industry from all over the globe.

- *Registration*. Unlike online forums, such as Slashdot, as of 2009 you had to register at least a fictitious name and e-mail address in order to post. That means you can have your anonymity and a secure online reputation on which other BOS readers can rely.

Here's another "Business of Software" online thingy in which you should consider participating: the **Business of Software Social Network** (`http://network.businessofsoftware.org`). Founded by Neil Davidson (whom we met in Chapter 1), this Ning-powered social network is 900+ members strong as of this writing and growing. It tends to cover more of the issues that existing software vendors face, such as e-mail campaigns to existing customers, using public webinars as marketing tools, and doing a better job as a product manager.

Speaking of **Ning** (`http://www.ning.com`)—which we do a bit more of in Chapter 6—take a moment and search for "startups" there. You'll find small local groups that might just be in your vicinity and a few large online social networks, such as Startup Net and EQ Connect.

When you talk about online social networks, the big gorilla is **Facebook** (`http://www.facebook.com`). You'll find over 500 results if you search Facebook Groups for "startup," groups such as Web Startups, Canadian Startups, LA Startups, StartupAfrica, Toronto Tech Startups, Sydney Web Startups, and the megagroup, Web 2.0 (Entrepreneurs).

If Facebook groups aren't for you, there's the other big gorilla in the social network: **LinkedIn** (`http://www.linkedin.com`). A quick search there recently yielded 212 "startup" groups. One I'd recommend is Darmish Shah's On Startups.

Annual Conferences

To wrap up this section on getting out more for the benefit of your startup, let me introduce you to three annual conferences you should know about.

First off is the **European Software Conference,** which is in its ninth year of providing two days of quality sessions for those building their own software businesses. With about 150 to 200 attendees, sessions range from web optimization techniques to excellent advice on AdWords to distributed agile development. I've attended twice and found the speakers knowledgeable, the vendors interesting, and the beer and camaraderie excellent. It is usually held the first weekend in November and costs 140 to 165. See `http://euroconference.org` for more information.

Next, on this side of the Atlantic, is the **Software Industry Conference**. A little larger than the European Software Conference, it runs two tracks of sessions for three days. The sessions are also very good, and they tend to cover a larger number of topics. It's usually held in July and costs $229. See `http://sic.org` for more information.

Both these conferences originated in the desktop shareware days of the last century and have their own awards ceremonies and a group of already-established small software firms that make up the organizational core. But much of the material is relevant to startups regardless of platform, and there's a lot to be learned from people already successful.

Finally, there's the three-year-old **Business of Software Conference**. Organized by Joel Spolsky (CEO of Fog Creek Software) and Neil Davidson (see Chapter 1), this conference is aimed at the founders and management of software companies, both established and new. If you're interested in the insights and wisdom of people such as Paul Graham, Don Norman, and Ryan Carson, insights that can galvanize your strategic vision for your startup, this is the place to be. In November 2008 it cost $1,495 to $1,995. See `http://www.businessofsoftware.org` for more information.

Large Vendor Programs for Startups

There are a couple more tools for startups you should know about, These are programs offered by major IT players designed especially for startups, not out of altruism but because startups are a key element in keeping these platform vendors healthy long term.

Microsoft BizSpark

Whereas Microsoft has offered startups deals on their development tools
and server licenses for years via something called the Empower[14] program,
BizSpark (http://www.microsoft.com/BizSpark) goes way beyond that
(Figure 4-22). If you get into the program, you'll get Microsoft's top-of-
the-line development tools (Visual Studio Team Foundation) with all the
trimmings, development server licenses for everything from SQL Server
2008 to SitePoint Server, and, most importantly, production licenses for as
many Windows Servers your startup needs to run for three years[15]—for free.

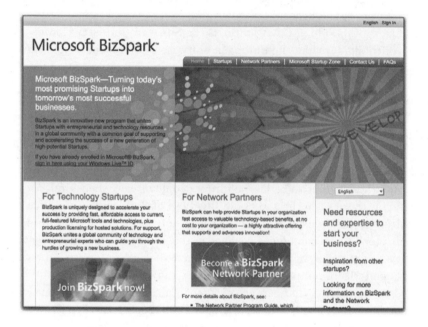

Figure 4-22. Microsoft BizSpark

How do you get into the program?

- Be a startup—that is, a business selling software, not doing custom
  or freelance development.

- Be in business less than three years—or be planning to do all the
  legal stuff to be a business in the eyes of the law in your country.

[14] https://partner.microsoft.com/40011351

[15] There's a "program termination fee" at the end of the three years of $100. I guess there's still one
bean counter somewhere in Microsoft!

- Make less than $1million a year.

- Get sponsored by an organization, group, or individual who is a BizSpark Network Partner.

How do you find a BizSpark Network Partner? You're reading a book from one. In fact, at least as of March 2009, I'm the single most active BizSpark Network Partner, sponsoring some 152 startups. Just e-mail me at bob.walsh@47hats.com, stick BizSpark in the subject, and tell me a bit about your startup and its (planned) app, and we'll get the ball rolling.

Since I don't get paid to do this, I should explain why I do it: for philosophical and business reasons both I and Microsofties who got the company to go for BizSpark want to see more developers, specifically.NET developers, become startups.

Until BizSpark, the production server licenses for, say, Windows Server and SQL Server were way too big an expense for a non-VC-funded startup to swallow, realistically meaning that if you and a buddy wanted to launch a startup and then attract capital, you'd better be planning to use Linux and other Open Source languages, IDEs, and technology.

From my point of view, BizSpark removes a huge roadblock for developers who happen to live in the .NET world but hunger for the chance to escape their cubicle farms and make it to entrepreneurial freedom. (You can get more info at http://www.microsoft.com/bizspark/Default.aspx.)

Sun Startup Essentials

Microsoft isn't the only big platform vendor who's realized that being nice to startups pays off. Sun Microsystems Startup Essentials Program (http://www.sun.com/emrkt/startupessentials) offers a tasty buffet of benefits for startups including the following:

- Hefty discounts on servers—for example, a well-provisioned Sun server with your choice of OS flavor for $750

- Deep discounts on Sun and MySQL software

- Big discounts from Sun partners for web hosting

- Free e-mail technical support from Sun engineers

- Free or discounted training on Sun's Open Source software and development tools

- Money

Figure 4-23. Sun Startup Essentials

Did that last bullet point catch your attention? It did mine, so I e-mailed Joann Yates, the marketing manager for the Sun Startup Essentials program. How does the VC funding aspect work? "We are partnering with Plug and Play Tech Center to leverage their vast network of investors," Joann replied. "Together with Plug and Play Tech Center [a Silicon Valley service provider for startups looking for hosting and funding] we evaluate each submitted Executive Summary of a startup's business, gather more information where necessary, and, for higher-potential ventures, attempt to match them against investors' business focus and goals. Investors can then review and meet with the startup for possible funding opportunities."

Since the program started in November 2006, it's expanded to 29 countries and thousands of startup companies.

Does Sun feel this program has been successful evangelizing Sun's platform? "Yes, although the primary purpose of the program is to bring Sun's great technologies to startups so that they can get off on a good footing that will allow them to grow quickly into a successful business," Joann replied. "We want to have the Fortune 100 companies of the future as Sun customers, and some of these startups will become just that."

Recap

One of the really nice things about launching a startup now is the wealth of great tools, groups, organizations, business programs, and company you find along the way. If anything, one real problem you need to face as a startup is that you're liable to drown in all the information to which you have access, at the expense of getting done the work you need to on your startup.

In this chapter, I've discussed a range of tools useful to your startup. Please feel free to ignore them, but if you do, you ignore the problems they address, at your startup's peril.

Besides a codebase, you're going to have to cover a wide variety of business bases. That's where the tools covered in this chapter can make a critical difference to getting to launch in a reasonable timeframe. Just in the past few years we're starting to see tools by startups for startups— congratulations, you're now a Market! ☺

There's another set of tools—better described as opportunities—for startups, and that's a huge explosion in ways to connect, face-to-face, with others seeking to build their own companies. It's been my observation that the more you put into face-to-face networking with other people in the Startup World, the more doors open to you for advice, funding, support, and opportunity. And, thanks to the Web, the days when you had to relocate to Silicon Valley to connect with other software entrepreneurs are well and truly over: *The Valley* is a global state of mind and set of values now, and that's a very, very good thing.

Finally, don't forget that at least two big companies are putting their money where their "we love startups" words are: Definitely check out both Microsoft BizSpark and Sun Startup Essentials as means to your ends.

Next up, we're finally going to get into a subject that should be near and dear to you—money—specifically, dissipating the air of mystery around exactly how to get friends, family, angel investors, and venture capitalists to put their money into your dream.

Money: Raise, Manage, Make

> *"Too much money is as demoralizing as too little,*
> *and there's no such thing as exactly enough."*
>
> —Mignon McLaughlin (American journalist and author, 1913–1983)

> *"The question isn't who is going to let me; it's who is going to stop me."*
>
> —Ayn Rand (American philosopher and author, 1905–1982),
> from *The Fountainhead*

Follow the Money

Odds are good you flipped to this chapter first, right? You were hoping that you'd find my patent-pending, supersecret, highly proprietary magic formula that, when cast over angel investors and venture capitalists, causes them to swoon and shower you with millions. Sorry to disappoint.

No magic formulas here, nor killer rules for VC presentations, nor amazing acts of prestidigitation—just a solid appraisal of the cold, hard reality of what it really takes to get funded, some very good advice on the legal and financial basics of a startup, and a few recommendations about what goes into that space between your customers' credit cards and your startup's bank account. If you're dreaming right now that tomorrow you'll see your startup glowingly described in *TechCrunch* as the latest canny investment to the tune of $5 million from a couple of VC outfits you've never heard of,[1] then you'd better wake up and smell the coffee.

---

[1] For example, Viximo Lands $5 Million for Virtual Goods Platform, http://www.techcrunch.com/2009/04/30/viximo-lands-5-million-for-virtual-goods-platform

If I can accomplish one thing in this chapter it's disabusing you of the mindset that funding is somehow an end in itself, that getting other people's equity money is the pot of gold at the end of your startup rainbow. It doesn't work that way, it has never worked that way, and thinking that way hangs a leper's bell around your neck that you can't hear but that every angel investor and VC can.

If, on the other hand, you want an introduction to the realities of how to fund your startup, then this chapter should get you started on the right road. Specifically I will focus on what happens after you've put your money and perhaps the money of family and friends into your startup.

And since we're playing for real money here, we will also cover how you as a startup need to manage your finances, and, by the way, how actually to make money. Teaching basic accounting and bookkeeping are beyond the scope of this book, but hopefully you'll finish this chapter with some idea of the difference between a profit/loss sheet and a balance sheet. Correctly forming your company and putting in place standard business practices isn't the game you want to play. But unless you get this stuff right, you won't even get to suit up.

Making money is what this entire book is about. But in this chapter, you'll get a rundown on five vendors who are in the business of converting your customers' money into your money: payment processors. Plus we'll take a quick look at a company that's found a way for you to get money from people who can't or won't buy your software.

Finally, we'll talk with one of the most knowledgeable people I know about something that just about every startup uses to connect to its market and make money: Google AdWords.

Raising the Money

In this section we're going to cover the basics of how, hypothetically, a first-time founder goes from "I want to build a startup" to preseed funding, angel investment, and then Series A funding in multiple tens of millions of dollars.

I need to make two things crystal clear. First, unlike a lot of the topics I talk about in this book, I myself have never raised outside funding. What I present here is a synthesis of the best information, advice, suggestions, and warnings I've accumulated while researching this book, not my personal experience. Second, I'm assuming we are in the same boat, that is, that this is your first startup, not your second or third, where a whole different set of rules apply.

Understanding the Funding Ladder

One of the first things you have to understand about getting money for your startup is that we're talking about four very different kinds of money, each with its own set of rules, motivations, and realities.

- **The 3 F's: family, friends, and fools (that's you).** This is the initial money you need to start, beginning with the first buck you spend on your startup. For most startups today that's something in the range of zero to $50,000. This is the money you (as a person) invest in you (as a business entity), and your cofounders do likewise.

- As a founder, you're going to want (and probably need) to structure any nonfounder 3F money as debt rather than sell a part of your company (equity), for several reasons, the most compelling being that potential angel/VC investors want it that way.

- Borrowing from friends and family obviously requires (1) friends and family who can afford to risk thousands of dollars on your dream and (2) some form of a promissory note detailing (a) the amount loaned, (b) the circumstances under which it will be paid back (your startup's hitting revenue targets is far better than a date certain), (c) whether you are personally guaranteeing the loan, and (d) the interest rate you'll pay for the use of this money (somewhere between the prevailing commercial loan rates and, say, 30%). In addition, at this point you should at least be able to state what you are attempting to build, why and how it's going to make money, and the gist of your startup in a couple of sentences.

- Keep in mind you're playing with fire here. If your startup crashes, you may kill a friendship or turn some or all of your family against you for the rest of your life. Fortunately, bootstrapping, which doesn't involve hitting up your friends and family for money, is a realistic way to go.

- **Angel round of investment ($50,000 to $5 million).** Now you're running with the Big Dogs, specifically with accredited and sophisticated investors.[2] Your angel funding (also called seed funding) might be because either one person has written you a check for $500,000 or you've made it to the final round of an arduous structured screening process.

---

[2] *Accredited and sophisticated has specific meanings—you're entering the world of equity funding, so you best start learning what these and many other terms mean.*

- You're going to need a lot of things to win this game: an executive summary that rivets attention, a totally credible business plan, a knockout presentation with a hundred researched, intelligent backup answers, and at least a working prototype if not actual proof of life.[3] But most of all you must be able to tell that angel investor (who was probably in your shoes a few years ago) how to turn his or her $200,000 into a minimum of $2 million in five years or less while enjoying living in your world.

- Don't underestimate that last point. I've been told by people who've secured their angel investment funding that for angels, it's not just the money; it's the desire to be back in the game. They want to contribute to the next (Internet) generation of founders, pay forward the help their angel investors and VCs gave them, solve problems, open doors, and convert the pain of hard lessons learned into the pleasure of helping you. Of course, don't think for one split second that the money isn't a prime issue here; it's just not the only issue.

- Out on the Internet you'll find angel groups that behave more like VCs, VCs interested and willing to fund very "early-stage" startups with angel-like money, and startup incubators and programs (see the later section "Startup Incubators") that sometimes precede or replace angel funding. This is the real world, not the API. One key fact that should help you understand the difference between angels and VCs is where they get the money they put into startups. Typically, angels are investing their own after-tax moolah, whereas VCs have raised a pool of funds from universities, pension funds, hedge funds, very rich investors, IT companies, and who knows where else. Venture capitalists have a very real fiduciary responsibility to return big globs of ROI to the people for whom they work; angels are betting their own money.

---

[3] No, I don't mean a picture of you holding today's newspaper. I mean either customers paying your startup money, registered people using your software, big-number page views and unique visitors, or some other metric indicating that there's a market, a big market, out there for what you're going to be selling.

- If you are a first-time founder and you can secure angel funding that lets you build a $20 million to $50 million company in five years' time, be happy. You've jumped through multiple hoops of fire and walked across burning coals unscathed. If your company (it's no longer a startup) needs to climb to the next rung of the funding ladder, you'd better have added to your skill set levitation, turning lead into gold, a whole team of advisors, executives, and directors, and a truly rare chance to create eight- or nine-figure wealth.

- **Series A funding ($1 million to around $6 million).** You've now entered the world of VCs—if and only if they think you can turn their $3 million into $80 million, $100 million, $300 million within three to around seven years. I say *around* because there's no such thing as hard-and-fast rules at this level of the funding game; different VCs invest in different sectors, represent different money pools, and have their own strategies for winning big.

- It's a gross but useful oversimplification that to secure this kind of funding in this era following the 2008 economic meltdown, you probably have done your angel investing round and that your company is a going concern that's producing revenue, has very good connections, and, if scaled to 10 times its current size, has a strong chance of being the global market leader in a significant market.

- **Series B, C funding ($8 million and up).** Think of this as Series A, part 2, funding and up.

You Are Not Alone

As with any unmet need, there are people out there to help you, the startup founder, succeed. One of them is Brandon Zeuner. Brandon is the cofounder of Venture51 (http://venture51.com; Figure 5-1), a venture/launch firm that helps early-stage tech startups go from idea to launch. Brandon's recent involvement in startups includes newly launched Republic Project (http://www.republicproject.com), PeopleJar (http://peoplejar.com), and Growth Panel (http://www.growthpanel.com). Before cofounding Venture51, he was on the founding executive team at Flypaper. Brandon and his team handle Growth Panel's Internet marketing and social media strategy. Brandon established his professional reputation as a software marketing and sales guy at SalesLogix and ACT! Software before turning in florescent lighting and corporate politics for the startup world and helping startups launch.

Figure 5-1. Venture51

Bob: What is Venture51, and what does it do for startups?

Brandon: Venture51 is a venture/launch firm that helps early-stage tech startups go from idea to launch. Venture51's philosophy is grounded in launching startups with minimal infusions of capital and includes an active involvement in executing the product development and launch strategy using emerging sales and marketing channels. As sales and marketing technologists, we believe that to improve the batting average of the portfolio, you must insulate good products with ongoing emerging sales and marketing activity. We help early-stage startups go from idea to launch, providing the support they need to be a great company and not simply another tech product.

Bob: What parts of the startup puzzle do you provide, and what do they cost?

Brandon: Software and Web development, user experience design, mentors and advisors, legal, accounting, and administrative help, launch and perpetual launch marketing services, perpetual launch strategy, social media marketing, search, web and interactive experiences, digital marketing, mobile, gaming, and emerging media, affiliate marketing sales and business development service, and investment strategy and enablement.

There are no set fees for our services. We work with the operators of these startups to identify the gaps in either product development or go-to-market. Depending on services needed, we then work out a hybrid equity/cash deal (with a heavier emphasis on the equity side) to keep burn low and runway extended.

Bob: What's your deal flow like these days?

Brandon: Deal flow has been great. We typically see 20–30 new deals per month. These deals are coming in from all over the country, but primarily the southwest. Out of the deals we see we intend to work with approximately 10 new startups per year.

Bob: Do you get involved with finding angel/VC funding for your clients? How does that work?

Brandon: Venture51 is not a fund and we are not finders. We work with startups to prepare them for varying levels of funding if needed. We have relationships with established angels and nontraditional VCs. We help to prepare the startup for the discussions but do not participate or take any fees in the capital formation process. We also identify whether the startup truly needs a cash infusion or if the gaps identified can be filled by efforts from our development team or marketing services.

The Basics of the Funding Game

Now that we've covered at least a working definition of what Other People's Money looks like to a first-time founder, I'd like to save you a few dozen hours Googling this subject by covering the basics of the funding. You will want those hours—and several hundred more—for doing the things necessary to actually get funded, but at least this section should give you a basic orientation to MoneyLand.

The Art of Raising Angel Capital, by Guy Kawasaki

When I interviewed Guy Kawasaki for Chapter 9, he was kind enough to grant permission to reprint several posts from his blog, How to Change the World. On these three topics—raising angel capital, the top ten lies of entrepreneurs, and the art of bootstrapping, I think Guy has written pretty near the final word—and words you should take to heart.

Make no mistake about it: There is an art to raising angel capital. Raising angel capital is not harder or easier than raising institutional venture capital—it's simply different. Here's how to do it.

1. **Make sure they are "accredited" investors.** "Accredited" is legalese for "rich enough never to get back a penny." Just read what the SEC says. You can get into a boatload of trouble for selling stock to the proverbial "little old lady in Florida," so don't do it. And get a good corporate finance attorney (as opposed to your aunt, the divorce lawyer) to advise you about the process of seeking investments.

2. **Make sure they're sophisticated investors.** I'm a masochist for hate e-mail, but I'll tell you anyway: the least desirable angel investor is a rich doctor or dentist—unless you're a life sciences entrepreneur. They will drive you crazy because they read how Ram Shriram made gazillions of dollars as an early investor in Google, and now, six months later, they want to know when you're going public too. Sophisticated angel investors have knowledge and expertise in your industry—they will have "been there and done that." Sure, you want their money, but you also want their expertise. Be warned: if you want to raise venture capital in later rounds, it's going to be much harder if you show up with a long list of unsophisticated investors.

3. **Don't underestimate them.** If I had a nickel for every time an entrepreneur told me that she was going to raise angel capital because it was easier than raising venture capital, I wouldn't have to run ads in this blog. Do everything on the venture capitalist wish list because the days of angel investors as "easy marks" are gone forever—if this was ever true. You can have an "early stage" company but not a "dumbass" company, and angels care as much about liquidity as venture capitalists—maybe even more since they're investing their personal, after-tax money. Angels do not consider investments to be "charitable contributions"—well, no angel whose money you'd want, anyway.

4. **Understand their motivation.** Here's how angel investors differ from venture capitalists. Typically, angel investors have a triple bottom line. First, they've "made it," so now they want to "pay back" society by helping the next generation of entrepreneurs. Second, they'd like to stay current with technology and tinker with interesting products and technologies. Finally, they want to make money. Thus, they are often willing to invest in less proven, more risky deals to provide entrepreneurs with the ability to get to the next stage. I know many nice venture capitalists, but I cannot tell you that many of them are motivated by the desire to pay back society or seek intellectual stimulation. :-)

5. **Enable them to live vicariously.** More on angel motivation: One of the rewards of angel investing is the ability to live vicariously through an entrepreneur's efforts. That is, angels want to relive the thrills of entrepreneurship while avoiding the firing line. Thus, you should frequently seek their guidance because they enjoy helping you. By contrast, most venture capitalists only want to get involved when things are going really well or really poorly.

6. **Make your story comprehensible to a spouse.** The investment committee for many venture capitalists works like this: "You vote for my deal, and I'll vote for yours." That's not how decisions are made by angel investors because the usual membership of an angel's investment committee consists of one person: a spouse. So, if you've got a "client-server Open Source OPML carrier-class enterprise software" product, you must make it comprehensible to the angel's husband when he asks, "What are we going to invest $100,000 into?"

7. **Sign up people that they've heard of.** Angel investors are also motivated by the social aspect of investing with buddies in startups run by bright, young people who are changing the world. Even if the other investors are not buddies, investing side by side with well-known angels is quite attractive. If you get one of these guys or gals, you're likely to attract a whole flock of angels too.

8. **Be nice.** More so than venture capitalists, angel investors fall in love with entrepreneurs. Often, the entrepreneurs remind them of their sons or daughters—or fill the position of the sons or daughters they never had. Venture capitalists will often invest in a schmuck if the schmuck is a proven money maker. If you're seeking angel capital, you're probably not proven, so you can't get away with acting like a schmuck. Therefore, be nice until you're proven—although I hope that when you're proven, you'll also realize that you should be a mensch.

Reprinted from the *How to Change the World* blog, by permission.

The process I describe next is what most startups would hypothetically go through when seeking their first taste of equity funding from angel investors and early-stage VCs.

1. What You're Building, What You Can Achieve, and How Valuable It'll Be

The very first step of a process that will span years of your life is to get a rock-solid understanding of what kind of startup you want to build, what you can realistically achieve, and what valuation others will see in your efforts.

- **What kind of startup do *you* want to create?** I assume you've read Chapter 1, but it's worth repeating: You (and your cofounders) need to decide at the get-go what you are building and why. *There is no single right answer.* Are you building a microISV that you will run yourself that yields an annual income—best case—something like $500,000 a year?

- Or are you building a software company with some number of employees that will have, say, $5 million in sales and, after all is said and done, create a sellable asset you might possibly be able to cash out one day for $15 million? Or do you honestly and truly believe with all your heart and soul that you've got an idea, the technical expertise, and the market opportunity to create another Google, YouTube, or Skype?

- **What kind of startup can you build this time around?**[4] Again, it's time for a dose of brutal self-honesty. What technical, financial, and social resources can you bring to bear on creating your startup? If you're an experienced, respected developer with more work offered you than you can do, with a good network among other experienced developers and six months savings in the bank, that's one thing. If you're a programmer with only a couple of years in the business who's just been laid off from your first postcollege job, that's another.

- Again, there's no right answer here; but the wrong answer is not being honest with yourself about what resources you have.

- **How valuable will your startup be in the eyes of others?** You may have hypnotized yourself into thinking that one-tenth of the human race will fork over money for your software; others may not be as optimistic. Forecast from the bottom up.

---

[4] *You may be planning your first startup, but nothing says it will be your last. In fact, a lot of first-time founders, regardless of outcome (acquisition, steady state, crash and burn) go on to launch their second, third, and nth startup or stay in the game as angel investors.*

- To add to the fun, your startup's valuation is anything but objective, static, or well defined. Depending on who's doing the valuation, everything gets thrown into the stewpot, from your financial forecasts to your office furniture (assuming you have an office, which you probably don't) to the price tag put on a "comparable" startup last week, to your YouNoodle Score.[5] Valuation is the basis for equity funding. And valuation—and what you can realistically raise from equity funding—changes as your startup grows and evolves. For more on what valuation means in the startup world, I'd recommend Cayenne Consulting's (http://www.caycon.com) **High Tech Startup Valuation Estimator** at (http://www.caycon.com/resources.php).[6]

- There's a fundamental economic reality here. When we're talking about equity funding (as opposed to debt funding), we are talking legalized gambling, with the bettors in the game in hopes their 10–60% of your company turns out to be worth at least 10 times what they paid you for it (angel investors), more like 50 times or hundreds of times (venture capitalists). If years down the road your company is going to be worth, say, a very respectable $50 million, the chances are close to zip that a VC will pony up $5 million in Series A funding. One of the biggest reasons startups that make it through the first VC meeting don't get a dime is not that they are bad people, but they just don't see how your potential valuation can get into the ballpark they need.

- The bottom line on valuation is whether your company is worth what the people you're trying to get funding from say it's worth. While you obviously need to put forward a credible estimate in your business plan (see next section), your potential investors are going to be far more interested in and accepting of your numbers if you make a compelling case and are not just spinning fantasies.

---

[5] We saw YouNoodle back in Chapter 4. YouNoodle's Startup Valuation Predictor is at http://younoodle.com/predictor. After completing a fairly detailed questionnaire, the Predictor weighs the team, financial factors, concept, and advisors of your startup and gives you its estimate of your startup's value in three years.

[6] Cayenne Consulting is in the business of writing business plans for the purpose of raising capital. The Entrepreneur Library section of their site is a first-class annotated megalist of other sites, nicely arranged for your edification. See and explore http://www.caycon.com/valuation.php.

2. Deciding and Documenting What You Need

"What do you want the money for?" You can expect to hear that from every single person, from your mother-in-law to the steely-eyed VC who looks like he's just dined on a buffet of livers ripped from the bodies of would-be founders. Answers to this question differ depending on where your startup is at, and they range from expanding your inbound sales team to further product development to committing to your share of a strategic partnership.

These questions should get answered, in enough detail to be credible, in your executive summary and your business plan. There's an infinitude of right answers, but here are two wrong answers and why they're wrong.

- **Pay back the founders.** Wrong answer! That's not how it works. The money you and your founders have invested up to this point is not going to be returned to you until and unless you sell your company— and, unless you had good legal/accounting counsel from before you took you first dollar, euro, or yen, maybe not even then.

- **Buying out a nonperforming partner.** Wrong answer! This should never have happened, and it's one of the reasons investors eyeball you and your cofounders so carefully before signing over the first tranche.[7] See the later interview of Gene Landy to learn what he has to say about avoiding this leg-breaker.

3. Writing an Executive Summary and a Business Plan

Achieving success in getting funded by an angel investor or getting into a startup incubator means preparing the time-tested document that makes this process work: the business plan.

There are two separate and distinct kinds of business plans in the startup world. One is the business plan that specifies what you are building, how it will operate, and what decisions you've made. We'll talk about these in Chapter 8. The second kind is the business plan and its executive summary that serve as your startup's API—how others will put money into your business and get anywhere from 10 to 1,000 times more money back in a specified number of years.

---

[7] *The equity funding world has as specialized a vocabulary as any you'll find in IT. If you want their money, you'd better learn to speak their language of deal flows, capital structure, accredited investors, and, yes, tranche, which is French for "slice." For the basics (since Google Translate does not yet cover this), check out the Venture Capital Glossary at FundingPost (http://www.fundingpost.com/ glossary/venture-glossary.asp) and the Glossary of Private Equity and Venture Capital at VC Experts (http://vcexperts.com/vce/library/encyclopedia/glossary.asp).*

Let's cover the executive summary first. It is, simply put, the one or two pages that sell your startup to the potential investor or that at least get your foot in the door. You can think of it as a written and more detailed version of the *elevator pitch*.[8] What goes into it? To find out, visit Guy Kawasaki's angel-funding Garage Technology Venture's web site at http://www.garage.com, and, under Resources, download "Writing a Compelling Executive Summary."[9]

As for the business plan, the archetypical[10] plan has the following sections.

- **Executive Summary:** This is the capstone of this particular edifice. You write it last, and in it, as concisely as possible, you explain what your selling and who, why, and how they're going to buy, how much you want from investors, and why they should invest in your startup.

- **Market Analysis:** Here's where you define and explain exactly who is going to buy from your startup and how you plan to go from zero market share to X% in, say, three years. But that's only the beginning. You're going to want to dissect your primary market—how it works, who makes the buying decision, what the typical price points are, what trends or changes are affecting this market—among another dozen or so questions that demonstrate you've thought through who's going to buy from you and why.

- **Company Description:** This section tells where you are in terms of staffing, state of development, milestones already reached, current objectives, and location.

---

[8] *Imagine you're walking on California Street in San Francisco and see VC legend John Doerr (http://en.wikipedia.org/wiki/John_Doerr) walking past the 200-ton black granite sculpture locals call "Banker's Heart" and into the landmark skyscraper that used to be the Bank of America's headquarters. You follow him into the lobby, where you both get into an elevator. He's heading to the Carnelian Room on the 52nd floor. You finally summon up the nerve to say to him, "Mr. Doerr, can I tell you about my startup?" Because he's been funding startups longer than you've been alive and is a true gentleman, he responds, "Sure. What's your pitch?" What you say to him before he exits on the 52nd floor is your elevator pitch. Good luck!*

[9] *Why don't I just tell you what Guy has to say? I do in Chapter 9. But Guy, who writes better than I do, has written nine books, two of which you'd better own already at this stage: Reality Check (Portfolio Hardcover, 2008) and The Art of the Start (Portfolio Hardcover, 2004. He also has a must-read blog: How to Change the World (http://blog.guykawasaki.com).*

[10] *See http://www.sba.gov/smallbusinessplanner/plan/writeabusinessplan/ SERV_ESSENTIAL.html.*

- **Organization and Management:** This section details who does what in your company and what their background, core competencies, and experience are. It tells how your company is structured, who owns it and in what proportions, and who sits on your Board of Directors and what they bring to the party.

- **Marketing and Sales Management:** This section describes your target market and explain exactly how you're going to sell to that market. It details your overall sales strategy, what channels you are using to implement that strategy (for example, whether you are going to have a sales force and, if so, how you will recruit, train, and compensate them). It specifies your sales funnel (from potential prospect through to customer) and how many people make it through each level of the process. Finally, it lists your competitors and your strategy for wresting market share from them.

- **Service or Product Line:** This section covers what you are selling. In it you describe your app or web service, what it provides to your customers, and how this connects to what you've identified as what the market needs and will pay for. By the way, while you'll be talking about your product or service from a technical perspective (technology, patents pending, trade secrets), what really matters is how what you sell looks from your customers' point of view.

- **Funding Request:** This section tells what you want the money for— not just how much, over what period, and how you propose that funding be structured and released to you, but exactly what the money will be used for to meet your company's objectives.

- **Financials:** This consists of two kinds of data: (1) a financial history of your firm to date (income and balance sheets, cash flow statements, profit and loss statements) and (2) your revenue forecasts for the next five years and the assumptions, logic, and key metrics that make those forecasts believable.

- **Appendix:** This is a grab bag of everything, from your company's and founders' credit reports to copies of favorable reviews, key legal documents, strategic partnership agreements, and who your attorney and accountant are.

Now, there are endless variations of the exact structure of a business plan. And depending on whether you start from scratch, use a software-driven template, or hire a business plan consultant, you are going to be investing a lot of time here. Writing a good business plan can make creating your software look easy.

Of course, the executive summary and business plan are the easy part of the funding process. Now the real fun begins.

4. The (Angel) Investment Process

There are two overlapping processes in this phase of the funding game: In theory, you'll do one thing. In reality, an entirely different set of things will likely happen. If this sounds a bit like the difference between getting a job by applying for one you see on Craigslist or monster.com and slipping in before there's a job opening posted because someone in your extended network of friends, buddies, ex-office mates, old girlfriends, old boyfriends, and family members gets you in, you're spot on.

In *theory*, you'll start by submitting your executive summary, business plan, and whatever else they want to numerous angel investor organizations such as you'll find listed in the Directory section of the Angel Capital Association (`http://www.angelcapitalassociation.org/dir_directory/directory.aspx`) or through Angelsoft (`http://angelsoft.net`[11]; see Figure 5-2).

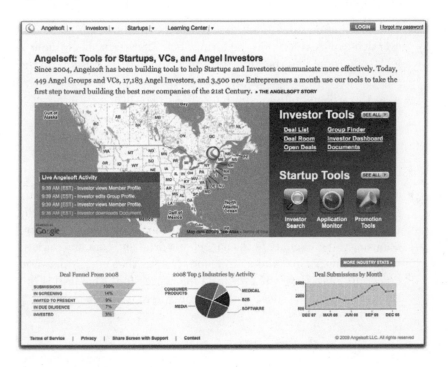

Figure 5-2. Angelsoft

---

[11] Not `http://angelsoft.com`! ☺

These angel groups will take your application and the following will happen.

- They will do some sort of initial screening before adding you to their deal flow. If you pass that,

- You will get presented to either the angel group at large or a screening committee to decide if you should actually meet with or talk to them. If you pass that,

- You will talk to one or more angels. If you pass that,

- You will get checked out more intensively on everything from your references to your financials (due diligence). If you pass that,

- You will be presented to the one or more angel investors in the group (individuals invest, not the group as a whole) who might be interested investing, and/or you will come up with a prefunding valuation and a term sheet that spells out the particular percentage of your company they will buy with their investment.

- That prefunding valuation is essentially the denominator for whatever deal you're offered in the term sheet. That term sheet might look something like the form term sheet Band of Angels has on its site (http://www.bandangels.com/entrepreneurs/index.php) or what the Wilson Sonini Goodrich & Rosati law firm's Term Sheet Generator will produce at http://www.wsgr.com/WSGR/Display.aspx?SectionName=practice/termsheet.htm or what you'll find at TheFunded (see http://www.thefunded.com/funds/item/2674 for details).

- The particulars of what's in a term sheet I leave for your attorney to explain, since he or she gets paid way more than I do.[12] In a nutshell, the term sheet will spell out the kind and amount of stock in your company you are selling to the angel investor(s) and contain a variety of conditions, rights, and contingency clauses that may or may not come into play. Have you ever used the expression "The devil is in the details"? Terms sheets are probably where it comes from.

---

[12] *If for some reason you don't already have an attorney who is savvy in tech/startup businesses, do not pass Go, do not sign, and get yourself one, pronto!*

- While your attorney—at a rate of probably over $500 an hour—is explaining to you the joys of drag-along rights, reverse vesting, and liquidation preferences, the investors will continue the due diligence process (think of it as a kind of legal/business colonoscopy).

- Assuming you reach a meeting of the minds on terms and that your startup is free of worrisome polyps such as a nonperforming cofounder, clouded intellectual property rights, or a few hundred other little items, the investor writes a check, probably takes a seat on your Board, starts opening doors you didn't know existed, and proffers sage advice, you get back to the business of scaling up your company while inspirational background music swells and the clouds part to reveal a sunny future.

Wasn't that a nice story? It's actually true, somewhat, some of the time, for some startups—maybe even yours.

The *reality* of the angel funding process is considerably different. First off, you didn't send off your executive summary and business plan to all and sundry angel groups; you bounced it off the startup founder you met a few months ago at an event you both attended and who you were able to intro to a really good JavaScript coder you know who was just what that startup needed. That founder, who's been through the angel funding mill, pointed out the 19 pieces of hype in your plan that actually were showstoppers and suggested that once you fixed the business strategy encapsulated in that plan, you talk to one of his investors, whom you actually know from a conference two years back.

The Top Ten Lies of Entrepreneurs, by Guy Kawasaki

I've included this post by Bill Reichert from Guy Kawasaki's blog because in this business there's a fine line between *dreaming big* and *dreaming on*. If you find you're telling one of these ten lies to yourself, that should be a your-house-is-on-fire wakeup call.

(Since I've antagonized the venture capital community with last week's blog [*The Top Ten Lies of Venture Capitalists*, http://blog.guykawasaki.com/ 2006/01/the_top_ten_lie.html], I thought I would complete the picture and "out" entrepreneurs to begin this week. The hard part about writing this blog was narrowing down these lies to ten. Luckily, my partner, Bill Reichert, had already documented this list of the top ten lies of entrepreneurs.)

We get pitched dozens of times every year, and every pitch contains at least three or four of these lies. We provide them not because we believe we can increase the level of honesty of entrepreneurs as much as to help entrepreneurs come up with new lies. At least new lies indicate a modicum of creativity!

1. **"Our projections are conservative."** An entrepreneur's projections are never conservative. If they were, they would be $0. I have never seen an entrepreneur achieve even her most conservative projections. Generally, an entrepreneur has no idea what sales will be, so she guesses: "Too little will make my deal uninteresting; too big, and I'll look hallucinogenic." The result is that everyone's projections are $50 million in year four. As a rule of thumb, when I see a projection, I add one year to delivery time and multiply by .1.

2. **"(Big name research firm) says our market will be $50 billion in 2010."** Every entrepreneur has a few slides about how the market potential for his segment is tens of billions. It doesn't matter if the product is bar mitzvah planning software or 802.11 chip sets. Venture capitalists don't believe this type of forecast because it's the fifth one of this magnitude that they've heard that day. Entrepreneurs would do themselves a favor by simply removing any reference to market size estimates from consulting firms.

3. **"(Big name company) is going to sign our purchase order next week."** This is the "I heard I have to show traction at a conference" lie of entrepreneurs. The funny thing is that next week, the purchase order still isn't signed. Nor the week after. The decision maker gets laid off, the CEO gets fired, there's a natural disaster, whatever. The only way to play this card is AFTER the purchase order is signed, because no investor whose money you'd want will fall for this one.

4. **"Key employees are set to join us as soon as we get funded."** More often than not when a venture capitalist calls these key employees who are VPs at Microsoft, Oracle, and Sun, he gets the following response: "Who said that? I recall meeting him at a Churchill Club meeting, but I certainly didn't say I would leave my cushy $250,000/year job at Adobe to join his startup." If it's true that key employees are ready to rock and roll, have them call the venture capitalist after the meeting and testify to this effect.

5. **"No one is doing what we're doing."** This is a bummer of a lie because there are only two logical conclusions. First, no one else is doing this because there is no market for it. Second, the entrepreneur is so clueless that he can't even use Google to figure out he has competition. Suffice it to say that the lack of a market and cluelessness is not conducive to securing an investment. As a rule of thumb, if you have a good idea, five companies are doing the same thing. If you have a great idea, 15 companies are doing the same thing.

6. **"No one can do what we're doing."** If there's anything worse than the lack of a market and cluelessness, it's arrogance. No one else can do this until the first company does it, and 10 others spring up in the next 90 days. Let's see, no one else ran a sub-four-minute mile after Roger Bannister. (It took only a month before John Landy did.) The world is a big place. There are lots of smart people in it. Entrepreneurs are kidding themselves if they think they have any kind of monopoly on knowledge. And, sure as I'm a Macintosh user, on the same day that an entrepreneur tells this lie, the venture capitalist will have met with another company that's doing the same thing.

7. **"Hurry because several other venture capital firms are interested."** The good news: There are maybe 100 entrepreneurs in the world who can make this claim. The bad news: The fact that you are reading a blog about venture capital means you're not one of them. As my mother used to say, "Never play Russian roulette with an Uzi." For the absolute cream of the crop, there is competition for a deal, and an entrepreneur can scare other investors to make a decision. For the rest of us, don't think one can create a sense of scarcity when it's not true. Reread the previous blog about the lies of venture capitalists to learn how entrepreneurs are hearing "maybe" when venture capitalists are saying "no."

8. **"Oracle is too big/dumb/slow to be a threat."** Larry Ellison has his own jet. He can keep the San Jose Airport open for his late-night landings. His boat is so big that it can barely get under the Golden Gate Bridge. Meanwhile, entrepreneurs are flying on Southwest out of Oakland and stealing the free peanuts. There's a reason why Larry is where he is and entrepreneurs are where they are, and it's not that he's big, dumb, and slow. Competing with Oracle, Microsoft, and other large companies is a very difficult task. Entrepreneurs who utter this lie look at best naive. You think it's bravado, but venture capitalists think it's stupidity.

9. **"We have a proven management team."** Says who? Because the founder worked at Morgan Stanley for a summer? Or McKinsey for two years? Or he made sure that John Sculley's Macintosh could power on? Truly "proven" in a venture capitalist's eyes is the founder of a company that returned billions to its investors. But if the entrepreneur were that proven, then he (a) probably wouldn't have to ask for money; (b) wouldn't be claiming that he's proven. (Do you think Wayne Gretzky went around saying "I am a good hockey player"?) A better strategy is for the entrepreneur to state that (a) she has relevant industry experience; (b) she is going to do whatever it takes to succeed; (c) she is going to surround herself with directors and advisors who are proven; and (d) she'll step aside whenever it becomes necessary. This is good enough for a venture capitalist that believes in what the entrepreneur is doing.

10. **"Patents make our product defensible."** The optimal number of times to use the P word in a presentation is one. Just once, say, "We have filed patents for what we are doing." Done. The second time you say it, venture capitalists begin to suspect that you are depending too much on patents for defensibility. The third time you say it, you are holding a sign above your head that says, "I am clueless." Sure, you should patent what you're doing—if for no other reason than to say it once in your presentation. But at the end, the patents are mostly good for impressing your parents. You won't have the time or money to sue anyone with a pocket deep enough to be worth suing.

11. **"All we have to do is get 1% of the market."** (Here's a bonus since I still have battery power.) This lie is the flip side of "The market will be $50 billion." There are two problems with this lie. First, no venture capitalist is interested in a company that is looking to get 1% or so of a market. Frankly, we want our companies to face the wrath of the antitrust division of the Department of Justice. Second, it's also not that easy to get 1% of any market, so you look silly pretending that it is. Generally, it's much better for entrepreneurs to show a realistic appreciation of the difficulty of building a successful company.

Reprinted from the *How to Change the World* blog, by permission.

Now, this investor—who got a sweet cashout when the startup of which he has a piece was gobbled up like one of those tasty little crab puff appetizers served at higher-end launch parties—isn't really interested in you. But he knows this other investor, who's just going crazy because she knows the right startup in your space is going to be another YouTube and she wants to be a player.

So the first investor gets you a warm intro to the second investor (paying off a favor). And now you and your team are sitting at a tiny table in some Starbucks trying to explain why your startup is worth their money. Maybe they like you. Maybe they don't. Let's say, for the sake of the story arc, that they do. Now, maybe this angel investor is a member of an angel investor group and talks you up at their next meeting and you jump the line in that group's deal flow, or maybe they tell their attorney to meet with your attorney to see if a deal can be made. And, assuming a wheel doesn't fall off the deal, you've checked out, they've checked out, and it all comes together. So now you have a real live angel on your side who not only funds your startup but connects you with some really good technical talent. The birds didn't sing, the clouds didn't part, and the challenges won't stop, but your startup has a real shot at being a contender. Congratulations are definitely in order.

The point I'm trying to make here is that in addition to doing all the impersonal business things that are required of a startup seeking angel or VC funding, you are going to need to network like crazy face-to-face because that's how this business works, and you're kidding yourself if you think otherwise.

Where do you start? Try one of the organizations described in Chapter 4, reach out to some other founders, sign up for some kind of startup event in your part of the world. Whatever works—just start.

What Angels and Venture Capitalists Want

OK, enough editorializing. Here's what three VCs and the founder of a prominent angel investor group told me to pass on to you about how getting funded really works. Once you've read this section, you might notice that these four incredibly sharp and successful people happen to be women. This is anything but a representative sampling of the angel/VC space, where you'll find at least four men to every woman in terms of company ownership, angels, VCs, you name it.

So what happened here? Well, angel investors and VCs are incredibly busy, successful people who by and large have zero bandwidth for snoopy authors pestering them for interviews for their upcoming books. That was true until I went to a Startup2Startup dinner where someone suggested I talk to Shaherose Charania, the managing director of Women 2.0 (see Chapter 4), who popped into the dinner for about 10 minutes. She was kind enough to answer my questions about Women 2.0 and then to reach out to her network to ask them, as a favor to her, to talk to me. Rebecca, Jo Anne, and Cindy gave me interviews, and Cindy made a warm intro to Stephanie. Beginning to get a sense of how this business works?

Rebecca Lynn, Principal, Morgenthaler Ventures

With over $2.5 billion invested in 300-plus companies over the years, Morgenthaler Ventures is one of the oldest VC firms in Silicon Valley, focusing on life sciences and IT. Here's what Rebecca Lynn, who focuses on early-stage investments in mobile, Internet services, digital media and financial services, had to say.

Bob: What do you look for in early-stage venture funding in the areas that you follow?

Rebecca: I think it's pretty core. There are a number of areas, but there are two core things. One is a truly disruptive technology or business model. The second is they have to address a very large market. Those are really, I think, always the two key contributors to what we look for when we're looking at early stage. Team is also a big factor. Market is a big factor and all of that.

But the vein that runs through everything are those two issues. Is it truly disruptive? And does it address a big market?

Bob: How often do you find what you are looking for in the course of a year?

Rebecca: It's funny, it goes in clusters. We will look at 100 or so deals where nothing is sort of what we were looking for. And then, it's funny; we will find two in a row. It seems to go that way to be honest. It's really a funny kind of business, but you just have to keep hunting and keep looking and be optimistic.

Bob: You're one of the people who would act as a gatekeeper, I would say. If they can't get past you, the odds that Morgenthaler Ventures, which is a 40-year-old VC firm, is going to consider them are pretty slim. What do you down-check people for?

Rebecca: What do we sort of count against people?

Bob: Yeah. What are the signs that these people are not going to make it for you.

Rebecca: There are a few things. One thing is, venture capital funding is not for everybody. Oftentimes you're better off just creating a really profitable business without creating the funding. When I say that, the reason is, when we look at a business idea, a lot of times we will see some great business ideas and we're like, "Yeah. These people are going to make money doing this." But it is not going to be enough for us to justify a venture investment.

We see so many ideas that we're like, "Yeah, we could see these people making a couple million dollars a year and being profitable," but we can't see them becoming a $100-million-a-year company.

I think that's the number one thing that we see. It's hard to sort good businesses. For us to back a company there has to be some way that we could envision—some low probability, perhaps—that the stars are lining up and it could be a billion-dollar company.

We know the likelihood of its being that big is small, but there has to be sort of a path that we believe it can get there. And then if it can't, then that is just not something that we can invest in as a VC business.

I tell entrepreneurs that all the time, that VC is not the only path for a lot of people. Oftentimes you can bootstrap companies, you can get angel investment. You could do things like that. But venture capital money is for capital-intensive businesses.

Bob: A small point that a lot of people seem to forget in this game is that really you have to be a startup that needs significant amounts of capital and have that possibility of returning a really significant value to the people who have the capital.

Rebecca: Yeah, absolutely. Like I said, I see a lot of good businesses day in and day out that are solid businesses. They're going to make somebody a pretty decent return. But the problem is, if somebody has a good idea and they come in and we write them a check for $3 million or $5 million, and the next day Google comes by the office and goes, "Oh, let's pay you $10 million for that," then the answer is no. I think a lot of entrepreneurs don't realize that they have to basically be in it for the bigger payout.

Bob: Now, if Google were to come by and you've written the check for $3 million, and they say, "We're prepared to pay $100 million, "then . . .

Rebecca: Oh, it would be done.

Bob: Then it's break out the champagne.

Rebecca: Yeah, we'd be done. Exactly. We have been around for a very long time. I think one of the reasons we have been around for so long is that we are known as very friendly to entrepreneurs. We are very collaborative with them. We have a lot of entrepreneurs who have come back to us several times. And we have those honest conversations with people. We lay that out for them. We are like, "OK. If you take this money and there are . . . " We want to make sure our goals are on the same page, and that's what creates our success. I think that's really important for people.

Bob: Can a startup still get funded if it has no actual revenue but a great technology and the potential to reach a market of the size you are looking for? Has the bar gone up?

Rebecca: I do think the bar has gone up in a lot of ways. Especially right now, since the funding situation is a lot tougher, companies have to have a way to support themselves and, if not support themselves, then have a way to sort of "make it through the desert," which is what you have people talk about on the low burn right now. Our portfolio companies have been pretty successful at doing that. Will a technology-only company still get funded? We funded a semiconductor company, believe it or not, in 2004 after the crash. It is going to be a while before they're profitable. But we believe in the technology and we think it's truly disruptive.

So, yes, it's still possible, but I think the bar is higher on a number of fronts. I just think there's more expected. And I think when you look at true consumer software plays, that bar is higher, for a few reasons. And one is, of course, the economy and just the tightness overall of credit and things. But the second reason is it's fundamentally cheaper by a lot, significantly cheaper, to start a company now, an Internet company especially.

You've got the cloud computing resources at Amazon. You don't have to go buy your own servers right now, which was a huge expense for startups in the past. You've got all kinds of Open Source available to you. Ten years ago, when I was with NextCard, everything was from scratch, absolutely everything. And now that's not as much the case.

There are all kinds of tools, and then you have platforms like the iPhone and Facebook that significantly help with marketing distribution, so the payment for the initial marketing fund is oftentimes not as great.

So I actually think it takes less money and I think when you look at the online space, expecting that somebody is scrappy enough to at least get a product and a prototype going is not unrealistic at all.

Bob: So the bar is raised. Are there more or less or maybe the same number of companies coming your way? In other words, on one hand the need for the type of capital that a firm like Morgenthaler can provide, in general, seems to be less. A lot of platforms have gotten pretty mature. No one's expecting a new Google to happen on Windows. Are you guys finding the opportunities drying up, or are they actually starting to cascade more than in the past?

Rebecca: No, I actually think it's been a pretty steady state, to be honest. To answer the question, I think we've seen a lot of very interesting opportunities lately. There's this weird phenomenon happening right now where people who have been successful entrepreneurs in the past, maybe checked out for a few years. They were kind of "on the beach," is how we talk about it. And now, all of a sudden, they're coming back. They're like, "Wow, I can hire engineering talent again. I couldn't hire it in here to save my life a year ago." And now that there's talent available and they can hire people, and their resources have become less expensive. We're seeing a lot of those people resurface. And they are starting to kick around what they want to do next. And so that's been really fun to see how that's evolved.

Bob: Would you say that perhaps a drop in personal worth might have something to do with that too?

Rebecca: Yeah, I know, probably, actually. Probably they are saying, they're probably like, "Hmm, maybe I'm not quite as done as I thought I was."

Bob: Yeah.

Rebecca: And it's kind of motivated them to come back and sort of try another shot at things.

Bob: For those people who are going out there and they're looking to raise their first round of capital —they may not be going to Morgenthaler or they may be going to a real early-seed- or angel-type investor—what advice would you have for them in general?

Rebecca: In terms of presentation or what?

Bob: Mistakes not to make. Maybe insights that they should really have clear in their mind before they go off and look for venture capital or significant angel capital.

Rebecca: Yeah, it's hard to say, because a lot of times different venture firms are different, to be honest. And some things that might work well with us I wouldn't suggest people do with other firms. For example, with us it's a good idea to come in really early, have a cup of coffee with us, talk to us about it in a casual way, so then we get a chance to know the entrepreneur over the next few months and see what they're delivering and see how they track.

And so I think it's good for the entrepreneur to come in. One of the recommendations that came from a panel discussion I was on last night was "Don't bring your entire team in." Really, just the one or two people, the key people in the venture, are pretty much all you want to bring in on your first pitch.

I come from a product background and product development background, and it amazes me how many times I see a technology and no real market assessment as yet. So that, to me, is very important. I want to know that they've gone out, have talked to the consumer, have the tested the faults to see if this is going to be something that people want.

And I think that's very important for people to do before they come in. And other than that, I think people need to be confident and be honest about what they're doing and how they got there. Every entrepreneur is a little different, and I think I would encourage . . . It's hard to give general blanket advice in terms of what to do and what not to do when you come in.

The other thing, too, that is a huge mistake is coming in with a 35-page deck. They should pretty much be able to say things in 10, maybe 15 slides, tops. And be prepared for lots of questions. I've sat through pitches before where the first half hour was telling me about the market segments. That should have taken two to five minutes maybe, tops.

So I think getting right at what's the need, what's their value proposition, and how they're the best at it, and let us ask questions.

Jo Anne Miller, Partner, Milk Street Ventures

Jo Anne Miller, a telecommunications/IT industry expert, has been, by turns, responsible for Nokia's portfolio of relationships, CEO of Gluon Networks (a startup providing voice/data-switching management systems for local telephone service providers), and now a partner at Milk Street Ventures (a specialized VC firm). She's also an investor in Sand Hill Angels and managing partner of Golden Seeds (see the later interview of Stephanie Hanbury-Brown).

Bob: You actually wear more than a few hats in the venture capital/angel world. Let's start with the angel side of things.

Jo Anne: OK.

Bob: One of the parts of that particular puzzle is getting their first chunk of outside funding. It seems, more and more, the right people they should be talking to for that are angel investors rather than VCs.

Jo Anne: Well, I think it depends on what kind of company and how much capital they're going to require and how far along they've been able to get themselves without looking for outside capital.

Bob: Let's say that they've got themselves an actual application. They've got perhaps even the start of a revenue base, and they're looking for something like $500,000, plus or minus $250,000. Would angels be the right place to go rather than VCs?

Jo Anne: Well, they would certainly be "a" place to go. If they're looking for half a million and then they think they're going to need another million in a year; if they look at their total capital requirements and they're probably looking at under 3 million, then I think angels are a really great place to start.

I'm only saying that because I think that angels, for a while, have sort of substituted for early-stage VC. But I just heard numbers today that said that early-stage VCs are actually putting as much money to work as angels.

I think if you are a first-time entrepreneur, I would start with angels. If you are a more experienced entrepreneur and you have other companies or you've been engaged with other companies, I would look at both angels and early-stage venture capitalists sort of equally.

Bob: What sort of odds does a first-time founder in our current, sort of post–boom times economy have with angels?

Jo Anne: One of the things that angels will do—angels will not be as risk-averse with a first-time entrepreneur as VCs will. That's my personal experience, because most angels are prepared to do a lot of measuring and a lot of active engagement with the company in trying to help them, as well as provide money. Even though venture capitalists will always want to help their companies, there are fewer hours for that measuring process, and there is more risk aversion, I think, with a first-time entrepreneur in a venture capitalist firm.

So it's hard to say what the odds are. I know that with an angel you may see 30, 40 deals a year, and you may fund five. You're not going to fund more than one a month, probably one every two months. So, five, six, I would say, would be probably the maximum that would be funded in a year by an angel group.

Bob: When founders make presentations to angels, what's the biggest mistake they tend to make over and over?

Jo Anne: Well, I think when entrepreneurs present to anybody, they need to understand everybody's motivation, the people in the audience's motivation. With venture capitalists that is "How are you going to help me make money?" With angels it's "How are you going to help me make money, and how are you going to make this be an interesting engagement for me?"

Bob: Well, lots of people have lots of good ideas. But how big an idea or how big a market potential does an angel investor basically set as the floor? In other words, are we talking about 10 times their potential investment? Fifty times their initial investment?

Jo Anne: Because angels are investing their own money rather than someone else's money in a fund, they are able to look at flexible rates of return over the time frame. Clearly, everybody's greedy and would like a bigger return. But angels don't have to have as large a market as many venture capitalists do, because they don't have to return to other people. They don't have to have the outsized returns for their limited capital.

Very often, angels will be satisfied with closer to a targeted 10x return, especially if they can foresee that return's coming sooner rather than later. If you're talking about bringing an angel into a pharmaceutical company, it's going to be a long way away. You're going to require a lot of capital, and you're going to get diluted along the way. They're going to look for the same kind of private market and outsized return that a venture capitalist is going to look for.

But if you're talking about a software company that might be able to be exited within five years, and you could get a 5x to 10x return within five years, and that is going to need 3 million to 5 million total capital in order to get there, then you don't necessarily have to have a huge, billion-dollar market.

Bob: There seems to be a lot more angel investors now than there were, let's say, two or three years ago. Is that correct?

Jo Anne: There are certainly a lot more angel investors than there were 10 years ago, and there are some more angel investors than there were two to three years ago. I saw statistics today, from the Angel Capital Association [http://www.angelcapitalassociation.org], that the average size of an angel investment in 2008 was $262,000.

Bob: Is Golden Seeds a network of investors or a single organization? I couldn't really figure that out.

Jo Anne: Golden Seeds was founded in New York. But you'll find Golden Seeds no matter where you are. There are four associations of meeting groups, one in Boston, one in Philadelphia, one in New York, and now one in San Francisco.

Bob: I guess there's two ways that I could look at this. One is, it's redressing the imbalance of how many women there are who are CEOs of software companies. Or is it a case that now that there are so many more women in the industry, this is sort of the natural culmination of that growth of women in the industry?

Jo Anne: Those who invest in women entrepreneurs are soft spaces. So we have women in life science, women in technology, women in consumer products, software IT, across all spaces. Our only criterion is that there is a woman founder or a woman CEO or a woman in another major team–level position.

That criterion is there because we think that women still only receive something south of 7% of the venture capital investments in the United States today. So we're looking for ways of helping the funding and mentoring to create more great women with capital.

Bob: But it's not altruism. There's the same . . .

Jo Anne: No, no, no. Believe me, at Golden Seeds, we invest . . .

Bob: I used the A word there, I guess.

Jo Anne: This is no charity. There's no altruism. This is about investment. We're investment bankers looking at it from the perspective of helping to make us money.

Bob: How should founders approach angels? Yes, they can e-mail them out of the clear blue sky, but what's a more intelligent way of doing it than that?

Jo Anne: We get deals three ways. We get introduced to people who know what we're doing and they know a women entrepreneur. They e-mail an introduction saying, "Here's a great entrepreneur. I think you ought to talk to them." We'll talk to them and find out what stage they're at, what they're about, and give them advice as to whether or not we think they are an investable idea in the place they're at, and ask them to then go ahead and apply.

We use Angelsoft [http://angelsoft.net] as our deal-training and deal-management software and ask them to apply through Angelsoft. Startups will find out about us and just apply through Angelsoft, or we'll actually meet somebody somewhere along the way, which is sort of a personal introduction. So, e-mail, Angelsoft, personal introduction.

Bob: Finally, what one or two things can a founder looking for investment do to really improve their odds? Is there any one thing that would improve their chances more than anything else?

Jo Anne: I think all entrepreneurs need to put themselves, for a few minutes, in the investor's shoes and think, "How is this going to not just save the world, but make money for an investor?" So that means, what's the pricing model that is required? What's my sweat equity? What problem am I solving?

I saw a very interesting situation last week at a training meeting. Beautiful stuff, a very interesting person from a team, dynamic perspective, we were very impressed. But she never told us what her revenue model was. So we had to go back and work with her on understanding how she prices that, what the revenue model is. She was all about the product and how the product team is great. But how she was going to make money for the company and, ultimately, how we were going to make money was lacking.

Bob: So one of the key fundamental things is that the founders have to get outside the shell of their startup. They have to understand the motivation of the people they're asking money from.

Jo Anne: Right, exactly. I don't know anyone who is investing just to have a social effect with an entrepreneur. This is not going to help people out of poverty. This is an investment decision. This is about making money.

Bob: One thing that's always kind of puzzled me is when a company comes to you and says, with a straight face, "We have no revenue yet, but we project the following numbers five years out." Are those numbers taken at all seriously?

Jo Anne: I think the only part of it ever taken seriously is the process that the entrepreneur goes through to create those numbers, because it gives you an insight into their mental ability. But the numbers are meaningless, in general.

It depends on how close people are to having some revenue. If somebody comes in with an idea on paper and says, "I think if I can do this and this, I can result in this much revenue." That's very different than somebody who says, "I've got this prototype, and I just signed these agreements to launch the prototype, therefore these revenues are anticipated. I can show you our P/L."

That's one thing. But those are two very different things, and I've seen both situations.

Bob: Anything else I should ask you?

Jo Anne: I don't know. I think that putting yourself in the feet of the investor is a very important thing for an entrepreneur to do. The team is very important because, frequently, what the product is and what the market is changes as things develop. So the team is very important, and market is very important—whatever you have done to validate your market and to show that the problem that you are solving is a real problem, and being realistic about who your competition is and might be. Those are all key criteria.

Cindy Padnos, Managing Director, Illuminate Ventures

Cindy Padnos is the founding managing partner of Illuminate Ventures, a startup VC fund focusing on women-led startups. With over 20 years of experience as a VC and a CEO of a software company, Cindy shares her experience about what gets startup founders venture capital.

Bob: What does a startup need today to be seriously considered for funding?

Cindy: Really today? Or you do mean over the longer period that you'd suspect?

Bob: Well, I have to think that the easy money of, let's say, 2007 and maybe part of 2008 and before, that's kind of gone. Now, maybe I'm wrong in that. And please correct me. You know and I don't.

Cindy: No, I think any category, though, tends to overreact, you know, whether that would be consumers overreacting to a downturn in the economy or investors overreacting to, you know, the unavailability of an IPOS tech market. So people do tend to overreact. And sometimes that will last a little bit longer than you expected. But it doesn't last forever. If it lasted forever, we wouldn't have had the easier years—let's put it that way—of maybe 2006–08 for startups to raise capital because investors would still be remembering 2001–03, when it was, you know, nuclear winter and you couldn't find capital for your company. Right?

Bob: So there are seasons in this game, I'd guess you'd say?

Cindy: I would say, like many other industries, it can be a bit cyclical. Yes.

Bob: Well, then I guess that's the question. Maybe it's one that's not just for right now, but just in general: What does a startup need to be considered—seriously considered—for funding?

Cindy: Well, I think the question depends on what kind of funding we're talking about. So, if we're going to assume venture funding for a minute, I think that you're talking about a company that has to have identified a large underserved target market segment. That segment can be defined by geography or by a product need or by the user type or, you know, by a variety of different factors. But it needs to be a substantial market opportunity that you can build a large business, not just a product, around. I think it has to have a credible team.

And *credible* doesn't necessarily mean a serial entrepreneur. But it means people who are bringing some combination of skills and experience to the table that allow that company to demonstrate that they have, you know, as an example, either deep market knowledge or deep technical expertise or great channel or distribution relationships, some kind of advantage that makes it logical for them to be targeted in that sector.

And so the credible team might have worked together before. They might have worked in startup environments before. There's going to have to be some combination of those factors. It doesn't have to be all of them, but some combination of those factors that make them a very credible team. So, big market, strong team that makes sense, and some demonstrated need in the market, I guess it's really maybe those three needs, those three things.

Bob: It's kind of interesting to me, being more of a developer-type person, that you don't mention in that list groundbreaking technology or innovative application. That seems to be less important?

Cindy: Well, I'm not sure that's—I think it's all about how you talk about things. So, as an example, I said it's got to be something people really need. And it's got to be a large market. Well, in order for something to—you know, a product and offering, whatever it might be—to be something people really need and a large market, the likelihood is that it's groundbreaking in one way or another. It may not be the newest technology. It may be a really differentiated business model. It may be a distribution strategy that's, you know, very economically advantaged.

It's not always purely about technology. But that certainly is a component of it. But there are times when there's just overall shifts in technology, right? Like when we went from main frames to client servers, and client server to the Internet, and the Internet to, you know—are we now at cloud computing? I don't know.

Bob: Getting there.

Cindy: Yeah, exactly. So my point is that those are kind of, you know, paradigm-shifting kind of underlying technologies. Sometimes it's just the same old application built on top of a new platform. I would say, you know, Salesforce.com is an interesting example of taking advantage of two things. It wasn't groundbreaking technology. But it was leveraging new technology, meaning the whole on-demand software as a service technology, in combination with a pay-as-you-go pricing mechanism that made the products that they built much more economical and accessible to a much broader market.

Bob: If you're creating a startup and you don't happen to be part of the Silicon Valley culture—in other words, you don't live somewhere between San Francisco and San Jose—what's the best way to approach venture capitalists? I mean, unsolicited e-mail does not seem the best way to do it.

Cindy: Well, I would say there are two answers to your question. One is, a venture capitalist is not always the right answer. And I don't think that's really your question.

Bob: OK.

Cindy: So I'm not going to go too far down that path. But the reality is that in the world we live in today, you can frequently bootstrap a company using Open Source technologies to get, to build a business in what could be a very attractive lucrative business for a small team and might never be an attractive venture investment.

So the first thing I would do is think really long and hard about whether you need venture capital or not, whether it's really the right way to go. If you're trying to build a big business that's going to be competitive on a national or a worldwide scale, then, sure, you may need capital to do that. And if you're in, you know, Grand Rapids, Michigan, or you're in Pittsburgh, Pennsylvania, whatever it may be, you know, there are typically business angels in those communities to help you get started.

Beyond that, there are frequently nationwide law firms who have practices both here in Silicon Valley, and in Boston and New York, which are other hubs of venture communities, that can make introductions for you. So use your network of who you went to school with, service providers, and national account firms with offices in all of these locations. These folks can and will make introductions, and that can be very meaningful in terms of getting you real access to Silicon Valley or other venture capital firms who may not be in your local community.

Bob: So, really, if you don't have a network, perhaps it's time to build one. That's what I'm hearing.

Cindy: Absolutely. Unsolicited e-mail is the easiest thing for an investor to ignore.

Bob: What does Illuminate Ventures invest in? What's the story there? I am frantically looking for the URL right now, and I'm not finding one.

Cindy: [laughs] You won't find it. We're a brand new firm that is just in the process of launching, so you won't find a URL today. I have been an investor since 2004 with Outlook Ventures, for which you will find a URL, where you will find my bio. But Outlook is not raising a new fund at this point, and I actually made the decision to launch a new firm, which is Illuminate Ventures, which will have an intentional focus on expanding our deal flow to be more inclusive of high-tech companies founded or led by women entrepreneurs.

Bob: So I guess it would be fair to say that you are a startup VC.

Cindy: I'm a startup VC. But I was a founder and CEO myself. I've been out there raising venture capital. This won't make me an entrepreneur for the first time.

Bob: I can understand the focus that you're going after. I presume that you think there's a real need for this type of venture capital firm. Are women discriminated today against in the VC world?

Cindy: I don't think that would be a fair representation of it. I think the reality is that venture capital is a world in which your network and your relationships make a tremendous amount of difference. It goes back to the question you were asking a minute ago. If you don't have a network, it's time to build one. That is true, but it is not easy to do overnight.

When you look at the dollars that are going into venture capital today, less than 3% of that in 2007 went into companies with women CEOs. If you add all the companies that had women cofounders—and I'm talking about in high tech—that number still goes up to under 10%. I think it's 6 or 7%. Then if you step out and look at what percentage of women are graduating from MBA programs, what percentage of women are officers of high-tech companies that have IPOs or big MNA assets, the number is certainly not 50%, but it is significantly higher and growing at a very substantial rate.

And so what I actually see is not an intentional bias or a need for women to have a handout or something else. I see an opportunity to frankly convince them to support women in a very unique way. By focusing on that market sector it will give us an opportunity to see the absolute best companies in that category. We're putting together an amazing advisory group to support that effort. It includes very successful women, entrepreneurs, investors, corporate executives in high-tech, etc. And not only women, but with a focus being perhaps stronger by identifying and having those folks participate in this process.

So for us it's about great deal flow. It's about great opportunities. It's not about lowering the bar for women.

Bob: From what you've said, I would actually think that you see an untapped resource, if you will. There is this network of women, and there is this difference between the venture capital firms that are out there now and what the reality is on the ground.

Cindy: That's exactly right. There are so many different things that you can attribute that to. Women have not built the same networks. If you even look at just the last 20 years of what percentage of the graduating classes at Stanford and Harvard—I got my masters at Carnegie Mellon—were women. I know my graduating class was under 15% women. Those numbers have changed pretty dramatically today. I think the average MBA program today is 35% women. It's still not 50%, but gaining traction. If you look at things like software patent filings, the percentage of women's names on them has grown astronomically over the last 10 years. Now, we are talking about who the very people are who have the skills, capabilities, and interest to go out and found companies.

Bob: Speaking as a white male, somewhat overweight person, I don't want to sound like I don't think people like me are good, but it's just that I think there's a lot to be said for diversity. I think that, from the get-go, this industry has taken a long time to grow up.

Cindy: Well, if you think about it, in the end this is a partnership business. In any partnership, that can take an extensive amount of time. This is an industry where the life cycle of a fund is 10 years on average. It is unlike a law partnership, where if someone doesn't perform or get along with the team or whatever it may be, that may change very rapidly. That can't happen.

The contracts and the complications of creating a venture fund are such that the transitions happen much more slowly, and there are a lot of dollars involved.

Even if you look at it today, there are fewer women partners in venture capital firms than there were back in 2000. Part of the reason for that is that when all of these firms were forced to downsize the size of their fund . . .

Bob: . . . the newest got cut first.

Cindy: That's right, because it's a partnership. There's nobody to blame for it. It's just a reality. Now we're just struggling back to where things were even 10 years ago.

Bob: One thing really strikes me about what you've said. I won't say it's the most critical factor, but if you are a founder, if you don't have a trusted network and the ability to build a trusted network of people who can connect with funding sources, your odds are just not very good. It's just that simple.

Cindy: Yeah, I agree. It's much, much harder.

Bob: You've sat through a lot of presentations from startups looking for funding. What are the really bonehead mistakes you've seen over and over again?

Cindy: Oh, there's quite a few that you could pick from.

Bob: Maybe we should ask, what would be the things that make for a really impressive presentation to you? There's always the question, does a business plan really make any difference?

Cindy: Well, I guess I could give you both sides of the equation. In terms of what can really impress an investor, I think it is how well prepared the team is, how consistent they are in their message. There are both sides of the equation here. When a team comes in and they're always contradicting one another or talking over the top of each other, you wonder and you worry about if this is a team that can work well together and whether they have made a decision about what they're going to focus on, do, and build.

I love to hear entrepreneurs come in and talk about their prospects or customers and the information they've gathered from them, rather than the greatest technology ever that they've developed, that they have no customer or user feedback on. I think that can be quite significant. The references that an individual can share of, not just prior success, but being able to recruit people onto the team that they worked with previously are very telling. If you have an entrepreneur who is having trouble building her team from the very beginning, that is going to cause some question marks. I look for people who surround themselves with other great people.

Bob: Any advice that you would give, other than that we already have covered, to founders when they are going to go for that first round of outside investment, whether they're talking to angels or VCs?

Cindy: I think there's several things. One, I think that entrepreneurs should be as careful about who they take money from as investors are about whom they give money to.

Bob: That makes sense.

Cindy: By that I mean that they should be doing their own reference checks. They should be calling the CEOs or founders of companies that these investors have invested in and talk to them about things like, "Well, Dash, when you had your first tough quarter and didn't make the numbers, how did they react?" That includes talking to people where the company did not succeed in the end. I think those are really important things for an entrepreneur to do.

Stephanie Hanbury-Brown, Founder and Managing Director, Golden Seeds

After 20 years in financial services in Sydney, London, and New York, Stephanie Hanbury-Brown founded Golden Seeds (http://www.goldenseeds.com), an angel investor group focused on women-led startups. Since its launch in 2004, it has grown to monthly angel investor screening meetings and entrepreneurial training sessions and other events in San Francisco, Boston, Philadelphia, and New York. I talked with Stephanie about Golden Seeds: its mission, and her take on the angel investment scene.

Bob: Can you tell me more about what Golden Seeds does?

Stephanie: We're an angel investor group, of which there are quite a few across the country, and we're fairly typical of the majority of angel groups in the country. If you know how angel groups operate, let me know because that will save me from saying to you stuff that you already know.

Bob: I know how angels operate but not necessarily angel groups. Is it a pooled sharing of risk and capital?

Stephanie: There are a couple of different models. So one model is that the angels will put their money into a fund and then review deals and vote on which deals the fund will invest in. A more typical model, which is like us, is that a group of individuals review, evaluate, invest together, and support the companies together, but each is more or less operating as an individual. So, investors decide which deal they want to go into, how much they are going to put in. They'll invest directly in the company, and one of them will go on the board to represent all of them.

Bob: OK.

Stephanie: That's how we operate.

Bob: How many investors do you have, and do you make your investment numbers public?

Stephanie: Yes, we have 110 members, and we've invested just over $10 million in the four years that we have been operating. They are public in that if you go to angelsoft.net you can see angel groups around the country. And there's quite a lot of data that's in there that includes how much has been invested in the last 12 months, how many applications a group received. If you go to angelsoft.net and look on "group finder," I think that the first thing you will see is groups in your location that you could ultimately . . .

There might be a way. I haven't tried it, but you could probably say, you know, most active groups in the U.S. or something. I'm sure you could sort of find that out. We would be one of those.

Bob: What does your group or your investors look for from startups today? Has the bar gone up from, let's say, where it was a year ago?

Stephanie: It depends on which bar you are referring to. The bar that is about valuation of the company has gone down.

Bob: OK. So, what companies are worth—estimates kind of dropped like property prices.

Stephanie: But I can't say that the bar has gone up because we were not investing in poor-quality companies 12 months ago. But what has gone up is the quality of deals that we see. Largely that's because companies that did not think they would need more capital now feel that they do need more capital, so raising capital when they might not have otherwise been going to do that.

Bob: How much would you say a first-time startup founder is typically likely to get from an angel group like Golden Seeds?

Stephanie: You know, it's typically between $300,000 and $700,000. We've put as much as $1 million into a first-round, early-stage deal. But it's more normal for us to do somewhere in that range of 300 to 750, let's say. So it depends a lot on what the entrepreneur needs, and it depends a lot on what the company is valued at when she is raising money, because if she needs a lot of money, then it's probably better to take it in small chunks so that she doesn't get diluted too much.

Bob: Does Golden Seeds, given its mission, only invest in women-led startups? If that's not the case, maybe, you can tell me what is the case.

Stephanie: We invest in companies that have a woman founder who still has a C-level operating position with the company and has significant equity. So she might be the CEO. If she was not the founding CEO, then she probably had been brought in and, therefore, might only have as much as 10% of the company. We'd be reluctant to invest if she has less than that, and it's more typical for our founders to have closer to 40% or 50%.

Bob: How would you characterize Golden Seeds when it comes to this question of investing in women-led companies? I understand from your site the need, the desire, the focus. But is it that you found a way to differentiate yourself from other angel investor groups or more that there's really an underrepresentation of women you are trying to address here?

Stephanie: It's because of the underrepresentation, and it's created sort of a niche investment strategy, which means that you do get to see your best field in your niche. So it's both of those. But the underrepresentation is that only between naught and 6% are venture capital dollars in any one year that go to women entrepreneurs. Angel money, it could be higher, closer to 13%. One of the issues is that not enough women entrepreneurs are out there looking for capital, for whatever reason. Maybe they are not interested in growing a company or don't know about it or don't have the right connections. So it is a combination of all of those things. But we feel that we are serving an underserved market as a starting point.

Bob: How should a startup go about securing angel capital from a group like Golden Seeds? That's a really large question, I realize. You can take either the positive way, the things they should do, or, maybe, the negative way, some of the things they shouldn't do.

Stephanie: Well, we have sort of a screening process. And because we are working with an underserved market, we place less emphasis on the need to have a warm introduction, because if you talk to a lot of investors they'll say, "Oh, you definitely need to get a warm introduction so that if one of the partners in this fund or one of the principals running the group knows you, you really want to be sponsored." We recognize that women don't necessarily have those connections, as one of the things holding them back, so we look at every single application very closely. We will say to them, "It is valuable if one of our members already knows your company or might have even invested in it." So do that if you can, but it's not a prerequisite by any means.

Bob: OK.

Stephanie: And so the thing that is important is to make sure that they've read our web site, understand the criteria, and know what to put in and pitch to investors. It's fairly easy to find this stuff out, a little bit of research and going to a couple of venture capital fairs or forums where you see entrepreneurs pitch to investors. That bit of homework, I think, is well worth doing. Having said that, if they come into us fairly unprepared, we will give them feedback and tell them, "You haven't blown your chances. Here's your feedback. If you can fix some of these things, we'll definitely have another look."

Bob: So there's no mystery. There's no magic. It's a matter of homework and being ready.

Stephanie: Yes and, well, having a great business.

Bob: That helps.

Stephanie: Those two things—great management team, great business plan—those are the two things that matter most. I don't mean a plan in terms of the paper. I mean in terms of what they're doing.

Bob: If it's not a business plan in terms of paper, do you mean basically their business structure in terms of how they are going to make money?

Stephanie: No, I basically mean whatever product they are trying to sell to customers, "Is this really, really compelling need that the customer has?" If it is, then people are going to buy it, and then they are going to start generating revenue. Then it's all going to fall into place very quickly. So that's really the main thing, that they have something really unique and different that they are trying to sell.

Bob: OK. Do they need to be selling it already to be considered in today's economic marketplace, or can they be pretty much . . .

Stephanie: Yeah, it makes it easier. It definitely makes it easier, because having a couple, even one or two, paying customers lowers the risk for investors and sort of validates that there's somebody out there who is paying real dollars to buy the product. Having said that, there are investors at both ends of the spectrum, and plenty of people are willing to make a bet alongside an entrepreneur with an idea that they have—if they think this is a very compelling product and if they think the idea is really good and if they think the entrepreneur is really able to take it to the next level. It's not a "must-have." It just increases your chances of getting funding.

Bob: Any final advice for founders who are still trepidacious about seeking venture capital?

Stephanie: Speak to other CEOs who have done it. They are going to be the best source of information about who was a good investor; how you go about finding the money, how long it took, what they had to give in on in order to get the capital, what they wished they had done differently. I really think that's the best thing, so, really, getting good input from peers would be very valuable.

Bob: Good advice. Thank you, Stephanie.

Startup Incubators

To close out this section about raising capital, it's time to have a look at just a few of the startup incubators out there. As I said in Chapter 1, you can definitely make the case that the modern, post-dot-com era of startups began in 2005, when Paul Graham, Robert Morris, Trevor Blackwell, and Jessica Livingston founded Y Combinator (Figure 5-3).

Figure 5-3. Y Combinator

Here's how Y Combinator works: Twice a year—from January through March and June through August—some 20 to 30 startup founders, most of them in their 20s, who've made the cut and cut the deal move to the San Francisco Bay Area to work full time on their startups, attend weekly dinners with primed investors, startup CEOs, and featured speakers, and get the business equivalent of an immersive language course where they eat, breathe, and drink "startup" 24/7. The deal part of this, in addition to the immersive program, getting these startups properly incorporated, and opening doors to prospective angels and VCs, is that Y Combinator provides something less than $20,000 funding for each startup in exchange for somewhere between 2% and 6% equity. As of May 2009, 118 startups had launched through Y Combinator, including RescueTime.com, whose cofounder Tony Wright talks about the experience in Chapter 7.[13]

Nor is Y Combinator the only entity out there to realize that there's money being left on the table by traditional VCs and angels: providing pre-seed funding of $5,000 or $10,000 in exchange for 5–10% of the founders' stock might be all that's needed to make some respectable money. Here are some of the other incubators out there.

- **NextStart** (http://www.nextstart.org), based in Greenville, South Carolina, offers a summer immersion entrepreneur program providing startup founders with 12 weeks of office space, Internet connectivity, and professional services.

- **Shotput Ventures** (http://www.shotputventures.com), in Atlanta, Georgia, was, as of May 2009, gearing up to help 8–10 teams of one to two persons launch their "capital-light" startups in summer 2009.

- **NYC SeedStart** (http://www.nycseed.com/seedstart.html) is an eight-week summer program in the Big Apple where 10 groups of two to four founders will find funding, mentorship, and access to New York City–based angels and VCs. NYC SeedStart is an outgrowth of NYC Seed, a public–private partnership focused on promoting manufacturing and technology companies in New York City.

- **LaunchBox Digital** (http://www.launchboxdigital.com), in Washington, D.C., had nine startups in its first summer program, in 2008; five of them have gone on to receive angel and VC funding.

---

[13] *You might be wondering where the Paul Graham and Jessica Livingston interviews are. Unfortunately, neither Paul nor Jessica was available during the two-month period I'd planned to interview them—totally my fault, not theirs.*

- **Capital Factory** (http://www.capitalfactory.com), based in Austin, Texas, screened over 250 applicants before picking five companies that would kick off its first summer program, in 2009. Each company gets—for 5% of their stock—$20,000 in funding, $20,000 in professional services, and 10 weeks of intense professional mentoring, culminating in a Demo Day during which each startup will strut its stuff to investors and the press.

- **TechStars** (http://www.techstars.org) describes itself as a mentorship-driven seed-stage investment fund that each summer will invest in about 20 startups (split between Boston and Boulder, Colorado), who, in exchange for a 6% equity stake, will get intensive help and the chance to pitch to a select group of angel investors and VCs.

- **iAccelerator** (http://iaccelerator.org), proving that startup incubators are not uniquely American, is a four-month intensive program designed to establish successful Indian tech companies by providing guidance, business connections, and funding. It is sponsored by the Indian Institute of Management at Ahmedabad's Incubation Center (CIIE).

Here's a prediction for you: There will be more, a lot more, startup incubators. Startup incubators make a great deal of sense for the entrepreneurial investors who want not only to fund startups but to help them succeed. It's a structured approach to what has in the past been very hit and miss: the process of turning developers into founders.

Managing the Money

If this book were an encyclopedia rather than a guided tour to Startupism, the accounting and general finance sections would be among the thickest and dullest entries. It's hard to get excited about setting up a chart of accounts, keeping Board of Director minutes, and filing annual ownership declarations.

Online resources abound for this kind of information: In the United States, the Small Business Administration (http://www.sba.gov) will give it to you straight; Business Link (http://www.businesslink.gov.uk) is where you start in the U.K.; and in the EU, have a look at the EC's SME Portal at http://ec.europa.eu/enterprise/sme/index_en.htm. In fact, it's a pretty safe bet that wherever you are in the world, a local or national government web site is just waiting to help you understand what you're going to need to do business.

Furthermore, between great sites such as StartupNation (http://www.startupnation.com), the resources put online by business publications ranging from *BusinessWeek* to your local newspaper (if it's still in business), the 5,119 books you'll find at Amazon under "small business accounting," let alone the 130,560 results you will find there for "small business," I can't help but feel that the mechanics of finance and accounting have been well and truly covered.

Instead of putting you into a coma, I called on two people who really do have a burning passion for these subjects to talk about some of the things you should watch out for. I chose these two individuals not just because they're walking, talking legal/financial startup encyclopedias, but because they are perfect examples of the kinds of legal and financial advisors you need to seek out and with whom to build a relationship to succeed as a startup.

Gene Landy, Attorney and Author of IT/Digital Legal Companion

In Chapter 4 we talked with Gene Landy, author of the *IT/Digital Legal Companion* (Syngress, 2008), about the proper care and feeding of Open Source code in your startup. But most of Gene's workload has to do with aligning legal ducks in a row for his startup clients at the Boston law firm Ruberto, Israel & Weiner, P.C. Here we turn the conversation to some of the things a startup needs to know to get funded, to incorporate correctly, to find an attorney, and more. Gene's answers deal with the general case; you're going to want to consult your startup's attorney on all the issues he raises and more.

Bob: What sort of things should a startup do to make themselves angel-investor fundable?

Gene: Well, I hate to tell you the most important things aren't legal. An investor will give you some slack to fix legal problems, if you have a dynamite application that hundreds of thousands of millions of people are using, right?

Bob: OK.

Gene: I think having legal noncompliance can really mess you up, but having perfect legal compliance cannot make you a success.

Bob: OK.

Gene: What makes you really successful is having a marketable product that the market really needs. If you sort of think about it, if you had a product that was no better than a product that's commercially available and not much cheaper, you would be crazy to deal with a startup because startups are thinly capitalized often. They don't often have a lot of personnel. They're often dependent on a key person, so if somebody dies, they'll disappear.

They might go bankrupt, and so forth and so on. There are a lot of risks in dealing with startups. So you normally will deal with a startup, if you're a customer, if the solution is compelling.

Bob: Well, does it make a difference, for purposes of raising capital, whether you're an S Corp or an LLC?

Gene: Yeah, sure does. Usually, the rule, basically, is that, as a practical matter, institutional investors don't want to invest in anything other than a C corporation, which is sort of the normal, default kind of company. LLCs and S corporations are mostly designed for either small service companies or, in some cases, for some private investors. They might have some kind of tax-shelter function; that is, they might be able to generate losses that an investor can use. But usually a company that's an investment target that's going to raise venture capital or going to get money from strategic investors like customers, they're going to be a C corporation, and even if they started out life as an LLC or an S corporation, they're probably going to convert.

Bob: So they can start off with a little more lightweight LLC and then convert to a C corporation?

Gene: Yeah. Although, it's not that much lighter-weight. [laughs]

Bob: So maybe they should just bite the bullet and become a full-fledged corporation.

Gene: Yeah. That's right. Because an LLC has some simplicity in terms of tax: you're basically taxed as a partnership. But the LLC agreement itself is more complicated than forming a corporation. Corporate law does a lot of things for you that you have to do by agreement with an LLC. And there are tax issues with LLC. So, certainly, when you start getting investors, you have to worry about stock options. And an LLC can earn money. If it's money that stays in the LLC but is not distributed, you'll be taxed on it anyway. So there are issues with LLCs.

Bob: OK.

Gene: You just have to talk to a tax accountant and make sure you know what you're getting into and whether it works for you. Usually, product companies want to raise money, and they usually shouldn't be LLCs. Service companies are much more likely to fit into that LLC mode.

Bob: Is a web service a service or a product?

Gene: In my scenario, a web company would be a product company, even though . . .

Bob: . . . even though it looks like a service to developers. Right.

Gene: It looks like a service company. What I mean as a service company, I mean it's a company that has a business model that is a professional service model, where they don't have to build a lot of stuff and they can start generating money on day one, and they don't have a lot of, especially, built-up capital or investment in their product. They're basically selling their time, right? Like some company that maybe does maintenance, or some company that does custom development, and doesn't have a product base, right? Those companies can function very well as quasi-partnerships, for tax purposes. But once you've started to invest a lot of money and you have capital and you need money to build up your infrastructure, that's when you need money.

So that would be true of a traditional software company. It would also be true of a software-as-a-service company that, from an operational point of view, they're a service, but they sure look a lot like a company that's a product company.

Bob: OK. How should a founder of a startup company find an attorney that does this? I mean, is there just a few people in the world that do it and they stick to them, or should they find somebody that they've already dealt with legally? What's the algorithm there, if you will?

Gene: I think there are two kinds of tasks that the attorneys do for you, and one is much more commoditized, and the other is much less. The one that's more commoditized is forming your company or doing your first deal with a venture capital or angel investor and so forth and so on. Lots and lots of companies know how to do that, because I would consider that sort of primarily legal.

What's harder is knowing how, for example, to do an online media distribution deal or how to do a deal for embedding software in a mobile phone product, mobile device, right? With those deals, you really need to have a much deeper understanding of both the intellectual property and the technology. And so there are fewer lawyers that have that skill set, because many lawyers have, essentially, a liberal arts education and haven't spent a lot of time really learning how technology works.

So, depending on your business model, you really want to look for somebody who's kind of done it before or something similar to what you've done before, particularly when you get beyond the kind of basics of formation and they're really doing your key deals.

What's a deal for a company could be very different. If you are a consumer product, maybe a deal is just putting your stuff online and I think people pay you with a credit card. But for many startup companies, there is a key strategic relationship they make that kind of makes or breaks the company: Their deal with Verizon, their deal with IBM or whatever, this is where they develop a channel and they get them to buy a lot of product and maybe invest some money, and then you need somebody who really understands your business.

Bob: So the key thing is somebody who understands your business, who understands the particulars of the deal that you are trying to put together?

Gene: That's right. I mean I don't want to overgeneralize here, but we find that people in cities that don't have a technology business base often don't have a lot of familiarity with how things work, particularly with regard to things other than—a lot of places around the country where people consume business software. So in most cities, their lawyers are people who would know how to license in or license out a business application. But that's very different than licensing software that will live in semiconductors, where we embed it in a system or firmware or something like that. And that's also very different than somebody who knows how to do media distribution or license widgets to be put into an application that would be server based and provide the service as well.

It is much more likely that people who know how to do that would be in the technology centers, which would be in California, northern California, and Boston and Research Triangle and Virginia and in Texas and in Austin, that's where those are.

Bob: Any final advice for startups?

Gene: So one thing that's very common is that people give away their ideas by not getting confidentiality agreements in place before they talk to people. I mean they are for protection and they only work if we sue on them, but they are certainly a lot better than nothing. And people should always do it, and it will scare your investors if you haven't used them.

Another thing is that technology doesn't automatically go into companies. You have technology that you have developed and you form a company; you still own the technology but the company doesn't own it. Very often what happens is a lot of people work together and then somewhere along the line after a few months they form a company. The company never grabs all the intellectual property they created. So that's a major issue. And then if they go off and get a job at Microsoft or something, you may never be able to get it. So you need to really get it early.

Bob: OK.

Gene: You can lose your patent ability on inventions if you disclose them too early and you don't file a patent application. So if it looks like you have developed something patentable, you need to talk to patent lawyers early. So the technology can end up in the public domain because you didn't file it right.

Bob: OK.

Gene: You need to remember that you can't use any old trademarks. Before you invest in a trademark, you got to register it and make sure you got rights to it. A lot of people get themselves cease-and-desist letters right after their project launched because they got a trademark problem, and that's relatively easy to avoid.

So the other kind of thing is I think people make mistakes in dealing with investors. And I think the most common mistake they make is only looking at the money and not looking at the rest of the deal. So the person that gives you the most money may be the best investor for you, but they may not be. And one thing that companies will have to understand is their investors often have the right to displace them. So doing due diligence on investors is very important.

Another really common mistake is not understanding vesting. So vesting is a concept that . . . for instance, when you found a company and you bring in somebody to be the VP of sales and you give him some stock. Well, the best way to do that is to make sure that he only gets the stock if it works out. If you give somebody a third of the stock of your company on Monday and you don't have a vesting schedule and then they leave your company on Tuesday, they still own the stock and they are no longer a contributor. So you really need to . . .

Bob: . . . have a vesting schedule.

Gene: Right. And I guess the final thing is if you came up with the idea in your current job and then you quit and form a company, you need to be very clear that you actually own the technology and it is not actually owned by the place where you used to work and that you can exploit it without violating whatever contract you signed with the place that you used to work.

Mairtini Ni Dhomhnaill, Senior Vice President, Accretive Solutions

Mairtini Ni Dhomhnaill heads up the startup practice in the San Francisco and Silicon Valley offices of the consulting firm Accretive Solutions (http://www.accretivesolutions.com), which provides accounting, financial, and other consulting services to over 500 startups. Put another way, Mairtini knows n^3 more about what startups need to do when it comes to handling their finances than you or I will ever know. For an episode of the *Startup Success Podcast*,[14] I asked Mairtini to help us out with some of the financial and legal basics a startup founder should know.

Bob: Mairtini, what's a balance sheet?

Mairtini: A balance sheet is a statement of your company's holdings at a given point in time. So it shows primarily two things. It shows your assets, which is what you own, and it shows your liabilities, which is what you owe. So it's a good indication of what the company is worth right now.

Bob: So it's a snapshot of your worth at that particular moment. Typically when a startup actually launches, do they begin with a balance sheet as their first sort of laying out the plumbing?

Mairtini: Absolutely. The first thing an investor is going to really want to see is a balance sheet, pertaining to the perspective of wanting to see how much money—usually the biggest asset on a balance sheet or the only asset would be cash in the bank. But the thing they're more interested in is how much you owe.

Bob: Ah, OK.

Mairtini: What liability you have.

---

[14] http://startuppodcast.wordpress.com/2008/10/30/show-3-news-from-pdc-getting-startup-accounting-right

Bob: Let's assume you've got a couple of founders sitting around a kitchen table. They're going to go after, let's say, the relatively or perhaps easier funding out there, angel investing, which nowadays typically goes up to about $1 million. Let's ask a couple of nitty-gritty questions here. Should people be listing their personal debt here, or should this all be about the company that they have created?

Mairtini: Oh, definitely not their personal debt. It should be about the company they've created. And I guess, on that point, they really should have created a legal entity for the company.

Bob: OK, let's discuss that point for a second. Any preferences out there? I started my consulting company as a subchapter S here in California, but that was back in 1994, before I became a microISV or anything else. It may be a bit old-fashioned, because I hear now more and more about limited liability companies, LLCs. What's been your experience for people who are startups?

Mairtini: In my experience, if you're a startup that wants to attract outside money, like a VC or an angel funding, you're more than likely going to have to be a C corp, a C-corporation. There are times when you might be a limited liability corporation, but there are certain tax reasons why you would be that. So it really is driven by the investors. But if you're looking for top-tier or even tier-2 or tier-3 VC money, you're going to have to be a C corp.

Bob: And they should probably get some professional help with that, because it sounds . . . You can do an S corp sort of pretty well, with maybe a bit of lawyering and a bit of accounting and especially with all of the online services now, but a C corp, that's a little bit more involved, to put it mildly.

Mairtini: It is a little bit more involved. I'm not suggesting that just one guy in his garage rushes out and starts a C corp. It might be OK to be an S corp or even a sole proprietor for the near term. But once you get to the point where you're going to need that money and bring it into the company, you'll then have to convert to a C corp.

Bob: Is there a good or a bad path to the C corp? In other words, should they start out as an LLC and then go to a C corp? Or should they start out as S corp, a subchapter S corporation in the in the U.S. tax code, and then convert that to a C corp? Is one harder or easier than the other?

Mairtini: No, it really depends on what you do while you're the S corp or the LLC, what kind of activity you have. So I wouldn't say one is harder or easier than the other. It just really does depend on the circumstances in each case. I've had both types of companies that I've rolled up into C corp. It was relatively painless as long as they had all of their records and had kept their numbers and their books in good shape.

Bob: Let's talk about records for just a second here. This may sound simple, but for a lot of startups today, because the cost has come down so far in what they need to put out, I mean they can pretty much launch a web site based on 2.0 for the cost of $400, $500 a month for a good host. When should they draw the line between their personal money and expenses and their company money and expenses?

Mairtini: Well, I am not quite sure what you mean when you ask, "When should they draw the line?" They should always draw a line. Even if you are spending your personal money, you should always keep it as a separate category as regards the receipts or the record of that money you spent, if it has to do with your company. By saying "when," I don't know whether you mean critical mass that comes to a point?

Bob: I guess I am thinking a bit of a leading question here. But I am under the impression that a single person who is going to start a company may not be sure yet of how big it is going to get. It's at the gleam-in-the-eye stage, if you will. It seems like that person should start tracking expenses separately from the very get-go, from the very first PayPal expense.

Mairtini: Absolutely. From day one, start tracking the expenses separately. Yes. Also, they should track their expenses separately from the beginning because you are going to need to get that activity into the records of your company when and if you do incorporate it or whatever.

Bob: OK.

Mairtini: And the way you would do that would be, say you spend four or five months and you haven't set up a legal entity. You are spending money on behalf of this new company you intend to start. You would spend the money maybe on your personal credit card or you might write checks; you will keep all of the receipts. And when you incorporate your company, whether you create an S corp or a C corp, you would do something pretty straightforward, like you would create an expense report and have the company now reimburse you through all of that spending you did.

Bob: Oh, OK, that makes sense.

Mairtini: But you just don't want to knock into your personal checking account.

Bob: OK.

Mairtini: And so, for example, when you talk about balance sheet, that would be something that would be on your balance sheet. When you first create your legal entity, if you haven't got the cash in the new entity to reimburse yourself, you would carry that as a liability, so that anyone looking at will see, "Oh this company owes the founder $10,000 or $20,000." But a new investor would look and see, "Well if I am going to put a $100,000 into the company, the first $10,000 or $20,000 is going straight out the door to the founder to reimburse him for prior expenses."

Bob: But that's the right way to do it, you are saying?

Mairtini: That is the right way to do it.

Bob: One more thing about balance sheets, and this is more my accounting ignorance than anything else. The only thing I sort of know about balance sheets is that some people try and put "goodwill" on it as some sort of asset. When you're talking, as a startup, when you're talking to people who have money that may or may not actually go into your company, do you think startup as an asset or strategic alliances, or are we talking cold, hard cash?

Mairtini: It is just cold, hard assets. There are very specific accounting rules, and you can have what's called an "intangible" asset on your balance sheet. Certain rules—actually almost all—boil down to if you purchase a company, you may be able to purchase a company and have some goodwill on your balance sheet, you may purchase a company and have some IP (intellectual property) on your balance sheet, but, overall, startups should never have an intangible asset on their balance sheet. There would be no reason for that. And not only would there be no reason for it, you can't do it, because it isn't GAAP, it is not generally accepted accounting policies.

Bob: Ah, and if you don't follow the rules, it doesn't count?

Mairtini: Pretty much.

Bob: Well, there are a couple of other things that you mentioned here as Financial Statements 101. What's an income statement? Is that basically a statement of your income?

Mairtini: An income statement, yeah, it's the results of the company's operations. It is: How did we do? What profits or income did we bring home after we sold stuff and spent stuff?

Bob: Is that what is also called a P&L?

Mairtini: Yes, the profit and loss or an income statement, they tend to be interchangeable.

Bob: That clarifies that for me. And this is basically showing what you have brought in or what you hope to bring in or both?

Mairtini: What you have brought in. It is not what you hope to bring in, it is what you have brought in.

Bob: OK.

Mairtini: In a specified period of time, say, from day one to day ten, here is what I actually did, here is what I actually sold, here is what I spent.

Bob: So it is a record rather than a projection?

Mairtini: Absolutely.

Bob: So you should keep the sales prediction stuff either on the shelf, along with the mysteries and the novels, or in your business plan for VCs and angel investors, but that doesn't go into your income statement?

Mairtini: No, it does not.

Bob: The third thing you mentioned is a cash flow statement. Now, how is that different from an income statement?

Mairtini: Well, a cash flow statement is kind of a weird little report, and really what it says is: what did I do with the money? So for an investor or an outside person looking at this, it basically starts with your profits and then it says of this profit, what happened to this cash. So in a lot of instances, a profit may not all have been in the cash in the door. So, for example, you may have made a profit on paper, but you haven't collected all of that cash yet. So there are some lines that back in and back out; these are what we call noncash or accrual items.

But then it kind of talks about, well, of my profits, I spent X amount on fixed assets or I spent X amount on purchases and/or I received new cash from an investor. So it sort of starts at your profit or loss and it brings you back to your cash position, and it talks about what happened in your cash account over this period.

Bob: Well, then, what do you do with a cash flow other than trying to keep it positive?

Mairtini: From a financing perspective and investors' perspective, your cash flow is a very important document. So I guess I would say the average nonfinancial person would not spend a lot of time looking at the cash flow statement. But you need to have it, because the cash flow statement is a byproduct of your balance sheet and P&L. It is a stand-alone entity. It is a result of the activity in both of those documents.

Bob: So it is the externally linked spreadsheet, if you will. Once you have got those three documents in some good form or another, either you'd pull templates off the Web for it or there are various packages out there of supposedly the startup documents you need. What else besides those three should you as a hopeful founder be doing as far as financial things, just the real basics when you get first started?

Mairtini: You're going to have to keep in mind: What are you doing it for? If you intend to attract investments, there's a certain set of material you'll be asked for in the due diligence process. And the set of financial statements is one part of it—and that is, show me how the company has done historically. And that's what your financial statements are. Financial statements are a historical record of how the company has performed. Now, in a lot of cases, when you're first going after your first round, it'll sort of be a lot of expenses. There's nothing to be revenue, because you may not be at revenue generation yet. So financial statements are just one piece of the puzzle that investors want to look at.

And the other side of that, which you alluded to earlier, is the financial forecast. So here's what you've done. But what do you expect to do? And that forecast needs to be in the same format as a P&L, a balance sheet, and a cash flow. It needs to be in hard, cold numbers.

So from a financial plan perspective, you need to have a model, an Excel spreadsheet, per se, that will run into a profit and loss of income statement, a balance sheet, and a cash flow statement.

Bob: OK. Now, I've never been part of the VC world or the angel investing world, so I'm a little hazy on the actual mechanics. Let's say that you go to an angel investor and you convince them, yeah, put $500,000 into this company I'm creating. I don't have a product yet, I don't have sales yet. What do they do? Do they write you a check, and you stick it in your pocket?

Mairtini: You know, there are angels out there that will do that, but not all of them. Even the angel world is becoming much more institutionalized—there's quite a number of angel bands sort of banded together. The reality is, you may sell someone just on the idea, and they won't want to see another thing. And I've had plans like that, that raised $500,000 to $1 million just on the idea.

But then there are people who are probably a little bit more cautious about where they put their money. They want to have some sense of the company they're investing in, and they may ask for more information, especially if they understand that some activity has already happened in the company—if it's not just an idea, at this point.

If you've actually been germinating that idea and working on the idea, they may ask to see . . . I've already talked about they'll ask to see the financial statements, the activity of what you've spent your money on, and, like I talked about, the balance sheet that shows how much you owe.

Because, really, a lot of new investors don't want to give you *X* amount of money and immediately have a portion of that walk out the door to existing liabilities. They're all about investing for the future. They want their money to bring you from the point you're at now to the point you want to get to. They don't want to pay for getting you to the point you're at now. Because to a certain extent, that's going to be rolled into your evaluation.

Bob: So that's kind of a sunk cost, as far as they're concerned.

Mairtini: It's a more complex conversation, but it is a very important point for any new entrepreneur to understand. An investor wants to invest in the future of your company, not in the past. So if you're coming to the table and you have bootstrapped the company to this point, if you expect to get paid back for that, you need to have it on the balance sheet, and it needs to be a point of negotiation.

Bob: OK.

Mairtini: You need to state very clearly that you owed *X* amount of money, and then that'll become part of the negotiation with the investor of what the valuation of the company should be and how much they're going to give you.

Bob: But from their point of view, they're looking at that as something that you've spent to get the company to that point. They want to put their money into the future, not into the past.

Mairtini: Absolutely.

Bob: And they look at it and say: OK, so you spent $10,000 or $20,000 getting here. But, hey, you're going to own the percentage of the company that I don't own, and that's how you get paid off on that.

Mairtini: Exactly. There are lots of ways that it could get resolved, and one could be that it means the valuation is higher, so you end up owning more of the company. Or it could be they say that you can convert that liability into preferred stock, if you're actually doing the stock round, if it's not an off-table for your first angel round. There are some tax ramifications to that, so this is not an area you should be advancing into without some legal advice.

Or they might say, "I'm OK with paying you back that money." It really just depends. But if they are paying you back the money, expect to get a lower valuation of your firm.

Bob: Let's talk about that advice for a moment. Let's take an example. Let's say they've got—I'll make it totally hypothetical here—they've got three founders, it's January 1st, 2009. They've lined up someone who's ready to put $250K into their company, and that's the thing that gets them moving to where they want to be. They've just decided they need that financing to make it happen. At what point should they have a lawyer? At what point should they have either an accountant or someone who says that he's a CFO—a chief financial officer? When do they need to lawyer up and accountant up here?

Mairtini: I would say once you've created the entity, you should have a lawyer on call. A lot of the law firms, they're willing to set you up initially, and then they don't have any ongoing expense until you have this transaction. So you absolutely do need a lawyer when you're at the point of negotiating the term sheet, for sure.

Bob: Ah, OK.

Mairtini: For sure you need the lawyer then. You may have used the lawyer to create your entity, or you may have done it yourself, but for sure you need a lawyer, at least on call, for when you're negotiating your term sheet. As regards the accountant, it really depends on the situation. If you have been spending money, or bootstrapping the company, you do need to have had at least a bookkeeper maintaining the numbers so that you can present the set of financials.

Unless you're able to run QuickBooks or a Microsoft product—some accounting product, I'm not quite sure what they have at this level. Unless you're able to run an accounting product yourself to come up with a P&L and a balance sheet—but you are going to have to produce one.

So I'm not saying that every investor's going to get hung up on that. It's certainly not about the financials for the company, when an investor comes to invest in the company, it's all about the idea, right? And the founders? It's just one of those things that you don't want to be the thing that tripped you up.

Bob: By the way, which is better for a software startup—cash-based accounting or accrual accounting? Or is it an individual case sort of thing?

Mairtini: It's really not an individual case. If you really want to be a real company, you should be doing accrual accounting.

Mairtini: There's really no reason to do cash-based accounting, unless you're just a sole proprietorship and you're never going to look for outside money, and you really only want to do a tax return. That's the driver for your accounting. But if you want to be able to tell, how is my company doing? What's my current situation? What's my true cash position? You really need to be doing accrual accounting.

Is There an Alternative?

If Gene's and Mairtini's ultracondensed introductions to standard company formation and accounting left you longing for a lightweight alternative to the whole traditional approach to business, you definitely want to learn more about FairSoftware (Figure 5-4).

Figure 5-4. FairSoftware

In a word, FairSoftware (http://fairsoftware.net) is a web app for creating monetized startup projects. Instead of forming a company, setting up bank accounts, issuing founder stock, and all the other ceremony, you create a FairSoftware project, divvy up on permanent shares (for your cofounders) or temporary shares (for freelancers helping you) of PayPal-powered revenue stream.

The flip side of FairSoftware is that it's a great way to find startups you can be a part of who are looking for specific kinds of help, from CEO to web site programmer to GFX designer to Ruby on Rails programmer.

Here's how Alain Raynaud, CEO and founder, describes FairSoftware.

Bob: What's the single biggest thing FairSoftware does for a developer who wants to create a startup, but doesn't want to incorporate a business?

Alain: The value of FairSoftware is that a developer can start a business immediately, without incurring any cost whatsoever, and start teaming up with other people to start building the product, legally and safely, because we crafted our terms very carefully. But saving money, while attractive, is not the main motivating factor. What really resonates with our users is that they finally have the freedom to associate with whomever they want online. Many developers see the 9-to-5 full-time job disappearing, and they look forward to a more "agile" form of work collaboration. In a few years, it will feel completely natural to be working on several projects in parallel, some successful, others not so much.

Bob: About how many active startup projects are now on FairSoftware?

Alain: We probably have about 80 really serious projects, plus another 20 or so web sites or blogs that share ad revenue. There are another 100 or more projects where I scratch my head and wonder how it could ever become a real business. But we don't intervene. People can start whatever they want.

Bob: FairSoftware costs 10% of each sale. Does that include what PayPal charges for each transaction?

Alain: FairSoftware takes a commission of 3.9% on sales from the projects we host. But we also pass along PayPal's costs, so in the worst case, where a payment crosses multiple continents between the consumer, us, and the contributor, the total charge reaches 10%. We have ways to lower this number for the United States. We are also introducing different pricing plans, where people can trade off commission and fixed hosting fees. Our goal is to find a price that works for everyone. It's very important for us to offer an option where creating a project is 100% free. We believe that students and people from poorer countries deserve their chance.

Bob: Have any FairSoftware projects "graduated" to the next level: become incorporated and raised angel money?

Alain: A handful of projects have "graduated." What happened typically is that people found each other through the site, started working together, and then partnered in real life. I can think of a few projects whose scope was outside our sweet spot. For instance, a nonprofit project gathered a lot of interest and FairSoftware helped set up the first few positions. But it was clear from the beginning that that project wouldn't remain hosted with us for long.

Bob: I know it's early yet, but have any FairSoftware projects started selling their software/SaaS to the public? Who?

Alain: The first projects to make money on FairSoftware were the bloggers, as we expected. FairSoftware has also become a meeting place for founders looking for their next idea. As you know, going from idea to paying customer is a long journey. On the other hand, we were impressed by some web projects (software) that took off really quickly. It's really only desktop software that takes forever to ship.

Making Money

Making money in your startup is another one of those jack-in-the-box topics: in a perfect world all you'd have to do is crank the wheel around and around and the money would pop out the top of the toy. In the real world, this little topic encompasses not just everything else in this book but anything at all that has to do with your startup.

So in this last section of the chapter let's focus on five companies that provide e-commerce solutions to startups, a company that's found a unique way for you to get paid by someone other than your customer, and a few things you need to know about one of the key infrastructures of more than a few startups: Google AdWords.

PayPal

Operating in 190 countries with 73 million accounts and $623 million in the last quarter of 2008,[15] PayPal in effect has become the Online World's banking system and an extremely popular e-commerce choice for startups not looking to join in the traditional credit card/payment authorization gateway/merchant account tango.

I have to interrupt myself here. If you thought equity funding was complicated, just wait until you have to dive into credit card processing. If you plan on making that particular dive and prefer not to smash into the bottom of the pool, go grab a copy of Amy Hoy's free e-book *Jump Start Credit Card Processing* at http://jumpstartcc.com. Amy wrote and illustrated this very cool and useful e-book as a way both to give back to the startup community and to attract worthy online attention to freckle time tracking (http://letsfreckle.com), the startup she and Thomas Fuchs (of script.aculo.us fame) started in 2008 (Figure 5-5).

---

[15] *http://en.wikipedia.org/wiki/PayPal*

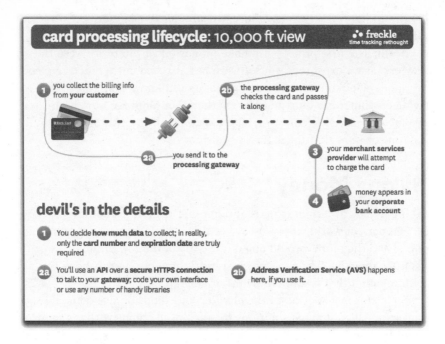

Figure 5-5. Jump Start Credit Card Processing e-book

OK, back to PayPal. In brief, PayPal lets people buy your software or subscribe to your service and easily and securely pay via either a major credit card or their PayPal account tied to a bank account and their credit card. Its fees—the slice of each and every money-receiving transaction it takes—are extremely competitive compared to traditional credit card processing: 1.9–2.9% + $0.30 USD for Premier/Business accounts.

In all the years I've been a microISV marketing software, a consultant hawking my services, an author selling e-books, and a buyer of way too many songs on iTunes (which translates into many hundreds of transactions), I have had no problems of any kind. None. Nada. Zip. If my body worked as well as PayPal does, I'd probably live to 250 and still get dates.

But other people will tell you a different tale: Horror stories of frozen accounts, uncaring customer support, and worse linger forever on the Internet, as they do for any company of this size. Furthermore, it's been my experience and that of dozens of other online sellers I've talked to that a small (and shrinking) percentage of consumers simply won't do business with PayPal. It's their money—it's their prerogative, and, as much as I like and recommend PayPal, I also urge you to provide your customers with an alternative. In fact, let me be specific: here are four software vendor–friendly e-commerce solutions I suggest.

Avangate

The first alternative to PayPal I recommend is Avangate (http://www.avangate.com),[16] for two reasons. First, over the years I've met and talked with a lot of Avangate's management and staff at all sorts of startup/microISV conferences and events they sponsor or at which they speak or participate. This is a company that well and truly likes and supports startups.

Second, and more tellingly, when people running startups and microISVs swap recommendations as to who to use for e-commerce at those various conferences or at huge public forums such as Joel on Software Business of Software (http://discuss.joelonsoftware.com/default.asp?biz) or private boards such as that run by the Association of Shareware Professionals (http://www.asp-shareware.org), you find nothing but positive recommendations when it comes to Avangate.

Avangate does more than process payments. From fielding a solid affiliate program to robust sales and lead analytics, software download, and physical fulfillment and registration key delivery, this company can make a lot of your startup's headaches go away. Of course, more service means you pay for more than bare-bones credit card processing—depending on which services you want, you'll pay somewhere between 4.9% and 8% per sale.

FastSpring

The second alternative to PayPal I recommend is FastSpring (http://www.fastspring.com/index.php). Again, this is a company with a good reputation, founded by people who years ago created and built two software e-commerce first movers, RegNow.com and RegSoft.com (now both part of Digital River, http://corporate.digitalriver.com). Being a second-generation e-commerce company in effect gives FastSpring a decided advantage over first-generation, some may say legacy, processors.

FastSpring's prices are straightforward: 5.9% plus $.95 per transaction or a flat rate of 8.9% (minimum fee of $0.75 per transaction).

iPortis

Number 3 on the alternative PayPal hit parade is iPortis.com (http://www.iportis.com). iPortis is yet another e-commerce provider that's part

---

[16] *Full-disclosure time: On occasion I've written for Avangate's startup-orientated blog at* http://blog.avangate.com, *and I've been paid for these posts, where I write about anything but Avangate.*

of the community of small software vendors and has a good, solid, positive reputation. iPortis is another second-generation e-commerce provider, started by two of the founders of Regsoft.com.

For 6.5% + $0.50 per transaction, you'll get great customer service from real people.

Zuora

Of the PayPal alternatives we've covered so far, as of this writing (May 2009) they all share a definite focus on supporting the sale of download-able desktop software. Zuora (http://zuora.com) focuses 100% on man-aging subscription billing for SaaS companies.

This well-funded outfit ($21.5 million, including $6.5 million from Salesforce CEO Marc Benioff)[17] aims to be the billing infrastructure of choice for not just web services, but the emerging ecology of social media apps, starting with Facebook. This is a different world than $24.95 desk-top software apps; for example, Zuora supports subscriptions for Facebook apps that are billed as little as 25 cents a year. Zuora handles the subscrip-tion process for a flat 2% before handing off the transaction to a payment processor such as authorize.net or PayPal.

TrialPay

No matter how cool and useful your startup's software, there's always going to be a percentage of potential customers who trial your software but can't or won't pay. Nothing new with that, right? Well, actually, there is something new: TrialPay (http://trialpay.com).

What TrialPay does is give your startup's potential customers a second chance to own your software by completing one offer from one of Trial-Pay's partners. Everything from becoming a Netflix customer to subscribing to the *New York Times* gets you paid—and you can get paid more than you normally charge for your software.

The magic words that make this possible are Customer Acquisition Cost and Customer Lifetime Value. How much it costs you to acquire a new customer and how much you'll make off them while they're your cus-tomer are key business metrics. Paying your startup for helping acquire a new customer when rendered frictionless through good software makes

---

[17] http://www.techcrunch.com/2008/10/28/zuora-raises-another-15-million-for-integrated-online-billing-and-payment-solution

perfect sense: the major league brand gets a new customer, you get paid, and the customer gets two things he or she wants instead of nothing.

Dave Collins, Founder, Shareware Promotions

In the online advertising world, where all things revolve around Google AdWords, Dave Collins is the skilled, proficient, and highly knowledgeable force behind Shareware Promotions (http://www.sharewarepromotions.com; Figure 5-6), which focuses on the arcane arts of AdWords, search engine optimization, and web analytics for small software companies like yours. I asked Dave to fill me in on the gist of what I—and you—need to understand about Google AdWords.

Figure 5-6. Shareware Promotions

Bob: Let's start with Google AdWords because that's the gorilla that owns this particular cage. When startups start thinking about their Google AdWords campaign, when is the right time to begin really considering what they need in this area?

Dave: I think as soon as they're ready to start selling. That's the time to start using AdWords. It can also be a very useful tool for actual market research. But basically, once you're web site is up and running and your product is available. There's absolutely no reason to wait. The sooner the better, really.

Bob: Let's talk about broad brush strokes here. When a startup is ready to go for a Google AdWords campaign and start using that as their main marketing tool, what should they know that Google won't tell them?

Dave: The two-word answer is *a lot*. There's a huge amount. I'd say the single most important fact, if you like, or point that should be behind every decision is that the whole AdWords system is set up for Google. It's a very obvious and very simplistic statement, that every aspect of the system is set up and geared heavily toward Google and their priorities.

There's an obvious overlap of priorities, and, for some matters, what's good for Google is good for you. But there are also a lot of times when you could be spending money on, for instance, keywords that aren't really relevant. Google is happy, and you are not.

So the key thing is, go with your eyes open, and understand that the system is not set up to be your friend, to be on your side at all.

Bob: That's a pretty harsh statement. Can you give me a couple of examples?

Dave: Don't call my bluff. I could probably come up with a list of 50. The two classic examples are: When you enter the keywords, these are the keywords that are going to trigger your ad to be displayed. By default, Google set these at broad match. So without getting bogged down by the technicalities, what this means is, you choose a phrase, for instance, "e-mail software for Mac" will be your keyword. By default, with broad match, someone searching for "Mac software" could see your ad. Someone searching for "software" could see your ad. And even, horrifically, someone searching for "e-mail software for Windows" could also see your ad, because of how broad matching works.

They have what's called "expanded matching," where they add more words to the phrase. But, bizarrely, expanded matching also includes taking words out of the phrase. So even though your keyword might be "e-mail software for Mac," the system could generate an ad impression and possibly a click that you're going to be charged for—someone searching for "Unix e-mail software," "Windows e-mail software."

Bob: It's a very powerful tool, but don't expect that Google is there to make your campaign as cost effective as possible.

Dave: Absolutely. I'm often saying that the absolute beauty, the sheer genius, of the AdWords system is that a lot of people think that they're doing very well from their AdWords account, that they're making a very good ROI. They walk away day after day, week after week, happy with the results, when in actual fact they're wasting a lot of money. So the true genius of the system is that, even though you're actually losing a lot of money, you think that you're not. It's little short of inspired. Your own analogy of a powerful tool is perfect. It's absolutely perfect.

It's a very, very powerful, but potentially dangerous tool, and it doesn't come with safety guards. It doesn't have big labels on it saying, "Warning, don't stick your finger here," and is potentially, very dangerous.

Bob: Let's start talking about reasonable expectations here. Let's say that I am a software-as-a-service web site. I'm selling a new, interesting app that my startup has developed. I put out a campaign to attract people. I don't go with the Google defaults. I work it pretty hard and try and nail down a very good list of keywords. I do my various A/B testing against my ads. I've also got several different dedicated landing pages for those ads, for people who click on them. What type of ROI should I be seeing? What should I be aiming for here?

Dave: It's a very commonly asked question. Unfortunately, it's almost impossible to answer. It's really like a software company turning around and saying, "If business is going well, what sort of profits should I be making, or what sort of profit margins should I be making?" The bottom line is, obviously, you need to be making a positive return, assuming you're not throwing money at the account purely from the point of view of branding and getting your name out there. But assuming the idea is to make money and sell, you obviously need to bring in more than you're spending.

But you can have an AdWords account that is highly, highly, profitable that's not even producing a 10% profit margin. Conversely you could have an AdWords account generating three, four, five times the amount that someone's spending that isn't really achieving anywhere near a fraction of its potential. Unfortunately, it's one of those politician-type answers. It just depends.

Bob: OK. Let's take the stages of life with the Google AdWords sale. We start with an ad that's shown on a Google search page or a content provider page. By the way, do you recommend content provider pages?

Dave: Absolutely. The content network is great, but the key thing is it has to be kept separate. There are different rules, very, very different budgets. You should be spending a lot less on the content network. As long you have to knit separate campaigns, you can track things separately, keep the bits down, control the budget. It can work very well. But, as in all things AdWords related and all things marketing related, it isn't for everyone. It really depends on what you're selling. As a general rule of thumb, yes, it can work very, very well.

Bob: The first step of the process is that we have the keywords that Google uses to place those ads on pages. Besides the tools that are within Google itself, what tools would you recommend to the startup who's going to put some significant money behind their AdWords campaign?

Dave: I'd say the starting point has to be subscribing to one of the keywords databases, because that's really where it all begins. If you get the keywords wrong, then everything else you do at that point is, more or less, a waste of time. So I would suggest that there are some very good databases, like Wordtracker.com and Keyworddiscovery.com. Wordtracker, in particular, offers even monthly subscriptions, if you only want to dip your toes in and see how worthwhile it is. It's very affordable. It's all about finding out exactly what people are searching for. So right from the beginning you know what people are actually looking for, as opposed to what you think people are probably looking for.

Bob: Let's talk about that keyword psychology for a moment. What's the big difference between the reality of what people are searching for and the ideas that developers and startups may think they are searching for?

Dave: The gap between the two can be incredible. It can be absolutely huge. The main point is that most software developers, irrespective of how long they've been in business or how big their company is, they probably can't even begin to imagine the terms people might be using when they're looking for the product that they're selling. Whether it's down to simply the mind shift of not understanding exactly the terms, the phrases, the problems people might have when they're looking for a solution. Or even such regional variations or different cultural, different countries have got different dialects and different slang.

There's an incredible, incredible number of variants, even on one or two basic keywords. And really the only way to find out is to use one of these databases.

Bob: And to use that as your tool to get within the mind of your potential customers.

Dave: Exactly. Because the key thing is, whichever tool you use, it always gives you some indication of what other terms are out there and how popular these phrases are. So there's no point in AdSense bidding on a phrase that maybe you think is a perfect fit for your product but maybe only one or two people a week or so are searching for.

Whereas these databases you can subscribe to, they show you different synonyms, different variations. You might find your phrase generates one or two impressions a week, but people who are looking for your product are using another phrase that could be literally thousands, tens of thousands of impressions a week. The only way to tap into that is to use one of these tools.

Bob: Let's take the next link in the chain, which is the ad itself. How much of a difference is there between your blah, vague ad versus something more snappy or humorous or what have you. In other words, are all ads pretty much alike, and this is not the big factor you should be spending your time on?

Dave: No, the ad really is vital. This is the classic scenario, if you like, of the weakest link in the chain: If you get the keywords wrong, the wrong people are going to be seeing your ads. If you get the ads wrong, no one's going to be clicking on it. We generally advise setting up for each keyword group around five or six or more ads. Try to have them as different, as varied, as possible. The difference can be astronomical.

You might have the lowest-performing ad—once you've built up some data, you might see the lowest-performing ad get something like 0.1% click-through rate. So, quite literally, for every thousand times the ad gets shown, one person clicks on it. Whereas other ads . . . we've worked with ads we've believed are in the 40%, 45% click-through rate, meaning that literally half the people can click on them. Generally for that sort of a difference, to go from 0.1% to 45%, the ads are going to be looking very, very different, as you can imagine.

But sometimes, with just a very small change, a really small, one-word change, juggling things around, stripping it down a little bit, you could easily make a difference. It could turn an ad with a 1% click-through rate to a 5% or 6% click-through rate, easily.

Bob: Google's AdWords has all these analytics built into it, so I guess that's going to be the way you know this. But for how long do you test an ad? What's a decent test period for an ad?

Dave: That will largely depend on how much demand there is for what you're looking for. So if you have a product, for instance, you're really perhaps only seeing 30 or 40 impressions a week. You're going to be looking, at the very, very minimum, a month, a month and a half before you have any sort of decent data you can work with. Whereas if you get a higher volume . . . we're having some accounts generate, quite literally, tens of thousands of impressions a day. So a week is more than adequate.

I do always recommend going for intervals of seven days, just because there's a seven-day pattern. If you, for instance, put up some new keywords on a Friday, then have a look at it on a Monday, you're really going to be seeing data from the weekend, which could be very, very different from the Monday through Friday.

Generally we always recommend working in units of seven days. As long as you've got enough impressions, seven days is enough. Really, I tend not to judge an ad until, at the very least; I've got a hundred impressions. That's an absolute bare minimum.

Bob: After they click on a startup's ad, what should happen next?

Dave: There's a whole process that should be a very smooth journey. The person goes to Google or whichever site they're going to be searching on with a phrase or a keyword or a solution and then type that in. There should be a very smooth transition from that to the ad. This is what makes the ad really get the attention. If the ad speaks to the phrase that they've actually entered and the solution they're looking for, they're more likely to click on it.

Once they click on the ad, it's the landing page that then carries on the work of the ad. So it carries on using the same term, the same language, the same tone, pushing the same product benefits. That's the page that they want to be on.

Sometimes just the regular web site's home page, sometimes that can work quite well. But more often than not it does need a specific landing page or a specific product page geared toward the ad. It's all about continuing the process, the keyword to ad to the landing page.

Bob: In the same way that a startup will basically do testing of their ads, should they also be doing testing of their landing pages?

Dave: Absolutely. We always say that the amount of data that Google gives you in the AdWords account is phenomenal. It's an incredible amount of different information, different reports, different graphs, trends that you can see. There are a huge number of columns of numerical data there. But that only takes you that far. Once they click on the ad, Google knows what happens next, up to a point, but you don't.

You have to continue the analysis once they get on the landing page. You have to see what happens next. At it's most basic, take an example of a keyword that generates a lot of impressions. Your ads are looking really well, they get a lot of clicks. Let's say each of the four ads is generating in the region of 1,500 to 2,000 clicks a day. Then you have a look at the data on the web site to find out that 99.5% of the people who land on that page leave within three seconds—you know that something's wrong. It's not necessarily the page, but chances are it's something in that whole process between the keyword, the ad, the landing page—something isn't right there.

Bob: Their expectations aren't being met.

Dave: Exactly. And it could be any number of reasons. It could even be as simple as the web page is just horrible. It could be ugly. People look at it, they like the idea, whatever you're selling is perfect. They land there and they think, "What on earth is this? This is horrible. It looks . . . " They think it's amateur. They go on. It could be the fact, when they get there, the first thing they see is "Voted by *PC World* the most powerful Windows system tool," but there is a Mac, but your ad didn't make that clear.

There's any number of reasons why it can go wrong, but you have to be looking at it most simply, at the very least, you need to know how long they're spending once they arrive.

Bob: Let's turn around on the other end of things for a moment, which is the idea of using Google AdWords or, I guess. actually AdSense as your revenue model as a startup. Realistically, how many page views—and we could probably use the definition of what we mean by page views, just so we're on the same page, pardon the pun—how many page views does a site that expects to live off Google ads need per month?

Dave: I risk sounding like a politician: it largely depends on what the site's actually pushing. The different products and markets can have a huge bearing. Say, for instance, if you're setting up, as an example, a software site, you're going to need a lot of traffic to start making some decent money from that. If it's . . .

Bob: How much is a lot?

Dave: Well, again, it's—I know exactly how slippery I'm sounding—but it depends. The ads have to be positioned well on the web site, and they have to be relevant to the web site. So, for instance, I know that legal services will generate a very large amount of money for each click. So I could set up a web site pushing legal services even though it's a software site. It's going to get me nowhere. We've seen web sites with traffic well in excess of 100,000 visitors a day that generate reasonable revenue. Nothing spectacular—you won't be upgrading your car or going somewhere fantastic for a vacation.

Bob: OK, so less than single-salary-type money.

Dave: Yeah, exactly. Especially nowadays, since AdSense has spread across the Internet. We're all used to seeing it; lots of people more or less automatically block them out. We don't need software to block them because we're used to ignoring them in the same way that we're very often used to seeing banner ads and we just don't even notice or register them. A few years ago, it was actually very easy to make some very nice money from AdSense.

Bob: Just because it hadn't spread so far.

Dave: Exactly. Also, to be completely honest, the rules were a lot more lax as well. Google was a lot more relaxed on what you could and couldn't do with the ads. So there are a lot of sites, for instance, who would get users to click on ads not realizing they were clicking on ads. By the time they realized it, it was too late, and they've got that click anyway. Whereas now, Google will absolutely stamp on that and will close down AdSense for behavior like that.

Bob: It sounds to me like the easy-money days with AdSense are over. At least as far as everybody except Google.

Dave: Yeah, exactly. They're still doing just fine.

Recap

Let me go back and make this point one more time: If your focus for building a startup is securing angel or VC funding, then stop, take your hands off the keyboard, and give yourself a hard reboot—you're not going to succeed that way.

The people you're approaching for money have heard it all before. They are not going to be impressed with your command of the latest buzzwords and technology, five-year revenue projections that one-half of the human race is your conservative market size, or any such nonsense. They will show you the door or hang up the phone and toss your business plan in the trashcan in a heartbeat. In fact, unless in their eyes your company has a good chance to make them really rich, out you go. Nothing personal—business is business.

Your business as a founder seeking funding to scale your dream into an honest-to-God company is to understand just what game you're in. It's a game where you, your cofounders, your team, and your advisors need to do a consummate job of not only writing software but doing all the other things expected of you. That's just the price of admission, and the odds are definitely not in your favor.

If that's the bad news, here's the good news: If you really do have a hot startup idea and put your heart and mind into executing it, and the people working with you do the same, and you do the things you need to do, someone is going to say yes, and you're going to cross that chasm from bootstrapping to true company building. It won't matter what the economy is like, what other companies are doing, what the latest media pronouncement is. You will get that first yes. And from there, I've been told by people I deeply respect, it gets a lot easier.

One last point. Remember that getting funded is about as objective as falling in love. Sure, you've got to be out there and doing the right things. But those things just set the stage for the real human drama—the stuff that happens person to person and face to face—because you're going to every social interaction you can get invited to or in the door of where you might find angels and VCs, entrepreneurs, and startups in the flesh.

It's an overgeneralization but a true one that people who love to code tend to be introverts, not extroverts, presidents of their high school math clubs, not picked as the most popular student in the school, which is why our next chapter is one you really need to read. We're going to be getting hot and social. OK, so it's online social, not the face-to-face stuff you need to get good at to woo investors. But it's definitely a step in the right direction. Onward and upward!

Social Media and Your Startup

"Tell me to what you pay attention and I will tell you who you are"
—Jose Ortega y Gasset (Spanish philosopher and humanist, 1883–1955)

"The simple act of paying attention can take you a long way."
—Keanu Reeves (actor)

It's All About Attention

Over the past few years the economics of attention has fundamentally changed—and that change has profound and deep implications for your startup. Sure, "building buzz around your startup" has always been high on every founder's to-do list. But what has changed is what works, what doesn't work, and what you need to do.

A decade ago, in the dot-com heyday, you built buzz by hiring a good public relations firm (for about $30,000 a month, minimum) that would woo and wheedle the computer trade press for a mention, a review, anything. And you could plan to spend a good $50,000 or more (way more) doing a launch event. Of course, all of this was just the prelude to a good web ad banner campaign chock-full of pop-ups, pop-downs, and pop-overs, all designed to scream louder than the other ads at the sucker watching the screen.

Back then, there was no Facebook or Twitter, no blogs or social networks, no news blogs, no social media. Attention was something you ripped out of (and ripped off) "consumers" with advertising and sycophant reviews in trade magazines while "harvesting their eyeballs."

The economics of attention online worked like strip mining: you blow up the attention of millions to garner a handful of sales, and who cared—everyone else did the same thing. You—the advertiser—were in the business of stealing attention, or at least appropriating it without consent, via the tried-and-true process of hammering your message into thick consumer skulls.

This same approach is alive and well today—just turn on your television—but something else has arisen. It's why Facebook has as many active users as Russia has "active citizens" and why social networks worldwide are growing, in terms of the number of participants, the depth of their participation, and the effect others in these networks have on opinion, values, and buying decisions.

What's developed is a different approach to attention, to markets, to people. And the cluetrain manifesto represents the theory, the instigator, and the clearest guide to that shift. What is the cluetrain manifesto? Back in 1999, Rick Levine, Christopher Locke, Doc Searls, and David Weinberger wrote the cluetrain manifesto (`http://cluetrain.com`) to nail on the door of the Holy Church of Advertising a list of tenets about markets and people in the Online World.

The preamble to the manifesto starts with: "We are not seats or eyeballs or end users or consumers. We are human beings—and our reach exceeds your grasp. *Deal with it.*"

The full list of 95 statements about the Online World reads like a social network Declaration of Independence from traditional marketing. Here are a few statements that should hit home if you're the founder of a startup.

- Markets are conversations.

- The Internet is enabling conversations among human beings that were simply not possible in the era of mass media.

- Corporations do not speak in the same voice as these new networked conversations. To their intended online audiences, companies sound hollow, flat, literally inhuman.

- To speak with a human voice, companies must share the concerns of their communities.

- But first, they must belong to a community.

- Companies that do not belong to a community of discourse will die.

- Markets do not want to talk to flacks and hucksters. They want to participate in the conversations going on behind the corporate firewall.

- We are immune to advertising. Just forget it.

- You want us to pay? We want you to pay attention.

- We know some people from your company. They're pretty cool online. Do you have any more like that you're hiding? Can they come out and play?

We now have a new economy of attention online. First and foremost, are you interesting? If you're not interesting, you'd better be prepared to work hard to bring interesting things to the global conversation to rescue your startup from obscurity.

The good news about how social networks have retooled who gets attention online is that the new rules favor startups.

The Big Idea

So here's the big idea we're going to be unpacking later in this chapter: The other critical job in a startup today (besides development) is that of *community manager*. That's the person or persons who do the work to connect your startup to social media so that it gets and continues to get that buzz it needs.

Unless you enjoy shoveling money into a wood stove to keep warm, social media replaces traditional advertising. Matter of fact, you'd probably get a better return on your initial investment by burning dollar bills than by paying for most online and all offline forms of interruption-based advertising. The return was never anything to brag about, and as traditional media (television, radio, print, newspapers) have declined, it's now abysmal.

So what this chapter is really about is what a community manager does, where she[1] or he does it, how, how often, and so on.

But before we get there, we need to cover a few things, the two key components of social media: blogs and Twitter. And we'll also dig into the one part of traditional marketing—PR—that has value and that is frantically trying to reinvent itself in a social world, talking with some of the people who's words online can make or break your startup.

Since time management is definitely an issue, let's start with the not-so-little problem of tracking what needs tracking in the social media world.

---

[1] *She? Absolutely. I'd argue that women in developed countries are by and large much better at working with people, creating conversations, and being community managers than alpha-male-developer-geek types. This is a generalization, but I think it's true. If you disagree, I suggest you get out more!*

Setting Up Your Social Media Basic Radar

I'm assuming that as a developer you are familiar with Twitter and Facebook and some of the other social media out there. But now, as you go from being a developer to being a startup founder, you have new needs and new concerns about who is saying what about your company and its product.

For starters, you need to erect what I call your *social media basic radar*. This is your startup's early warning system that good or bad things are about to rain down on your head or server. There are lots of ways of building this radar and lots of nice add-ons you can devise and install once you have the basic system working. And, as with all things Internet, what does the job today can easily be supplanted tomorrow by something that does the job even better.

For this section I'm going to use Mint.com (which we will get to know better in Chapter 7) because one of the things their CEO, Aaron Patzer, does well is social media. So here's a list of components from which to assemble your radar. Feel free to substitute parts that suit you better.

- iGoogle as your home page (there are alternatives, but this is the leader)

- Google Blog Search

- Twitter Search and TweetGrid

- BackType

- FriendFeed

- gReader and PostRank

I'm assuming that, as someone technically with it, you don't need step-by-step instructions here. Instead I'm going to focus on how each of these components works.

iGoogle

URL: http://www.google.com/ig

What it is: Free widget/RSS multitab home page for any and all browsers.

What it does: For our purposes, it's the canvas onto which all the other components deliver their data.

Setup: iGoogle is part of your Google account. You want to set it as your start page for whatever browsers/boxes you use in the course of the day. Then create or add tabs for at least the following: "Our Startup," "Our Industry," "Me," and "Competitors." These tabs are going to be the endpoints for a number of RSS feeds from the other components, all with the goal of making it easy to know what people are saying about your startup, your competition, and you.

Keep in mind that, in iGoogle Settings, you can choose which tabs and tab components you want to share with specific people, such as the rest of your startup team. Day by day, Google gets more social. You can also import/export tabs, and you can backup your radar.

Google Blog Search

URL: http://blogsearch.google.com

What it is: Google search, but only for blogs and with a very handy search by time period.

What it does: It let's you create ongoing RSS feeds for search terms as they appear on blogs.

Setup: Start with your startup's name, if it was mentioned in the past week. Mentions a week or less old are still fresh enough to get into the conversation. At some point you're going to want to add a feed for the last day, the last 12 hours, and, when you have your launch or a major release, the last hour.

Each search has a unique RSS feed (see your browser's address bar) that when clicked lets you add it to iGoogle (Figure 6-1).

Keep adding Google Blog Search feeds for your name, your competitor's name, and other keywords that make sense. Once you're done, it's time to move on to provisioning the next part of your radar.

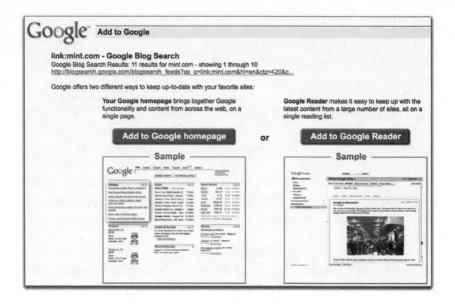

Figure 6-1. Adding a feed from Google Blog Search

Twitter Search and TweetGrid

URL: http://search.twitter.com and http://tweetgrid.com

What it is: Real-time search of Twitter and then, with TweetGrid, a way to bundle multiple searches on one page.

What it does: Gives you a powerful communication tool for starting Twitter conversations (Figure 6-2). As to why you'd want to do this, see the section "Welcome to the Land of Twitter," later in this chapter.

Now, you could pull a feed from this page onto your iGoogle, but unless you are going to sit there and hit Refresh several hundred times a day, you'll lose the real-time-ness of this search engine. Better still, add it as another start page for your browser so that you can pay continuous partial attention to it throughout the day.[2]

Now, TweetGrid lets you pipe in up to 12 real-time searches of Twitter. This is perfect if your startup's product is getting noticed in multiple ways in Twitterland; it's overkill for most people (Figure 6-3).

---

[2] You can add multiple start pages in Firefox as follows: Go to http://www.google.com/ig and then to http://search.twitter.com/search?q=mint.com. In IE, go to the page you want to add, click the down arrow next to the Home Page icon, choose Add or Change Home Page, and then choose Add this webpage to your home page tabs.

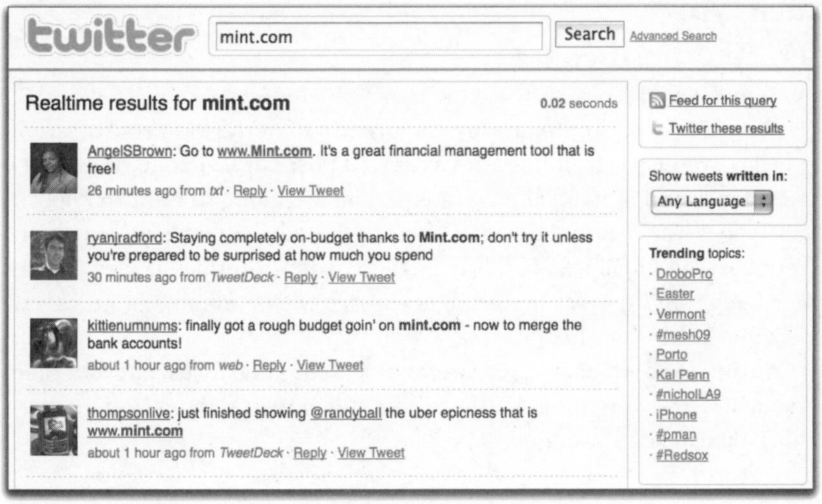

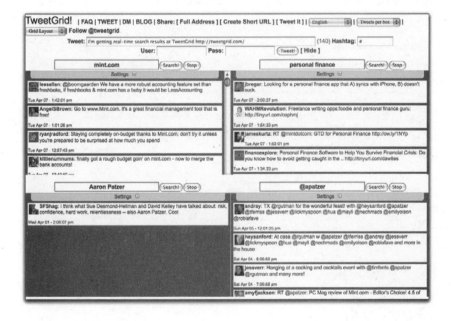

Figure 6-2. *Mint.com* results on Twitter Search

Figure 6-3. TweetGrid

BackType

URL: http://backtype.com

What it is: Free search engine for blog comments.

What it does: Comments are the other half of the blog conversation, and they are nearly as influential as actual posts. If someone praises or rants about your startup as a comment, you are going to want to know it. BackType doesn't cover the entire blogosphere by any means, but their list of covered blogs is constantly growing, their interface is clean, and their BackType Connect feature lets you see who's talking about a given post or article—very handy.

Setup: Go to BackType, create your searches and feeds, and add them to your iGoogle (Figure 6-4). If you're really nervous about comments, BackType can send you e-mail.

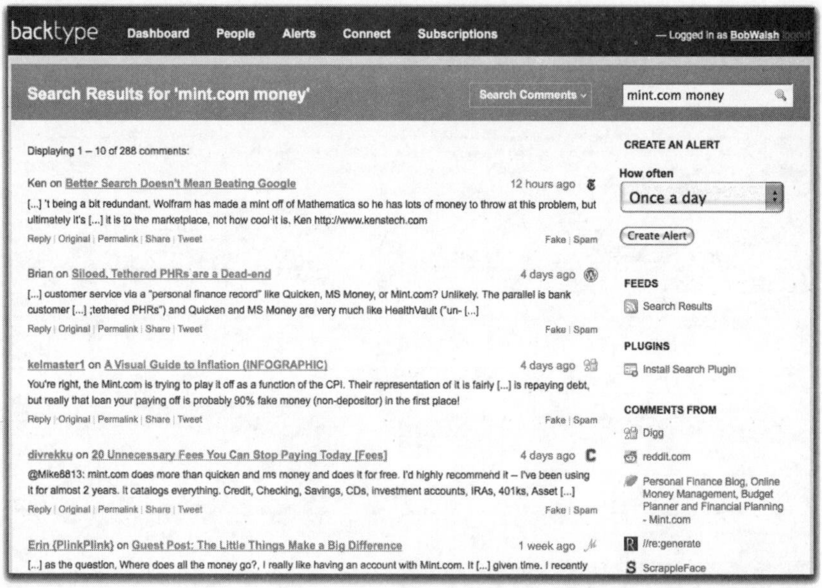

Figure 6-4. BackType

FriendFeed

URL: http://friendfeed.com

What it is: Free life-stream/social media tool.

What it does: A lot of social media data ends up in FriendFeed. You want to mine that data for bits that are relevant to your startup.

Setup: Set up an account, start adding friends, and then begin creating custom searches and capturing the RSS feeds to iGoogle. I say "add friends" because there are two kinds of searches that interest you here: searching everyone's feed of social items and searches of your friends, colleagues, and cofounders, who are likely to include higher-quality, more relevant items (Figure 6-5).

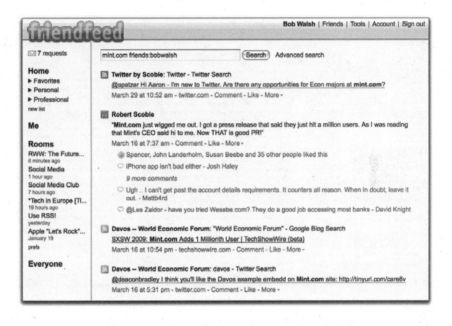

Figure 6-5. FriendFeed

Google Reader with PostRank

URL: http://www.google.com/reader and http://postrank.com

What it is: RSS reader combined with a popularity filter.

What it does: Finally, besides pinpointing who exactly you should be talking to online, you need to step back and get the broader picture. Following the right posts for your given market or industry is a great way to do that, and RSS makes it easy.

However, it actually makes it too easy. Most people I know are in RSS bankruptcy—too many feeds to follow—or have given up on RSS entirely. Too much—much too much—information is at your fingertips. Unless you live and breathe this stuff—and make a living from doing so—you need to throttle this fire hose down to something manageable. That's where PostRank comes in. PostRank will take your feeds in Google Reader and other popular RSS readers and add an orange PostRank rating badge to each item. This rating in turn is determined by how much play a given post, comment, or news story gets in the world of social media.

For example, Figure 6-6 shows my Google Reader, equipped with PostRank. Now, I could have spent 90 minutes trying to catch up on the 237 posts from my 32 favorite bloggers, or I could look at a single screen utilizing PostRank and pick the best of the best.

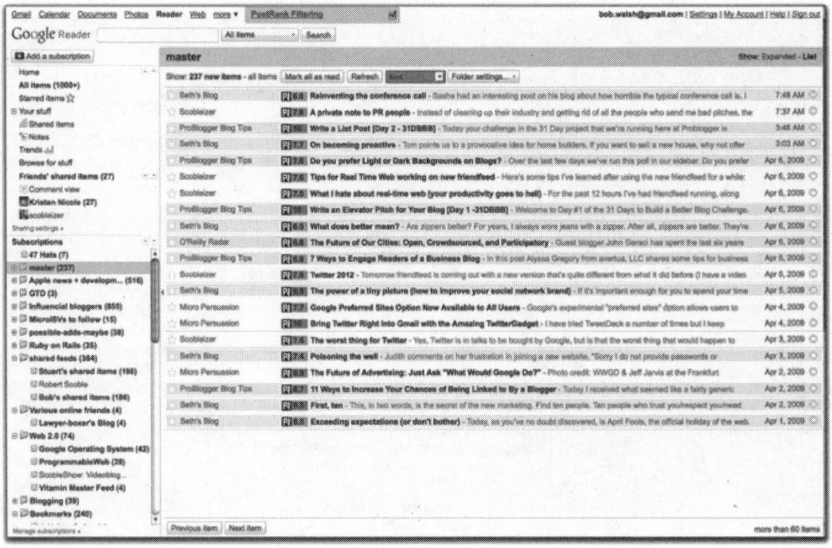

Figure 6-6. Google Reader with PostRank

So there you have it: a fairly clean, free way to filter an enormous flood of information for the tiny little bits that have to do with your startup. And it's easily accessorized with a feed from Digg and one from, say, Get Satisfaction (see Chapter 4) so that you'll know when you are about to get whacked by 10,000 hits or one really angry customer.

The trick here is to make checking your radar a standard workday routine without getting sucked into endless hours of surfing the Web. Here are a few points concerning what you're looking for in all this data (and definitely check out the next three sections of this chapter).

What to Look for on Your Social Media Radar

1. *Any factually incorrect information about your startup's app*, such as new comments referring to old bugs that have been fixed, misstatements about what your software can do, mistruths (inadvertent or not), etc. These kind of information bugs are like single broken windows in a skyscraper—soon, no one wants to go in the front door.

2. *Extremely happy, enthusiastic users of your software's service or product.* By reaching out to these people and expressing humility and offering a little gratitude, you get a positive opinion and a mindset of "I must tell others" and build up your legion of online influencers.

3. *People with the problems your software solves.* These are known as *customers.* Connecting to people on blogs, Twitter, Facebook, and other social media in a low-key, nonselling way works wonders. Don't dump a sales message on them and run. Let them know you sell a solution, and ask politely if you can help them.

4. *Other ways of offering value to people.* As we'll cover in the later section "Your Other Title: Chief Community Officer," you have more value to people than just the software or service your startup sells. From a pure dollars-and-cents point of view, it makes sense to share that value—expertise, experience, contacts, insight—with others who, though not necessarily a prospective customer today, may be one tomorrow. Consider it enlightened self-interest—adding value to people's lives, work, and online experience is good business.

The Startup Company Blog

I can go on for quite a while about the what and how of blogging—in fact I did just that in my previous Apress book, *Clear Blogging: How People Are Changing the World and How You Can Join Them* (Apress, 2007). In this section, however, I'd like to focus on the why—why the founders of your startup should blog, and why they should blog instead of or in addition to using Twitter or Facebook or participating in any number of social networks and media: **because it works!**

When people buy a product or service, they are in a sense buying the people who make that offering and brought it into the world. This is true for the largest of the large companies—who, you may notice, make a point of putting real people in their television commercials—to the smallest, newest business entity on the block. That's you.

By blogging, you, as the founder of your startup, can communicate and spread the passion, excitement, and expertise that made that startup possible. You are on a mission (or should be) to share this exciting new thing with as many people as you can.

One thing I need to warn you about: If you think your blog is a place where you can get results by just touting your "marketing message," you will be very disappointed in the results you get—like disappointed right out of business. Blogging is a person-to-person thing; no smooth, third-person marketing pronouncements need apply.

There's no one right way to do a startup blog. A huge amount depends on who you and, by extension, your company are, who you'd like to converse with at your blog, and the tone, frequency, and length that feel right for that conversation. But there are some basic guidelines, some proven rules of thumb, that will help you structure and execute a good startup blog, With work, passion, and a bit of luck, it will be a great startup blog.

Here are my recommendations about what makes for a good startup blog.

- Let your customer know what's going on. I don't mean posting about what you're going to do for them; I mean posting about what you've done for them to make your software/service easier/better/more usable/more valuable.

- Definitely use your blog to ask for and listen to feedback from prospective and actual customers.

- Provide real value. Long gone are the days when blogs were novel and read just because the concept was new. If your market is reading blogs—and more and more people in general are doing just that—they are reading a lot of blogs. You need to provide real substance and worth in your posts, about your startup's software, about the problem(s) it addresses, about the lives and livelihoods of the people who have those problems.

- Take the high road, not the low. That means do write posts that dig deep into topics your customers care about; don't pick fights with straw men or real competitors. Do explain what makes your product valuable, meaningful, and worthy of attention, but don't trash other companies in the process. By all means, do explain what it is that got you excited enough to take the huge leap of creating a startup, but don't bore your readers with mundane bits of your life.

- Use your blog as part of your customer support and product improvement workflows. That's a fancy way of saying that when you notice customers are stumbling over a particular feature or defect, talk about it on your blog and how you're working to resolve it. That can be as small and quick as posting a 20-second video on how to do something in your app (Jing, at http://www.jingproject.com, works really well for this) to asking your readers what they think should be the next big feature you add.

- Spend a good one-third of your "blogging" time adding value to other blogs by commenting and eventually doing guest posts. Whose blogs? The blogs your prospective customers are already likely to be reading. Blogging is not doing a monologue. And if you've not yet launched your startup's product or service, you should be spending half of your blogging time doing this.

- Be emphatic in inviting comments. Comments are hugely important in a blog. To be blunt, they are what adds to your Google page rank, what ignites more inbound traffic, what prompts other readers to comment, what makes the blogging world go around. This means that when you're first starting out, use other social media, such as Twitter and Facebook, to inform people you know personally that you want comments. If that doesn't work, don't be too proud to e-mail them. Getting those first few comments is the hardest, so be prepared to work for them. Of course, the easiest way to get people to comment on your blog is to comment on their blogs first.

- Keep to your focus. At times, you will be tempted to post about all sorts of things that happen in the world, good and bad. Think twice, maybe three times, before doing so. On occasion I've succumbed to the temptation to use my blog as a soapbox on which to stand and shout; invariably I regretted it later. Remember, you're not writing for yourself; you're writing for your readers. You deliver what they're interested in, they pay you attention: that's the deal.

- Avoid the topics of sex, religion, and politics—they have no place in a startup blog, unless you sell a product that improves sex, manages churches, or keeps politicians out of jail.

Startup Blogs—Three Examples

Just about every startup has a blog—for good reason—so there's no shortage of examples out there. I wanted to focus on just three here, because they each exemplify something you should know about startup blogs.

First up we have the Rising Tide blog, from Tugboat Enterprises. Tugboat makes Selkie Software, a line of data-rescue and -migration products for business and consumers—not necessarily the most exciting or attention-getting subject out there (Figure 6-7).

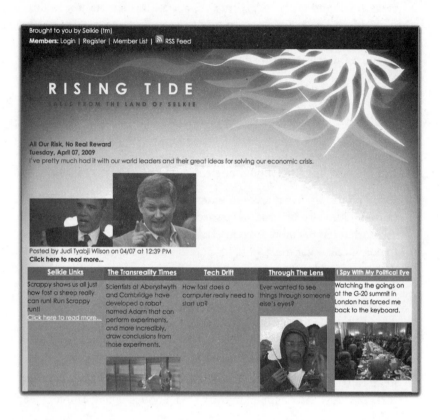

Figure 6-7. Rising Tide

I asked Matthew Bleicher, Tugboat Enterprises online marketing manager, about Rising Tide.[3]

"Your timing on these questions is good," replied Matthew. "Our blog reached a milestone of sorts this past month. It has now passed all of our product sites and our corporate site in traffic. A very small percentage of our visitors are checking out our product sites from the blog. As our blog traffic grows we certainly expect that number to grow.

---

[3] A note of disclosure here: I consulted with Tugboat about how to position their blog, its structure and focus.

"For the most part we use the blog to post topics not directly related to our product. We have done some posting in regards to our product on there, but that is not the focus of the site. We would rather pull in a larger audience than just those seeking recovery and migration software. What I am hoping to see, and honestly expect to see, is that in the coming months more and more people will come back to us by way of our product sites to purchase the product. I expect this, since it is a rare computer user that doesn't require software like ours."

The lesson here is twofold: (1) Passion attracts, even when it has little to do with your software. And (2) every rule (even the ones I suggest in this book) has an exception. If your software isn't exactly something people get excited about, blog about what you and they do get excited about, because that shared passion let's you start a conversation that can move on to other, more business-oriented topics.

Next up we have Ian Landsman, founder of UserScape. UserScape sells HelpSpot, a help desk system. Way back in 2004, before launching HelpSpot, Ian began to blog about its features, tease with revealing screenshots, and discuss why things would work in certain ways in his startup's software. He successfully engaged with his market before he had a product (Figure 6-8).

"My prelaunch blog made all the difference in the world. It's why I'm still in business today, it's as simple as that," Ian replied to my e-mail. "I was entering an extremely competitive software niche. Help desk software has thousands of competitors, from small startups to billion-dollar public companies. My personal blog allowed me to zig while the competitors were still zagging. Blogs were just really getting going in business in 2005, and few of my competitors had them.

"The blog allowed me to build up a small following which helped evangelize the product, linked to the product, helped my search engine rank, and also provided a place for a mental release. Starting a company is very stressful, and my readers were great at lightening my mood and listening to my ongoing trials and frustrations."

However, that was then and this is now. What does Ian blog about today, and how many people read his blog?

"My blogging has fallen off a lot. I think there are a few reasons for this. Primarily it's a lack of time. We've been very successful, and that's limited the time I have to write more in-depth posts. I also think many bloggers go through cycles. It's hard to always be on top of your game, so I think mentally it's good to get away from it a bit and then return when you're jazzed to post. The rise of Twitter has also had an impact on me. Doing a quick Tweet is so much faster and less formal than a full blog post, so Twitter has replaced a lot of my smaller blog posts.

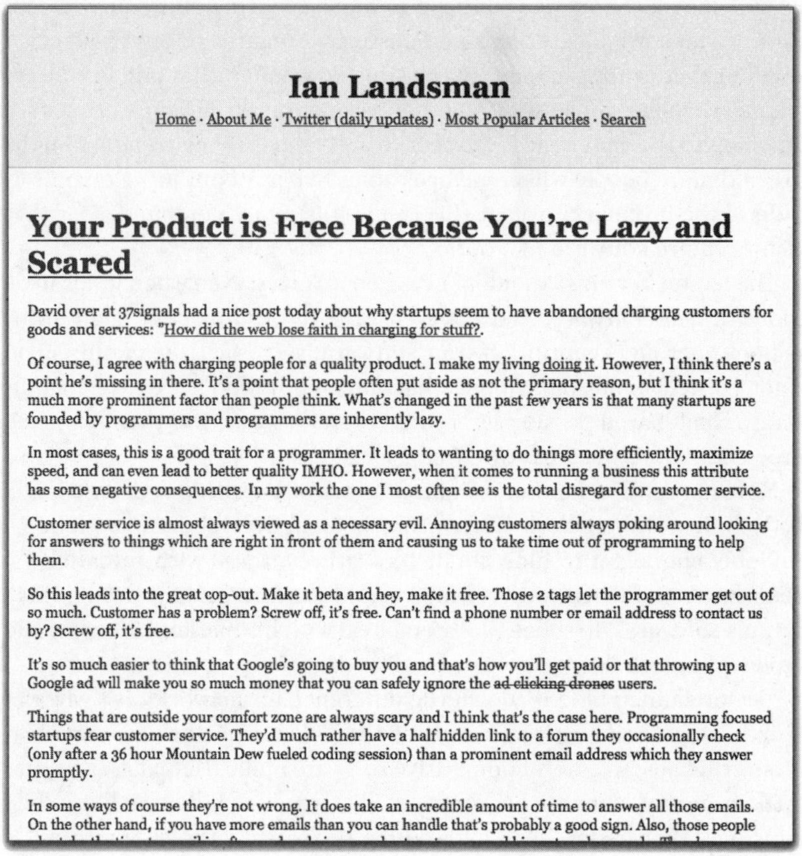

Ian Landsman

Home · About Me · Twitter (daily updates) · Most Popular Articles · Search

---

Your Product is Free Because You're Lazy and Scared

David over at 37signals had a nice post today about why startups seem to have abandoned charging customers for goods and services: "How did the web lose faith in charging for stuff?".

Of course, I agree with charging people for a quality product. I make my living doing it. However, I think there's a point he's missing in there. It's a point that people often put aside as not the primary reason, but I think it's a much more prominent factor than people think. What's changed in the past few years is that many startups are founded by programmers and programmers are inherently lazy.

In most cases, this is a good trait for a programmer. It leads to wanting to do things more efficiently, maximize speed, and can even lead to better quality IMHO. However, when it comes to running a business this attribute has some negative consequences. In my work the one I most often see is the total disregard for customer service.

Customer service is almost always viewed as a necessary evil. Annoying customers always poking around looking for answers to things which are right in front of them and causing us to take time out of programming to help them.

So this leads into the great cop-out. Make it beta and hey, make it free. Those 2 tags let the programmer get out of so much. Customer has a problem? Screw off, it's free. Can't find a phone number or email address to contact us by? Screw off, it's free.

It's so much easier to think that Google's going to buy you and that's how you'll get paid or that throwing up a Google ad will make you so much money that you can safely ignore the ad clicking drones users.

Things that are outside your comfort zone are always scary and I think that's the case here. Programming focused startups fear customer service. They'd much rather have a half hidden link to a forum they occasionally check (only after a 36 hour Mountain Dew fueled coding session) than a prominent email address which they answer promptly.

In some ways of course they're not wrong. It does take an incredible amount of time to answer all those emails. On the other hand, if you have more emails than you can handle that's probably a good sign. Also, those people

Figure 6-8. Ian Landsman's UserScape blog

"As for readership, it's in the thousands, but honestly I don't have any stats on it. I don't think the quantity is that important really; too much emphasis is placed on it. What you really want is quality. From a business perspective, 10 readers, all with their own blogs, all who post about what you're writing and what you're doing, is far more valuable than 10,000 readers who just browse your RSS feed (though I still appreciate those readers!)."

OK. But having been through the experience, would Ian recommend that startups blog prelaunch and about major upcoming releases?

"Yes and no. To the first part of your question, absolutely yes. A prelaunch blog is critical. It's perhaps not as unique as a few years ago, but it's still a great way to get the word out, build up a following, and, if you do a good job, it will have huge benefits to your business.

"To the second part I think you need to be much more careful. Pre-launch you have no customers to disappoint, you're in 100% publicity mode. You need to let everyone know what you're doing and how great it's going to be. Getting new customers is your entire focus, getting people to take a chance on you.

"Once you're established, though, the risk of disappointing customers should your release plan not work out is huge. I would much rather underpromise and overdeliver. Also, in a small startup or MicroISV there's always a good chance you're not going to get all the features done you think you will, or you'll hit an impasse where you'll have to delay or remove features from a new release. You don't want to have been blogging about those features for six months to not deliver them."

Again, we get two lessons for the price of one: Ian started blogging before releasing and this was critical for his success: he amassed attention, potential customers, and valuable product feedback prior to launch. The second lesson is that over the years, Ian has experimented with I think about five blog layouts before arriving at his current, shall we say minimalist layout shown in Figure 6-8. Great content trumps web design when it comes to blogs—invest your time in the content, not trying to look amazingly great.

Finally, let's turn to another startup's blog: RescueTime. We'll go into more detail about RescueTime and its CEO, Tony Wright, in Chapter 7, but I think RescueTime's blog is notable, for several reasons.

- It's not an overt product blog—it's a developer blog in many ways. Posts like the following don't, on their face, have a lot to do with time management: "Extend Rails ActiveRecord and Connection-Adapter to support dirty reads on MySQL."

- Certain posts—and I think this is the core of the blog—reveal surprising information about how time gets spent. And these posts get a sizable number of comments. For example, a few posts past the foregoing, which got zero comments, is this post: "Daylight Savings Time costs the United States $480,000,000." It got 28 comments. This is in line with Tony's strategy of garnering attention by using surprising information amassed from RescueTime's raw anonymous data.

- The blog is not all Tony. RescueTime's other two founders—Joe Hrusha and Brian Floca—as well as Montana Low, Sr. (software development engineer) and Mark Wolgemuth (chief architect) share some of the burden.

- The RescueTime blog is hosted at `WordPress.com`, which will host your blog Google ad-free for $30 a year. You don't have the creative freedom or the attendant time sink of a self-hosted, all the plug-ins you can eat, `WordPress.org` blog, and that's probably a good thing.

I asked Tony how much of a role RescueTime's blog has had in its success.

"I wouldn't say too much, though if you add all of our blogs into the mix, it might go up a touch," Tony replied. "For us, it's a valuable channel for announcements. Note that we also use Get Satisfaction, which we love for public, two-way conversations." As for why the blog covers developer issues rather than customer issues on occasion: "Mostly because our developers want to write about it sometimes. Our customer base is pretty developer heavy right now, so interesting tech stuff is a bit of a draw for that. Anything link-worthy is good (SEO, etc.)."

How does it work having five bloggers under one URL roof? "It's 95% me, though everyone is welcome to blog. We'll generally send out e-mail drafts."

And finally, what's his take on hosting his blog at `WordPress.com`? "We LOVE `wordpress.com`. It's not QUITE as customizable as we'd like, due to the hosted nature of it, but it makes up for it by not requiring any effort/maintenance."

Andy Wibbels, Six Apart

One of the most thoughtful bloggers on what blogging is all about is Andy Wibbels. Andy, now the product manager for `blogs.com` at Six Apart (the makers of TypePad), is the author of *Blogwild!: A Guide for Small Business* (Portfolio, 2006) and a clear and passionate advocate for blogging.

Although I've written extensively on blogging, I wanted to get Andy's take on blogging for startups, especially on how blogging and microblogging at sites such as Twitter interact.

Bob: Let's start with the big picture. What should startups understand about the strategic value of doing a blog today?

Andy: I think that the strategic value is how easily you can put stuff online. I always think about that with an online business, unless you can put stuff online quickly, you don't have a business. A blog is often the fastest and quickest way to simply get stuff online. I think that's kind of the foundation of it: quick publishing, cheap publishing, and just get it up and get it going. That is the foundation, for me, about why startups should be looking at blogs.

Another part of the puzzle is that it provides this inside view into a company. For a startup, a lot of times with the marketing PR, they want to convey this sense that the company or the project or the product is really something that's going to be new and fresh and exciting. It's coming from people who are innovators or have a particular cache of inventors.

So I think that is kind of the second part. The first part is getting stuff online quickly, the second part is providing this warmth and this depth that a larger company can't replicate easily. That can be a strategic advantage for a company.

Bob: One question that comes up nowadays for some people who are, let's say, on Twitter 18 times a day or 1,800 times a day . . .

Andy: Right.

Bob: . . . is do blogs really matter in a world of Twitter?

Andy: Well, I think that these are all part of a larger trend that some folks are calling the social web, or social publishing. We had a Facebook, we have Twitter. We have all of these different conduits, so we have these different media formats that have these little bits of information and pictures and text and video. And then we have all the connections between them. So I think that blogging is kind of nested inside all of these trends.

With Twitter, it's going to depend on if your audience, your future customers, the journalists that you want to reach, and the people who you want to track your company, are those people on Twitter? I think part of it is, is your audience even on Twitter yet? I think Twitter can take up a lot of your time every day, and I think the value of Twitter is really for networking and starting to get to know people who may be useful for your business, for future employees, for press coverage, and just gently introducing them to who the heck you are.

But I think it can definitely be a time sink for a lot of people, because it provides that quick hit of instant publishing that I think blogging grew away from, which is why we even have Twitter in the first place. Blogging used to be white box: type what you think and click Save. And then we added categories and rich text editor. And we have to add images and tags and permissions and themes and templates. I think the advantage of tools like Twitter and the new blogging platforms Posterous and Tumblr, they've really stripped blogging down back to a white box you throw stuff into.

Bob: So if Twitter is how we get ourselves out there, assuming that the people we want to talk to are on Twitter, is our blog then sort of the backbone of our online persona?

Andy: I think it can be. I think a blog is becoming a more useful place to have much more thoughtful essays that go beyond 140 characters, that go beyond "Oh, I found this cool thing. Here's a link to it," which is what blogging sort of started off as. A blog can still be an anchor for the rest of your world, because with a Twitter profile, you don't own that profile, Twitter does. You don't own your Facebook profile, Mark Zuckerberg does. You don't own all of these online profiles unless you own -- you don't have domain over those profiles. But if you anchor them all to your online identity on a blog or a web site, then you truly own all these different pieces of your online life.

I think that's going to be a big issue coming up, maybe sooner than later. I'm not really sure. People get a bit nutty about privacy and who owns their profiles. We just had that big bad crash with Facebook, where they said we can own your information, even after you've deleted your account. The users went crazy. So I think there is a privacy backlash brewing as people start to realize their exposure and how they don't own their online identities when it's owned by a service like Twitter or Facebook.

So I think a blog can still be the anchor for all these other parts of your online persona.

Bob: Let's talk about just the idea of a blog for your "product" at a startup. Should blogs really function in the role as basically places to flog your product?
Andy: They can. It will not be very popular. I think part of a company's blog is focused on "Yes, here's what we're working on," but also "Here are the greater trends that we're seeing." "Here is information that our customers need to know," whether or not it's linked to the product. So we all have customers that we reach and people that we touch every day. That may or may not be fine, boosting our products right then and there. But if we can become the authoritative voice, then when a customer or reader has a need that we can fill, he'll think of us and come grab our product or service. I think part of it is about cultivating intending.

A blog is not a place to constantly talk about only what you're working on. But it can be a place to say, "Here's what we're thinking of working on" or "You know, a year ago we had this experience, and, wow, did we learn from that."

So it's a way to show the expertise as well as become this authoritative voice on your particular segment of the market.

Bob: Do you have any preference as to whether you have "a company blog" that a variety of people write for or, let's say, each founder having his own blog? Is there an advantage to one or the other?
Andy: I waffle back and forth on that. Here we sort of have the slogan that it's about the blogger, not the blog. That all this social media stuff is about connecting individuals who have individual voices, who may work for companies. So if you've got a company blog, you could have multiple authors, and each of them could have a certain space on the blog or a certain archive or a certain way to communicate that this is this particular person's voice. But with a startup, if you've got a kind of rambunctious leader, and that's part of your marketing edge, that you're working with an innovator, somebody that's the hot, young innovator, or sort of the old guard coming back, then that's part of that particular story and that particular perspective. So you may keep that on a separate blog. And it's going to depend on if the blogger is going to stay totally on topic all the time.

That's why I have a personal blog and a professional blog, because I like to rant about crazy things, and I keep that off of the professional blog because it's just not stuff that businesspeople really want to read unless they think I'm worth reading about.

Bob: So I guess one of the things you're talking about is, first off, that you have a separation between your company and yourself, which is why we have companies, and to carry that division over to the online world.

Andy: Right. And this is part of, I think, the friction between personality and company, is if you're running a startup and are wanting to be seen as this on-the-go company that's creating brand new visions, then you may want your blog to be all you all the time, and how dedicated you are toward your service or product or company. So it's going to depend on the goals of the particular blog. I go back and forth on if it should be totally separate or totally together. I think it depends on the persona of the company that's putting out the blog.

Bob: Where does Six Apart fit in all this, now that we've reached a point of maturity of what blogs are about.

Andy: We are really seeing blogging, I guess in this overall social publishing, social web blanket or cloud, I guess, of trends, that people need to have the ability to publish anything to anyone anywhere and have full control over how that's going to appear. That's one reason why we've worked very hard on the OpenID standard, because that's kind of a way that people can continue to own their online identity.

We worked with a lot of large media companies; they're seeing this trend and saying, well, how do we build a community around a certain artist or a certain movie or a certain piece of entertainment? That dichotomy that we have at Six Apart is we have a services team that usually works with pretty large companies and pretty large organizations, and then we have been working with Moveable Type. The reason we launched a production called Motion that brings the idea of a friend and news feed, like the Facebook feed, and my microblogging into a product, into a blog that a company can own. So like I said, instead of having Facebook own all of your customer data, you can.

So large companies really get excited about that. And then on the flip side, toward individual bloggers, we are really retooling what TypePad can do and TypePad is. So it can integrate with all these new services and new products and new ways of publishing online. They can connect Twitter and Facebook, and it can reach out to all these other services that didn't exist a couple of years ago.

We also have launched a media division that is focusing on developing these bloggers and these publishers. So we're able to serve the large companies that want to reach out to these bloggers, but also we work on publisher development, which is just fancy speak for we help bloggers cultivate their audience and their blogs.

And also I guess a footnote is we're trying to go beyond just servicing people on Six Apart platforms. Part of what I 'm working with is a new service called TypePad One, which is going to be growing past training and services just for TypePad users, and how we can help people using WordPress or Blogger or Tumblr. How can we help all the bloggers out there? So, yes, of course we would love for them to be in our media program and to use our products. But at the base, we remain an advocate for blogging in all of its formats and social publishing in all of its formats.

Bob: OK. Any final advice that you would give people who want to go from being a developer to being a startup founder when it comes to social media?

Andy: I think it can be a very different mindset. If you're an engineer, you may be very focused on the things that are shiny and cool to you. And sometimes I find myself reflecting on a lot during meetings about our products or developments or features, who is this product for? And if you can, keep asking yourself who are you really making something for? I know here in the Silicon Valley area, I see—I came from Chicago about a year ago, so I feel like there's kind of a disconnect between what Silicon Valley people think users do and the rest of the population does online and then what I call real people do online. I think there's a lot of friction between—you have to recognize that not everybody lives online all the time, and they don't see that as something that they really want to do.

So I think with software developing and technology development, it's really asking, "Who are you developing for?" Is it the early adopters, is it real people, is it people who watch network TV or cable TV, and having a pretty good idea of who you're serving and what their problems are. And how you help solve those problems better than anybody else, I think, is pretty valuable.

To sum up our discussion of startup blogs, this is something that should be at the very top of your nondevelopment to-do list, from before you launch. The key thing is that your blog isn't about you and your startup; it's about your customers and potential customers who are paying you extremely valuable attention. You'll need to work hard for that attention, but, as we've seen, the payoffs of doing your startup's blog right are huge.

Welcome to the Land of Twitter

Unless you've been locked in your basement with a pallet of Meals Ready to Eat, a chemical toilet, and your codebase for the past few years, you've heard about Twitter, the microblogging platform without a revenue model.[4]

If you've stoutly resisted—like Joel Spolsky,[5] for example—this giant timewaster on the grounds that it doesn't matter to your startup if a few

---

[4] As of May 17, 2009—but that will change, just as soon as it drives all the mainstream media nuts that one of the most popular and newsworthy startups doesn't have a revenue model!

[5] Now at http://twitter.com/spolsky with 7,925 followers, and counting.

hundred people know what you had for breakfast, then for a start let me refer you to my and Nicole Kristen's *The Twitter Survival Guide* e-book, available at `http://multisocialmedia.com`.

For everyone else, let's get specific about why you want to be on Twitter as a startup, why, in fact, you *need* to be on Twitter. It's not just that Twitter has taken off—adding 6 million users in just January and February 2009 alone—or that its demographics are shifting past the traditional early adopters of social media.[6] It's that Twitter can bring your startup sales. But it's *not* going to do it in a traditionally measurable way (spend *x* on advertising, get *y* customers). Social media doesn't work by herding cattle.

Consider Giacomo "Peldi" Guilizzoni's experience with Twitter. He's the founder of Balsamiq Studios, LLC, a self-funded startup that sells a great mockup/wireframing application that had already become profitable enough in its first six months to hire its first employee.

"My use of Twitter has evolved over time (`http://www.balsamiq.com/blog/?p=1025`)," Peldi e-mailed back from Italy. "At first I used it mostly as a way to announce new features and blog posts . . . microblogging, if you will.

"Then I read your book on Twitter and it opened my eyes. I was doing it all wrong! Now I see Twitter as a way to stay close to the community of my product's users and customers. I use it to answer their questions, ask them for feedback early in the design process, ask them for recommendations on products or services to use . . . it's a wonderful group of people sharing my company's shared interests. I also try to retweet as much as I can, to provide value to my followers. Thanks to TwitterSheep [`http://twittersheep.com`], I know what their interests are, so I can cater my tweets to them."

Does the time Peldi spends on Twitter translate into sales for his startup?

"I don't really know, but I'm sure it doesn't hurt. Twitter is definitely one of my top referral web sites, and I know people appreciate being able to reach me via Twitter when they need to. It's like IM, but in the open, which makes me more accountable. I like that."

Figure 6-9 illustrates one specific case of how Twitter can improve your startup's reputation: It shows a tweet that Joel Spolsky (highly influential ex-Twitter hater and one of our wise people interviewed in Chapter 9) posted about Balsamiq Mockups. This is the kind of positive mention you dream about as a founder.

---

[6] *"Twitter Traffic Explodes . . . and Not Being Driven by the Usual Suspects!"*—`http://www.comscore.com/blog/2009/04/twitter_traffic_explodes.html`

Figure 6-9. You can only wish your startup was this lucky.

The bottom line on Twitter for startups is simply this: Whether or not you participate, people are going to be tweeting about your startup and its service or product. You have their attention—ignoring them by not talking to them is a crazy bad idea for any startup.

The New News Media

Let's turn our attention to another, older part of what gets people talking about a startup: it's in the news. Maybe it makes CNN or a major newspaper or maybe it gets favorable coverage in one of the leading technology news blogs that have readerships now surpassing major mainstream media news outlets, but getting press attention can make or break your startup.

Having been a full-time reporter for a major news organization (United Press International) before succumbing a very long time ago to the siren call of technology, and having written over the last few years for Lifehacker.org (http://lifehacker.com), Web Worker Daily (http://webworkerdaily.com), and CNET Webware (http://news.cnet.com/webware), I've seen and continue to see more press releases than I care to remember. They suck!

Something like 95% of the time startups get it wrong when trying to get media attention. They—or their PR agency—e-mail blast every reporter on earth with the shattering non-news that they've moved from version 3.21 to 3.22 and that humanity is far better for it. Or those same, mostly brain-dead PR people whine and beg that you're life as a news blogger is simply not complete without spending at least an hour of a workday engaged in valuable virtual face time with the CEO, who will repeat the marketing message verbatim to you.

If it sounds like I have some very definite opinions about this, you're right. But my opinions aren't going to give you what you need in order to be in that 5% who win the media attention lottery. For that, if you want to know how your startup can get media attention, go ask them. That's what this section is all about: how online and mainstream editors, writers, and reporters decide what startups to cover and which to ignore.

First up, I talked to a friend of mine, Mike Gunderloy. Mike is an accomplished software developer, news blogger, and book author who up until recently was the lead writer for one of the major startup-covering news blogs: Web Worker Daily. I've known Mike over the years and also worked with him for a time as WWD writer; but for every post I'd do, Mike would crank out 10 (and they were way better) and still keep his programming contract clients happy and coming back for more. We did this interview via IM.[7]

Bob: When you were lead writer at Web Worker Daily, what was the right way to pitch a story to you, and what were the wrong ways? Besides always starting with an e-mail, what did you look for in a pitch?

Mike: Had to have some relevance to the readers, of course. Let's see: I threw pitches away for a bunch of reasons: more than one follow-up (if I'm not interested, I'm not interested), lack of any evidence that the pr person had done any research on us (i.e., getting pitched on stuff we'd already covered), didn't get to the point quickly, expected me to go online or call or get to a conference or listen to a briefing before I knew whether I was interested.

Bob: All good to know. So if a startup wanted to pitch a story to you, they'd better do their research, get to the point, not angle for you to talk to their CEO or do a demo before they knew you're interested and not to pester you?

Mike: Yup. Send over the basic facts, and let me decide whether it's worth following up on, and "XYZ signs 478th user" or "Big Company buys license for XYZ" is not newsworthy. Too many invented excuses for sending out the release of the week, even though no changes in the product.

---

[7] *If you don't use IM as part of your social media mix, you're missing out. Check out Adium if you're OS in life is Mac (http://adium.im/) or Pidgin (http://www.pidgin.im) if it's not.*

Bob: Gotcha. Were there any PR people you thought got it right?

Mike: Probably, but I don't remember PR people by name. I probably got 90% of my leads from my own research, rather than being pitched, even though I was reading 50+ releases per day for a while there.

Bob: How did you/do you do your research? Five hundred RSS feeds?

Mike: Mainly. RSS feeds, a few newsletters, Twitter mentions. Sites like MOMB too.

Bob: MOMB?

Mike: Museum of Modern Betas [http://momb.socio-kybernetics. net].

Bob: Aha—another add for the book!

Mike: Their RSS feed is pretty high quality for web apps. There are a few others similar: KillerStartups, Listio, SimpleSpark.

Bob: For startups doing their own PR, should they try to build relationships with writers or not?

Mike: I'm sure there are **some** writers that works with. But I'm not one of them. I suspect it works better with the sites that are on the "We must cover everything first" treadmill.

Bob: Besides your WWD work and other writing, you run a news site of sorts, A Fresh Cup, for the Ruby on Rails community. Why, and has it opened up any opportunities for you?

Mike: I'm a believer that one way to find clients is to be visible in multiple places. So I've got AFC, an active Twitter account, a professional site, all the stuff I do for Rails . . . it all adds up. People know I'm out there, they can recommend me.

Plus, for me AFC serves the same purpose as Delicious bookmarks do for some people—a long list of stuff I might want to get back to someday. Seems to serve the same purpose for some other folks too, which is nice.

Bob: While you're not doing a startup, you've found a solution to the problem they have: getting attention in a very noisy world. If a startup has solid expertise in a given technology or industry, would you as a writer be impressed if they were sharing that online actively?

Mike: Well, I'd be more likely to keep an eye on them if they were writing stuff about a technology I care about. There is a batch of rails startups— pivotal, exceptional, etc.—that I end up keeping track of because one of their devs is blogging

Bob: Any final advice for startups?

Mikes: You're better off getting noticed for something useful than for stunts—in today's world, I don't think stuff like tradeshow giveaways or imprinted pens or whatever is as important as having an authentic online presence.

Marshall Kirkpatrick, Lead Writer, ReadWriteWeb

Marshall Kirkpatrick broke into the news-blogging business at *TechCrunch*, fast becoming the lead blogger there before moving on to *ReadWriteWeb* as that blog's lead blogger and VP for content development.

Marshall's based in Portland, Oregon, far from Silicon Valley, but his virtuoso RSS/Web 2.0 research skills let him consistently leave more connected newspeople in his dust.

Bob: What's the right way for startups to approach you who want you to write about them? What's the wrong way?

Marshall: Sending an email to tips@readwriteweb.com at any time is appropriate. Sending your company's blog or news release RSS feed is the best way to keep us in the loop. Otherwise, we like to get an e-mail three or four days before a news event. Send us info about what you're doing, login access to see it, and contact info to reach out with any questions. If we can get the full picture without a briefing (we're pretty good at looking at startups), then that's great.

We don't appreciate it when a company expects an hour of our time to ramble on the phone in order for us to find out what they are doing.

Bob: Do you prefer hearing from startup founders or PR people working for startups?

Marshall: People working for them, especially not salespeople. Talking to engineers is ideal. If we must talk to a CEO or salesperson, though, we'll live.

Bob: How many startups do you hear about in a week? How do you decide what to write about?

Marshall: It's hard to say, probably about 200. We're looking for a news hook and an innovation hook. We're much more interested in the tech of tech than in the business of tech.

Bob: What mistakes do startups make approaching news bloggers and for that matter regular trade/general reporters?

Marshall: Don't send us an e-mail with a link to our competitors' coverage of you—that drives us nuts. Also, tell us honestly what you are doing, quickly, and if we say no—accept that and come back later with something better suited for us.

Bob: Any advice for startup founders?

Marshall: Please give me really interesting stories about innovation so I can make us both look great. Try not to neglect your families, too. That's just a bad thing to do.

Bob: What question should I ask that I haven't?

Marshall: Q: Do you think this is a wildly disruptive time in technology that we're living through? A: Yes I do, it's very exciting. The possibilities are mind-blowing, and the ISV community is really at the forefront of it. Keep up the great work out there!

The Editor Is In

Let's move up the new food chain in our search for getting your startup star power attention: Rafe Needleman has been covering startups and technology for a good 20 years for InfoWorld, Byte, Red Herring, Business 2.0, and, since 2004, CNET. He's the editor in charge of CNET's Webware blog (http://news.cnet.com/webware) (See Figure 6-10.). Webware is one of the top news blogs, and now that CBS owns CNET, coverage of a startup at Webware has a huge reach.

Figure 6-10. CNET Webware

Rafe's both a writer and the managing editor of Webware: setting the tone, managing about a dozen CNET and freelance bloggers, and deciding what gets covered.

Bob: What would be your dream day, as far as the startups that you would see and how they came to you? In other words, what should a startup be doing that's smart, rather than some of the less intelligent approaches that you've seen?

Rafe: Well, you know it's the product that matters. When I hear about a new product ahead of anybody else in a way that makes me sit up and take notice, that's good. I love hearing from people who are passionate about a product, and that's generally a founder or CEO of a company. That's ideal.

Bob: Is it better if they talk to you directly? What about the various PR firms that are out there that get into the mix?

Rafe: I think PR has a lot of value. There are some PR people who I really do like to hear from. But, like I said, when I get a personal pitch from somebody who's actually built a product and wants to talk to me about it, that means more to me than getting what I know is probably a pitch that's going out to 100 people or more at the same time.

Bob: Should these CEOs of startups introduce themselves before they have something really to say? Or should they just knock on your door when they're ready?

Rafe: Well, *ready* is a relative term. I like talking to companies at all stages, and the earlier the better. If we're going to be reviewing a product, then of course the product should be something that's in a reviewable state and something that's close to availability. But when is the right time to talk to me depends on the company, the technology, what they're trying to do, and what I'm trying to write about.

Bob: What sort of things do you like to hear about? Is there any particular type of startups that will really get your attention?

Rafe: Well, if I knew that, I would be building it myself.

Bob: [laughs]

Rafe: I'm always looking to have my eyes opened.

Bob: So it's sort of the new and novel and different effect that matters? Is it harder to generate much excitement over yet another CRM system?

Rafe: Fair to say, yeah. Difficult, but there is innovation in every category. It's possible to knock my socks off with a CRM. It's also quite likely that there is a product that you might think that I would find tedious. Then three people who are unaware of each other are announcing similar things at the same time, and boom! I've got a trend. Now it's interesting.

Bob: Where do you find new things to write about? Besides the people coming to you, where do you go look for them?

Rafe: I have a pretty extensive collection of contacts, entrepreneurs, investors, and funders. You'd be surprised how many readers reach out to me saying that they've seen something. I scour a lot of sources, a lot of feeds, and a lot of aggregation sites. I go to events and parties. This stuff comes in all the time from everywhere.

Bob: Do you find that Twitter is a useful way for people to contact you? Or is that not a good way to try to pitch you on a story idea?

Rafe: No. I don't like Twitter as a way to try to contact me for a pitch. I don't think it's very effective for that. I like to control my incoming information through e-mail, just because it's easier to file, keep track of, and respond to. However, I find Twitter extremely valuable as a way to reach out to people en masse. I monitor Twitter all the time. When there's an interesting trend or something that's very timely, I set up a filter in Twitter—a search field—and I watch to see what's happening there. So I find Twitter extremely valuable.

I do get a lot of tips from it, and I do get a lot of feedback from it, from readers and things. But I don't think it's appropriate to pitch someone. Well, it's not appropriate to pitch *me* on Twitter. Other people do like it. I don't.

Bob: How about Facebook?

Rafe: Well, you know I'm not very active on Facebook, except through Twitter. My Twitter feed goes into Facebook, and I see a lot of replies to it on Facebook. But I'm not particularly active on Facebook. People do, occasionally, pitch me on Facebook, which is a really bad idea. I don't like being pitched on Facebook, because it's not in my e-mail system.

Bob: These are good things to know. A while back, you put together a blog, and actually it continues to this day, Pro PR Tips [http://proprtips.com]. Why do you do this?

Rafe: [laughs] Because it's fun. Honestly, I like what I do, and I find it sometimes amusing, the bonehead moves that PR people make in trying to get their story out. I don't think that PR people are evil. I don't think they're stupid. But every now and then, somebody makes an interesting blunder. I thought it would be both funny and educational to chronicle it as it went. I'm going to do more with Pro PR Tips in the future, because I think it's a good way to get the word out and for everybody to learn.

Bob: You've been in the journalism business now for a long time. Has what PR firms done changed that much in the last few years? Or is it pretty much what they've been doing all along?

Rafe: The fundamentals of public relations and of any kind of communications have not changed, which is this: The best way to communicate with somebody is to know them and to tell them something that is personally relevant to them, either because it's something that they find personally interesting or because it's related to the work that they do. Everybody does different work. So the blanket pitch is generally pretty ineffective, except when it's not. Except when you're Google or Microsoft, and you have a story that you want to tell to everybody at the same time.

The tools and the technologies have made a big difference, as witnessed by your questions when you were asking me about people trying to reach me on Twitter or Facebook.

The ways to get a hold of people, the number of people who are trying to get a hold of people, and the number of people who are there to be got hold of have all increased dramatically. There is a lot of noise, and there's a lot of information flying around.

The fundamentals are the direct connection. When Joe, the entrepreneur, says, "Hey, I've got this incredible, cool new product, new web service that will automatically make your food taste better at restaurants," I'm going to pay attention. He sends it to me, and he says, "I know that you like eating, let me show this to you before anybody else," I'm going to notice. That has not changed.

Bob: So that really comes under the heading of PR firms that know what interests journalists.

Rafe: Yeah. I think there's a big value in PR. I think that some companies overuse it and use PR as their mouthpieces. I don't always think that's wise. Sometimes it is, but in many cases it's not. Most companies trying to get noticed could use professional PR counsel. That doesn't mean that they should give the PR company the microphone and have them speak on their behalf. The demo and the pitch are always more effective coming from the person who built the product, the person who started the company, or the person who's passionate about it.

How that person gets in touch with people, how he crafts his message, and who he talks to, that is advice that a PR person can give them. But, it doesn't mean that the PR person has to be front and center in the communications, in the dialogue.

Bob: So you see more of the value PR people as advisors rather than mouthpieces.

Rafe: Yes, although I'm talking about in an ideal world. I realize that it isn't.

Bob: OK, any advice to startups?

Rafe: Yeah. My best advice for startups is to build a good product and don't fall back on PR to make a sucky product good. If the product is good, then you need good PR to support it. If the product is not good, no amount of PR is going to make it succeed. The journalists will find out. The bloggers will find out. People will find out, and the product will die. If the product is good, you want it to get out to as many people as possible.

Al Harberg, President, DP Directory, Inc.

Press releases are part and parcel of any company's effort to be in the public eye, and for nearly 25 years Al Harberg has been in the business of creating effective press releases. Al's company, DP Directory, specializes in creating and distributing press releases for software/IT companies, so I asked him a few questions about the realities and mechanics of doing good press releases.

Bob: How effective are wholesale press releases?

Al: Sending well-written press releases to well-targeted editors has been a cost-effective publicity tactic for nearly a century. And it continues to be effective today.

Millions of software buyers make their software-buying decisions based on what they read in magazines and newspapers. And these publications' editors continue to rely upon press releases to learn about the latest computer software.

I'm not sure what you mean by "wholesale" press releases, Bob. There are some awful services available on the Internet. These services blindly send poorly written so-called press releases to magazine writers and columnists, regardless of these editors' "beats" or specialties. They often mass-mail the press releases using bcc: or "undisclosed recipient" lists, giving the editors the impression that they've been spammed. Using such a service is a waste of time and money, and it can damage your reputation with the editors.

Make sure the person who writes your press release is an experienced marketing professional. If that's not in your budget, be sure the company that e-mails your press releases to the editors is run by an experienced marketing professional who will take the time to review your press release for you, free. My company, DP Directory, Inc. (http://www.dpdirectory.com), reviews our customers' press releases before we send them to the editors. We correct our clients' grammar, usage, and agreement errors, and we "Americanize" their writing, free. From the editors' perspective, they're receiving an individual e-mail from the developer and not a mass-mailed spam.

We offer more than 100 categories of editors for software developers, ensuring that each press release is sent to well-targeted publications.

Again, the two keys to success are a well-written press release and a list that is targeted to editors in your niche.

Bob: Are press releases as effective today as they were, say, a decade ago?
Al: There have been a lot of changes in the press release business since I started full time more than 24 years ago.

The Internet has changed the method of delivery from postal mail to e-mail.

The biggest change, however, has been the economic stress that has been placed on magazines and newspapers. For the past two decades, these publi-cations have been under tremendous pressure from cable news and enter-tainment and from the Internet. Readership is down for both magazines and newspapers as people turn on their TVs and computers for information and relaxation.

In general, this is good news for software developers. Editors simply don't have time to do market research, investigative reporting, or any in-depth work to uncover the newest software. They rely more and more upon software developers' press releases to learn about new applications.

The other big change in the marketplace in recent years has been the addition of computer reporters to smaller newspapers. Twenty years ago, computers were expensive and complicated. Today, even the smallest business has multiple computers, and most homes have more than one machine, too. To respond to this proliferation of technology, small-town newspapers and general-interest magazines have reporters who cover the computer beat. More dedicated computer editors means more opportunities for software developers to use press releases to get free publicity.

Bob: Have you expanded your lists to include tech blogs? And are bloggers more or less likely to use a press release?

Al: Many computer magazine editors write blogs. Similarly, many newspapers now have tech blogs. I include these bloggers in my press release distribution lists.

There are quite a few bloggers who welcome press releases from distribution services like mine—services that ensure that only well-written New Product Announcements are sent. These bloggers are on my list.

Some bloggers have a narrow focus for their writing, and they don't enjoy receiving press releases that are about software that is not in their particular niche. They only want to hear from software developers whose applications are a perfect match for their blogs. So the best way for software developers to reach these specialized bloggers is to develop a "house list" and contact these bloggers individually and personally.

So Is the Reporter

I've known Leslie Suzukamo, a *St. Paul Pioneer Press* reporter on telecom, technology, and energy, since we bumped into each other heading for UCLA's *Daily Bruin* many, many years ago. I got out of journalism, he stayed in. That he's still a reporter in today's era of shriveling newspapers is proof positive he works five times harder than most people. I asked Les to spill the beans on exactly how he picks and chooses what to cover.

  Bob: What's the best way for startups to pitch reporters today? Formal press release, e-mail you, call?

  Les: You know all this anyway, but for what it's worth . . . We are, for better and for worse, tied to our e-mail now, the way reporters a generation ago were tied to the phone. Formal press release [paper, I assume] is too slow for daily work and usually means it's not urgent. If it can wait and you want something thoughtful, there's still a place for paper. But that place is rapidly shrinking because so many newspaper reporters are doubling (or, in my case, tripling) up on beats. Calls are OK, but I usually tell them to send me an e-mail anyway. Calls work best after an e-mail, but they tell me something that brings it into immediate focus. The newsroom is an ADHD environment, and if we sound gruff and impatient on the line, it's because we've got one of those Indiana Jones–size rocks rolling behind us. It's called *deadline*. Get to the point, be knowledgeable enough to answer a few questions in more detail than you've done in the press release (I hate it when I get PR people who obviously don't know anything beyond what they've already written you—it's like talking to a parrot), and don't call in the late afternoon or whenever it's deadline (I say that because web operations and TV have their own separate sets of deadlines).

Bob: What do you want to know from companies pitching you? What do you not want to hear about?

Les: I want to know about something that would surprise people, something I didn't know (and people in general don't know), something that matters to people, or something that would startle them. I want a good story—and that's where the problem lies. PR folks are looking to tell me how wonderful their company is. Most of the time, the average person. Just. Doesn't. Care. Doesn't mean the company isn't wonderful, but they don't care. On the other hand, the average person cares mightily about something that affects them or their lives directly. So if it involves layoffs from their company, they care. If it involves a CEO's getting a million-dollar bonus while everyone else took a pay cut, they care. They care more than ever about companies behaving badly. They care about good companies taking care of their employees too, but it's got to be newsworthy, like that banker in Florida who cashed out when he retired, and, rather than just keeping the money, he spread the wealth among all his bank's employees, even the ones who had retired. It's got to have drama and conflict and, hopefully, resolution, but certainly the first two. Companies doing PR hate the idea of drama and conflict because it implies trouble. But people know that life is trouble. It insults their intelligence to pretend otherwise.

Bob: Are their any PR people you know who do a really good job for their clients in your estimation? If so, how?

Les: There are a few that I know and work with regularly. One—they don't waste my time much with stuff that doesn't matter. They know me, know my paper, so they know what we like and what we ignore. They answer my calls, even when it's bad news, especially when it's bad news. A couple have taken the bullet for not just their companies but for their entire industries, and their counterparts are laying low and refusing to return my calls. I give those bullet-takers respect back when it counts. I sometimes think their companies don't get that, though. Which is a shame.

Bob: Should a startup contact their local mainstream media newspaper, news blog? Does being local count?

Les: Can't speak about others, but for us, local is the first, second, and third reason we do stories about companies. If you're not local, there'd better be a good overarching reason for the story, like you represent a service that is ubiquitous. My best example of that would be cell phone service. None of the majors are local, but everyone has a cell phone, so they're always high-reader-interest stories. Ditto with cable (though I focus on Comcast because it is the dominant cable provider for Minnesota) and home phone service (Qwest Communications International, of Denver, dominant phone provider in the state). For startups, local newspapers or news outlets of any kind are a good place to start. News blogs aren't necessarily local, but that's an emerging forum for publicity, as you well know. Get the right blogs behind you, and you can leverage for better positioning with bigger blogs, etc. Know who you want to reach too. Too often I get releases that are written as a one-size-fits-all and is mainly for the tech press or the trades. They're dense, hard to read, and, for me, anyway, a waste of time. If you want to reach a trade audience, go for that and don't waste my time. And vice versa. I imagine that something I'm interested in may not be of much use to something like, say, Light Reading, or Heavy Reading, to name two trade sites that do a lot on the telecom world.

Bob: How do you find startups to write about?

Les: I look at press releases, I pay attention to the blogs like *TechCrunch* and *VentureBeat*, I use my powers of mental telepathy, read the tarot, and scrutinize chicken entrails. Seriously, this is one of the few areas where PR actually helps a lot. Because I can't read minds and unless someone I know tips me off, I'll have no clue you're out there. We welcome tips—the juicier the better. If you want to really be my friend, tip me off about juicy things that maybe don't involve your company directly but are in your sphere of knowledge. Get me interested. Make yourself memorable, and I may have more time to spend with you trying to figure out if there's an interesting story to dig out from your company. Many times, I've found that the most interesting thing an executive says is as I'm getting up to leave. Often, he doesn't know it's that interesting because it's around him all the time so much that it becomes like wallpaper—you don't see it anymore. But for the outsider, like me or the reader, it's a fascinating glimpse into another world.

Bob: Any advice for startups?

Les: See above. And don't get discouraged. I often don't write about startups right away because I want to see if they make it past the first year. It's a way to reality-check the business. But I save a lot of press releases by creating e-mail folders in Outlook so I don't forget who they are a year later if or when they call back to remind me that they're still alive. That's another reason why e-mail is so important, for me, anyway. It is my electronic memory. (My IT guys hate me, though, because I'm one of the top three users of network space. Can't say I blame them either, but it's the way I work.)

Luke Armour, PR Coordinator, blogtalkradio.com

Luke Armour is a PR blogger and podcaster and the PR coordinator for BlogTalkRadio, the first citizen broadcasting network built on a web-based platform. It allows any user with a phone and a computer to host a live, interactive Internet radio show; and it is the home of Cinch, the simplest podcasting tool ever. He can be reached at LukeArmour@blogtalkradio.com.

I ran into Luke when, as a writer for *Web Worker Daily,* I got his press release for BlogTalkRadio. I was so impressed with how he crafted that PR that I asked him if he'd share some of his expertise at my blog, 47hats.com and now this book. Here's Luke's post.

Luke Armour's Post

So you've got a killer app. Now what?

I guess the first thing would be to tell someone, right? Right. But shouting out the window and e-mailing every e-mail address you can find on the Internet are not likely your best options. What are your best options? First I'm going to assume that what you've got is worth having. If what you're shilling isn't new or newsworthy (to someone other than you), go back to the drawing board. I mean it.

As a MicroISV your goal is to get your products into the hands—and minds—of those who can best use it, best share it with others, or both. To do that, you must (1) pitch the story of your product to the (2) right people (3) in the proper manner. Your target audience might include a high-profile blogger, an online news site, or a tech reporter for a print publication.

Remember, you are competing with hundreds of other people and thousands of other messages. And while a great, attractive product will speak for itself, getting it into the hands of the proper people will really help spread the word. When BlogTalkRadio unveiled Cinch, it was referred to as "the simplest podcast API ever." Word spread quickly, especially when we released some additional developments and told a handful of relevant people.

You may only get one shot at cutting through the clutter and reaching the eyes of your audience until the next update, product, or service—so do it right. Let's talk about sending a quick pitch e-mail to introduce yourself and your product. Since any good outreach begins with understanding your target audience, let's start there.

Tailored/Relevant

Great outreach begins with a relationship, but we don't always have that association to the media or the end users we need to reach. Without that connection, you first need to make sure what you're offering is of interest. Every new name in the e-mail inbox is a potential groan-and-delete for the media. Save yourself the bridge-burning and e-mail the right people.

Doing a little bit of homework on each outlet or reporter is essential. That reporter who covers the education beat? Probably not your best bet unless you can make the connection. That mommy blogger? Probably not, but that social media marketing guy who loves the newest tools might be a good bet. Be creative and be energetic, but don't be unrealistic.

Laziness is probably the biggest culprit here. You've compiled a list of e-mail addresses. Why not just send the note to them all? Because that's why we don't open 85% of our postal mail—it's junk. Only, it's a lot easier to block an e-mail address than to move, so take the time to make sure the outlet is suitable. Draw that connection between them and your offering if you have to.

Concise

As Bob Walsh notes in his book *MicroISV Sites that Sell!* a big mistake with many sites is "drowning your visitor with words." That same principle can be said with any pitch letter. Brevity is your friend. Introduce your product and call the readers to action. That's it.

Do not tell them everything there is to know about your product or service; your goal is to get them to want more information. At that point you can sell it to them in person, by offering more information or by welcoming them to the site for a trial. Mark Twain said, "I didn't have time to write a short letter, so I wrote a long one instead." Writing succinctly is difficult because it takes time and energy to write short, tight sentences. Strip out the unnecessary and get to the core of your message as quickly as possible.

Keep *relevant* and *concise* in mind before you even sit down at the computer.

Now let's focus on how to craft your message. A good pitch letter should do two things: indicate your credibility and provide benefits to your audience.

Credibility

"Who are you, and what reason do I have to believe anything you say?" This can be done easily with a few relevant facts or statistics. For BlogTalkRadio, I've written:

The site was launched in August 2006, redesigned with social-networking components in September 2007, and released from Beta in November 2007. Today, over 66,000 shows have been streamed from the BlogTalkRadio site. January logged 2.4 million listeners across the site, a 40% increase in listeners since the site came out of Beta.

That demonstrates that we've been around, that hosts and listeners are using us, and that we're growing. I did all that in three sentences.

Think Benefits, Not Features

Remember, end users aren't interested in how many buttons something has; they're interested in how it makes their lives better. Even if you're writing to the media, always keep your end user in mind. For example:

BlogTalkRadio allows anyone—worldwide—to host his or her own talk radio show with just a phone and computer. It's completely web-based, so there are no downloads and no recording equipment to buy, which makes it a perfect business or personal tool for today's online enthusiast, like your readers. Want to talk politics? Cover your favorite sports beat? Rant and rave about today's headlines or celebrity gossip? Now you can, from the comfort of your home—for free.

And then know when to stop (remember *concise?*). No one knows your product like you do, but you've got to stick to the core message in this initial pitch e-mail. And the core can change with each message, because each e-mail is relevant to the receiver of the e-mail.

Call to Action

At the end you must call the reader to action with a simple way to get more information and an incentive to do so. From "Drop me a line if you'd like more information" to "Contact me today for a free 30-day trial," you must prod them to act. Watch some late-night infomercials for more examples.

Subject Line

All of these tips won't mean anything unless someone actually opens the e-mail. Fortunately, these same guidelines apply to your subject line, which itself is a mini-pitch. It should be short, relevant, and catchy. Your subject line teases the pitch e-mail, which teases what you really want to say on your site or on the phone. Write for the end user.

Conclusion

So do your homework and make it relevant to your audience. Keep it concise with your core information, facts, and why this person should care. Finish with a call to action, and wrap it in a punchy subject line.

Be creative. Media and end users often don't even know they want your product yet. Follow up a week or so later with a second e-mail that includes an additional feature or core message. If they say "not interested," thank them for their time and move on. But don't count them out for version 2.0 or that other application you're tinkering with.

For more information about public relations, Brian Solis has a free eBook called *PR Tips for Startups* that provides a great introduction to approaching PR. It's a must-read.

Good luck and good pitching.

Startup PR the Right Way

So what's the bottom line takeaway from the five people we've just covered about how a startup can "generate media buzz"? Here's what I see.

1. Take the time to get to know the reporter or blogger you're trying to reach. If you don't, your chances of getting anywhere approximate zero.

2. News—something interesting, surprising, worth readers' attention because they're interested in it, not because you want them to be—is a must-have. Don't waste your time churning out PR about moving from 2.31 to 2.32. Instead, find a customer who's using your product in a surprising or moving way, a really new feature or feature set, or stats that surprise or at least intrigue.

3. Get right to the point. Zero fluff. Don't try to do their job for them—give them facts with which they can work.

4. If writing doesn't come easily to you, accept that, hire a pro, and tell that professional what news you want to release.

5. If you're funded, it's worth the outlay to hire a PR agency that focuses on building relationships with both the press and bloggers to whom your customers pay attention. But if you just hand off PR to them, you may see a lot of press releases but not much value.

6. Be cheerful and upbeat, and have a thick, thick skin. You are going to be told no a lot more than yes; your job is to first make sure you don't provoke a "Hell, no!" by angering the reporter or blogger. And keep swinging your bat at the ball.

Your Other Title: Chief Community Officer

So far we've covered blogs, Twitter, and getting in the news, both online and off. I haven't even touched on Facebook, MySpace, Hi5, Ning's network of over a hundred thousand social networks, all of the specialized social networks (such as StartupToDo.com—I couldn't resist), all of the other microblogging startups, such as Posterous and Identica, let alone how every major online company from Amazon to Google is adding more and more social media features. My poor bleeding fingers! Let's step back and look at where all this is heading and what that means for your startup.

What it all comes down to, as I said at the beginning of this chapter, is that you'll need to fulfill a whole new role if you want your startup to succeed: *chief community officer* (CCO). Just as there was a time when there was no such box on a corporate organization chart as *chief technology officer,* because technology wasn't critical, you are seeing more and more

CCOs, more community managers, popping up at companies that recognize the value and importance of social media.

So what does a community manager or CCO do? Blogs. Twitter. Facebook. GetSatisfaction.com and UserVoice.com. Podcasts. All that social media work that needs to land on someone's desk if it's going to get done and get done right. Add it all up, and it's easily a full-time job that's critical to a startup from day 1. And that means either you need a partner who's going to make this rock, or you've some rocky times ahead.

Speaking of getting it all done right, let's talk to three of these community managers in the wild.

Ginevra Whalen, TypePad Community Manager, Six Apart

Ginevra Whalen (@miz_ginevra and http://ginevra.typepad.com) is the community manager for Six Apart's flagship product, the TypePad blogging service. I heard about her both from other Six Apart employees and on Twitter as the go-to person if you needed help from that company (Figure 6-11).

Figure 6-11. Six Apart's Ginevra Whalen

Bob: So what do you do as TypePad's community manager?

Ginevra: I do a lot of things! Mostly, I invest a lot of time and effort into building up a positive community around our products. I do the one-to-many communication via our Everything TypePad blog and one-to-one communication via Twitter, Facebook, Get Satisfaction, and many other social media channels.

Bob: What social networks do you monitor, and how?

Ginevra: Facebook, Twitter, Get Satisfaction, Yahoo Answers, and the blogosphere. I've got a complicated tangle of RSS feeds/searches that I run to see who is saying what about who. I usually reach out to customers with issues individually, and if the problem is more widespread, then I know to address it publically.

Bob: Is being a community manager more than just reacting to the negative comments people make about Six Apart online?

Ginevra: Yes, of course it is. Reacting to negative comments isn't even how I'd term it; it's listening to feedback and turning it into something useful and actionable. I see community management as the future of marketing and customer service. People really want the products they care enough to spend money on to have a responsive, personal, personable voice to speak with them like humans.

I think this is a result of a lot of innovation in the space, but also a reaction to the endless phone-tree runaround frustration people experience. I have a far better time talking with @comcastcares on Twitter than I do simply punching numbers into the phone. The connection is more valuable because of the human interaction.

Bob: Do you ever find yourself in the role of customer advocate? How's that worked out?

Ginevra: Yes! I frequently call myself "our most annoying customer." :) I've been using TypePad for five years, and I use it daily for our blogs, so I really do feel all the same delights and pain points as our customers do.

Bob: Given how much social media has grown in the last few years, should a startup seek out someone like you to be their community manager? Where should they look?

Ginevra: I grew my experience and aptitude for this by working in restaurants, actually. It's a very similar personality type! When I was a bartender, I ran into so many people all day long that I was invariably fascinated by their stories and how to help them solve problems. Not all bartenders are this way, of course. There's something one of our bloggers wrote that was very smart called "the service heart" that I think sums it up: http://www.happiness-project.com/happiness_project/2007/07/the-happiness-o.html

Bob: Any social media advice to share with startups?

Ginevra: Be interested. Be genuine. Talk to people how you want to be talked to by a company you're interacting with. Be human.

Matt Johnston, VP of Marketing & Community, uTest, Inc.

We took a look at uTest in Chapter 4—crowd-based white-box testing at way below traditional cost. For uTest, building and adding to its community of over *15,000* testers (as of just a year after launching) is a must-have: no testers, no company. It's Matt's job to build that community (Figure 6-12).[8]

Figure 6-12. uTest: The community is the product.

Bob: What's different about running a business based on an online community instead of employees and contractors?

---

[8] *If you'd like to know more about how uTest works, check out this podcast: http://startuppodcast. wordpress.com/2009/04/15/show-22-crowdsourced-bug-detection-with-utest*

Matt: When you're building a traditional business that fulfills its services through employees or contractors, you only have one set of customers: your customers. In this traditional type of company, you have direct, contractual control over your employees or contractors. And so, oftentimes, companies don't concern themselves with serving the needs of these audiences.

When building a community-driven business, however, you have two sets of customers that you must serve: the companies who need work done, and the community who supplies the skills and experience. Also, when leveraging an online community, the ultimate arbiter of your best performers is made by customers who rate members of the community, not by an employer who manages and evaluates his/her employees.

Bob: What advice would you give those who want to build their startups based on an online community?

Matt: First, you have to understand, appreciate, and model around the fact that you have two customer constituencies (see preceding answer). Second, it's important to note that there is a subtle science to effective community-building. It's much more than just acquiring a big group of people who share a common interest or skill set. In order to build an effective community, you need to account for things like structured user profiles, reputation systems, carrots and sticks, and community programs to increase the level of skill and engagement.

Veronica Jorden, Communications Manager, Blellow

Blellow (http://blellow.com) is a just-launched community for freelancers and professionals, focusing on helping freelancers, entrepreneurs, and professionals build a list of trusted friends who can help you solve problems, give feedback when you need it, and even help you find work (Figure 6-13).

Bob: Tell me about your job for Blellow. Are you both community manager and communications manager?

Veronica: I am by title the communications manager and do spend a lot of time in the typical sales and marketing type of role, but we are a small team and so we all wear many hats. In a sense our entire core staff acts as community managers. We all have different backgrounds and different work experience and so we all contribute to managing the community in different ways.

Bob: Blellow's "product" is its community. How do you get more people into a startup's community?

Figure 6-13. Blellow: building a trusted community

Veronica: That is our daily challenge, giving people a reason to join yet another community. During development we worked to identify what was missing from some of the other communities out there, what we wanted but just weren't getting out of them. Taking those ideas and building them into Blellow has helped us to clearly identify why being a part of our community can actually help others in their professional life. We take those same ideas and the features that resulted and use them in our marketing messages.

Getting people to sign up for another community has been tough, but we one thing we did was to use development as a way to bring folks in. We launched a closed beta to a small group of "early adopters" who were willing to take a look at our community and give us some feedback. That gave us a great base of members to start with. From there we tried to identify the best way for us to talk to lots of people about what we were doing; for us that was the 2009 SxSWi event in Austin, Texas. Beyond that we have also embraced a very "grassroots" type of marketing strategy and use other networks, like Twitter, Facebook, and Yahoo and Google Groups, to reach out and talk to potential new community members.

Bob: Is it all about getting them to join? What else do you have to do to keep their attention and participation?

Veronica: Great question! Numbers are great motivating factors, but they are by no means the real "meat" of a community. You could have a community of 10K members, but if only a third of them are actually participating, then the community isn't as active as the numbers would lead you to believe.

Getting people to sign up for something doesn't necessarily mean that they will participate. For us, once we get new members, we work to keep them engaged. Because we are a community of collaboration and sharing of knowledge, we try to make sure that every person that comes into our community is acknowledged and made to feel welcome. We are very open about the core team participation within the community and offer direct and open lines of communication between our staff and the community members.

We spend a lot of our time listening to our members, what features they like, what features they wish we would add, and other ideas about how to make the community better. What is really great is that we are starting to be able to identify the community members who really are championing for us both internally and externally.

We try to recognize those people and work with them; their enthusiasm is contagious, and it is that kind of positive word-of-mouth advertising that helps us to gain new members who actually want to participate in the community. We are also working on some other projects, things like widgets for posting on other social networks and blogs, contests and community projects, guest blog postings to our main blog, and a bimonthly newsletter, just to name a few.

Bob: How do you deal with people who are "off message"? I noticed, for example, some posts from what looks like typical "Work at home make money on the Internet" types. What do you do?

Veronica: For us I honestly think the key to keeping the community "on message" is allowing the community to govern itself. In our community we have grouping capabilities, and each group has a moderator. We are almost finished developing our group management functionality, but the plan is to give a group owner/moderator the ability to delete messages that are inappropriate, to form rules for group conduct, and, if necessary, to boot or ban a member from participating in a group.

Beyond that from a total community perspective we will be implementing a process for community members to flag posts and members for inappropriate or "off message" posts. Again this goes back to allowing the community to set their own rules for conduct. That's not to say that we won't be involved—ultimately the power to remove messages and members lies with us and who we delegate it to—but we want to give our members what they want.

If it turns out that our community wants a whole bunch of those work-from-home type of opportunities, then so be it. On Blellow we also have job and project boards, so you question applies to us in that respect as well. Currently while still in open beta we are not charging a fee to post projects and jobs. Once we have finished building out functionality of those features, we will be charging a small fee to help keep the junk and scam postings off of those boards as well.

Bob: Any advice for other startups trying to build/amass online communities?

Veronica: I think there are really two big lessons I have learned from our process so far. One is to clearly identify who your audience is and to keep them in mind at all times when building your community. Creating new features and functionality is only a good thing if they really benefit your members; try to see things from your users' point of view so you can concentrate on the things they most need and want.

And two, don't be afraid to talk with people about your community. It really just takes a few people on your side to help start spreading the word, so while I don't think it is necessarily a good idea to give your sales pitch to everyone you meet in every situation, be open to talking to people about things they are working on . . . ask for their opinion, ask for their ideas, ask for their insight. We have met so many brilliant, creative, and helpful people in this process who have given us advice that has helped us to both avoid mistakes and create a great community. You honestly never know who you are going to meet, and the most random person can sometimes be the key to getting your community to really grow and succeed.

So how do you become a community manager? It's definitely on-the-job-training time—it's so new that the traditional offline economy is barely aware of it. Of course, you're halfway there if you've been reading the pdf version of this book while keeping one eye on TweetDeck!

Maria Sipka, CEO, Linqia

Now I'd like to introduce you to a friend of mine who lives and breathes community and is focused like a laser beam on making a better world by connecting people online. Maria Sipka is the CEO of a startup called Linqia (http://Linqia.com), about which I think you'll be hearing more—a lot more—in the next few years.

Maria's story is an interesting one. At 18 Maria set the goal of becoming financially independent in her family's adopted country of Australia. She then proceeded to build four businesses, including a property portfolio with 35 properties and a web design shop. By 28, she'd hit her financial goal, decided life wasn't just about money, and found her calling going to work for XING, a European social network platform company.

In short order, as director of community building at XING, she founded four of its most successful online communities before moving on to launch Linqia.com—a marketplace for and to online communities. And in March 2009, Linqia launched Moderator Community—the online community for community managers (http://www.themoderatorcommunity.com/).

Maria now makes her home in Barcelona, Spain. I interviewed her for this book via Skype (Figure 6-14).

Figure 6-14. The Moderator Community

Bob: OK. Let's talk about the Moderator Community. What is it? Why is it, and how is that going? How did you get it started? You know, good stuff like that.

Maria: OK. With the Moderator Community it was always part of our core vision when we started Linqia [http://www.linqia.com] to provide an independent place where we could capture all of the value that we were stumbling across, because many people within our company are community builders as well, and we have been working with clients all around the world, helping them build their communities.

It's a space that we have spent countless hours researching, so we are continually reading blog articles, we are reviewing presentations, listening to podcasts, we are conversing with experts. You can say that the people within Linqia are at the forefront of what's going on in the community space.

We've listed over 700 resources, probably close to 800 or 900 with blogs and podcasts and presentations. Anybody can upload those resources. Right now, we are doing 95% of the activity, like, within any community. In the first six months, most of the activity is the people who have been championing it right from the beginning, and then you reach that tip where the community starts to generate the discussions and upload the content.

We are also listing all the events that are related to communities and social media, but it does have a community edge to it. We are also scouting around what jobs are available. I mean, that's one of the most popular sections. Funny enough we have only been launched for a month and we have a look at our Google Analytics. A lot of people are searching for community management jobs, and, yeah, as I said, it's just a rich, resource bustling place where people can come to and extract a lot of value without any expectation in return from us other than just contributing and drawing upon those resources.

Bob: Yeah, the thing that strikes me is that, let's say two years ago, if you asked people who their community manager was, they would go "Huh?" Tell me what you think has led to this rise of the community manager role within companies.

Maria: Well, I've just finished reading Seth Godin's book *The Purple Cow,* and he talks about marketers and salespeople and how both of those roles have now evolved. The days of just pushing out communication messages via press releases, via newspapers, television, radio, and spending bulk amounts of money, those days are gone because people no longer have the attention to be receptive to that, no matter how targeted it is.

The bulk of the people that they want to target are spending so much time in social networks. The numbers are astounding. We have got 1.4 billion people that are on the Internet, of which 700 million belong to social networks, of which over 300 million belong to communities and groups. And they're spending more time in platforms such as Digg, such as Twitter, such as bookmarking via del.icio.us [now `Delicious.com`]. People are really changing their whole way of communicating with each other and with brands and companies and absorbing information.

And so, many of these companies come to the realization of "We have to join the conversation. This is no longer about just having a blog and one person or a number of people within the company who are just publishing blogs and have a following. It's a holistic approach. We need to have blogs. We need to have communities and groups. We need to have Twitter."

To cut a long story short, the short answer is that companies realize they need to start conversing with their key stakeholders. They need to establish relationships with them. It's no longer about pushing their company or their products or the benefits of their products. It's about understanding the behaviors of their key stakeholders and fulfilling on the needs of their key stakeholders by adding value and sparking the conversation that then has them have a loyal following. Because it's so transparent. The days of just having a database and attracting e-mail addresses and then pushing messages is no longer there. If somebody follows you on Twitter and you're not interesting, they're going to immediately disconnect. If they're following your blog and you're publishing just commercial-angled stories, they're going to disconnect.

It's extremely cutthroat. So, that's why a lot of these companies now are employing full-time community managers, Twitter reporters. Like, Dunkin' Donuts is really the best example of people that represent the brand, but their intention is not to sell, but rather converse and say, "Hey, I'm just like you. How can I reach the small attention span that you're willing to dedicate towards my brand or business?"

Bob: So, it really is a battle for attention. That's what it comes down to.

Maria: Spot on. Spot on.

Building Your Pre-Community

Bob: OK. Let's talk about startups and community here for a moment. Let's say that you were doing a startup, a software startup of some sort. What should be your first move in terms of community?

Maria: I'm so glad you asked that question, because we've been experimenting a lot in the last month, specifically on "How do you really start out?" OK? The trick here is that, depending on what your focus is . . . I mean, I'll share the example of us. In a way, we're a startup. We haven't done any major push to position ourselves in the marketplace until we're confident that we actually are building a product that's going to be of value and we know how we're going to execute on that. So, we're at a stage of certainty, of we know what we're doing is going to be valuable.

We've pinpointed who our key stakeholders are, and we want to build a relationship with these people. We know that these people . . . I'm sorry?

Bob: In other words, you know who you want to talk to.

Maria: We know who we want to talk to. And, Bob, we know that these people have limited attention. They are scratching around for minutes. OK? The issue becomes how do we position ourselves? How do we get credibility? How do we gain their trust? How do we gain their loyalty? How do we become a go-to point, specifically that's going to benefit us and benefit them?

We are not going to go and create a group around Linqia and start to push our product or the benefits of using our product. Sure, we might have a Facebook fan page around Linqia, but that's . . .

Bob: That's different, yeah.

Maria: That's different. That's more just affiliation. It's more just gathering people that already know who you are to say, "Hey, yep," on the side. It's on a badge. It's just wearing a badge on a jacket.

Bob: OK.

Maria: What we want to do is we want to deepen the trust and the loyalty with these people. What are the channels to our key stakeholders? Where are they living? They're living on Twitter, they're living on LinkedIn, some of them are on Facebook, and then special-interest blogs and communities that are out there. How do we reach and put our tentacles into all of those different spaces and, at the same time, add significant value to those people? The Moderator Community is very generic and very broad. OK? Those people who are joining our Moderator Community, it's more like a very, very big umbrella. I want to get focused.

So the expertise that's at the core of what we're offering is around influence in marketing. OK? Because we're building a channel that will be able to offer the connection between what Seth Godin calls these *sneezers*, these highly influential people. And our technology will be able to pinpoint exactly what the members of those communities and groups are talking about. But at no point in time are we going to mention our product.

So, I've created a group, in LinkedIn, called Influence in Marketing, and it's around that topic. And again, I'm sharing a lot of resources that are related to influence in marketing, so I'm uploading reports. I'm uploading blogs, news articles. I'm sparking discussions around the topic so that people see this group as a go-to place to, number 1: learn, and number 2: also connect with other people that are interested in that topic.

It took me two hours to create that community, to think about it, to write the short description, long description, find a logo, think about "What's the content? How often am I going to contribute?," invite the people within my network. And overnight, 50 people joined that group. And we're talking very high-profile, key, key, key stakeholders. This is not about getting the masses. This is about getting the most important people.

Every day, we have now 5 to 10 people who join that are not even part of my network but that have seen, by other member profiles, "Oh, what's this Influence in Marketing?" Or they've searched for "influence in marketing."

And we're getting, again, the most high-profile people that are joining this group. And it's like honey to the bee. You've got this captive, captive audience. You're contributing content and valuable resources into that community, and every week these now 70-odd people are "A newsletter from LinkedIn. Here are all the discussions that are taking place."

And then those people are coming back into that group. They're reading that content. And every single second that they have an interaction with Influence in Marketing, they're going to relate that to me as a person as well as to our company. And when the moment is right, you can activate that network to say, "Hey, you people are special. We've spent the last six months together learning about influence in marketing. Here's a special invitation. As a very exclusive group, you get a sneak peak at what it is that we're creating." You can blend in one of your commercial messages.

Bob: Well, not to be crass about it, but it sounds like the first step is to engage in conversation with these people and establish some value with them. In other words, before you even talk about your product or your service, you've got to establish some value.

Maria: Yes. And we're talking real value. OK? This is not just like something on the surface.

Bob: OK.

Maria: It has to be, like, "Wow! I have not read this before" or "Yes. I've read five of these articles already. Then this group must be . . ." "It's this group's like me." That's the kind of value.

Bob: In terms of a strategy for establishing the value, are we really only talking about acting as sort of an Internet editor, where you're pooling resources that they may not have seen together? Or is it a question of your own, original content? Or is it a mix of both?

Maria: Well, not all of us are great writers. Let's face it. Most companies, most individuals don't know how to write. They don't even know how to articulate what it is that they know.

So, it goes back to Malcolm Gladwell's "Tipping Point." Are you a maven? Are you a connector? Are you a super-spreader? What are you?

What's the value that you have as a person? If you, as Bob Walsh, have the capability to articulate what it is that you know and you can write a blog every week, then great. You're going to be able to add even more value to that group.

I can half-write, 50% of your capability. So I will, for example . . .

Bob: You're too kind.

Maria: [laughs] So I'll spark discussions. I won't go and write blog articles, because I just don't know how to research or articulate the message. But I know how to ask good questions. So you've got to know what value either you have or somebody in your company has, and gather those people together to say, "Right, this is how you're going to contribute to this particular community here or this particular group." And then you need to do it consistently. OK? So that means being habitual about, if you stumble across a resource, the first thing that comes to mind is, "Oh, I want to share it with the group!"

So it's about saying, what value, what gifts do we have, and how can we present that and share that with this following of people to gain their loyalty and trust?

Bob: OK. So, in terms of the life of a startup, that actually begins before they release, before they launch. This is because, to be a little bit mercenary about it, they want to have that community in place when they're about to launch because they're the people who are going to launch too.

Maria: Exactly. Yeah. They're the people that become the early adopters, the sneezers.

The Post-Startup Community

Bob: OK. Now, let's say that you get to that point where you've launched. You've got your core community of people who have found value in what you had to say about the things that you're interested in, which probably are about the things that your startup is interested in. Is it just, from there, rinse, lather, and repeat? Do you just keep doing what you're doing, or do you need to change focus?

Maria: Yeah, the communities evolve. Because what we're talking about are startups that haven't launched a product. If you have a look at a Twitter that is already launched, well, one of their communities might be purely all about educational resources around how do you Twitter. And another community may be . . . It's understanding the different needs of your key stakeholders. The second version is, "How do I use this product? And how is it really valuable in maximizing the experience?"

Another community might be, for example, the bigger brands, like the Procter & Gambles. They've created nonprofit communities. So it's all about positioning themselves as being the saviors in the world, and it's about gaining the loyalty of these people as "Hey, we don't only offer you education, we don't only offer you a great product, but we're doing good in the world. And here are some of our initiatives. Come and participate in supporting teenage girls in developing countries."

So community-building has to serve the business needs. There's no illusion about "Hey, let's just go and do good and invest all of this money and time and not be clear on what the business outcomes are." OK? So you've got to be able to set a very clear purpose and set up multiple communities that meet different needs and try not to mix them together, because otherwise you start to dilute the experience of those key stakeholders.

Bob: So you might end up with, actually, a couple of different communities, depending on exactly what your focus is. I mean, doing good for good's sake is one thing. Doing good to get attention on the Internet, because good things do tend to get attention, is another, and perhaps something more that startups should be thinking about.

Maria: Exactly. Procter & Gamble have 2,000 communities.

Bob: What? [laughs] Wait a minute. Huh?

Maria: They have 2,000 communities.

Bob: What are these people talking about? Procter & Gamble, I mean, they make soap.

Maria: That's the point. They have one of the most successful communities that's ever been launched. It's called `BeingGirl.com`, and it's for teenage girls. Procter & Gamble wanted to create a community around hygiene. OK? But, hey, are you going to create a community where you're going to sell your tampons and all of these are areas that teenage girls like, "Oh my God, I don't even want to hear that word"? It's a very, very sensitive topic.

But what Procter & Gamble found was that these teenage girls want a place where they can talk about "What happens when I first get my period? What do I do here?" Because they're too afraid to talk about it either among their friends or to their mother. So this community has attracted hundreds of thousands of girls that have found a way to communicate with one another and to share their stories and ask the questions.

Procter & Gamble has doctors that are in there that are, like, "Ask Anne." And then that doctor has to respond to these messages. And then, very subtly, in a signature, it is, "Oh, by the way, use Tampax." It's because Procter & Gamble know that the lifetime value of one of their customers is around about $4,000. So they know that they can afford to spend a certain percentage, say, per member, to create this community.

And this community has become one of the most successful and most profitable communities. And you could never achieve the same results if you were to go to Stardoll or Piczo or one of the other teenage sites, because they're too generic and broad.

So what they've done is . . . Procter & Gamble is one of the largest packaged-goods companies in the world. They have hundreds of products. So they've gone and created either these big, massive, official communities like BeingGirl, or what they've done is they've sponsored smaller groups or communities so that they get a positioning in there. And what they do is they purely focus on adding value. None of their communities are heavily product-focused, unless the customers want product conversations.

The Build-or-Buy Decision

Bob: OK. Well, what's your recommendation right now for a startup? Should they build their own site, or should they go with Ning or one of Ning's competitors? Or does the software for this really matter?

Maria: This is the big misconception about community-building. The first question that I often get asked is "What technology should we use?" And it's, like, forget about the technology. Have a look at the purpose, have a look at the people, have a look at the whole community experience, and then think about the technology that you need. For example, we've just built our own community. It's expensive. We've even used a free software. We've used Open Source Drupal. But it cost us around about 30,000 euros just to get it to this point. It's expensive.

We have one full-time resource that's on the community. We have another resource that spends 20% to 50 % of her time on the community. I spend 20% of my time on the community. It's really expensive, because once you've set up the community, you then have to nurture it, and you have to keep iterating, whether it be by features, whether it be by content.

So building your own community, I would only recommend if it's absolutely core to your business, because building your own community has its upsides, in that you then get to retain the IP of that community, whereas you get to retain the database of that community. If you go and set up a community on Ning or Facebook, then they own that database. They own the content. It depends on the conditions and the rules. But if you have a look at the fine print, most of those community platforms own that content.

So once you have gone and identified what your purpose is and really identified what value this community is going to add: What are the metrics that you are going to sift for success? If your community is going to be the place where you can confidently retain all of your key stakeholders and converse with them on a regular basis, then what are those key stake-holders worth to you?

Are they potentially worth 100,000 euros per annum because you're spending that sort of money? OK. Then you might invest into building your own community and building your own community will cost you any-where from 10,000 euros to a million Euros. It's like how long is a piece of string?

There are so many solutions out there. There are 120 different white label platforms that you can build your community on. That's really the most robust side of community building. But if you realize that you just want to build some special-interest groups like what I did with influence in marketing, and that's really for our marketplace. It had nothing to do with the Moderator Community.

Then that took me two hours. It was free. I had already built my network over the last three years. So it was overnight I activated that community, and it's very straightforward and extremely powerful. So that's the other end of the extreme.

Bob: If I were to summarize your advice, I think what you are getting to here is this. We're talking about business and community, so the first question is, what is the lifetime value of one of your customers? You should know what that is.

If it's a small amount, if you are in the consumer space, that by its nature leads to one type of approach. If it's a large amount of money, let's say you're more the enterprise space, where you are going to have fewer conversations and the conversations you are having are, quite frankly, worth a lot more to you, then maybe it makes sense to build something where you own the IP, where you can absolutely customize it to the con-versation that you want. Is that a fair summation?

Maria: Exactly. You are spot on it. It's identifying who your key stake-holders are, what the value of those key stakeholders is. What's the purpose of building your community? What is it that you have to offer? On a scale of 1 to 10, how much of a need is there for your offering? Like "Influence in Marketing" is the hot topic, so people are going to bust down the doors to get into that group. But if you've got something around dental care, then maybe it might not be so exciting. Maybe your key stakeholders spend very little time on the Internet. So you've got to identify the risk of what your purpose is. What's the need for the marketplace, and how receptive are they going to be to that?

It's about building satellites in multiple different platforms where you are going to be to attract those people who are interested in your topic. So you might have a group on Facebook, a fan page on Facebook, a group in LinkedIn, a community on Ning. You might have seven different places, a Twitter following. You could have a Flicker group or a YouTube group.

There are so many different platforms out there. You have got to choose: Where are we going to be? Who's going to take care of this? What budget are we going to set? What metrics are we going to set?

And then you might start off really small. You might just start off with something really straightforward like a LinkedIn group and then that might grow into a much bigger community where you do invest money to build big.

Finding Your Community Manager

Bob: OK, well let me ask you one last question. Let's say you're a developer/founder. In other words, you're a software geek here. You've decided that, yes, a core part of what your company needs to do is to be talking to people online. You need to build all these conversations. You need basically a community manager.

What experience or characteristics should you look for in, let's say, a cofounder whose main role is going to be community manager?

Maria: Community managers are very special people. And not everybody can do it. Because you need, first and foremost, somebody who's very good with people and can connect and communicate with people. That's something that has to come naturally. You want to find somebody who is natural at that. If you find somebody who's an extrovert who just rubs people the wrong way, it can be disastrous. So finding that person is . . . it could be internal. It could be, hey, if you can have the CEO or founder of the company play that role, wonderful. But then the other thing is that that person is going to need to be consistent. Consistency is the second biggest key to community, being a community manager.

If you are going to be sending a message to people to say, hey, come and hang out with me, then those people are going to want to hang out with you; and if you are not in your community for two weeks, then that starts to have a detrimental effect on your community.

Then thirdly it's being a good manager. Because as your community starts to grow, you need to juggle a lot of plates. You are going to be needing to welcome people, respond to people's comments, making sure they are posting in the right categories, posting the right type of resources.

You yourself are going need to gather valuable content to bring back into your community. So eventually, the bigger the community grows, you can pretty much almost spend almost full time just managing or moderating your community.

Then the question becomes, well, where do you find those people if you don't have them in-house? The Web works with companies where they have been shared by 10 different people within the company. So we have identified all the different roles that need to exist for this community, and then each of those people has been responsible for contributing a bit into that community.

So it's been shared among many, many people, and it hasn't been a full-time role of any one person. If you are a company that wants to hire somebody, my preference would be to just hire one person that has a lot of those, who can wear all of those hats.

The best place to find those people is within those communities and groups. These people need to already understand social media, understand the rules of engagement. They would have built their own community or group or participated in at least 8 to 10 groups. They would have spent at least one or two hours a day discussing . . . that's a breeding ground for finding these community managers.

Although they might not see themselves as a community manager, if they get approached by somebody to say: "Hey, you're really good at what you. I've noticed that you belong to a number of groups. You're posting a lot of content. You seem to really understand this topic. We would like to hire you." [laughs]

Bob: OK, so first off they have to be great with people. Second, they need to be consistent. They need to be able to work this day in and day out. How would you summarize that third point, though?

Maria: Good with people, they need consistency. Third is experience. They need to be experienced with social media. They need to know how to use the tools and leverage the tools. And join the Moderator Community, for example, so that they're at the forefront of knowing how to maximize the value and the experience of the members of that community and group. The manager or motivator can make or break a community. If you aren't getting it right, you can say goodbye to that community.

Recap

In this chapter we've been exploring the make-or-break question for a startup: How do you get attention in an uncaring world? Without that attention, nothing happens. Without that attention, no matter how long your financial runway, you're going to crash and burn.

The way to get attention in this business used to be through traditional news organizations, such as trade magazines and newspapers. Those still work, but less and less so. Whereas newspapers are falling over like porcelain dolls in a 7.5 quake, online news blogs are coming on strong and very much want to hear your story.

But they don't want their time wasted. Clueless PR efforts are worse than no PR efforts—you're going to need to take the time or buy the expertise to know who in the news business is interested in what, and what they—not you—define as news.

Meanwhile, when hundreds of millions of people start spending their attention and time in social networks, social media, social ways online, that is something you as a startup founder cannot afford to ignore.

The bad news is that connecting to this new social media thing—this arc of change and disruption, from Twitter at one end to blogs, to "socialized" major sites, to social sites the size of countries—is a full-time job. It's a lot of work spending the time to scan your social media radar and participating in hundreds—thousands—of overlapping conversations. You are going to need help. That means either bringing in a partner who's going to do this 24/7 or making your first hire, not another developer and certainly not a VP for marketing, but a community manager who gets it.

The good news in this era where attention is dear and markets are conversations is that the social media playing field favors tiny companies with passionate people on a mission to bring something new into the world. That's you—if you're willing to jettison the whole marketing mentality with which big companies blanket our lives.

Next up, we dig in deep on exactly how to communicate your startup's message. This is a subject that has tripped up many a startup. I don't want your startup to end up on that casualty list.

Clarity Matters

"Four basic premises of writing: clarity, brevity, simplicity, and humanity."
—William Zinsser (American author and editor)

If You're Not Clear, You're Not Selling

In this chapter, we're going to dig into a subject almost every startup gets wrong the first time around. Some recover, many don't. The subject is how well you present your startup's software to first-time visitors to your site. The goal is to make that case in the right order, with the right parts, so that those prospective customers become actual customers.

Describing clearly why someone should give you money for your software is a skill that doesn't come naturally to most developers and startups. It makes us somewhat uncomfortable to do so, probably because we're too close to see the benefits of what we've created, apart from the flaws. But if you're going to succeed, you need to be able to step back, look with the eyes of your prospective customers at what you're going to be selling, and then know how to present your case.

Before we get to two case studies illustrating how to make a case for your software, let's examine a couple of assumptions and a design pattern I and others call the Unique Selling Proposition.

First off, I'm assuming you've got no desire to inflate, overplay, or exaggerate what your software does and no interest in bamboozling, conniving, or manipulating though yard-long web pages of screaming headlines, coercive text, pop-ups demanding your visitors' e-mail address, gushing testimonials, multiple bonuses, and hidden prices. In other words, you're not interested in the *Internet Marketing* approach to marketing your software: Make! Money! Now! (see Figure 7-1). If you are, then return this book. You probably wanted *MindControlMarketing.com*[1] (Steel Icarus, 2003) by

---

[1] `http://www.markjoyner.name//logs/mj_books.php`

Mark Joyner or some lesser practitioner of the Dark Arts. Internet Marketing is the evil mutant digital offspring of the first kind of spam—direct mail advertising. And though I'd like to tell you that approach doesn't work, someone is nonetheless making money from it and those late-night television ads.

Figure 7-1. We are not talking about this kind of approach.

You see, I'm assuming you have an application with some real benefits to the right people and that those people would probably be extremely interested in your web or desktop app if they were properly introduced. The point of this chapter is to help you understand and structure honestly the prospective customer's initial experience with your software—your home page—and communicate clearly your value to them.

With that out of the way, let's take a quick look at something I've written about elsewhere[2] at much greater length: the Unique Selling Proposition pattern.

The Unique Selling Proposition Pattern

Let me put what I'm talking about here into programmer-speak. The Unique Selling Proposition (USP) is a **robust and powerful marketing design pattern** that can effectively save you from designing spaghetti-like marketing that's hard to understand, let alone maintain. It's a pattern for connecting what you are selling to the right people in the right way so that they are eager to purchase.

What's more, it's an extremely efficient, effective, and elegant pattern that can be used and reused in a wide variety of circumstances. It's a pattern that has been employed successfully on literally thousands of projects worldwide. Marketing is just another programming language. And the USP pattern is one of its most useful and flexible design patterns.

Another way to describe the USP is that it's the set of expectations most people have about what is—and is not—good software from a trustworthy vendor worth their attention.

All right, enough chatter. Let's walk through the components of a USP, the timeline of how a typical prospective customer sees—or doesn't see—these components, and what the USP means for your startup web site's home page.

The Hook

When people go to a web site for the first time, there's logically going to be one thing they perceive and comprehend first. They are going to glance at the site and make—literally—a split-second decision to stay or go based on the first thing they see. Your job as a founder of a startup that wants to succeed is to control as much as possible the first thing prospective customers see on your web site and to make sure that what they see or read connects with them so that they keep reading. It's a big Internet out there, and that new arrival to your wonderful web site **cares not one bit** about it, about you, or about your startup—yet.

The job of the hook is to give potential customers a reason to care (a little), to read on (a little), and to think that there might be some value at your site that's worth a few seconds more of their valuable time.

Now, before you mentally complain that your startup is different, that your app is so interesting that, of course, prospective customers are going

---

[2] *MicroISVs Sites That Sell!*, and I apologize for the exclamation mark. `http://www.47hats.com/?page_id=534.`

to analyze your 23 bullet points and decipher your 193 industry-specific terms, ask yourself what you did the last time you went looking for something on the Web. You probably did a Google search, opened a bunch of pages, quickly scanned through the lot, with your fingers poised to press Ctrl-W, and without a second's hesitation chopped any page that didn't look right, didn't tell you that you were on the right page for what you wanted, didn't make unequivocally clear what it was offering. Why would your prospective customers act any differently?

Let's take a closer look at what your prospective customers are looking for in the first couple of seconds.

- They want to know that they haven't navigated to some weird, spammy, amateur, possibly dangerous site.

- They want to know that the site is relevant, that it relates to what they want.

- They want to know what you intend to offer them.

Here, then, are the three key elements of the hook: **credibility**, **relevant value**, and a **clear offer**. These are also the main components of a compelling Unique Selling Proposition.

The hook needs to be the first words to which the prospective customer's eye is drawn. That's usually accomplished by making its text three times larger than any other headline on the page, with plenty of white space around it to set it off. But the right text size isn't enough. Let's look at each of these elements in turn.

Credibility

Whatever you say in that one- or two-sentence hook should be honest, not hyperbole, believable, not bull. Claims such as "Best," "Revolutionary," "Industry Leader," "Unique," and "Easy to Use" immediately trigger most people's MFR—marketing filter response.[3] Now, maybe your web app *is* revolutionary, unique, easy to use, and more. Fine. But first you have to establish some trust between you and would-be buyers, and then you must introduce and back up your claims. Remember, they've just opened a bunch of web sites via Google, and they're itching for a reason to close your page. Don't give them one.

---

[3] *Did you think it was an accident that all those weird television ads with impossible claims and promises are on late-night television?*

Instead, here are three good ways to establish your credibility via your hook.

- Show that you speak their language, that you understand the need that brought them to your page, their mindset, their vocabulary for describing things in this part of their world.

- Don't use terms at the beginning of the sales conversation that blow your credibility.

- Don't try the patience of your prospective customer. Get to the point.

I know, I know, you want to mention in your hook all your software's really cool features, because, well, they're cool. Don't! Your prospective customers need to grasp easily why you matter to them, what in the news business is called the "So what?" test.

Relevant Value

Let's move on to the second component of the hook and, for that matter, of you're entire site: relevant value. Value depends on relevance. Relevance can be as simple as "I'm a happy Windows user. What do I care about Mac apps?" [4] It's all about what's at the top of the pain/I Want list of your customers-to-be when they arrive at your web site.

Some of my clients initially want to try to be as relevant as possible to anyone and everyone having any need, however tangential, for what they're selling. Doesn't work—and it costs credibility points. Let's put it this way: What's the one thing about your web or desktop app that matters most to the one or two kinds of people who constitute your collection of market segments? That's the relevant value you want to put upfront and center in your hook.

What Are You Trying to Sell Them?

Are you trying to sell a web app, a Windows or Mac app, an Apple iPhone or Google Android or Windows Smartphone app? Do you want people to buy it, subscribe to it, get consulting on it, or consume it for free? Given the number of ways software is being delivered today, people visiting this site need to know what platform your startup's software is for and how you intend to charge them for it.

---

[4] *Of course, there are no happy Windows users, just some who have a higher pain threshold and can endure almost anything before they beg for mercy (joke!).*

So you should tell them they can choose a free 30-day trial or a free account, right? Nope. Those are things in your marketing toolbox, just as glossy brochures and info packets were during the last century. Worse, including the *F*-word (free) in the hook, only to have potential customers find out that you're talking about a limited account or a trial version, is like sticking a hard drive in a microwave: the results are *not* pretty.

When you walk into a store, you know you're going to grab things off the shelves, walk to the front of the store, and pay for them. If you go to Amazon, you're going to click a button to put the item into your Amazon cart or, if you're logged in, you're going to click one of the three orange Buy Now buttons to do your business. Your customers need the same kind of guidance from you when they are comprehending your hook; they need to know you are selling them something and what form that something is going to take.

Credibility Markers

OK, enough about the hook. Let's look at the other parts of the Unique Selling Proposition pattern, starting with an expanded view of this whole "Should I trust you?" thing: *credibility markers*. There are two aspects to this part of the USP: (1) what you say and how you say it and (2) whether you've competently included the standard things most online buyers look for in order to pass judgment on a site. Let's deal with the latter first. Here's the short list.

- Do you identify your company by providing its logo, physical/mailing address, phone number, and general e-mail? If not, why would you expect people to give an anonymous page their credit card info? Now, I realize that startups in some parts of the world—eastern Europe and Russia come to mind—think their customers in the United States will penalize them. Some will, although not as many as you think and not if you do the right things.[5] But the cost of not having this information on your site is far higher.

- Did you include a copyright notice and, if you mention other companies' products on the page, a trademark disclaimer? You're running a business; these are the signposts of a business.

---

[5] Such as having a very detailed About page showing who you are and where; making sure your site's text is written in grammatically perfect English; using a blog and other social media so that people can get to know you; and having a product that's loaded with real value.

- Is the price of what you are selling shown either on the home page or where you expect people to sign up?

- Is it clear and unmistakable what people have to do to buy your app or service and, for that matter, to try it?

- When a person goes to buy your app or web service, do you make clear what your refund policy is and, if you are using a third-party payment processor (see Chapter 5), who that processor is?

- Does the site look professional and businesslike, whatever that means in your particular online industry?

- Do you have testimonials praising your product or web app from other people who visitors may already trust or with whom they can at least associate themselves? Is at least one of those testimonials on the home page?

The people looking at your web site expect and understand that they are involved in a specific social situation called a *sale*. This sale situation has its own etiquette, its own rhythm, its own do's and don'ts—ignore them at your financial peril.

Famous People Saying Nice Things About You

Testimonials and (positive) reviews are a big part of establishing the overall credibility of your offering. The comfort factor goes way up when prospective customers see the name of a media organization or a prominent blog or logo on your home page. We covered this in some depth in Chapter 6, but in this context the thing to know is that no matter how many steps it takes, you want those media/blogger reviews—they really matter.

The word *famous* has a television definition like everything else, but don't forget that *famous* could mean the head of surgery at a major hospital if you are selling surgery-related software or, for that matter, the head tree surgeon at a well-known landscaping company if you're selling software to landscaping companies.

It's all about relevance—and since many of your customers may not take what "authorities" say seriously, positive quotes from real people who use your software and are willing to say, they use and like your software can be just as important. Notice that I didn't say "purchased your software" in that last sentence. The catch-22 of not getting sales because you have zero testimonials and having zero testimonials because you have no sales is best fixed when you do either your initial or your major release public beta.

Of course, if you establish your credibility but don't communicate your relevant value, your job's at best half done.

Relevant Value

Once a visitor is past the hook, relevant value is all about bullet points. No, I'm not talking about bullet points that escaped a corporate PowerPoint presentation. I'm talking about a modern startup benefit and customer-centric bullet points.

Let's look at a good example from the startup freckle time tracking. First off, a good modern bullet point isn't just text, it's a headline to preview the message and give it a mental peg to hang on to. And it's small visual image to associate with the feature. And it's ultra-easy to read and comprehend block of text that is about you the prospective customer, not me the amazing startup (see Figure 7-2).

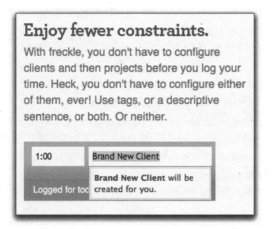

Figure 7-2. The ammo for your startup: benefit bullet points

The word *you* appears four times in this one bullet point. Amy Hoy, Thomas Fuchs, and the two other founders use the word *you* or the like *31 times* on freckle's home page.[6] It's all about the customer, not about your product and certainly not about your startup.

Something else you should notice about this benefit bullet point: it's simple—no jargon, no long sentences. The goal is customer comprehension, not data packing.

---

[6] As of May 1, 2009.

You'll have to visit freckle time tracking (http://letsfreckle.com) to realize how each of its four bullet points—that's right, only four—backs up and buttresses the site's hook ("freckle time tracking helps *you do more of what you love,* and *less of what you don't.*"). If you haven't nailed the customer after that many shots, something is wrong with your ammunition.

The Final Piece of the USP Puzzle

Before we get to the Case Studies there's the last component of the process: asking for the sale. You are selling, they're (maybe) buying, and it's your job to ask nicely for their money.

Should you do this by having an unmissable Buy Now button, or should you go for the sale via the indirect route of the free 30-day trial? Do both, because you're dealing with the entire bell curve here, from the earliest adopters who will buy anything they consider shiny to the middle-of-the-road folks who've been burned and want to taste your wine before they buy a case.[7]

And what if your startup doesn't actually sell something, like our first case study, Mint.com? You don't actually have to have to sell, do you? Yes, you do. If you don't ask for the sale, whatever that means for your startup, then you leave visitors hanging, wondering what they are supposed to do next. So even if you've found a cool way to get someone other than your customers to pay for your startup, get comfortable asking them to take the next step leading where you want them to go; it's the only way they'll get there.

Case Study: Mint.com

URL: http://mint.com

    Area: Personal financial management.

    Platform(s): Web, Apple iPhone, and SMS text.

    Summary: At the time of this writing (mid-January 2009), Mint.com had gone from zero users to over 800,000, with a whopping 23,000 people signing up the day before my interview with 28-year-old CEO Aaron Patzer. The free consumer personal financial manager makes its revenue when its patent-pending search algorithm finds a way to save money for a customer

---

[7] *This raises an interesting point I'll leave up to you to think about: What's the bell curve of your primary market segment? Are you going for the early adopters, the online mainstream where the money is, or those just now joining the show. It's a good thing to know in terms of how you construct your USP.*

and that customer chooses to accept that offer. Since starting in November 2006, Mint.com has raised a total of $17.45 million in three rounds of equity funding.[8] Those are impressive numbers.

For purposes of this chapter, let's have a look at the home page of Mint.com (see Figure 7-3).

- Any chance you'll miss the hook of *Mint.com*? Nope. And while it's a pretty big claim, notice how it's buttressed by great major media quotes right under it? That deactivates most people's marketing filter response.

- The PC Editor's Choice award certainly helps, as does the customer testimonial that leads to an entire page of both test and video customer testimonials.[9]

- The VeriSign, TRUSTe, and McAfee badges at the bottom help further establish the credibility of Mint.com.

- Aaron would agree with you that establishing Mint.com's credibility was the hardest hurdle to jump (see the upcoming interview). If you click down to their Privacy and Security page, you won't get privacy boilerplate. Instead, you get a video of Aaron talking about security and, page after page, covering exactly why you can trust Mint.com with your financial data and bank passwords.

Bank passwords? *Danger! Danger!* We've all been trained by authorities and spammers never, ever, ever to give out that information. Yet people are doing just that—in droves. Partly because Mint.com spells out exactly what happens to that information, how it is a read-only app (you can't move money around), how while your financial data is in the cloud, your identity is never asked for.

Here's what Aaron had to say about the trust issue, what it took to get his initial funding, and why he decided to build Mint.com.

---

[8] *http://www.crunchbase.com/company/mint is wrong: First Round Capital's investment was part of the angel round, not separate. So says Aaron, and he should know.*

[9] *I love those MintFanatic videos. If your market is comfortable with videos of themselves online, these are powerful. Check out 12seconds and, of course, YouTube.*

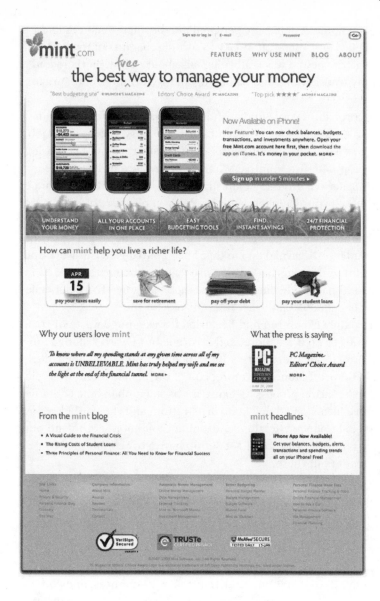

Figure 7-3. Mint.com

Interview with Aaron Patzer, CEO, Mint.com

Bob: Let's start with how you decided that Mint.com was something you wanted to do.

Aaron: Yes, I had started a couple of businesses back in high school, building web sites and doing online marketing. When the Internet was quite new, I guess, it was back in sort of the 1996–97 era. And that's how I put myself through college, went to Duke and then to Princeton.

So I was combining doing my personal and business finances and I was using Quicken and Microsoft Money to sort of separate out my personal and my business finances. I was really religious about getting in there and entering all my transactions and balancing all my accounts, categorizing everything.

I did that probably every Sunday afternoon, for an hour every Sunday, every week for about eight years. Then I got really busy with another job. I was working as a software architect for another startup, and I didn't log into Quicken for, like, five months. When I got in there it downloaded about 500 transactions from my banks that said, hey, your bank balance just doesn't match your Quicken balance. Will you please reconcile these 500 transactions.

I thought, man, that's going to take me all weekend to get back to square one. And it just dawned on me that I been putting all this work and all this effort into a system that really wasn't giving me anything back in return. Why did I have to balance my checkbook anyway? The electronic version of my checkbook can't just figure it out for me?

I was incredibly frustrated and I realized it was a huge waste of time and I didn't want to do it anymore, and it turned out I wasn't alone in my frustration. Turned out there were a lot of people who really didn't like Quicken and Microsoft Money anymore, half of the people didn't even get through the installation process, because it was so cumbersome to set up.

So the core idea started out in my frustration, and the core idea was to make personal finance effortless and simple. You know, get in and out in five minutes a week or less and get set up in five to ten minutes to get all of your accounts in there.

Bob: OK, well, I've used Quicken and I actually used Microsoft Money and I don't do it on Sundays; I do it on Fridays. But I know exactly the frustration you're talking about. How does Mint.com solve the problem?

Aaron: Yes, it's a free online application and links to 7,500 banks, credit cards, loans, and brokerages. So instead of the setup process you go through with, say, Microsoft Money, where you buy the software in the store, you install it on your computer that takes 20 minutes, and you go through 30 different setup screens, search for your bank, enter your credentials, what you want to rename and call these bank accounts, how you want to rename transactions.

Mint.com basically makes intelligent decisions for you. All you have to do is search for your bank and enter your username and password; after that point it will update your balances, your transactions, your bill-due dates. It will pull it in every single night, whether you logged in or not, sends you bill reminders, low-balance alerts, credit alerts. Things that the desktop program can't do because a desktop program is only running when that application is open. So it's always up to date and it's always watching your back, 24/7, making sure you don't have any late fees, making sure the bank doesn't charge you any fee, and it categorizes everything for you.

So I spent about three or four months alone in a room working on a patent pending categorization program so that it knows that when you go to Rose's Café, that's a coffee shop, or that the "Superior Court" entry, despite its name, is actually a racquetball court and not a traffic ticket or something. So there is a tremendous amount of technology behind it. We get five patents in what were doing.

Bob: Whoa! Let me ask you about something, from sort of the marketing point of view here. Financial tracking desktop software has been around for, well, at least 15 years that I know of.

Aaron: Yup.

Bob: But nobody seemed to have the right mix of message and features to convince people to put their financial information on a web site, somewhere that we don't even know where they exist. How do you deal with this issue of credibility?

Aaron: Yeah. I mean, every venture capitalist I talked to in the early days said that Mint.com would definitely fail because people would never trust a startup with their financial information, and certainly they were never going to enter their bank username and password. But we need your bank username and bank password if were going to sort of essentially get your information out.

The banks need to know it's you that's authorized it. So there are a number of things we did with our messaging. Every reporter asks about security, so we spent a lot of time talking about what to do with security from an engineering standpoint and then how to brand that.

Mint.com has bank-level security. We have all the same encryption and backend protections that a bank would. We have outside security auditing, by hacker-safe outfits, and we verify signing outside, *late-night hackers,* they're called, who try to break into the system, who haven't so far.

We are a read-only system, so you can't actually move money around. So even if somebody breaks in, that person can't drain your accounts. And we're anonymous, so we made a conscious decision not to request name, age, address, phone number, social security number, anything like that; we only ask for e-mail and a zip code.

So even if somebody broke in, got into our database, he wouldn't know who you are; he just knows happygirl17@yahoo drinks a lot of Starbucks coffee or something.

Bob: So like cutting off the head of the information, who you are actually are . . .

Aaron: Exactly, but no personal identifying information. And then the other thing is Mint.com helps actually protect you. So we've turned the security issue 180° into a strength because Mint.com is going out and monitoring your four or five different credit cards that you have in your wallet, every single night.

And so 90% of all fraud occurs offline, not online. You're much more likely to get your credit card stolen at a restaurant or a gas station or if somebody is actually physically handling your card. The alternative is you can log into four or five different web sites every day and check for fraud, or you link them into Mint.com and Mint.com will just tell you if there's suspicious activity on your card.

Bob: Hence the alerts about these 25-cent charges that started popping up on various people's accounts.

Aaron: Yes, and on our database; and we let those users know that their accounts may have been compromised, certainly not at Mint.com, but somewhere else. Well, I guess they lost 25 cents in it, but they should probably have those credit cards reissued by their provider.

Bob: OK, let's talk more about money. Specifically you're saying that when you talked to VCs, they were of the attitude that this is never going to fly because nobody is going to give you any personal financial information.

Aaron: Yes.

Bob: When you got your first round of capital, which according to CrunchBase was $325,000, how did you sell that?

Aaron: I found one guy who believed in the vision or was willing to take a bet on me and the team that I put together. Here's the catch of venture funding. It was in spring of 2006. I went to see Sequoia. And I came in and gave them a pitch, and they said, good idea, but no one will trust it and, by the way, you have no team and no product, so there's no way we can ever give you money. The catch-22 is they only want to invest in something they know will work or is starting to work.

Bob: Right.

Aaron: But you need money in order to get it to that point. We won't invest in the company unless they've built a product, but you need money to build the product. I built Mint.com off my own savings and sat alone in a room for seven months and worked 14 hours a day, seven days a week, until I basically got a prototype of the system—front end, graphics, functionality, everything.

Then I was able to do a demo in front an investor, Josh Kopelman (First Round Capital), who's the founder of half.com. He said, yes, I think this might work, but, to help with the trust aspect, don't use the domain mymint.com, which is from before; mint.com is much more valuable. We spent three months negotiating for mint.com because that's a much better name and a more trustworthy name.

Bob: Was Josh the person you were referring to that was your first VC believer?

Aaron: Yes, he was.

Bob: And just to clarify here, what then was the $325,000 that CrunchBase is referring to? Is that the money and time you put into it?

Aaron: That's how much that First Round Capital themselves put in.

Bob: OK.

Aaron: The $750,000 was $325,000 from First Round Capital and $425,000 from other investors.

Bob: Hence don't always believe what you read on the Web. Let me ask you: How about when you went to talk to the banks and the credit cards and Visa International and you're saying, hey, look, we want to put all this information online, how about it? How did you convince what is basically a whole bunch of conservative people that this was in their interest?

Aaron: Yes, there's a way around that, in that someone else had already solved that problem. In the late 1990s Microsoft and Intuit developed the OFX standard, which was the Open Financial Exchange. That lets you sync up with bank servers and, if you have credentials, download transactions and balances and things like that.

Some banks use that. And the banks that didn't support that, we partnered with a company called Yodlee [http://www.yodlee.com], and they do what's known as *screen scrapping,* which is essentially logging in as the user; they pull down the web pages and pull out the columns of data representing your transactions and your balances.

They already had those relationships set up, and they were already partnered with Bank of America and some of the large institutions.

Bob: So, bottom line, it wasn't a problem. It was basically outsourced to Yodlee for those people who don't use the sort of standard industry format.

Aaron: That's right.

Bob: There's not that many people in their mid-20s who already have 800,000 users. To what do you attribute your success?

Aaron: Well, first and foremost, solving a real need and a real pain point that people have. I mean, every adult in the Free World needs to manage his money, and existing tools just made it way too difficult. Then bank web sites, well, they only show you your balance for a particular credit card or a particular account.

The average American has 11 different accounts where they need some way to track all of it. All their loans, all their investments, their

401Ks, their IRAs, their credit cards, their checking and savings accounts. We just made it really easy to do that, really easy navigation. We hired a designer, a user action designer, who built `apple.com,` so we took our inspiration from Apple and then we focused a lot on the product and the usability and the user interface.

We brought actual people in to help with software, like right off the street. A woman brought her kid with a stroller in and tested `mint.com` out while the kid was screaming. We brought people who were in their 40s and 50s and people who were in their 20s, men and women. Got a diverse set of people in and saw where they were using the software well and the places where things weren't going well. Just took a really user-centric approach.

Once we launched, I will basically do any and every interview from any blogger or any press.

Bob: [laughs] OK, that helps.

Aaron: Yes.

Bob: One more question on that. Did going multiplatform . . . In other words, you start as a web app and now you've added an iPhone interface. How much did that help?

Aaron: Well, it's been four weeks, but it's helped tremendously. We are the number 1 finance application in the finance category in the apps store, which means we've beaten Bank of America, Wells Fargo, PayPal, the AT&T mobile banking system. At one point we were ranked as high as number 30 on the top 100 free applications overall, and we're the only finance app ever to have done that. We were almost as high as Pandora and Facebook at one point.

Bob: Was this part of your strategy way back when, that you wanted to diversify across platforms, or was it, Hey, wow, this iPhone is incredibly cool. Lots of people are buying them. Let's go for it.

Aaron: Well, we didn't launch right when the iPhone launched. What we did was we did some user research and found out that 40% of our users had iPhones. And of the 60% who didn't have them, half of them were planning to buy one within the next year.

The overlap between Mint.com's user base and iPhone usage was insane, it was phenomenal. It was a highly requested feature, so we put some engineers on it and got it out in very short order and launched it. I always knew that I wanted Mint.com to be mobile, but originally I thought that was going to be text message based.

You can actually—and you've been able to do this for four months now—you can get text message alerts and little reminders and you can query for your balances. You just text *shortcode mymint*.

Bob: OK.

Aaron: And type the word **balance** or **bal**. It'll send you your balances back when you're at a restaurant and you want to figure if you have enough money to pick up the tab. Or if you're in a store and you want to make a purchase and you want to see how much you've got on your credit card bill, it will tell you your balances right then.

Bob: OK. If you're sitting down with yourself right now and you're going to do another type of startup, another whole new venture, what lessons have you learned that you'd want to pass on to avoid some pain?

Aaron: Well, managing, raising capital, and figuring out what value the company should be at and when you should raise and when you shouldn't is definitely a big lesson that I didn't entirely understand until after raising a couple of rounds of financing.

The other lesson would be: hiring people is the very most important thing that you do at a company, a greater focus on the interview process, and training everyone to interview people well and deliberately. A lot of times people interview and they get into a room and they're, like, Well, I thought that guy sounded like he knew what he was talking about.

You need well-defined criteria for how you evaluate: who asks what questions. Make sure you cover all areas of technical and management skills. Ask the same sort of technical questions between two engineering candidates so that you can compare them head to head accurately, efficiently. All those things matter, but they're actually not done all that well in most companies.

Bob: Well, there is one more question that I really should ask: Here we are in 2009; the offline economy is looking like a train wreck.

Aaron: Yes.

Bob: Do you think it's a good, or a bad, or a great, or a horrible time to create a startup?

Aaron: I think if you're solving a real problem, it's always a good time to start a company, because if you don't do it, someone else will.

Case Study: RescueTime

URL: `http://www.rescuetime.com/`

Disclosure: I did some strategy/positioning consulting with Tony Wright in 2008.

Area: Time management—individual, small business, and enterprise.

Platform(s): Web, with GUI-less Windows and Mac clients.

Summary: RescueTime puts a new spin on time management: target people who live at their keyboards and require zip effort on their part to track how much time they're spending on which apps and web sites.

Now, it may seem that CEO and founder Tony Wright has built a YARTTA—yet another Rails time tracking app. Well, the investors who've put up $900,000 after the initial Y Combinator seed round of funding beg to differ.

Chris Sacca, one of RescueTime's investors, had this to say about the Seattle-based startup to the BBC's Business Daily podcast.[10]

> *I have a little company called RescueTime. It's free for individuals and $4 to $8 a month. It watches and helps you understand where you spend your time online. So you're able to set time goals and targets for yourself so you realize, "Wow. I'm spending a lot of time on Twitter; maybe I need to focus back on my [business] Gmail account."*
>
> *So that actually make employees 9% more efficient in the first month they use it. So companies are really excited to pay for it. They pay such a small fee for it, so the company does really well, despite being such a small company, and all the users are very happy to use it.*

RescueTime's challenge, and why they're a case study for this chapter, is how you communicate clearly your startup's value to three different audiences, all of which have seen so many time management apps they've lost count (see Figure 7-4).

- Start with a simple, brief hook, essentially the same for all three market segments.

- Next, talk about what matters to each market segment. Effortless Time Tracking for individuals and small businesses; Business Intelligence You've Never Had Before for enterprise.

- The AS SEEN IN bar has some very heavy media hitters: check out the following interview with Tony for how he got these positive mentions.

- Make your web site's layout back up your message. Here, Tony is selling *effortlessness*, and the site could not be easier to understand or navigate.

Time management has been around for over a century. But what Tony and RescueTime are doing here is addressing the relatively new problem of reduced productivity, due primarily to oversurfing the Web, while steering well clear of evil software that involuntarily tracks employees' every keystroke, glance, and moment.

---

[10] *January 6, 2009. If you're not listening to this podcast and the BBC's Peter Day's World of Business, you should be.*

Figure 7-4. RescueTime

Here's what Tony had to say about how he got into Y Combinator, what that did for him, how he raised $900,000 after that, and what's left on his to-do list.

Tony Wright, CEO, RescueTime

Bob: Let me ask you about RescueTime. First off, where did you get the idea?

Tony: It was born out of our personal inability to understand how we spend our time. Every day we had a scrum agile meeting. We're a bunch of software geeks. Everyone's job would say what they'd accomplished in the last 24 hours and what they were going to do in the next 24. We found that people's ability to articulate what they'd done, literally, just in the last workday, was terrible. People would say, well, I felt busy but I can't really articulate what I did.

We wanted to understand that, but we recognize that despite all these time management books that say keep a log of how you spend your time, that's incredibly impractical for a technology worker who's shifting between applications and websites, sometimes in 10-, 20-second blocks.

We wanted something that was totally passive that would answer those questions for us and for our business without actually requiring data entry, which is no fun.

Bob: So the biggest point was making it, as you say in your first bullet here, effortless.

Tony: Well, yeah. From a business perspective, whether you're a freelancer or a business, the idea is that time is precious. It's really hard to do a good job. If you screw up and don't do a good job for a couple of days, that data is irrecoverable. The effort was the thing that we thought prevented all knowledge workers from having this data at their fingertips—it's just too much of a pain in the butt.

Bob: Time management has actually been around for over a century now in one form or another. How did you break through people's resistance to, oh, it's just another time tracking application?

Tony: I'm not entirely sure we're done breaking through, but we're still trying. I think we've done a good job on a couple of fronts. I think one of the biggest things for us is that it does have a twist. I don't know if you've read the book called *Made to Stick*,[11] but it's about sticky ideas. One of the things that makes an idea sticky is that it's surprising. What we've done is put a surprising twist of—everyone's done time entry at one point or another in his or her life, or a lot of people have. Everyone's familiar with the concept. We've basically said this is just going to happen.

We also have some surprising stuff, in the sense of people who use it tend to be shocked by what they see. People have a picture in their head of what they think they do with their time. What they actually do with their time has only a bare relationship to that sometimes.

We get a lot of credibility and a lot of breakthrough, in that people talk about this. So they use RescueTime, they may go on Twitter, or they go on their blog, or they sit down at a bar somewhere and say, "Dear Lord, look what I found out. I had no idea." And that creates questions in other people's minds.

I think that part of the breakthrough comes from the kind of word-of-mouth engine; if you hear about something from someone else whom you trust, that's huge. That's basically them saying, "Yes, I understand that time management is something that everyone's tried and looked at and

---

[11] *"Made to Stick: Why Some Ideas Survive and Others Die"* by Chip and Dan Heath (Random House, 2007), http://www.madetostick.com

paid attention to and gotten frustrated with. But look what I did. It worked. I learned some things. I'm now smarter about myself."

The way we talked about is important, but I think the way we created something that made other people talk about it was arguably more important.

Bob: OK. Well, part of the credibility that really comes across when I look at this web site . . . By the way, I am disclosing we've done a little business together here. I look and I see *New York Times*, the *BBC*, *PC World*, *Lifehacker*, *U.S. News*, *BusinessWeek*, *TechCrunch*. How do you get all these major media brands to talk about you? Is there a strategy there, or did it happen by chance?

Tony: I would love to pat myself on the back for that or pat someone on our team on the back for that. I think, what we did, again, was, if I could give one bit of marketing advice for people, I would say get the book *Made to Stick*. It is absolutely awesome. I think we kind of stumbled into that. But that's how I map it—we really, again, created surprising data and we have some surprising data in aggregate. This is kind of a web-based service. This is in the cloud and has all the advantages web-based e-mail has over Outlook, for example.

And what we get as a result of that is the ability to say that the average person spends X hours in e-mail. Or the average person shifts to an instant message window 77 times per day. So, if you use IM, you're shifting to an instant message window 77 times per day on average.

Now there's obviously a mean. That kind of data, I think, really . . .

Bob: . . . creates headlines.

Tony: If you mention that to a reporter or a blogger and they say, "I can build an article around that," whether it's an article on how people could sort of manage instant message more effectively or just a sort of shock piece of, gosh, look how knowledge workers aren't getting stuff done.

Bob: Are these media brands calling you, or are you calling them? Do you send out press releases? Walk me through here.

Tony: Yeah, so we're not doing anything. We don't have anyone who's dedicated PR. I'm probably the closest thing to that as CEO. There are a couple overt things that we did. For example, we took this data that we thought was pretty shocking, the aggregate data of the entire user base, and made a little spreadsheet of: here are the top 100 applications and web sites that people are spending time on. We kind of made a list of that and what percentage they work. You could see, like, how much percentage time people spent on communication stuff or productivity stuff or word processing or what have you, or Google.

Then whatever we found, a surprising bit like that with that particular list, we sent that to *TechCrunch*. *TechCrunch* said, "Oh, we can build an article around that." I believe it was called "Early Adopters Still Sticking with Microsoft" or desktop products, or some such.

Showing the idea that, hey, while there is all this wonderful stuff in the cloud where you can word process and do spreadsheets and stuff, people are still really using the old-style desktop software for this stuff. Outlook is more dominant than Gmail. And, you know, we have pretty early-adopter audience yet.

So we would do stuff like that. I've done a speaking engagement as a result of the Y Combinator thing, because we were kind of in the productivity space. I think we got tapped for that. Someone asked Paul Graham if he knew a good startup to be on a panel at the Churchill Club, so I did a speaking engagement at the Churchill Club.

Bob: It sounds to me like one of your core strategies was to be remarkable.

Tony: Yeah, and, really, the subset of remarkable of the sort of surprising kind. Obviously, we could be incredibly beautiful. I mean, we try to focus a little bit on graphic design, but I don't think we're anywhere in the top 5% of most stunning web sites out there. But there's lots of remarkable things. We've really focused on the sort of surprising, and I think that's the sort of asset we have.

Bob: OK.

Tony: Really, I think that's one of the lessons that I really learned is that you need to have that twist, that hook that makes someone do a double take, and whether they say, "Wait a minute. There's no data entry" or "Wait a minute. People spend that much time doing that?" Something that basically makes someone give that second look, because of just the noise level out there, you need to have something like that.

Bob: You mentioned Y Combinator. Tell me what your experience was like.

Tony: It was kind of a forcing function for us. Y Combinator's basically a software incubator in the Valley that basically takes you into the Valley. You have to be down there for three months. So we relocated from Seattle to do this.

Bob: Now, who is "we"—you, or you and your partner?

Tony: Yeah. I had two cofounders. We were getting some traction and some exciting interest in our product. We had done a permission-marketing kind of campaign. At the very beginning of this, we weren't sure that anybody wanted it. So we put up a little, three-page splash site that said, "Hey, here's some screenshots that are fake of what we're building, and if you'd like to have this, give us your e-mail address and we'll let you know when we launch."

Bob: And how many people responded?

Tony: Well, on the basis of literally that three-page HTML site with no code behind it, we got on *TechCrunch*. And the way we got on *TechCrunch* was, again, very organic. We didn't pitch them. We posted on a couple of forums in various places: "Hey, here's a site." And all we really wanted to do was measure, for every 100 people who we can get to come to the site, what percentage of them will give us their e-mail address? What is their sort of take rate for this value proposition and these screenshots that we're pitching?

And we found that about a third of the users who came to the site would give us their e-mail address, which was very encouraging. *TechCrunch* will give you 12,000 to 14,000 uniques over a weeklong period. I mean, we got about 4,000 from *TechCrunch*, and then a lot of splash coverage from that.

Bob: So you started by saying to the world, "This is what we're going to do. Do you want us to do it?"

Tony: Yeah. [laughs]

Bob: And no code, other than whatever form you had.

Tony: Yep.

Bob: And from there you got press, because *TechCrunch* picked it up, because they decided to pick it up. Did you apply to Y Combinator? Did they come to you? How did that happen?

Tony: Y Combinator has an application process. And the Y Combinator thing was kind of my idea to my cofounders to say, "Hey, I want us all to jump into this full time." And we all had full-time jobs. We were fairly well compensated for what we did. So Y Combinator was sort of a, "Hey, if Y Combinator accepts our application, that will be sort of the thing that pushes us out of the nest, so to speak." [laughs] So we did apply. It's a one-and-a-half-page application, very small. It takes probably a couple hours to fill out well. And so the process, they won't publish how many people apply, but it's in the sort of thousands of people apply for about 20-ish company slots.

Bob: OK.

Tony: And they will basically call you if they like your application and fly out—I think, for us, it was about 50 or 60 people—to go through a 10-minute interview process. We managed to get 17 minutes, so we were fairly encouraged by that. But that is the amount of time that they give to you. And that interview process is just riotous in its chaos. It's pretty amazing. So you go in, and you think you have this agenda and this demo that you're going to pitch. And they very strongly emphasize that if you're going to go to Y Combinator for this interview that you'd darn well better have a demo.

So we had this demo and this flow that we were going to show them through the demo. We got about two minutes into the demo, and then we start getting peppered with questions. And it goes off on tangents. It's really just total stream of consciousness from Paul Graham and the other interviewers, just peppering us with questions.

So the agenda that we had sort of set up and the practice that we did was not—I mean, it was valuable, I think, but it had very little resemblance to reality.

So if you're going to practice for that particular interview, I would practice—find someone who will pretend to interview you and constantly pepper you with questions.

Bob: You mean, like, grill you unmercifully?

Tony: Yeah. [laughs] I would say that's pretty safe. And they ask very good questions. When you get the gist of a demo, it doesn't make sense to get into the sort of details of what the software does, because the software's going to change dramatically.

Bob: OK.

Tony: So the sort of central tenets of Y Combinator are "Build something people want," which is seemingly obvious, but so many people build things that are neat that no one actually wants, that are technologically impressive that no one has an itch for. So "Build something that people want" is really the sort of core thing that they're after. And beyond that, [laughs] they don't have a lot of criteria.

Bob: And what were the top three things or one thing or five things that you got out of Y Combinator?

Tony: It's a pretty long list. Toward the top, a real quick one is obviously just the credibility. This is a pretty exclusive club that Y Combinator has kind of built. So if you've made it through there, that immediately gets you access to reporters and investors and bloggers and things that you wouldn't otherwise have easy access to. It's a bit of a leg up, there. There's obviously the huge mentorship that Paul Graham, Trevor Blackwell, and Jessica Livingston all provide. They are very generous on that front.

These guys, obviously . . . You think about what most mentors have. They have maybe one startup under their belt or maybe two. I think with that, oftentimes you don't necessarily have great pattern recognition. You might have seen one way that things succeeded. But you've only really seen one kind of success.

Paul Graham, having mentored, literally—I think he's into about 150 of these companies. I think Paul Graham and all of these guys have a really unique perspective. They can see patterns in startups that other people can't see because they don't have the depth of the variety of startup vision that Paul had.

Bob: Right. OK.

Tony: I think that's really powerful. I think one of the hugest lessons was: Build something that a small number of people want a lot rather than a lot of people want a little. Find a small audience that would literally chew off their own leg to have what you are building.

Bob: [laughs] OK.

Tony: The idea there is that once you find a heart of people who are madly in love with what you are doing, then to get bigger and more successful as a startup, all you need to do is find more people like that or move laterally to serve a slightly different type of audience. An example is, you might say, "Gosh, we serve a small audience. You're making a small product." Craigslist launched serving San Francisco. They are a little bit bigger than that now. Amazon launched selling books. Gosh, they are doing a little bit more than books now.

If you do it the other way, and you make something that everyone kind of thinks is neat, then what is the action item for you to get more successful? What do you do? You basically have to make them want it more. What is the formula for making them want it more? It's a hard formula to know. You don't know what's missing from your product to make them love it, because right now they only just like it.

Bob: I see where you're going with this.

Tony: That was really kind of a neat thing to hear. We focused on our core users, the users who are really enjoying it and yelling at us to build certain things and add certain things to the product. Yeah, and Paul, the other thing that he really focuses on is to listen to your users. If you aren't building something that you yourself are madly in love with . . . Paul built Viaweb, which was an e-commerce platform.

Bob: I remember it.

Tony: He wasn't necessarily a shop owner. He was a software developer who saw a need. So when you aren't building something that you yourself are a passionate user for, listen to your users. Be constantly engaged with them, and make sure you understand what they need. It's not always what they say they need. That's an art form in and of itself.

Bob: How much did that $20,000 help?

Tony: Part of the Y Combinator thing is that they do you give you money. You notice that I didn't list that on the valuable assets that we got from Y Combinator. For us, Y Combinator attracts a bunch of different types of people, ranging from 20 years old to I think the oldest is 40. You don't want to talk about it too much, but some of those guys are going to the Y Combinator meetings driving Mercedes SLKs. Especially as Y Combinator gets more and more credibility, you get higher- and higher-end people applying.

I don't think the financial motivation is that it's nice for someone, some wunderkind, applying out of college and wanting to live in an apartment and eat Ramen. We live pretty cheaply, but obviously the money doesn't get you far. It gets you three months' worth of server bills, rent, and Ramen. [laughs] That's how I always put it.

Bob: Were you building RescueTime while you were in the Y Combinator program, or did that come later? In other words, how long before you launched 1.0?

Tony: That's the other thing that Paul emphasizes. I keep saying Paul and that's wrong. It should be Y Combinator.

Bob: OK. We'll take that as the entire Y Combinator team.

Tony: He is the squeakiest wheel there. One of the other things that he emphasizes is to release early. Get something out the door. Because before you get it out the door, you are operating on theories. Just like no battle plan survives contact with the enemy, no product plan survives contact with the users. Yeah. Basically, the idea with Y Combinator is almost everybody . . . He'll push really hard and at the end of three months, you'd better have launched your product. Some people take a little bit longer.

Certain products are more ambitious, obviously, than others. But really, finding that barest iota of value that you can create and trimming your feature set down so that you can launch it. Start getting that user feedback and that market understanding that you are just guessing at now.

Bob: Were you able to launch?

Tony: Yeah, we sure were. We weren't unique; this is happening more and more with Y Combinator. We had a moderately flushed-out alpha release even before we interviewed. We had a richer demo than a lot of people did. Some people apply literally with just an idea, and then have two weeks between their application and their interview to build some sort of demo.

That is the other kind of pattern recognition that Y Combinator tries to do: trying to understand what the recipe for a successful entrepreneur is.

I think initially they had a stronger bias toward education than they do. They used to think, "Oh, Ivy League is a good thing." I think, at this point they think it is a nonsignificant thing. It's not a bad thing, but it's not a serious determiner of success.

One of the things that they really focus on now is people who can't stop building stuff. If you can build a demo of something even moderately interesting in two weeks, that's encouraging. If you've actually got something out in the world, that's encouraging. That is a lot of what Y Combinator is a test of. Can you build something that people want in two weeks or three months?

Bob: OK.

Tony: Just about everybody did. I think there is one team that hasn't launched and a couple of teams that launched a little bit afterward.

Bob: Let me ask you a couple of more questions, and I think that will wrap it up.

Tony: Sure.

Bob: If you and your partners had not gone down to Silicon Valley and made this commitment to jump in to doing this app pretty much full time, do you think you would have succeeded?

Tony: I don't think so. I still think success is not a foregone conclusion. But I don't think we would have had the shot that we do. One of the things—and this is another Paul Graham-ism that I constantly parrot—the biggest motivator for most people isn't financial. It isn't building cool stuff. For a lot of people it is fear of public shame.

Bob: [laughs]

Tony: The way you hack this is . . . This is a life hack, right? People do this for weight loss and other things—they make a public declaration of intent. It means that if your startup fails, you are a failure. And if we hadn't jumped in full time, it would have been a side project. There have been times with RescueTime where things looked tough, right? We had a hard time.

Bob: Right.

Tony: It wasn't fun anymore. You push through those walls. But if it's just a side project, you don't have a ton of incentive to push through those walls. Because, gosh, you have this other idea that sounds like a lot of fun—your day job.

Bob: There is always another technology to chase.

Tony: Yeah. There is always something else fun to do. Now, if I publicly say, "RescueTime and Tony Wright are the exact same thing. When RescueTime fails, Tony Wright fails. This is now my livelihood." It is no longer the side project that didn't work out. It's the livelihood or core thing that is failing in Tony's life. That is a huge motivator, I think. Could we have done that without Y Combinator? Certainly. I think the cash didn't hurt. One of the things that I probably didn't list on the Y Combinator advantages that I could is that, after Y Combinator, about six months after Y Combinator ended, we raised a small Series A—very small and small on purpose. But nonetheless, it gave us the ability to have actual paychecks for the foreseeable future.

Bob: According to CrunchBase, your Series A was $900,000.

Tony: Yeah.

Bob: Let me ask it this way. Did Y Combinator up open doors you wouldn't have known about otherwise?

Tony: Absolutely.

Bob: For that's Series A.

Tony: Yeah, for the fundraising stuff, absolutely. Fundraising is hard. If anyone says, "Tell me the bullet points about fundraising that I should care about." For early-stage fundraising, the only bullet point you should care about is that there are two things that can allow you to raise early-stage funding. One is traction: people who are either paying for or using—whether you are a consumer or a business—either paying for or actively using your application and a growth curve that keeps growing. Or a rock star team, basically. You have Bill Gates coming out of retirement to help you with your product, or what have you.

Bob: How did you get Tim Ferriss, who I assume is the same Tim Ferriss we all know and love from "The 4-Hour Workweek"?

Tony: Yeah, that is. [laughs] Tim was interesting. He was introduced through another angel. This is really awesome. It's a great story. Tim actually was evangelizing RescueTime before we ever said a word to him. We saw in a *US News and World Report* interview with him that he was recommending Rescue Time. I was, like, "Oh my God, Ferriss is recommending us. How awesome is that?" I tried to e-mail him a thank you and never got anything back. The guy obviously gets as much e-mail as anybody.

Bob: Yeah.

Tony: When we were actually fundraising, one of the guys who did express interest in being an angel said, "Do you know who you should talk to is Tim Ferriss, and let me make an introduction." That is another lesson in fundraising: introductions win big. If you have an introduction from someone they trust, that is 90% of the battle.

On Y Combinator demo day, which is the big coming-out party at the end of Y Combinator, where you present to 100 to 150 investors. From that we maybe landed, ultimately, one or two investors. Every one of the other investors that we landed was an introduction chain from those initial investors.

So (a) introductions win and (b) you have to ask for them. If you have someone onboard who is willing to fund you, you say, "Can you give me five names of people who you think might be a good fit as an investor, and can you make that introduction? That is your first job as an investor." [laughs]

Bob: I think the key thing, to roll this all the way back, is you wouldn't have gotten those introductions—you probably wouldn't have gotten into Y Combinator—if you hadn't started with something that was remarkable and made people double take, based on what you could show them there.

Tony: Right. Absolutely. I think that making something remarkable and not underestimating the challenges of an early-stage startup are critical. If you are going to be funded, I think Y Combinator, TechStars, or anything of that sort is so incredibly valuable.

Recap

In this chapter we've discussed just how you go about marketing your startup's product with clarity and results. I've suggested that the right way forward is to understand and craft what I call a Unique Selling Proposition, and to make sure your web site delivers the components of that offer in the right way, in the right order.

We've talked to two startups who have made the leap from "I want" to "I am," and seen the outlines of how they got there while we've examined their web sites and how they communicate their USPs.

In the next chapter, we'll talk to a different kind of startup and arguably one of the foremost leaders in personal productivity, David Allen. And, standing on the shoulders of giants, I'll offer some suggestions on how you can and how you must improve your online, developer, and startup founder productivity.

Getting It Done

"If you spend too much time thinking about a thing, you'll never get it done."

—Bruce Lee (Martial artist/actor.)

"Nothing worthwhile comes easily. Half effort does not produce half results, it produces no results. Work, continuous work and hard work, is the only way to accomplish results that last."

—Hamilton Holt (American educator and author)

This Might Hurt

So far in this book, you've gotten off easy. Sure, you've learned a lot, had plenty to ponder, hopefully been somewhat entertained. None of that is going to make your startup a reality.

The sharp, hard truth is that building an app worth other people's money and wrapping a successful business venture around it means you are going to be working harder, more productively, and longer than you ever thought possible. And, yes, I know, you already work longer hours than any of your non-IT friends. I'm sorry to be the bearer of bad news, but that's the reality.

Nor will it be enough just to work real hard. Unless you're already the most productive person you know, you're not where you need to be to succeed. *Productive* here means, not how much information you consume, but the quality and quantity of what you produce.

For starters, we're going to cover some basic rules of productivity that, though widespread in the IT and business world, you might never have dug into. (If you're already familiar with David Allen and use his Getting Things Done (GTD) system for managing your workload, you can save some time by skipping ahead to the interview with David.)

Next, we're going to dig into this issue of productivity three times: first in terms of your online productivity, then in terms of you as a productive developer, and finally in terms of you as a productive startup founder. As we do so, I'm going to ask you to take stock of where you are, suggest some specific behaviors to adopt or change, check out a few select tools that I'll argue can make a huge difference in the quality and quantity of what you get done, and talk to a few people who have some real insights to share.

I think you'll find this an interesting and useful chapter. But I should point out something we both know: unless you actually follow the suggestions and perform the recommended actions that make sense to you, you're not going to get the results.

GTD in Summary

Here's the background on David Allen and GTD. Over the past decade, productivity expert David Allen has become something of the living patron saint of the IT world. His methodology—expressed first in *Getting Things Done—The Art of Stress-Free Productivity* (Penguin Books, 2001), then in *Ready for Anything: 52 Productivity Principles for Work and Life* (Penguin Books, 2004), and most recently in *Making It All Work: Winning at the Game of Work and Business of Life* (Viking Adult, 2008)—has taken hold in the business world, especially in the tech sector.

Although the details, nuances, and practical application of GTD fill not just David Allen's three books but dozens of other books[1] and hundreds of thoughtful blogs (see http://gtd.alltop.com) and spawned more than 300 GTD-centric applications, the core of GTD can be expressed in a single sentence:

> *You need to establish and maintain a comprehensive process for collecting, processing, organizing, reviewing, and doing all of the tasks and commitments in your life if you want to achieve results.*

---

[1] *If you're looking for the least amount of documentation to read before you start getting some results, I strongly recommend Leo Babauta's Zen to Done [http://www.47hats.com/?page_id=521] e-book ($9.50 USD). Leo has taken GTD and integrated it into the goal-setting and prioritization methods that made Steven Covey's The Seven Habits of Highly Effective People so popular. Think of it as a lightweight implementation of the more powerful GTD framework.*

Expanding this sentence touches on everything from striving to have no e-mails in your inbox to picking which software systems you'll put in place to manage your startup. We shall cover the core first.

GTD's Five Core Principles

- **Collecting.** For GTD to work—for *your life* to work—you need a comprehensive set of physical, digital, and online buckets for all the things on which you have to act. These buckets are anything but your memory and your mind, where—like a software process run amok—they would suck up focus and energy.

- **Processing.** At least weekly—and in some cases, such as e-mail, much more often—you should empty these collection points by systematically processing their contents. If an item requires action, you either do it (if it's something that can be completed in two minutes), delegate it to someone else, defer it to a specific date and time, add it to a new or ongoing project, or file it under Someday/Maybe. If an item requires no action, then file it as reference information, delete it, or let it stew for possible action later.

- **Organizing.** Mistaking projects for tasks can make the difference between creating a flow of actionable and achievable units of work and producing a morass of indigestible and stressful mini-crises ripe for procrastination. Some tasks are simple, atomic, binary; anything that takes more than one physical action is not a task but a project. Every project has at any given time one *next action*—a physical task that should be completed next to move the project toward completion. At any given time, you might have hundreds of multiple-step projects in progress and dozens of items that are waiting for someone else to do something. Although every project needs regular oversight and perhaps a plan, tracking those "waiting for" items is especially useful. So, too, is building your task-organizing system such that you can pull out similar tasks from different projects that make sense to do in a given context, such as running errands and meeting with your cofounders or working in your e-mail program.

- **Reviewing.** For GTD to work for you, you need a systematic approach to reviewing all tasks and projects at appropriate intervals. The reviewing process keeps you and your multitude of projects and tasks on course. Actual reviews can be as fleeting as deciding what your next action is to a more structured weekly review that ensures not only that things are getting done, but that the right things are getting the attention needed to advance objectives, goals, and values, this week, this month, and this year.

- **Doing.** Collecting, processing, organizing, and reviewing the things you need to do is not a substitute for actually doing them. But performing these processes consistently will give you the best chance to do what needs doing, with clarity, focus, and perhaps even fun.

What I've just presented is the briefest of summaries, summarized further into a great one-page cheat sheet in Figure 8-1. For more information, definitely get one or more of David's books and visit `http://gtd.alltop.com`.

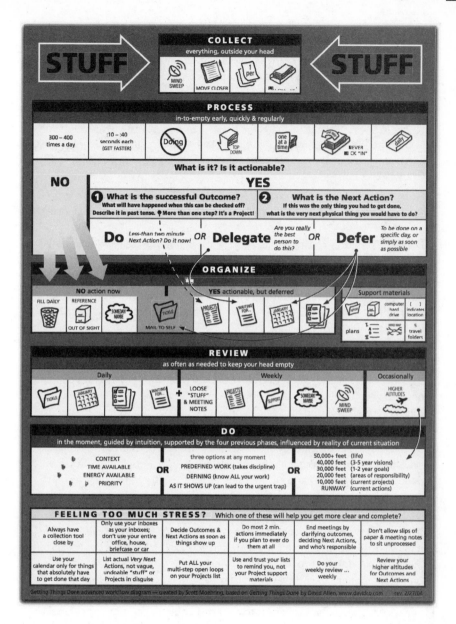

Figure 8-1. The GTD Advanced Workflow[2]

---

[2] *Used with permission of David Allen.*

David Allen, Author, Speaker

David Allen has been one of my personal heroes since I came across his 2001 book *Getting Things Done—The Art of Stress-Free Productivity*. For a long time I've felt that any startup that hopes to succeed needs to adopt GTD as a way of managing the very large load of tasks, open commitments, and responsibilities that go with creating a company.

In this interview, I was fortunate enough to be able focus with David on just what startups can and should expect from GTD. I got a lot out of it; I think you will too.

Bob: Maybe the place to start is in your new book, where you look at GTD from the points of view of control and perspective. What does that really mean?

David: Well, they're the two aspects of managing yourself and managing a company. If you're starting tabula rasa, you start with perspective. "Hey, I've got a vision. I woke up; I've got a fire in my belly. I've got to go do this thing."

Now you've got a vision, but now you just threw yourself into being a potential victim of modality because now you're the victim of your own creativity. Like what have I done, right?

Bob: The 10,000 things you need to do to get it done.

David: Yes, but the "it" is the starting point. It's just that if you already have an entity or it's already got legs of any sort and it's moving, oftentimes people need to get it under control. In other words, if your ship is sinking, you don't care where it's pointed. But once you plug it up, you'd better point it in the right direction or you'll keep hitting stuff that you don't want to hit.

So they're both key aspects of managing anything. It's kind of the simplicity on the other side of complexity—those two things. People say, "Look, we need to get organized and get focused." That's what you're going to tell anybody who's in: "Hey, let's get organized. Let's get focused. Let's try to start a company or have a party."

Any and all of that will require those two elements. So what I did in making it all work was just define How simple can you get? What does get organized mean? What does get focused mean? Actually, as you know, organization is only a component of getting control. So control is actually a better word. So if I'm trying to get control of it, those are five very distinct kinds of practices, behaviors, that require different tools, etc. I couldn't get it any simpler than those five.

The six horizons are basically the different conversations that you need to have in order to feel comfortable that this thing is in alignment, on track, headed in the right direction, and that you make choices about how you allocate your resources.

Bob: You and your company have worked with literally tens of thousands of people, applying GTD. Do entrepreneurs and/or high-tech people have an easier or harder time getting GTD right?

David: Yes.

Bob: [laughs] Let's unpack that a little further. I mean, what are the characteristics there?

David: One of my favorite sayings is "The better you get, the better you better get." So it's all relative to what you're doing. If you're not playing a big enough game, it's easy to stay in control and it's easy to stay focused. If you're playing a big enough game, you're going to throw yourself out of control and be losing your focus regularly. If you're not, you're stale.

So obviously, people in an entrepreneurial modality are going to be losing control probably faster, quicker, and in grander ways than almost anybody else, simply because of their nature. They've thrown themselves out into the world that doesn't exist. They've got to make things happen. They've got to make it up. Mission-critical stuff is showing up by surprise almost with every e-mail download.

That's no different than anybody in terms of what they're dealing with. So it's almost like the better you get, the more you're willing to take those kinds of risks, then the more you throw focus and control, or perspective and control, potentially at risk. In other words, it's not an either-or. It's not like, well, OK. Those people are better or worse at this. Other people need this more than anybody else. It just means that it's in a more intense situation where the necessity to do this is—the cycle for applying it—is perhaps a lot quicker and perhaps more important.

Bob: Sounds like they need to be—whatever way you'd like to say this—a hell of a lot better than people who are dealing with a lower threshold of change, of creation, of making things happen. I guess one question that comes to mind is, does GTD scale? That's a question that we always ask in the software world. Does this or that scale? Take the example of when you built GTD Connect [https://secure.davidco.com/connect], where you were basically a startup. How did that work out?

David: Well, it worked out very well. It was a component of a bigger thing that we needed to do, which was to provide ongoing support. I've been pretty much market-driven from the very beginning. It wasn't like I went out to make something up and then said, "OK, let me go see if anybody wants this." It was mostly just paying attention to what seemed to be needed, and if I had value to add to that: How could I do that? How do I create or maintain some business model so that I don't go broke in the process?

On a very big scale, 50,000 feet, our whole vision is, let's get GTD out there to the end of the world, to as many people as want or can use it. So how do you do that? How do you decide who it goes to, and how do you put a cash register on this process, our intellectual property?

Essentially, it's just common sense. But it's how it's packaged, how the methodology has been defined, and how we can help people deliver and implement that that is the value of our company. So this is just another modality. I said, "OK, I think we need something like that," so that's where that came from. I don't know if that answered your question.

Bob: I think it did. You've been (for lack of a better term) a startup founder. Yes, you had DavidCo before that, and it was a thriving business before that, but you've been into the hurly-burly of making a software thing happen now, an online software thing, at that. In that process, did anything stand out that kind of surprised you as far as different ways that you need to apply GTD as a startup founder, rather than, let's say, somebody who works at a corporation?

David: No, it's all the same thing. GTD is really nothing more than asking what the best questions are that you need to be asking yourself about anything, from a business standpoint. What are we trying to accomplish? How do you allocate resources to make it happen?

In a way, that's not rocket science, unless you're a jet propulsion lab, but it's essentially those questions we had to ask ourselves. So we are constantly having to eat our own dog food. Let's sit down and go, "Wait a minute! What's the purpose of that?" We're rethinking it right now, because as we move forward, we constantly need to keep ourselves honest and real and say, "Wait a minute! Is it fulfilling the purpose that was started? Is that still the viable purpose? What other purposes could this fulfill?"

Many times, there is a lot of ready, fire, aim: "Hey, let's put it out there. Let's get some feedback. Let's see what happens and iterate this thing." We've got our own version of sort of radical programming, which is "Yeah, let's build something, put it out there, and then reiterate the model."

So we're constantly doing that. We're constantly rethinking, reworking: Is this supposed to be? Is it what it needs to be? Is it what it's supposed to be? I think that's the only way you're going to keep anything vital and alive, especially in the world of the Internet and the Web and so forth, which is a constantly moving, changing event.

So you'd better be clear about what your purpose is. That's why I think GTD has been so sustainable, because it's very clear what its purpose is, and it's not about any particular system because systems always get out of date. Somebody is always going to come up with a sleeker, slicker, sexier way to keep a list. [laughs]

Bob: OK.

David: Ultimately, that's still what it's going to be, the very simple idea that people just need tools to help them focus. That's no different than it's been since dirt. So there's nothing new about the principles that we're trying to apply. How you engage with that, with the technology, in a way that makes it work best, that's another story.

Bob: Speaking of lists and tools, one thing that I picked up from *Making It All Work* was that it may not be possible or desirable to have just one GTD system, that is, one place where all tasks and projects go to live. Did I get that right?

David: Well, you just need reminders where you need reminders. I mean, if you pay your bills every Friday afternoon, you don't need to schlep your bills around for six and a half days. Just keep them where you pay your bills, and Friday afternoon sit down and pay them. So there's a big "duh" factor there. No need to carry them, unless you need to carry them. If you need to have ubiquity in terms of "At any point and time, I might need to be reminded about this," then you need to have that in a tool that you have at any point and time.

Bob: OK.

David: If that's true, you just need to make sure your system matches its purpose. See, most people never figured out what the purpose of this is; that's why productivity porn exists out there—everybody wants what's the latest, newest new thing. Is there a better way to get this done? If they figured out what the purpose of this was, they could fulfill the purpose with whatever they've got.

Bob: Are all those blogs that I guess are purveyors of productivity porn (try saying that three times fast), are they missing the point?

David: They might be, I don't know. It depends on what their point is. If all they're doing is saying, "Look, I've got my own spin about how to do this, and here's a cool way to do it. So I'm going to find all the people that happen to like it and do it my way, and I'll make some money off that." God bless them. I mean, that's cool. Why not? I mean, how many different kinds of gum can you chew? Lots of them. But that's more stylistic, it's not necessarily functional.

Bob: So it doesn't really matter whether they use (to put it in programmer terms) a defect-tracking ticketing system for those sort of tasks versus an agile scrum system for those other types of tasks. The goal here is not beauty and elegance. It's more along the lines of function and functionality.

David: Absolutely. There's an article in the new *Wired U.K.* magazine, by the way, that I highly recommend. I am now writing a column for them, and they have some very cool stuff. A new article on the new Paper-Net, for the web-based paper stuff. In other words, your printer—your aunt is going to send you a little thank you note through your printer. So it has nothing to do with what the tool is itself; it has to do with the functionality of it.

The truth of it is, a lot of people still like the touch and feel of paper. As a matter of fact, it's easier for the brain to integrate multiple horizons of information on paper than it is any other way. I love these companies that say, "We're going paperless." I go, "Grow up!"

Bob: It's not going to happen, huh?

David: It might, but only if the function the paper is serving can be better served some other way. But then, you have to come back to, what's the function?

Bob: So this is all about function here, not ceremony?

David: Right, function with a "K."

Bob: OK, function with a "K"?

David: Yeah. It's going to be funky and cool, isn't it? You know what I mean?

Bob: Oh, OK.

David: That's all it's about, really, come on! I'm into cool gear as much as anybody else. Anything small, black, high-tech, and expensive I just want. Later on I'll figure out if it does anything. Unfortunately, I just don't have the bandwidth to go test them out, because you truly have to try out all these things before you can find out how usable they really are.

Bob: Well, I'm not looking for a product endorsement for Apple, but what do you think of the Apple iPhone and all those GTD apps that are now available for it?

David: Well, the reason is that Apple basically has productivity as its third priority, entertainment first and communication second, and third is productivity. So productivity sucks on the Apple, because they haven't integrated the productivity functions as have Outlook and Lotus Notes.

That's why everybody is doing all of those apps, because Apple didn't give you a way to tie iCal to e-mail, to tasks lists; so everybody had to build it in. It will be cool when they get it, because they'll probably get it and add an elegant and stylistic factor that's really cool. Obviously, the visibility of the iPhone was probably a game changer, because that meant you could handle a lot more data well without going nuts trying to read it or trying to function with it is available through more portable devices. I'd say that's the real breakthrough, not the function.

Bob: I read recently that there's something over 300 desktop, web, mobile, and software applications that tout their "GTDness." How do you feel about that, being the spiritual founder of all that?

David: Yeah, it's cool! It's kind of amusing. It depends on what side of the bed I get up, in terms of whether I get up with my small ego or my big ego. If I get up with my big ego, I go, "Look, only a million and a half people have bought GTD and probably a lot of them haven't read it yet. We've got about 5.9 billion to go, wake up!" One part of it says, "Who doesn't need this? Anybody who's got to keep track of more than one thing at a time needs this methodology."

On the other side, I'm sort of amused that anybody catches this, because it's so subtle and on the surface looks like every other time management, personal organization thing that doesn't work out there. So it's kind of, which day are you asking me how I feel about it?

Bob: Well, there are things that are new out there. Since we last talked, there is something I would describe as a new kind of "human activity," online social media, such as Twitter, and, more importantly, the much, much larger networks, such as Facebook. How do you apply GTD to Twitter?

David: The way you apply GTD to a cocktail party or to your laundromat's bulletin board.

Bob: Well, how would you apply it to a cocktail party? I mean, you sit there and make a list, take everybody's input, and put that into your process bag?

David: Yeah, you carry a little David Allan NoteTaker Wallet with you, and in the cocktail party if somebody says, "By the way, you should read this book," write it down. I mean, what is social media but a global cocktail party, just through a different medium? What's the difference between that and a bulletin board in the laundromat? Same thing, just different medium. There's no qualitatively different thing about what that is.

Bob: I guess I'm hearing two things here. One is that you see online social media as something that people have been doing for, you know, 10,000 years, but in a new form now. Still, it's the same thing—social interaction. The other part of that is that the social interaction is one thing, but the things that become actionable out of that social interaction are another, and they should go in the hopper with everything else—digital, analog, online, offline.

David: Sure. But what the social media has done—to be a little more practical and *au courant* to what you're really asking—what social media has done is the same thing the Web and everything else has done: They've made input easy, sexy, cool, fun, a whole lot of potentially meaningful things.

Come on, how many links on Twitter can you see that could be cool, that could be worth reading, that could be "Oh my God!"

Bob: [laughs]

David: What that does is force you to read the back part of *Making It All Work*, which is, OK, what horizon am I really focused on right now? What's the purpose of my hanging out and allowing myself essentially to graze intuitively?

You can go to the cocktail party to avoid your life, or you can go there to find an investor in your new startup. Those are two very different purposes for going to the same event. Exactly the same thing with Twitter. Why are you doing it?

Bob: This is where we come back to control and perspective, I guess.

David: Sure.

Bob: Basically, if you're involved in an online activity such as Twitter and you're not clear about what it is you're doing there, well, you may get some good results, but they're going to be more by pure dumb luck than anything else.

David: Yes. There's a lot of ready, fire, aim-ness. I think you should just go out and do what you feel like doing, and then learn from your experiences. Don't make the same mistakes twice. So, yes, throw yourself into it.

I did. I wasn't sure how this was all going to work. My nephew, Scott Allen, was a big proponent to begin with. He turned me on to it. I interviewed Scott in my GTD Connect forum. Scott was doing a lot of early writing about the social media. What's the business application of social media?

I was not even clear myself. So I got onto LinkedIn, because I figured it was the most professional of all of those. Still, the jury's out for me about whether it is still worth it. Not a whole lot has necessarily come across there.

But I hopped onto Twitter about, I guess, two or three months ago. I had a sense intuitively that there was something there. I couldn't put my finger on it. But I'm staring now at 398,826 followers I've got. It turned out to be that this kind of little haiku format where I could do my little David Allen-isms and allow people to stay somewhat intimately involved with my thought process. That helps GTD stick a lot when you get around it.

So there's a service factor there just in giving people access to me and a sense of familiarity and informality that I think is important to wrap around GTD, so people don't get too wrapped up. I can hold that standard out there. It makes it a lot easier for people to engage and get access to it.

It's always a great thing to do while I'm standing in an airport security line. I just sit down, and pop something out, and just glance at all that. It is truly a global cocktail party. I happen to like to hang out. But sometimes I like to stand in the corner and just watch. Sometimes I get engaged in conversations. I think that's the best analogy I can give for it.

Bob: Now, it may be productivity porn, but one of the things that always seems to come up in the second or third paragraph when people are talking about GTD is information overload, especially online information overload, especially online information overload when you're browsing the Web.

I wonder, is there a way, be it a general idea or a specific tool, that you've come across for applying GTD to web browsing, to this wonderful idea of bookmarks and favorites? At least everyone I know, including me, ends up with thousands of these indigestible to-dos that are called Bookmarks.

David: Well, if they're reference, they're not to-dos. If they're to-dos and you can grab the to-do, that's a problem. It's kind of like people filing an e-mail that they need to respond to over in their reference e-mail. It's like, "Whoa! Wrong." You've now mixed up meanings.

Bob: Comingling of purposes there, huh?

David: That's exactly it. That's what disorganization is, where things don't match what they mean to you. So if you have two different things that mean two different things in the same place, that's, by definition, disorganized, and the brain gets confused. It has to re-sort it every time it looks at it.

That's why you don't want to open your Favorites list, because you've still got actions, you've told yourself subliminally, that are embedded in there and that you haven't pulled them off where you want to see reminders of actions to do.

But once you've filtered it like I have—look, I have two years of e-mail on my laptop here because I can. Why not? It's a library. I'm a serious pack rat. I keep all kinds of things. It's a good idea to purge that every once in a while, just so that it's not too big a black hole. If you have trouble finding things or if you've got a bunch of irrelevant things, then every once in a while it's kind of nice to clean the trunk of your car, your tackle box, and stuff like that.

Bob: I've noticed that one thing a lot of people get very excited about when they get into GTD is when it gets applied to e-mail. They are just liberated and energized by the idea of an actual day when they have achieved an empty inbox.

Now, we've got all these other types of digital communication, RSS, all the online social stuff. Is there any guiding principle there, other than you'd really need to be clear whether the place you're looking at is a point of collection or a point where it's going to be reference or a list of actual things that fit into the projects of your life?

David: Yes, well, that's back to the point that what most people don't do with e-mail is, they think a medium is one thing. No, it's a medium through which you then have reference material, and you have actionable stuff, and you have trash, and you have all kinds of things. You just have to put it through the same drill.

To me, it's just bizarre that people . . . I have never heard anybody say, "I get too many messages on my answering machine. I get too many voicemails." Well, some people say voicemails, but frankly, nobody complains about those. What's the difference? There's no difference. Each one of them, you get stuff that's just reference stuff, that's just trash, and stuff you need to act on.

What people don't do is leave it there, undecided. But they do about e-mail. They also do it by paper. That's why most people are highly voice-addicted, and most cultures are voice-addicted. That's why interruptitis is so huge out there, because if you have something you consider timely and meaningful that somebody needs to know and hear, you've got to deliver it to them by some sort of auditory means, because that's the only thing they're processing.

Well, I just go, "Duh! Somebody give me the rationale for this." And there is none. E-mail wouldn't be a problem if it blew up like your answering machine did once you got more than a screen full.

Bob: [laughs]

David: People go, "Oh, I guess I better empty this," thus allowing them the luxury of nondecision. That is not e-mail's fault. That is theirs.

Bob: OK. So it is a case of "Doctor, heal thyself."

David: Sure, and I understand it is a beast because there is a lot of stuff and you better be fast and you better be typing 60 words a minute. You better stop using your mouse. You better use speed keys.

I mean there is a little bit of a grow-up factor here. This is going to be a significant factor and the keyboard is still going to be the most important tool you'll have the rest of your life. So if anybody doesn't get that, then wake up.

Bob: A couple more questions. One thing that popped out of *Making It All Work* is that you sort of trashed that there is an idea of a life–work balance. You called it a hoax. Isn't that basically like saying Santa Claus doesn't exist?

David: Well, no. I didn't say balance didn't exist. Balance is actually what you're after. But you should make life and work two different things. The truth is that most people go somewhat dead when they go to work. So I suppose it is more of a descriptive term than a prescriptive term. You know?

Yeah, I guess a lot of people just don't consider those the same thing. But once you are in your zone, once you really get this, when time disappears, you are not making any qualitative distinction internally between "Is this work?" or "Is this play?" or "What is this?" You don't care. [laughs]

That is only an issue when there is no balance and then you say, "Well, I need to get balance." For some people, balance is 98% of what you'd call work. You know they're 24. It is all an adrenaline rush. They get bored when they go home because there is nobody there but the cat and they don't even like the cat. So they would just as soon stay at work the whole time because it is more fun. So when I say it is a hoax, I was just making a point, obviously, that the fact that you even set up that dichotomy is very, very unusual in the history of the world.

As I say, farmers have never split that. Just What's next? What's next? What's next? It's all work. That is why the kind of play on words I've in the title *Making It All Work*. It is all work.

Bob: [laughs]

David: Make your life the work you have to do on the planet, and then . . . Look, some of it you get paid for and some of it you don't. Some it you are just moving through.

Bob: Any final advice for people who are creating startups on how GTD can help them succeed?

David: I've talked to VCs who have been involved with a lot of startups. There are two or three things that will cause a startup to crash. One is if you haven't protected your intellectual property.

Bob: OK.

David: So make sure that is handled. The other is lack of funding and resources, you know, enough to get it off the ground. And the third is execution. Most of the VCs that I've talked to will tell you that number three is the biggest issue. They don't get the thing done. They've got the plan. They've got the money. They've got the IP protection. But they just don't get the stuff off the ground the way they need to.

GTD is the execution methodology. It is how you get stuff done. Define what *done* means and what *doing* looks like and where it happens, and that is a constant, ongoing set of best practices. Most people don't sit down and do that kind of thinking until the heat of the situation forces them to.

This is opposed to, I need to train myself to be thinking outcome–action, outcome–action, outcome–action on a consistent basis. And constantly, as I get new meaningful input, constantly recalibrating all of the mix I've got about all my commitments. And then refocusing and point and shoot again.

So that's where, as I say, on the part of the entrepreneur, it isn't a nice-to-have, it is a must-have as a success factor to make sure these things get done.

Bob: OK. David, thank you very much. I think that when people read this interview, it is going to open some eyes, especially among all the startups, who basically live in a whirlwind of things to do and who wonder just how to execute that whirlwind.

David: Yep. Well, my parting words are just these: Read *Making It All Work,* especially the chapter where I focus on paying attention to what has your attention. Because if you don't give appropriate attention to what has your attention, it will start to take more of your attention then it deserves.

So as my last tweet says, "When you know what you are doing, efficiency and style are your only opportunities."

Bob: There you go. Thanks so much.

David: Most people don't know what they are doing, so [laughs] that's their problem.

Bob: There are times when I fit into that category too. But I think that, for entrepreneurs, for founders who sometimes feel that they are running on a tightrope across the Grand Canyon, the end that they've started at is already on fire.

David: Yeah, I know the feeling. I'm a 30-year overnight success. I'm still in it.

Bob: And I think that one of the things that keeps coming back to me is that this isn't something that you do once. You keep coming back to it and you keep finding more and more levels of understanding in application to your own life. And whether you are building a startup or you are still working in a nice structured somebody else's corporation environment, the principles apply. And you need to practice the skills that make it possible to apply those principles, even if you are under duress and stress of, let's say, massive change in your life.

David: Another way to say that, Bob, is that when you are under massive stress, it is too late. You are going to be in survival mode, so you just have to hope that what you've built in as your default best practices and systemic responses are the best. So the trick is, when you are not in crisis mode, what part of your process do you need to be working on so that when the next surprise hits you'll deal with it with more efficiency and elegance.

Bob: Well, maybe that raises one last question, which is, how do you get out of crisis mode? Let's say you've got your startup, you've got your vision, but it is not getting executed. How do you get out of this?

David: Back to pay attention to what has your attention, what most would relieve the biggest amount of pressure if you made progress on it. And get a next action on it and go.

Bob: And that's it.

David: That's it.

GTD Recommended Software

As contrarian as it may sound, the best way of tracking your GTD data might be with a paper notepad, index cards, or any kind of notebook you fancy. As the sayings go, the devil is in the details, your mileage will differ, and no two computers have exactly the same configuration.

There are hundreds of software applications (including one I wrote[3]) on every platform, from the Apple iPhone to Lotus Notes. And, unfortunately, to my knowledge no one tool is powerful, flexible, and comprehensive enough to work for all people in all circumstances. But whether it's a Moleskine notebook, a hybrid desktop/mobile app, or something else, the more effectively it works for you to implement these five principles, the better.

That said, I would like to commend two GTD-friendly apps to your attention if you want to get on the GTD train via software: *Remember the Milk* (RTM) and *Things*. Remember the Milk (http://www.rememberthemilk.com; see Figure 8-2) is a simple and elegant online task manager with over 750,000 users of their free and Pro ($25/year) plans, mobile clients for

---

[3] *MasterList Professional for Windows, now sold by masterlistpro.com at* http://masterlistpro.com.

the Apple iPhone and BlackBerry. RTM's simplicity, its integration with Google Maps and Twitter, and its robust functionality make it a good choice.

Figure 8-2. Remember the Milk.

If you use a Mac for your desktop and an iPhone as your mobile platform—as I do nowadays—let me recommend Things, from Cultured Code (http://culturedcode.com/things) Although there are other very good GTD apps for the Mac—notably OmniFocus (http://www.omnigroup.com/applications/omnifocus) and Midnight Inbox (http://www.midnightbeep.com), I've found Things to be an extremely lightweight application, with a fast and reliable iPhone client. Figure 8-3 presents a screenshot of my copy of Things, to give you a taste of the application.

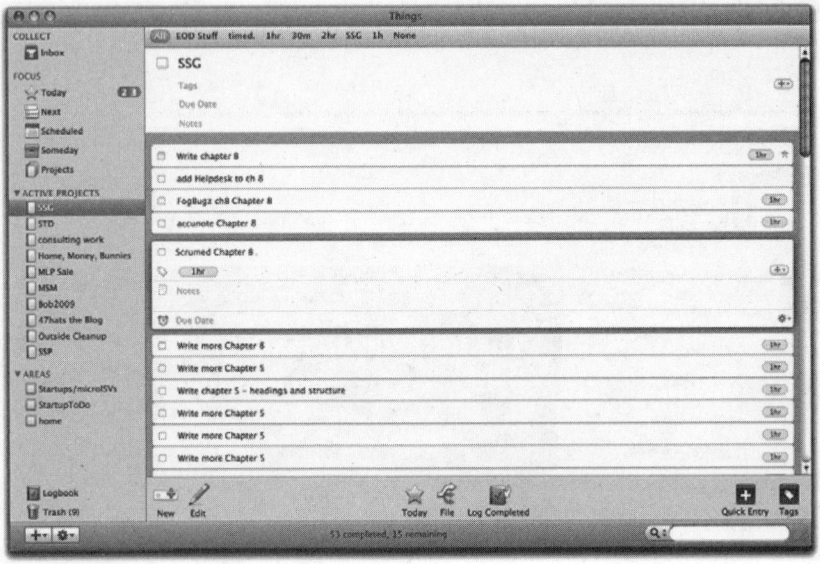

Figure 8-3. Things

After many years and many applications, I've come around to the position that, at least for me, the best GTD software is the software that adds the absolute least amount of overhead to managing a task load, a conclusion that may or may not work for you.

For Windows, a large number[4] of choices are available, including David Allen's own Getting Things Done Outlook Add-in (https://secure.davidco.com/store/other.php). Patrick Foley, my cohost at the Startup Success Podcast, swears by AbstractSpoon Software's ToDoList (http://www.abstractspoon.com).

Having been keenly interested in GTD for many years, I consider the major trend to be pairing either a desktop or web-based main application with a lightweight app for your mobile device of choice. But, again, it's all about what works for you.

---

[4] Priacta's list of 111 reviewed GTD software apps includes 52 for Windows: http://www.priacta.com/Articles/Comparison_of_GTD_Software.php

Matt Cornell, Productivity Expert

Matt Cornell (http://matthewcornell.org) is a Massachusetts-based consultant who regularly trains teams at NASA and elsewhere on the finer points of personal and small-team productivity. If his advice can make rocket scientists more productive, it should be just what you need for your startup.

Matt has three big pieces of advice for software developers who are now going from established work environments to a situation where they're building not only a specific product but the set of business practices, informal rules, and values that define a particular corporate culture.

1. **Use micro-experiments to amass actionable, non-emotionally charged information about your own productivity first.** Most of those who work online have no idea of how fractured our attention spans have become. "Bad habits are what we're talking about," Matt said. "Just keep a little timer, an online timer or whatever. And when you start a project, like you're starting coding some module or fixing a bug, just start your timer, and then catch yourself, the next time you think about switching to e-mail or you actually do switch over and check your inbox, right? And look at that number. And I bet you'll be very surprised at how few minutes transpire before you switch."

2. **Build a set of agreements with your fellow founders on how and when you're going to communicate.** "You need to start having some, I won't say policies, but some understandings about interruptibility," Matt suggests. "It's very tempting—and you see this all the time—to just shout over the cubicle or do an instant message and say, 'Hey, got a second for this?' And everybody says yes.

    "But for the company, that's not the best answer, unless it's urgent. A better answer is: 'I'll be taking a break at noon. Let's talk then. Can it wait?' An even better answer is not even having to answer. In other words, people know: save up your questions. Use a GTD agenda, for example, and save it up till you have a regular meeting.

    "I think one of the things we're talking about here in terms of moving from personal productivity to group productivity is that the group has to set some boundaries as far as interruptibility. And it's actually a pretty explicit agreement that, 'OK, from this period to this period a day, at noon or whatever, these are the times I can answer those questions, I can deal with those interruptions. That's all I'm doing is that stuff.'"

3. **DRY (don't repeat yourself) applies to business, not just writing software.** This is a two-for-one point: certain kinds of information work best when housed in an application that is designed for effectively processing that information. A prime example is bug defects. "One of the most common GTD frequently asked questions is, 'How do I integrate with my sales system, my bug-tracking system, my ticketing system, and customer support?' This comes up all the time."

4. Instead of moving information from your bug-tracking system, to e-mail, to your own GTD system, time-block your work. "Say, 'OK, in the morning I'm going to work strictly from a ticketing system. That's my to-do list. And in the afternoon I'm going to work from the rest of my list.' Because it doesn't make sense to pull out tickets into a GTD-like system. You want to work within the ticketing system or the bug-tracking system. Let them be separate islands of tasks or actions or activity is my thinking. And then integrate them into your workday as needed, whether it's doing it by blocking by time, or we can brainstorm other ways to do that. But, yeah, let them be separate islands of tasks or whatever, and then bounce around as you need."

The second point Matt makes about keeping information DRY in a small team is establishing conventions about communicating information that save everyone time. "You want to limit how much interaction you have of the mundane sort so that you can prioritize the kind of human interaction that makes a group function well," Matt said. "There are certain kinds of things, like sharing documents and such, that you don't want to have to be sending an e-mail necessarily, because you need to get together when you're making decisions."

Online Productivity

Now that we've covered basic task management, it's time to focus on what I like to call *online productivity*. Online productivity is all about focus, taking conscious control of how you work and communicate online. Let's start with five simple questions about your current state of online productivity.

- How often do you interrupt your work to check e-mail? (a) Three times a day. (b) Three times an hour. (c) Constantly.

- When reading RSS feeds, which do you do? (a) Set a time limit and cull out a few select posts that I want to act on. (b) Skim posts for interesting items a few times a day. (c) Read everything and anything until my brain is mush.

■ When do you check in with your social networks on services such as Twitter and Facebook? (a) When I have specific things I want to share or am not at work. (b) Regularly to catch up with what everyone I know online is doing. (c) They're always on because it's more fun than working.

■ How many e-mails do you have in your inbox right now? (a) Only those that I haven't processed already today. (b) Only those I processed this week. (c) So many I don't even want to think about this question.

■ When's the last time you cleaned up your browser's bookmarks or favorites? (a) I do it weekly as part of clearing and processing sites into reference information and tasks to act on. (b) I have a system for organizing my URLS, but it needs a good cleanup. (c) It's a hopeless mess.

If you answered (a) to all of these questions, then congratulations! If you answered (b) to most or all of them, then maybe it's time to start noticing how much of your attention is being consumed by communication instead of by work. If you answered (c) to most or all of them, then it's time to reinvent how you work online because your present approach is not going to serve your startup aspirations.

Online productivity means being in control of how much information you consume, when, and for what purpose. Now, maybe you're an incredibly intelligent person with so much brainpower and focus that you can constantly bombard yourself with web-based information and e-mails while powering through, with single-minded determination, one task after another all day long. But I wouldn't bet on it. And it's hard to believe that you're doing your best work with a fire hose of information turned on full power and aimed square at your face.

Taming the Info Beast

Unfortunately, this book does not come equipped with a magic wand you can use to cast a spell around yourself that changes behavior, protects you from the crises of the moment, and neatly orders up the Online World. But there are ways you can improve your online productivity by making—and when necessary remaking—a few simple changes in how you interact online. Note: These nine steps are simple, and they will significantly improve your online productivity, but it's not easy breaking old habits.

1. **Create a firebreak.** If your e-mail inbox has hundreds of unhandled messages, your RSS feeds are beyond control, and your bookmarks have run amok, you need to create some breathing space for yourself. Change your online IM status to "unavailable," Stick your unhandled e-mail into a folder labeled "e-mail bankruptcy," export your current RSS subscribes to an OPML file, and zero out your subscriptions. Yes, this is pretty drastic stuff, but half efforts are inadequate to the challenge at hand.

2. **Reset e-mail expectations.** First, change your automatic signature or add one to every e-mail (all e-mail clients can do this) so that it lets the world know what to expect when it communicates with you via e-mail. Nothing elaborate—I use "(I check e-mail several times during the business day.)"—but something to make clear that your days of always-on-e-mail are over.

3. **Reset e-mail usage.** How many e-mails do you get that are self-inflicted time-management wounds? You know what I mean: all those subscriber e-mails that over the years you either signed up for or passively let happen, from every Web 2.0 site on the planet, every online retailer of any size, every single news site. These aren't communications—their info dumps at your expense.

   Here's the algorithm: For each subscribed e-mail, unsubscribe unless it still has real value for you. If it does have value, switch to their RSS feed or use Page2RSS (http://page2rss.com), FeedYes (http://www.feedyes.com), or a similar tool[5] to force a feed out them. Repeat until the queue of attention-draining e-mail infomercials is empty.

4. **Repurpose your RSS Reader with PostRank.** See Chapter 6 for details on how to use PostRank to attach a filtering system to you RSS reader of choice.

5. **Set IM/Skype boundaries.** Whatever instant messaging client(s) you use, set the default status to something that makes clear that you're less than immediately available. This may cut into your social life (startups, by the way, don't have social lives), but it will cut down the number of times friends and family interrupt your workflow because you've given them permission.

---

[5] See http://techpp.com/2009/04/27/top-10-free-tools-to-create-rss-for-any-website-2.

6. **Time-box and group your social media interactions.** For example, morning and night I go on Twitter with Tweetie (Mac: `http://www.atebits.com/tweetie-mac`, $19.95), respond to direct messages and mentions, lightly scan the timeline for anything worth spending time to investigate, retweeting, or commenting on, and then log off. I limit my Twitter time to my communication periods (see item 8), and that's it, except when I am completing a task such as "Tweet finished Chapter 8."

   Again, the idea here is that when you're communicating, you're not working. You can no more expect to get a day's work done with Twitter—or Facebook or whatever—on continuously than you could with your phone to your ear for eight hours.

7. **Set your public telephony to voicemail.** I have a business telephone number. I don't answer it—ever! My voicemail message makes clear that the best way to reach me is via e-mail—on my terms. Unless you're behind a corporate telephony firewall, landlines in the United States are hopelessly pawned to robo-dialing telemarketers. I have a mobile phone. Only my family, friends, and the handful of people with whom I work day in and day out have that number.

8. **Schedule communication periods.** In whatever calendar app you use to track appointments, create two to three 45-minute appointments for each day for the next week during which you will turn on e-mail, surfing, IM, Twitter, and all the rest. These are your communication periods, when—and only when—you process e-mail, chat with friends and coworkers, check sites, Twitter for fun, and generally be a social animal.

   By scheduling this behavior, you start to get a handle on it—and realistically take it into account when estimating how much work you can get done in a day. I need between one and two hours a day for communication; you may need more or less than that.

9. **Go to the bank and get $100 in dollar bills.** Then stack those nice crisp dollars (or pounds or euros) on one side of your desktop or notebook computer. Every time you check e-mail impulsively or use Google or another search engine to find a site that doesn't have to do with what you are working on, take a dollar and throw it in the trashcan under your desk.

10. Huh? Did he just say *throw away* money? That's exactly what I said—it's time to do a little psychological makeover on yourself. After all, you're wasting time and time is money—your money. This exercise just makes painfully explicit what you're really doing, and it connects the near-universal socially instilled abhorrence of denigrating money with the reality of what you're doing. Believe me, your behavior will change, and right quick.

Tools That Help

Improving your online productivity is not easy, but certain tools are out there that can be of help, and you should know about and consider using them if you don't already. Here are four suggestions.

- For Microsoft Outlook users, I strongly recommend Claritude Software's **Speedfiler 2.0 Professional** (http://www.claritude.com, $39.95). Before I switched over to Macs, Speedfiler week in and week out saved me about 25% of the total time I'd spend in Outlook by making it possible to file e-mail fast. I figured it paid for itself in the first two days.

- For Mac Mail users, depending on whether you prefer to file or tag your e-mail, get either **MailAct-On** or **MailTags** from Indev Software (http://www.indev.ca/MailActOn.html, $24.95, or http://www.indev.ca/MailTags.html, $29.95). In different ways, these two Mail add-ons speed up the processing of e-mail—a good thing.[6]

- David Allen's **GTD Connect** (http://gtdconnect.com, $48/month or $480/year). If you've read the books and the blogs about GTD but are still struggling to make it work in your life, I'd recommend GTD Connect, David Allen's online offering. GTD combines a huge library of video, audio, and text from Allen and other GTD trainers with a 16-module Getting Started course and member forums where you can learn from and share with others.

---

[6] *Full-disclosure time: Scott Morrison, Indev Software's founder, became a consulting client of mine after I bought Mail Act-On.*

- **TimeBoxed** on the Mac (http://www.macmation.com/TimeBoxed, 14.99), **TimeBox for Windows** (http://www.taubler.com/timebox/newuser.shtml, $9) or **TimeBox for Linux** (http://www.brothersoft.com/timebox-for-linux-69058.html, free), **Talk Timer** for the iPhone (http://www.inuse.se/talktimer, free). All of these tools do the essentially the same thing—help you focus on a given task or activity for a given period of time. Yes, this is simple stuff, but having a reminder visible helps you to refocus.

Before we move on to developer productivity, one final point. Since you are presumably not an AI, don't expect your productivity to go in one day from where it is to where it could be. You will experience setbacks. You will backslide. You will find old, ineffective habits reasserting themselves. That doesn't matter. What matters is that you get up one more time than you fall down.

Developer Productivity

The next level of productivity improvement that will aid your startup effort is developer productivity. Simply put, programming is one of those activities in life where small differences in input can make huge differences in quality and quantity of output.

Let's start with a bit of honest self-examination. It's time to take Joel Spolsky's **The Joel Test**.[7]

1. Do you use source control?

2. Can you make a build in one step?

3. Do you make daily builds?

4. Do you have a bug database?

5. Do you fix bugs before writing new code?

6. Do you have an up-to-date schedule?

---

[7] See http://www.joelonsoftware.com/articles/fog0000000043.html.

7. Do you have a spec?

8. Do your programmers have quiet working conditions?

9. Do you use the best tools money can buy?

10. Do you have testers?

11. Do new candidates write code during their interview?

12. Do you do hallway usability testing?

With the deferred exception of item 11, you should be answering yes to all of these questions. If you've ever wondered why Joel Spolsky is so popular with his fellow programmers, posts like The Joel Test are why—they offer great advice that makes a real difference in one's ability to execute.

Now, you may want to argue with some of the items on the Joel Test, but can you honestly say that if you're going to be a professional developer they don't apply? I don't think so.

Beating the Google Loop

Joel posted his test to Joel on Software way back in 2000. (You could do a lot worse in terms of professional education reading his posts from that era on.) Meanwhile, Joel and well-known programmer Jeff Atwood have tackled a major inefficiency in how most developers develop. Tell me if this sounds familiar: You're programming away in your language of choice and you hit a roadblock, a bug you can't figure out, a hole in your mental database of programming expertise. So you Google it. And before you know it, you're sifting through umpteen blog posts, code snippets, forum posts trying to figure out which pages have information that's valid and pertinent today. Guess what? You've just spent an hour on this one problem, because Google shows answers based, not on how correct they are today, but on how many hits and links they've received cumulatively. You've just—again—gotten into the **Google loop**.

Joel's and Jeff's—and your—antidote to the Google loop is Stack Overflow (http://stackoverflow.com; Figure 8-4). Begun in 2008, Stack Overflow is an intelligent way for programmers to ask specific technical questions and get them answered in a timely way. Stack Overflow now gets over 600,000 page views and 250,000 visitors a day—a substantial portion of all programmers.

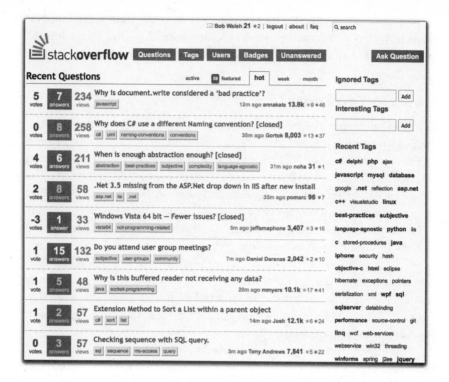

Figure 8-4. Stack Overflow

The mechanism behind Stack Overflow is deceptively simple: You post a technical question such as "Which table plug-in for jQuery are developers using?" or "Can I preemptively do caching in Django?" or "Why is WCF throwing an `Exceptions.DataSourceNotFoundException` in my code?" You tag it, and, as with a wiki, others can edit your question to improve it. Other developers gain reputation points by offering up answers, which range from RTFM to specific code examples, in a matter of minutes, hours, or days, and you decide which is the best answer offered. If you've been answering other people's questions, then your reputation is higher, other developers working in the same area are more likely to respond, and you can offer a bounty of reputation points to them.

As of April 2009, how much was a reputation point worth? Zip. But it's easy to see—given the success of the job board at Joel on Software—how these reputation points and community badges could easily ascend into what Alvin Toffler calls a para-currency[8] that has real, extrinsic value.

If you're not using Stack Overflow to reduce the number of Google loops in your development process, you are shortchanging yourself in a major way—it's that useful, that good, that comprehensive.

How Do You Learn?

Besides finding specific bits of information about the programming languages with which you are working in your startup, a larger, deeper problem is at work here: the half-life of technical information has plummeted this century. Back in the 20th century, entire years would go by when the definition of a programming language and what the best ways of using that language were would remain virtually unchanged. This gave programmers a chance to learn a language and gain some proficiency in it before having to retool to the next major version.

Now, regardless of what language or platform we are talking about, you're lucky if you can go three months without a major change in what's on offer. For example, during the 18 months I went from total Rails newbie to moderately competent midlevel proficiency, no less than five significant new versions were released.

Making matters worse from a productivity perspective, the number of specific languages and frameworks in which you need to be competent in order to build a monetizeable codebase has grown. For example, for a web app, in addition to your main programming language, at a bare minimum you'll probably need JavaScript, a JavaScript framework such as jQuery, and CSS.

So how do you cope with rapid technical change? You could opt out: work with what you know, ignore new stuff, and get done. That will work (if getting to 1.0 is a matter of months, not years), but that new stuff can sometimes save you 10 to 50 times its weight in development time, avoid your getting caught in a bug bottle that was fixed in a later version, and open new functionalities your app could use. In sum, not a great choice.

---

[8] *Revolutionary Wealth: How It Will Be Created and How It Will Change Our Lives*, by Alvin and Heidi Toffler (Broadway Business, 2007).

Or you could just try to swot up whatever you need to improvise as you go along. That works, so long as you're honest with yourself that you're building in a variable amount of overhead to every programming task you tackle and that the overhead on any given day might explode in your face.

Or you can block out some percentage of your week just for keeping an active watch on the core languages and frameworks in which you're working, running a quick scan of a core group of developer blogs that report new and relevant software developments, and playing with new code samples.

For example, I try to spend somewhere between one and two hours each week doing the following:

- Listening to the Rails Envy Podcast (http://www.railsenvy.com) and watching every single Railscast by Ryan Bates (http://railscasts.com)

- Reading through Mike Gunderloy's A Fresh Cup (http://afreshcup.com)

- Doing a quick PostRank-powered scan of the feeds from RubyInside (http://www.rubyinside.com), ajaxian (http://ajaxian.com), nettuts+ (http://net.tutsplus.com), and a few other rails bloggers I follow[9]

- Eyeballing what's new and popular at GitHub for Ruby (http://github.com/languages/Ruby) and JavaScript (http://github.com/languages/JavaScript)

The more consistently I work through the foregoing as a specific task, the less of a nagging feeling I have that I'm missing some important technical development or time-saving Open Source project.

Now, which online technical sources make sense for you to follow will in all likelihood be different. But I think taking a systematic, timeboxable, scheduled approach to keeping up technically has a lot to offer.

---

[9] *Alltop.com*—if it has a page for what you're interested in—is a high-speed way of sampling bloggers worth following.

Into the Heart of Darkness:
Startup Developer Methodologies

So far in this section we've been talking about effective ways of gaining useful technical information in a systematic way—good stuff, useful, not particularly controversial. Here's where that changes.

Ask five developers whether one specific developer methodology is better than others and you'll get 10 opinions, ranging from passionate paeans to vehement denouncements of any and all. Now, I'm not here to pick a fight with you—after all, you were nice enough to buy this book— but let me offer for your consideration the following.

- The methodology (or none) you use at your day job, be it as corporate code monkey or independent custom developer, serves the interests of the person who signs your check. However, for a small startup development team it may be exactly the wrong approach.

- You—and your cofounders if you have any—get to decide the software methodology. And not deciding is a decision in itself.

- The appropriate software methodology for a given project can make the difference between success and failure.

All that said, I'd strongly recommend that you consider adopting an Agile development approach to your startup. I'm not saying that Waterfall, V-Model, RUP, or Cleanroom are bad methodologies. But I do believe that a methodology that adheres to principles contained in the Agile Manifesto[10] is more likely to fit what a startup needs and that Scrum in particular makes a great fit for startup software development.

Here's the Wikipedia summary of Scrum:

"During each 'sprint,' typically a two- to four-week period (with the length being decided by the team), the team creates an increment of usable software. The set of features that go into a sprint come from the product 'backlog,' which is a prioritized set of high-level requirements of work to be done. Which backlog items go into the sprint is determined during the sprint planning meeting. During this meeting, the product owner informs the team of the items in the product backlog that he wants completed. The team then determines how much of this they can commit to complete during the next sprint. During a sprint, no one is allowed to change the sprint backlog, which means that the requirements are frozen for that sprint. After a sprint is completed, the team demonstrates the use of the software."[11]

---

[10] See http://agilemanifesto.org/ and, of course, Wikipedia.

Detailing Agile development in theory and Scrum in particular has been done already by many other, more skillful programmers than I. In fact, there's a mere 88 Scrum project management books currently listed at Amazon.com. Let me recommend exactly one to you, since you're reading this book: Dan Pilone's and Russ Miles' *Head First Software Development* (O'Reilly, 2008). Now, *Head First* books aren't everyone's favorite approach, and you barely find mention of Agile in it. But that's what this book convincingly lays out.

Another good source to check out is Tim Haughton's *The Agile Micro ISV Blog* at http://www.agilemicroisv.com. Up until just recently, Tim made his living helping British companies adopt and implement Agile software development methodologies.

For this book I asked Tim two questions: First, if you're creating a startup with, say, up to three developers, why should you adopt an Agile methodology from the start?

"When any project is led by the developers, as is usually the case with small software startups, there is always the temptation to start coding way too early." Tim replied. "One of the core aims of any creative project, software or otherwise, is so obvious it is often overlooked: Build the Right Thing! By following an Agile method, you will be forced to have an understanding of your whole product, know what the high-value bits are, what the high-risk bits are, and have prioritized accordingly.

"By breaking the application's functionality down into more finely grained 'stories,' you will again be hammering home the core message of "Build the Right Thing." The stories will direct a developer's hour-by-hour activities. One of a startup's strengths is focus. Using an Agile method will turn the focus dial up to 10; not a moment will be wasted on frivolous, unfocused development activities.

"Other Agile techniques, such as Test Driven Development, ensure you do the next important thing: Build the Right Thing Right!

Second I asked Tim, in his knowledgeable opinion, which Agile methodology offers the most bang to a startup?

"Ideally, any startup wanting to use an Agile method would understand the key methods like eXtreme Programming and Scrum. But it's more important to understand the synergies between the different practices within the methods; understanding how they play off each other. By embracing continuous improvement and tweaking the process as they go, the startup will end up at the right method for them."

---

[11] http://en.wikipedia.org/wiki/Scrum_(development)

Once you've absorbed the basics of Agile and perhaps Scrum, I recommend two web apps to provide support for your startup: **Acunote** and **scrum'd**. Acunote (http://www.acunote.com, from free to $99 a month) is designed specifically to support Scrum, provides motivating burn-down charts, integrates with other tools you're likely to use (Subversion, Trac, FogBugz, for example), and offers a generous free plan.

I used Acunote to plan and track StartupToDo's development and found it a very lightweight and productive tool. Figure 8-5 presents a screenshot from one Acunote sprint.

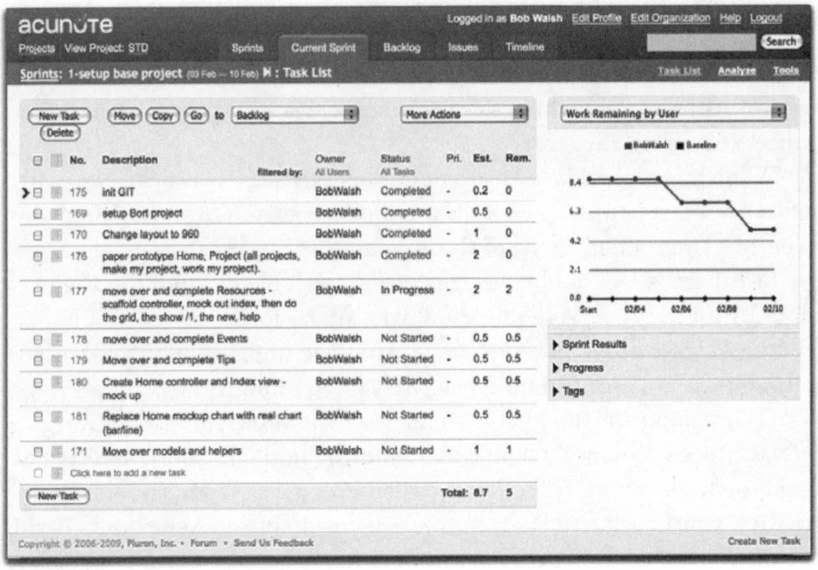

Figure 8-5. Acunote

In 2009, a new tool came out that was a worthy competitor to Acunote: scrum'd (http://scrumd.com, from $6 to $79 a month, depending on the number of projects). Whereas Acunote focuses on sprints, tasks, and burn-down rates, scrum'd adds a level above this by supporting easy creation of user stories, assigning user stories to sprints, and employing user story points to estimate amounts of work (Figure 8-6).

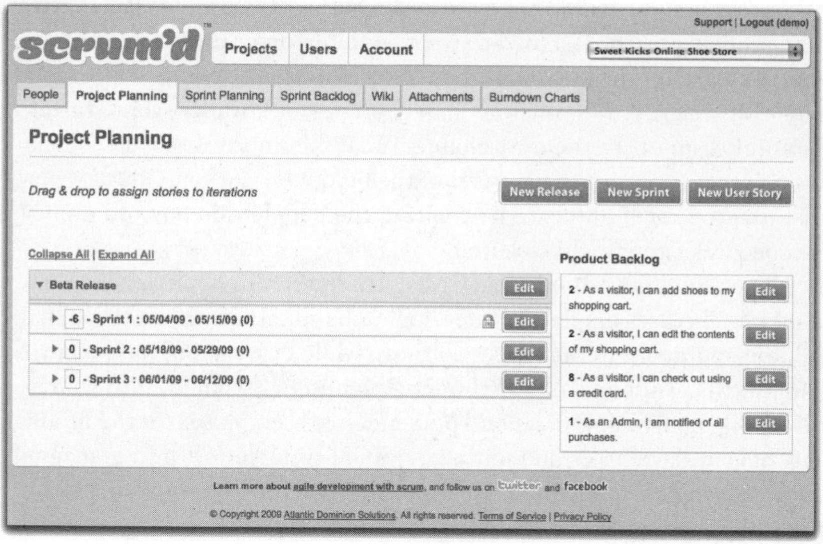

Figure 8-6. scrum'd

Your Least Favorite Subject

There's one final component of developer productivity we should discuss: tracking defects and providing tech support to your customers. Simply put, this is the yin to software development methodology yang, the other indispensable system you need in place before you launch. The more proficiently you and the rest of your startup team uses whatever system for collecting and processing bug reports, customer requests, and other inquiries, the less friction involved in delivering better software, creating happier customers, and exploiting new opportunities.

Somehow you are going to have to track, prioritize, process, and close each and every reported bug. Somehow, each time a customer contacts your company, you need to understand what they want, treat them well, and ensure not only that the issue they brought to the table is resolved, but that their irritation, anger, and sometimes outright rage are replaced to the degree possible with passion, enthusiasm, and maybe a bit of gratitude. These are big "somehows."

Unfortunately, many bug-tracking/customer-ticketing systems out there seem expressly designed to treat your customer like something you want to scrape off the bottom of your shoe. While large companies can get away with treating their customers like crap—for a while—your startup absolutely cannot. In the next chapter, we'll talk more about customer experience with one of the masters of the field, Lou Carbone. But for now, trust me, you do *not* want to be treating the people who pay you money like speeders caught and ticketed.

Depending on your customer base, there are two approaches I'd recommend. The first emphasizes developing happier customers through building and maintaining better software while creating an online environment that supports converting complaining customers into your startup's supporters. The second puts much less emphasis on the productivity of your developers and more functionality and effort into managing and improving each customer relationship that your startup has. Both approaches work; they are both better than competing and Open Source solutions. The key is what you sell and which approach is a better fit for *your customers*, not for you.

Fog Creek's FogBugz

Since its first release in November 2000, FogBugz (http://www.fogcreek. com/FogBugz, either $25 per month per SaaS user or $199 per year per user if you host[12]) has become a finely tuned tool for capturing and processing defect reports, feature requests, and inquiries in the most developer-effective way possible (Figure 8-7).

The core of FogBugz is bug tracking. Bug reports—from your customers via e-mail, from your application, from within your startup—are collected and put through a process that ensures that whoever reported the bug has final say-so on whether it has been corrected. This one design point ensures that with FogBugz you don't just file bug reports, you solve them.

Much of the depth of this product is its very careful design to make a team of people more effective at enhancing and developing a software application: from near-autonomous evidence-based work scheduling and estimation, to spam-proof customer e-mail, discussion group, and wiki functionality.

---

[12] *And you can convert your hosted trial FogBugz account into a Student and Startup Edition supporting two active users for free.*

Figure 8-7. FogBugz

I've used FogBugz over the years—as a microISV supporting a Windows desktop application and now as a startup improving and maintaining a web-based app and as a moderator at the large and popular Joel on Software Business of Software forum. When I say spam-free, results-oriented, low overhead, that's exactly what I've seen.

That said, there are functionality decisions built into FogBugz that may not work for you. Some people want their system to provide more functionality directly to customers, such as a knowledgebase or a more traditional forum functionality. If that's the case, UserScape's HelpSpot (http://www.userscape.com, $199 or less per user) is a help-desk system you should definitely look into (Figure 8-8). With it's customizable customer portals, support for mobile devices such as the Apple iPhone, rules-based workflow logic, and robust case management functionality, I think HelpSpot is a serious competitor of FogBugz's and will fit people and startups that FogBugz does not.

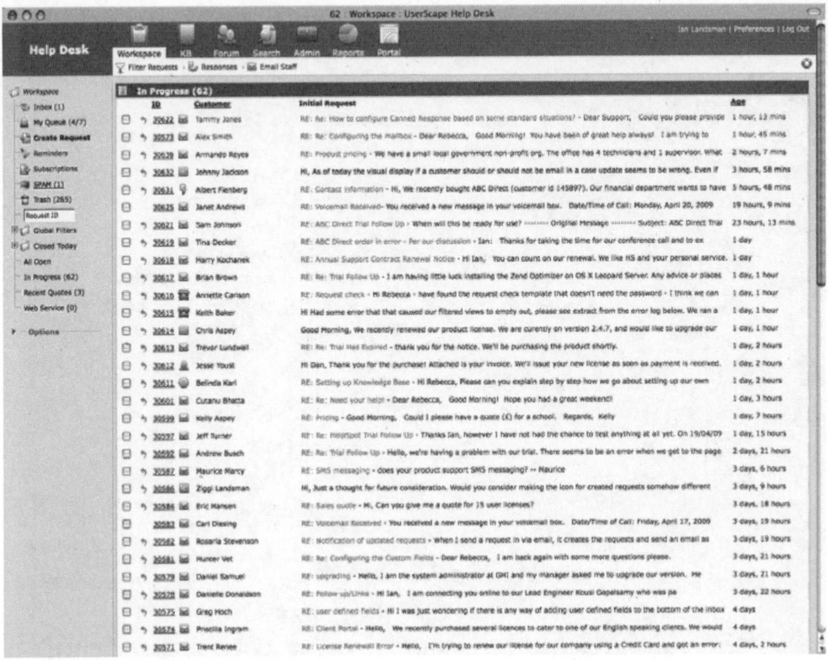

Figure 8-8. HelpSpot

Now, both of these applications are well supplemented by one or more of the Startup Tools we covered in Chapter 4, specifically UserVoice and Get Satisfaction or both. I hope to see application programming interfaces (APIs) from both of these tools by the time you read this book so that both Fog Creek Software and UserScape can extend their software to connect to them.

Next Floor, Please

I consider improving developer productivity a major leverage point: small amounts of effort can have a positive effect on a multitude of projects and areas of your startup. You can improve the quality and quantity of your LOC (lines of code) by producing a yes on each of the questions in The Joel Test and by actively participating in Stack Overflow, not by 10 or 20% but by 300 or 400% percent.

Having a systematic approach to monitoring new developments and practices in the community surrounding the software languages, frameworks, and tools you're using daily to build your startup can let you deliver more useful functionality with less code and in less time than trying to shut out new developments.

Though no development methodology is going to build your app for you, picking an inappropriate methodology—or defaulting to no methodology—lengthens the odds against your startup. If Scrum or Agile in general is not the approach for you, find something else that works. And adopting, using, and mastering a comprehensive bug-tracking system that synchs with the kind of customers your startup hopes to have comes under the heading of critical startup infrastructure, not an afterthought to development.

OK, enough said about developer productivity. It's time to get back in the elevator and move to the next floor: how to be a productive startup founder.

Startup Founder Productivity

So you've got a GTD system in place that works for you, you no longer check e-mail 50 times a day like a crazed chimpanzee, and you understand what you need to know—and just as much as you need to know—about new stuff going on in your software language(s)/framework(s). Now what?

We got into this a bit in Chapter 5, but now that you are running a company (even if it's a company of one or you've yet to make your first sale), you need to compartmentalize your usual work perspective and add to your repertoire a few new, CEO-like ways of doing things. No, I don't mean you should turn into your last boss, but I do mean it's time to start thinking like a founder of a software company, not as developer and certainly not as an employee or a contractor. If you're going to build a successful startup, you must learn how to do some things that will run against your developer sensibilities.

Let's start by making explicit five traits or practices about which you should be thinking hard and long. These new ways of thinking and acting are at the core of fulfilling your role in your startup.

- **Focus on more than your app.** As a developer, the right and proper thing to do is to focus, sometimes to the point of obsession, on the software you are creating. But if you focus solely on your app instead of on the overall business and the business you are in, odds are your startup is going to crash and burn. Creating and maintaining the software can only be one of several core things on which you need to focus. Just as important are communicating and sharing the value of your company's product or service, improving and deepening the relationship between your company and your customers, and creating and maintaining a good work environment and healthy relationships within that environment.

- **Analog beats digital.** This is one point with which we coders tend to have a lot of trouble. We live in a professional world where, from the simplest routine to the largest system, every part of it is determinant. There is no ambiguity. In the business world, in the larger world in which you've chosen to participate, damn few things are black or white, 100% or zero percent. You're going to have to get comfortable with large amounts of ambiguity, from what your customers see in your product or service that makes them open their wallets to herding like cats all the trade-offs you'll have to make when allocating your and other people's time, effort, and money.

- **Get used to—and seek out—not being the smartest person in the room.** Admit it: You harbor more than a little smugness and pride that you know how software and information technology work whereas nongeeks don't. You're just a little bit (hell, a lot) smarter than all those nonsoftware types—at least up until the moment you happen to talk to someone running a hundred-million-dollar company. Then you realize (a) you're not at the top of the food chain and (b) you'd better start spending as much time as you can with your peers and above if you're going to get the insights, mentorship, and wisdom you need to succeed.

- **You're going to need to be tough in general, sometimes downright ruthless.** If you move past the microISV stage and hire people, you can bet that at some point you'll need to fire people—even if they're someone you've known for years. Even if you are your only employee, you're going to have to be as ultrahard on yourself at times, owning up to mistakes you've made and opportunities you've missed, and getting the work done that needs doing, whether you like it or not. Startups aren't for sissies.

- **You will be discovering new levels of obsession and work.** Back in your day job, you might have moaned and whined about how many hours you worked. As founder of a startup, that level of effort and focus is the warm-up act. Of the scores of successful founders I've talked to, read about,[13] and listened to, exactly none of them got there without working brain-exploding amounts of time and obsessing totally over their startups. Not one.

---

[13] *This is a good point to add another book to your reading list: Founders at Work by Jessica Livingston (Apress, 2008).*

- **You're the leader, so lead.** As founder, you no longer have the luxury and comfort of having a manager tell you what to do. You—and your cofounders—are it. That sudden heaviness you feel on your shoulders is called *responsibility* and the sure and certain knowledge that you're going to make some bad decisions along the way. You might as well get used to it, because it's part and parcel of running a business.

- **You're going to have to be confident to just this side of arrogant.** Don't expect customers to buy, investors to put up their money, partners to execute, or contractors to perform unless you exude confidence from every pore. If you don't believe totally that you're going to succeed, how can you expect others to? Two further pieces of advice regarding confidence: First, if you're not 100% confident in your software idea and its execution, then fake it. Seriously. Act the part and you will become the part. Second, there are two occupational health hazards to starting a company—heart attacks brought on by high stress, junk food, and no exercise and ego inflation until you look like and act like a giant balloon in a parade. We can all name names here—just don't make the mistake that arrogance causes success.

Tools for Founder Productivity

I have three tools to suggest for improving your founder productivity, and, yes, one of them is mine (I did, after all, write the preceding section!). The first tool is a **notebook**. It can be a real, live physical notebook (check out Moleskines at http://www.moleskines.com), or it can be digital, such as Circus Ponies Software's Notebook for the Mac (http://www.circusponies.com, $49.95), which I use.

This particular notebook is going to have (at least) three main sections: Your Business Plan, Weekly Progress Reports, and an Assumptions and Decisions section. Let's examine each of those a bit more closely.

Your Business Plan. No, this is not the raising capital-type business plan we discussed in Chapter 5; this is your *real* business plan. Specifically, it's a structured, constantly updated document that records your *business planning*, not something you create with which to impress the money people. It's not polished, it's not professionally formatted, and it doesn't have to be neat or clean any more than the working drawings of an architect once the house is under construction.

Since this document is not for anyone but you and your cofounders, it's entirely up to you how it's structured. That said, the purpose of this tool is find the answers—and to keep finding the answers—to a set of very fundamental questions.

- Why are we building this company?

- What exactly are we selling?

- Who will buy what we are selling and why?

- How are we going connect what we are selling to the people who we think will buy?

- How do we measure success?

Answering these questions will lead to all sorts of other questions.

- What parts of doing this business do we really care about and consider core company functions, and which parts should we outsource one way or another?

- What are the characteristics, traits, attitudes, buying habits, and expectations of a typical person in our primary market?

- What makes this startup different from all the other software companies out there?

- What are the strengths and weaknesses of myself and my cofounders? How and when will we add the services of others to augment those strengths and compensate for those weaknesses?

- What's our competition?

- What needs and desires of our target market does our software address? And how well does it address them as of launch, at the first major upgrade, and further down the road?

You see, a business plan is all about asking—and answering—the questions you know you need to ask. It's an iterative process: the questions don't stop coming, and the answers change over time.

Weekly Progress Reports. If you can't or won't measure what you are doing, then you're not building a startup, your enjoying a hobby. That means holding yourself accountable for whether you execute. And that means defining on a regular basis—weekly works for most people—what you as a founder are going to accomplish in the next seven days and what you as a founder did accomplish in the past seven days.

Note the "you as a founder" construction. This is more—a lot more—than how many lines of code you write; it needs to cover the gamut of roles you undertake in your company.

A good format for your weekly progress report is a set of your top six (no more) planned accomplishments for the week ahead, in enough specificity so that you will be able to measure what you've accomplished. Here's a sampling of what I mean.

1. As developer, I will complete the beta build sprint of StartupToDo.com, with all tests passing, and deploy it to the VPS.

2. As community manager, I invite the first 10 beta testers to log into StartupToDo and to get their initial feedback either by speaking with them via Skype or by discussing via e-mail.

3. As blogger, I will post a description of what the problem is with asking others for feedback on your startup or microISV site at a public forum and how StartupToDo provides a more powerful and functional environment for transactions such as this to occur.

4. As content developer, I will complete and proof another five StartupToDo Public Projects and add them to the production build.

5. As system admin, I will review the New Relic RPM Lite data to identify the three slowest controller queries and improve their performance.

(Not shown, but important: Leave space to answer each objective: done, or not done and why not done. The "why not done" can be as important as the objective itself.)

Assumptions and Decisions. Here's something curious I've noticed that's true for most startups: The initial assumptions about what your market really wants, which features they'll especially like, how long it will take to build the app, and so forth tend to be dead wrong. That's OK, so long as you know what your assumptions are, review them on a periodic basis and in light of empirical evidence, and adjust as needed.

Reviewing and "tuning" your assumptions gets a lot easier when you've externalized them—and that means writing them down in a somewhat structured way (Date, Area, and Assumption works for me and will probably work for you) and reviewing them at least once a month. These are, after all, the facts on which you are building your business.

Decisions go hand-in-hand with assumptions—sometimes right off a cliff. By definition, your job as founder is to make decisions—hopefully more good, accurate, useful, effective decisions than bad, unrealistic, ineffective, unproductive decisions. But you won't know if they are good or bad if you don't keep score. It's like estimating how long it will take to write a given chunk of functionality. Until and unless you start measuring your estimates against your reality, you are in the Land of Make-Believe. What's more, the more feedback you get, the better your estimating—or your decision making—gets.

Again, this notebook is highly proprietary information. You should not share its existence, let alone its contents, with anyone except perhaps your partners. But used correctly it will close the loop between what you plan and what actually happens. And closing this loop helps you improve your business planning, objective setting, and decision making—all things at the top of your founder job description.

He's at It Again!

Okay, one more plug for StartupToDo.com (http://startuptodo.com). Hopefully by now you've checked it out and joined (thank you!). But if you haven't or you hated it, I think the reasoning behind it stands on its own as your second startup founder productivity tool.

- **If your startup is going to succeed, you have to build momentum.** You're going nowhere but in circles if you work on your startup fitfully, taking weeks off from it. That won't work before launch, and it certainly won't work after. The StartupToDo point system builds momentum by giving you an easy way to compare what you've accomplished this week to what you accomplished last week, to your friends in the StartupToDo community and to other startups like you.

- **You need to separate research/analysis from execution.** Building a startup involves hundreds of specific, multiple-task projects of huge variety; for each project, you need to know what you are going to do *before* you do it. The research/discovery/Google-it-to-death phase, if not managed, will eat all of your implementation/execution time, especially if you're bootstrapping your startup. StartupToDo's core goodness is its hundreds of projects containing specific steps, recommendations, and URLs to content on the Web written by myself and other fellow startup founders. Since things change fast in this business, these projects get updated by members as they work on them via comments, whereas only people you explicitly allow (your partners) can see the details of your projects.

- **There are no absolute answers in this business.** There is no one right way to picking a company name, creating a deployment checklist, working with a graphic designer, communicating your startup's core message. Your job as a startup founder is to sift, weigh, and judge and jiggle multiple approaches and then to execute what you think is the right approach for your startup. That's why you'll find at StartupToDo multiple projects written by many different people in the community, often taking different approaches to the same desired outcome—and why we're all looking forward to your contributed Public Projects.

- **You need honest feedback.** You definitely need honest feedback on your app, on your site, on your value proposition, on your market. That's why StartupToDo has Review Requests and makes its dirt easy to get constructive criticism from your peers in a trusted environment instead of a public, search-engine-indexed forum.

- **Startups can be lonely.** A lot of the people you know probably don't understand what you're attempting to do or why. Hanging out with other entrepreneurs and being able to get and give advice, technical pointers, ideas, and support is a huge help. That's why the social side of StartupToDo—Groups, where you can share online discussions, specific resources and finds, Friends, with whom you can (in a friendly way) compete and cooperate, and Partners (others who are actually working with you on your startup)—is so important.

Okay, enough about Startuptodo. There's one last "tool" to increase your startup founder productivity I strongly recommend—**other startup founders**. Go back to Chapter 4 as one place to begin. But make a commitment to start spending some time, in person, with other startup founders, entrepreneurs, and people who run their own companies. Make the effort to get physically involved in groups and organizations of other people who share your passion for self-determination. While I'm a big believer in all things online, face-to-face beats it cold when it comes to this.

Recap

In some ways, building a startup is the reverse of nuclear fission. Instead of converting some tiny amount of matter into an explosive amount of energy, you're going to convert a huge amount of your personal energy into an actual thing.

Each and every way you can be more efficient with that energy—be it your time, your attention, or your intelligence—means a faster and better conversion process. Improving your productivity—in general, online, as a developer, as a founder—is the gift that keeps on giving.

In this chapter we started with the basics one step above getting out of bed in the morning: how you collect, manage, and process tasks. As a lightweight, agnostic methodology for that, David Allen's Getting Things Done is the best we've got, and it's something you should get into as well.

In this business, online productivity is not a nice-to-have, it is a must-have. Taming your e-mail, RSS feeds, and online social interactions is a key milestone to reclaiming enough time and attention to build your startup.

Developer productivity—seeking out and adopting activities that other developers use to be productive and opting out of the Google loop via Stack Overflow—goes to the heart of what you do and what you offer. Two of the most important of those adoptions are a development methodology and a-bug tracking system that fits your startup.

Finally, becoming a founder of a company of whatever initial size means you need to plan, to lead, to assess, to act in new and perhaps uncomfortable ways. You grow into this new role in life by adopting practices and tools that help you act like a founder and by seeking out other founders and executives.

All right, I think you've heard quite enough from me. In the next chapter we sit down with—and I get out of the way of—six very successful people from whom we can learn a lot. Grab your highlighter, refill that caffeine container: next up, Six Wise People.

Six Wise People

> *"Someone's hindsight can become your foresight."*
> —Anonymous

> *"Don't follow any advice, no matter how good, until you feel as deeply
> in your spirit as you think in your mind that the counsel is wise."*
> —Joan Rivers, American comedian

Some People You Ought to Listen To

How do people accomplish big things like building a company? There's
no one formula, but there are common ingredients—perseverance, large
amounts of hard work, listening keenly to others who've succeeded.

That last bit is what we get into in this chapter, in the form of six
interviews with people from whom I think you'll learn valuable lessons,
cheaply. I say *cheaply* because each of these people has already paid the
price to learn what he or she is most generously sharing with you here.

So what can four successful software company founders, a highly
respected Fortune 500 consultant, and a writer and blogger on how to
break free of other people's companies teach you? Quite a bit actually.
Time to get out the highlighter or to turn it on in your pdf reader and get
to work.

Dharmesh Shah, Founder, Chief Software Architect, HubSpot

Let's start with a number: $17.5 million. That's how much Dharmesh Shah (Figure 9-1) has raised for his third startup, HubSpot, an inbound-marketing system designed to help businesses get found on the net by prospective customers and to turn those prospective customers into actual customers.

Figure 9-1. Dharmesh Shaw

Like most "instant successes," Dharmesh is anything but. Back in 1992, he was a typical programmer working for a large enterprise. By 1994, at age 24, he'd become bored with his programming job and launched his first startup, Pyramid Digital Solutions, with $10,000 of his own money. Pyramid took off, winning awards and customers by creating and selling a web-based retirement plan industry application. In October 2005 Dharmesh sold Pyramid to SunGard Business Systems, a large IT services firm (and the same company he had worked for 11 years earlier).

I first got to know Dharmesh in 2006 when he contacted me for his master's thesis on startup companies, on his way to an M.S. in innovation and global leadership in the MIT Sloan Fellows Program.

In 2006, besides working on his M.S. and launching HubSpot (http://www.hubspot.com), Dharmesh launched his blog OnStartups (http://onstartups.com) as both a place to share his entrepreneurial insights and experience and a forum to challenge some of the conventional wisdom about what founders needed to do to be successful.

A Nagging Feeling

Bob: So, Dharmesh, you've started three startups. You've created 10 commercial applications. You've now raised over $17 million in funding. How's life going?

Dharmesh: Life is going well. It keeps me busy, but I have the same genetic flaw that I think a lot of your readers have, which is that we're just gluttons for punishment. So we continue to do the startup thing over and over again. It's hard to stop at just one.

Bob: How did you decide to get into your first startup?

Dharmesh: I did my first startup right out of computer science undergrad work. There was no big idea for that first startup. I was working with, obviously, a bunch of programmers. I was a software developer myself, and I was working in a big multibillion-dollar company. Although the company itself was doing well and the environment was good, I just didn't see that it was really leveraging all of the kinds of talents and skills of the other programmers. I'm like, "It doesn't seem like we're as productive as we could be. It doesn't seem like we're solving the problems as efficiently as we would like them to be."

So the original startup was really around "Can we take some smart people and solve interesting problems? We'll make money along the way, someway, somehow." The idea that the company then formed around came after the company formation.

Bob: It wasn't a case of "I have this burning passion to create a particular solution." It was more a desire to build something plus using underutilized resources?

Dharmesh: Yes, it's not so much underutilized. You have to be a programmer, which you are. But it's that when you write code and you're in team environments and you're working for a company, you have this nagging feeling that there's a better way to produce highly profitable software. The genesis of a lot of software developers is, if you want to do things well, you're, like, "OK, I'm not sure of the approach that we're taking, whether it's product management or whatever it is. It's like we're just not doing things as well as we could be."

The concept wasn't a product idea. It was "Can we create an environment for really smart developers?" We were all in our early 20s, ready "to go off and solve big problems for big companies," but to do it in ways that we thought were much more productive, essentially. That wasn't really possible in a big company.

So we're solving more for the culture than we were for any given product idea in that first startup.

Bob: In that first startup, did you self-fund, or did you go looking for money?

Dharmesh: Self-funded it. So we started with $10,000 in capital. I was relatively new to the country at the time. I honestly did not know what venture capital was. The term had never entered my vocabulary. I had never read about it, never heard about it, never talked to anyone about it. So the sheer notion that you'd go off and raise capital to fund something just hadn't been part of my mindset at all. I didn't know of any other way than saying, "I've got this much cash. I put it in. I've got to go off and find customers in order to be able to really do anything." It was bootstrapped simply because I didn't know any other way.

To Raise or Not to Raise—That Is the Question

Bob: What was the first startup that you actually went out and got some outside funding for? Was that HubSpot?

Dharmesh: HubSpot's the first company I raised outside capital for, which was my third startup.

Bob: How did you do it?

Dharmesh: In terms of raising capital, it's interesting. The first decision is around deciding you actually want to do it. It sounds glamorous. It's like, "Oh, you go off and raise venture capital." It's great to get really smart people involved. Obviously the money's nice, too. You can go off and do all these wonderful things with the money. But there's actually a decision process around whether you do or don't want to raise capital. Lots of trade-offs. The big one is really around deciding what it is you're trying to build and what success looks like. For instance, there are two broadly defined outcomes. You can say, "I'm going to do," which is what I did for my first and second startups. "I'm going to do a bootstrap company with a modest outcome," which I'll define, let's say, as between $10 million and $50 million outcome.

It's OK by me. I'm going to own most of that pie. I'm not going to become famous, but I can make some cash, get an exit, and get some money, even if it's a small part of something really, really, really big, and that's fine too. I think what entrepreneurs fail to do sometimes is think through, "Do they really want to raise capital or not?"

Once you decide that "I want to swing really big, really hard, and go after something really big, then it's a matter of finding an idea, essentially, that has that large-magnitude opportunity, and then demonstrating a passion around it. I don't know how deep you want to go into that. We can talk for hours about raising venture capital.

Bob: Let's talk a little further because there is this air of mystery, I would describe it, around the process of successfully getting that first initial round of somebody else's money to put into your idea. I'm hearing two things here. One is that it's got to be an idea that has a huge payout potential, if you're going to attract any type of investment, especially insofar as that's a very risky investment by anybody's standards. The other thing I'm hearing is that you didn't do this the first time around or the second. This was on your third startup.

Dharmesh: Yes, and I almost didn't do it on the third one as well. I did the seed-round funding for my third startup and then did an angel-round funding, just by networking. It was $1.5 million of capital later that we actually decided to bring a VC into the mix. Even then, I was not 100% certain that I even wanted to raise venture capital for my third one, because the trade-offs are significant.

Bob: Of equity for that funding?

Dharmesh: Not just a matter of equity. Obviously, you're going to give up some portion of your company in terms of just shares and percentage, but the dynamics of the business do change. Now you have different parties at the table in terms of having institutional investors. For the most part, your goals are aligned. You both want to create a really big, successful company. But there is a certain dynamic to remembering that venture capitalists have a portfolio of startups that they're investing in. So they'll have 10, 20, 50 startup companies that they're invested in, where you have only one.

This goes to how you actually raise capital. You have to understand this dynamic, which is VCs saying, "We're going to go off and invest, say, 20 different startup opportunities." Their expectation is that each of those 20 startup opportunities has a chance, however small, of being really, really big, of being the next Google, of being the next YouTube or something like that, in the hopes that if one or two of them actually pulls that off, it carries the rest of the portfolio.

What VCs are not doing is, "Oh, I'm going to invest in these 20 startups, all of which have a decent chance of a modest outcome." Because what ends up happening is the risk is so high that most of them, even though they have a decent chance, are going to fail to pull off even that modest outcome. The ones that are successful are not successful enough to really create the return that's necessary for them to demonstrate to their investors.

Bob: So they're hoping for the grand slam, but they're taking the approach that there's going to be a whole lot of outs as well.

Dharmesh: Absolutely. You have to demonstrate that your opportunity, your idea, has the potential to be big enough to carry, essentially, close to the rest of the portfolio, that you have to be that one. You're going to passionately work at being that one. The VCs recognize that they're not going to be able to get several of these big outcomes, but they're expecting some small percentage of their portfolio is going to actually pull it off. It's very rare that anyone pulls it off, if no one's actually swinging hard and trying. It doesn't happen, for the most part, accidentally.

What About Angel Investors?

Bob: Are angel investors like VCs, only smaller? Or are they fundamentally different? Is there something that startups need to know?

Dharmesh: The thing that startups need to know is that this particular dynamic is very different. Other than just the magnitude of capital that they'll invest, angels are different. I'm an angel investor as well. I've got an investment in, I think, nine startups now. The way the angels look at it is that, for the most part, they're entrepreneurs themselves that have made some money along the way. They're living vicariously through the entrepreneurs again. That's essentially what I do. That's what a lot of angels do.

It's not their job. They're not saying, "OK, it's 2009, I've got this much money to deploy. That means I can make three investments this year, and I'm out there looking, actively seeking. I have to 'deploy' this capital efficiently into opportunities."

Angels are much more opportunistic. They invest in startups because they really love the people. They really love the idea. They're just jumping in because they really want to be involved in some small way.

It's a very different dynamic. Angels don't really have to demonstrate in order for them to kind of maintain being who they are, like a VC does. They don't have to demonstrate that big outcome. They're not necessarily looking for that grand slam.

Even a series of modest outcomes is actually often sufficient. Often, they're not even necessarily looking for pure financial returns. There's something beyond that. VCs, at the end of the day, are measured completely based on the returns that they're generating for their limited partners. Angels, not so much. There's a variety of things that can matter to an angel investor.

Bob: Let's talk, for a moment; to you in your angel investor hat. Two questions: One, if I'm a startup looking for an angel, should I come knock on your door? Two, the flip side of that: What got you interested in the nine startups that you presently are invested in?

Dharmesh: Actually, I don't actively seek. I have enough in the network right now, people that I'll come across. Because it's more me looking at ideas and finding people that I'm interested in, versus the other way around. That's the candid response. Although people are welcome to send me an e-mail, my take rate is actually very, very low because I don't do that many deals. I'll do probably one or two a year. That's the first thing.

What I am generally looking for are passionate entrepreneurs that just need a little bit of capital to pull something off. They've made it a little bit of the way there. I invest exclusively in software companies or tech companies, mostly web-based or Internet-based, because they're capital efficient.

What attracts me to a particular opportunity is when I see this glimmer of what could be a really big idea, so there's that little bit of VC in me. I want that big outcome, but there's something really practical about the entrepreneur.

There are some entrepreneurs that you meet with or have a conversation with and there's something about them that signals, "I'm going to find a way to make this successful, and successful to me even means just having a modest outcome."

There are certain entrepreneurs that will end up making money. It may not be the idea that you're talking about right now, but they will handle their path through the woods and somehow emerge.

I've seen this over 15 or 20 years of being in the software business. Of all the people that you would expect, here's a woman that's just going to make money. I like that gene. I have a tendency to invest in pragmatic entrepreneurs, essentially.

It's Not the Concept

Bob: So it's more than just the concept. It's the person behind the concept or the people behind the concept. That's what you're investing in.

Dharmesh: Very much so. So the concept itself, although interesting and it can be appealing, changes so often. If you are a student of the startup game, most of these successful startups that you encounter, that are even big names, if you dig a little bit deeper, they didn't start with that idea. They evolved into it or fell into it or came across it as a result of something else that they were doing. I think that's typical. So investing in just a specific idea, I don't think is particularly effective. What I like to do is what the idea is representative of the entrepreneur often. Here's a class of problem this entrepreneur is interested in solving. Is that particular class of problem something worthwhile or something that I could get excited about?

Bob: This ability to make money as a founder, in other words, not the idea, but this character trait. What does that look like when it's at home? Is that perseverance, determination, flexibility, obsession? How would you describe that to people?

Dharmesh: If I had to describe it, I would describe it in two ways. One would be objectivity, in terms of being objective about the world around you and saying, "The world really doesn't owe me anything. I have this idea, which I think is decent." But they can see all the flaws and all the hardships that are ahead. They're basically realists. They're not living this distorted reality. They're not reading all these articles about multibillion-dollar software startups and thinking they're going to pull it off. They're realists and objective about how hard it's going to be. That's part one.

Part two is that they're just optimistic enough to actually do what most people would consider to be semicrazy things. So if you're in it just to make money, if you could have been a great entrepreneur—I'm talking specifically about software entrepreneurs—you could have made money just working for other people the rest of your life. Probably, in the whole grand scheme of things, you probably would have made more money.

Software entrepreneurs don't get into it for the money. They get into it because there's something else. You have to have this naive optimism about you, coupled with this objective to see the world as it is, and react accordingly. It's that mix that I think really pulls off that pragmatic entrepreneur.

Finding Founders and First Hires

Bob: Let's turn, for a moment, to HubSpot. How do you build a team around, or in, a startup? You've started with a couple of other founders. How did you end up picking those people to build HubSpot?

Dharmesh: There are two founders in the company. My cofounder and I actually met in grad school at MIT. So we had to be thrown together. We had similar, overlapping passions around the software industry and small business, which was the market we were going after. But we were both very different. He has a sales and distribution background. I have a software development and technology background. It comes back to the same kinds of traits I look for if I'm looking for an investment. They're the kinds of people I think do really well joining an early startup team. If you look at both my cofounder and then the management team that we've built out, they've all that entrepreneurial kind of mindset.

In the early days of most startups, if you have to choose between hiring generalists and specialists, my leaning in the early days is always to hire generalists, people who wear several hats, whether it's doing finance stuff or accounting, selling or marketing, or writing code, whatever it happens to be.

Most startups can't afford to hire a person that's really, really good at just one thing. That's all they really want to do. Because there's just not enough resources to really do that.

Just find those practical people that have a passion for building something and pull them in. They already have a genetic flaw, because that's what makes them entrepreneurs. You just have to figure out how to detect it and then tap into that and give them something fun to work on. Tap the passion.

Bob: I'm not sure if it's a flaw or an evolutionary advantage, but I get the feeling that you're really talking about a certain type of person. That's what attracts you, whether they are going to be your cofounder or whether they're going to be somebody that works in your company or whether you think they're worth putting your money into as an investor.

Dharmesh: That's exactly it.

Getting Them to Come to You

Bob: I've noticed that you're doing a variety of things at HubSpot that don't seem to have a lot to do, necessarily, with the idea of inbound marketing for small and middle-sized companies. There's the Website Grader (http://website.grader.com). There's the Twitter Grader (http://twitter.grader.com). Are these just tactics to pull eyeballs, and are they working?

Dharmesh: If you look at the greater family of free tools that we have, the original genesis of Website Grader is where it all started. The idea originally was related to the business around marketing, because what we were doing is spending a lot of time looking at small business web sites, trying to figure out how effective those web sites were from a marketing perspective. This was in the early days of HubSpot. Primarily to get an assessment of "Is there a good fit here? Can we help? How far along in the evolutionary process, as far as inbound marketing, is this particular small business?"

What we found ourselves doing is the same kind of repetitive lookup. "Let's look at their Alexa traffic ranking. Let's look at their SEO. Let's look at the HTML code and all these things."

It wouldn't be that hard to automate some of this stuff. It was done originally to basically save me time, since we're talking to all these prospective customers. Around the same time that this was happening, I was looking at a lot of these things, and so I hoped that it wouldn't be that hard to automate some of this stuff. It was done originally just to save me time. We're talking to all these prospective customers, and it's interesting that, around the same time that this was happening, I was looking at a lot of potential angel investments.

I was doing the same kinds of things to look at as if I was going to put money into a web startup, "OK, where are they on the overall inbound marketing spectrum? Are they really, really sophisticated? Do they have really high search engine rankings? How's the company doing?" So I wrote a script, essentially a small tool just to automate the things I was doing, primarily for my own use.

It was about a week or so later, and I'm like, "This is kind of semiuseful. Maybe other people will find it useful too and we can just put it out there on the Web." It's interesting, in the early days of Website Grader, it didn't even ask for an e-mail address, there was no lead generation. I had no concept as to what I wanted to do with it; it was just a tool that I have found useful that I thought others might as well.

Fast-forward a little bit: at this point now we've graded, or Website Grader has graded, 800,000 web sites and is the single largest lead generation source for HubSpot. We generate a lot of leads, because we've got 1,200 customers, 20 inside salespeople. It's been a phenomenal success for us.

Bob: There's Website Grader, but then there's Twitter Grader.
Dharmesh: There is.
Bob: What's the genesis of that? That gets us into the whole social media question.
Dharmesh: Sure, so a couple of things, if you go back through history, you've got this Website Grader tool that made us a bunch of money in terms of being able to drive lots of qualified leads to HubSpot and help us find customers. What I was looking to do was to say, "OK. How can we repeat that pattern? What is it about Website Grader that people liked? We were looking basically

for another hit, that says, "Well, can we create other grading tools, and what is it about that particular tool that people are finding interesting?" So we essentially said, "OK." I was just getting into Twitter at the time. I'm like, "Oh well, maybe we could do something. Instead of grading a web site, we could grade someone's Twitter profile." It sounded kind of silly at the time. Right now, I guess, it still sounds a little bit silly, and I get lots of controversy around it. But that was the original idea.

I was like, "OK, well let's just look at someone's you know. What kind of attributes of a Twitter profile would we look at?" In terms of number of followers, what kind of followers? How often are they Tweeting? How often are they being reTweeted? Let's check out all of those things and attach a score to that (Figure 9-2).

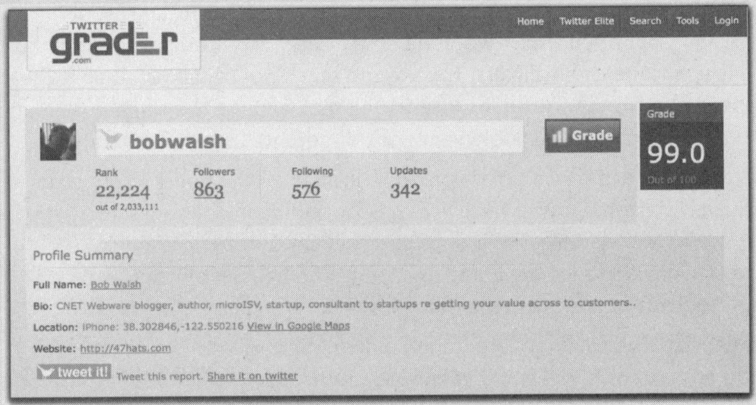

Figure 9-2. HubSpot's Twitter Grader

Twitter Grader has really, really taken off. It actually generates more traffic, in terms of just raw eyeballs, than Website Grader does. It gets over 1 million page views and 30,000 uses a day, for just Twitter grader.

Bob: Wow!

Dharmesh: So it's been a phenomenal success in terms of just raw activity. Now it's on the top 10 sources of lead generation for HubSpot as well. It's not quite a moneymaking machine, as Website Grader was, but still profitable in terms of how easy it was to develop and how much traffic and leads it was generating.

Bob: Well, let me ask you this: Among the things you're doing at HubSpot is trying to help small, medium businesses with their marketing. Is traditional marketing dead, given social networking? Should companies use Twitter and Facebook and all the other social tools, instead of traditional marketing and advertising? Do you buy into that, or do you see it differently?

Dharmesh: I do buy in to that. I don't think it's dead, but I think it's becoming increasingly less effective. So just look at our own individual behaviors. What we have now is all of these outbound messages, people targeting us and sending us junk mail or telemarketers calling us or e-mail spam. All of those kinds of things are becoming increasingly less effective simply because we, as consumers, are now very, very good at blocking those messages out. We have spam protection, we don't go through our junk mail anymore, we've got caller ID on our phones. So it's much harder to get to us as consumers now through those classic outbound channels. What I think the world is kind of moving toward is where the consumer has much more control and says, "OK, I'm actually looking for something; and when I'm looking for it, then I'm much more likely to respond to marketing information and to actually buy something."

So we think this is actually a very good thing for small businesses and startups. The reason is that outbound marketing historically was always defined by how big of a marketing budget you had. Could you afford to advertise? Could you afford to hire a bank of telemarketers just to cold-call people? How successful you were in terms of getting market share and then customers was the definition of what we like to call "the width of your wallet."

Which is, basically, if you have a big budget, you had a chance. If you didn't have a big budget, it was really hard to kind of get any attention. With inbound marketing now, it's becoming much more about your creativity and your openness and the degree to which you can actually engage people and establish some trust and authority on the Web.

We think that's a much more effective way these days, instead of spending all this money trying to have your message broadcast to people far and wide in a hope that some small percentage of them who care will actually call you or buy from you. We think it's just much more fruitful to say, "OK, we'll set up your web site correctly, put yourself out there in the social media web site. So those that are already looking for you or what you have to offer will actually find it."

Bob: That kind of brings us around to your blog on startups. I know from my own experience how much time and effort it takes to do a good blog. That's got to be eating a good chunk of your total time. You obviously have other things to do. Why do you keep working that since you surely don't need it anymore? Or do you?

Dharmesh: I don't. OnStartups was actually originally begun as part of my MIT graduate thesis. It wasn't really business related. It's interesting how that evolved. Ultimately OnStartups and the lessons from the blog itself were some of the original genesis for the HubSpot idea. We're, like, "OK. Well, this blog is actually able to attract traffic," and I was seeing it attract more traffic in some cases than some of the venture-backed startups that I knew had relatively large budgets. What we were trying to do is bottle up the lessons from blogging on startups and figure out how we can help small businesses do that. In terms of why I still do it today, because I just have it in me. I've got this propensity to try and say semiuseful things as fun. Even from a raw business perspective, for me personally, it is still profitable. All of the deals that I do generally will originate on Startups.com; that's where I find entrepreneurs that are interesting.

We still get leads for HubSpot through that and it's still a productive use of time. Even if it wasn't, I probably would do it anyway. As it turns out, it is.

Final Advice

Bob: Let's go on, at this point, to just what lessons you've learned that you would like to pass on to other startups who are at that point where you began as a startup.

Dharmesh: Sure. A couple of things. Number one is don't waste time writing a business plan. If you have the need to write and say things, write a blog instead. The short, mid-, and long term, however you slice it, a blog is going to be much more helpful for startups than the business plan is. No one reads business plans; someone might actually read your blog. That's number one. Number two is to try to be on the constant lookout for other, like-minded people that are practical, that share your passions, and that you would want to build something with, whether you do a startup this year with them or you do it two or five years from now.

Odds are, If you're going to do a startup at all, you will likely not do just one. You will have a series of startups over your professional career. It's helpful to start thinking about that stuff long term. So if you are a young entrepreneur, you're still in school, start having conversations with other entrepreneurial folks that are in your class, start to get to know them. It's a great environment.

Anytime you have an opportunity to be in and around other entrepreneurs, A, you'll have much better times with those people anyway because they have shared interests. But, B, those are the people you'll likely start companies with or be involved in projects of some sort.

Third would be, don't automatically jump to the conclusion that you need to raise capital to do a startup. Especially for software startups, it doesn't take that much money. Most people overestimate the value of raising venture capital, and you can always do that later if things are successful. Don't waste your time raising capital too early. You're better off solving the customer's problem than the investor's problem.

Work on the actual product, toil away at it, get something semiworking, get it—and I'll close with this—get something out there into real people's hands as early as possible. If by the time you launch your software product as a startup, if you're not completely embarrassed by it, you waited too long. The winners tend to release it very, very early and then iterate it very, very quickly.

Eric Sink, Founder/Ceo, SourceGear

In some ways, Eric Sink's to blame for the microISV arc of my life over the years since I read his "Exploring Micro-ISVs" post in September 2004 (http://www.ericsink.com/bos/Micro_ISV.html). He coined the term, and he breathed life into the idea that a single-person, self-funded software company was something doable.

Although Eric's microISV experiment, Winnable Solitaire, was a bust, it was probably because he was putting too much time into his "day job" as founder and CEO of SourceGear, a software company filling a need left unfulfilled by Microsoft (Figure 9-3).

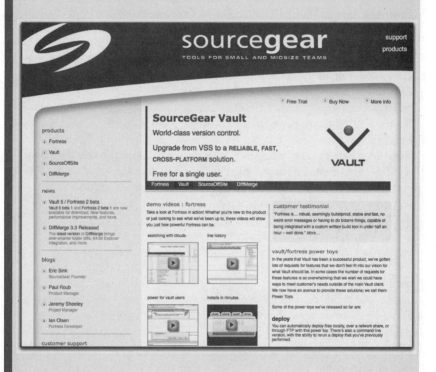

Figure 9-3. SourceGear

Back in the late 1990s, working with Microsoft's version control software, SourceSafe, was a major exercise in frustration. SourceGear's first product was SourceOffSite, which for the first time gave offsite developers access to SourceSafe via the Internet.

Year after year, Microsoft's myopia continued when it came to the critical need of version control software, and SourceGear grew: improving SourceOffSite, then taking on the near-senile SourceSafe with Vault, source control done right for Windows, and then adding Fortress, a cross-platform application lifecycle management solution for small and medium-size developer teams. Along the way, Eric collected his essays and blog posts into *Eric Sink on the Business of Software* (Apress, 2006), a book you most definitely should buy.

Eric and SourceGear also are the case that disproves the dictum that you absolutely, positively have to live in Silicon Valley if you're going to succeed: Eric went to college at the University of Illinois, Urbana-Champaign, where he headed up the team that created what was to become Microsoft's Internet Explorer. SourceGear's offices are located nearby.

Going Against Microsoft—and Winning

Bob: Maybe we should start with where SourceGear is these days in terms of size and number of employees, that sort of thing.

Eric: Sure. I think our employee count is 26 or 27. It bounces around a little bit.

Bob: OK. And SourceGear started how many years ago?

Eric: 12.

Bob: That is pretty impressive, for anybody in this business to be able to get that big in that period of time. Maybe the question to ask overall here is how you did it. Because SourceGear got its start with going against the largest software company in the world, Microsoft. How did you manage to make this happen?

Eric: Well, to be fair, I should point out that we did a fair amount of consulting work in our early days to keep the bills paid. And we gave that up right around 2000, I believe it was. There was a bit of a recession or at least a tech pull-back in 2000 and 2001. We stopped the consulting at that point and focused just on our products. But for probably the first four years we were doing a lot of rent-a-brain type of work just to keep the cash flow going.

And then as far as SourceOffSite, we've been shipping that product for over 10 years now. In fact, we're preparing another release even now. That's just a story of plugging a hole that a big player didn't fill. We thought that product was probably dead the day we shipped it. And there is still, to this day, no product at SourceGear has made more aggregate revenue than SourceOffSite.

Bob: So it was a gamble.

Eric: Yes.

Bob: Because, at anytime, Microsoft could just have added the feature you have in SourceOffSite to their offering, and that would have been that.

Eric: That's right.

Bob: How do you live with that type of uncertainty?

Eric: There were a lot of times we didn't. We didn't live with it well. We learned a lesson here along the way that I think is very important. When we first shipped, like I said, we thought we had a two-year window right off the bat. And over time that window just kept looking longer and longer. And now what's happened is that Microsoft has added those features to SourceSafe and they've discontinued SourceSafe, and we still sell the thing.

I think one of the things that we've learned is that a product has a certain life cycle to it. If it's a successful product, it's going to run for quite a few years. The way I think I'm starting to explain it these days is that a lot of the revenue potential of your product is going to start happening right about the time the developers lose interest in it. [laughter]

Bob: Oh, that's cruel.

Eric: Well, it's true. It's the latter half of a product's life that makes so much money.

Bob: And maybe that's what startups need to be thinking about: It's not just about getting to 1.0 and getting it out the door. That's only the beginning of the story.

Eric: That's right.

What Comes After 1.0?

Bob: If that's the beginning of the story, what would you say is the continuation of that? In other words, once you got SourceOffSite out the door and you thought you had a two-year window, you started generating revenue. What was the next priority? Was it the product or building the team or finding new ways of selling it? What were the things you went for after you started up business?

Eric: Once we got SourceOffSite out the door and we thought it was going to die soon after we released it, I spent probably my time from 1998 until 2002—about four years there—trying to figure out what our next product was. I tried several things. I can think of three or four products I created there that never made it to market. We finally ended up trying to choose something that was a bit more of a follow-on to SourceOffSite, something that was a bit more evolutionary than revolutionary. But, yeah, that was what we did: what's our next product? To go on and try to figure that out.

Bob: Why do you think that was? Was it that it wasn't obvious, or the thing that you wanted to do didn't really have that much potential commercially?

Eric: I think a lot of it was just me being a bonehead. [laughter]

The fact is, figuring out products is hard enough. And then what happens is you start getting advice from all sorts of people whose situation is different than yours. The recipes for failure in a software startup far outnumber the recipes for success. And a lot of the recipes for failure looked exactly like really great ideas. For example, say your recipe is "Do what PayPal did." Well, that's only going to work once. Or suppose your recipe is "Whatever Microsoft is doing these days, I'm going to follow them and do something very similar."

Well, the fact is you're different, your situation is different. A lot of business advice actually flying around these days is "Hey, here's what I learned at IBM; you can apply this to your startup." But the fact is you can't; it doesn't apply.

Bob: Is it more a case of the lessons from large corporations don't apply when you get down to a small software company? Or is it that plus things have changed since, let's say, the mid-1990s to now in terms of what works or doesn't work?

Eric: I think there's some of both. Certainly things have changed. A lot of money these days can be made using web applications, which in 1992 didn't exist. So obviously things have changed. But at the same time—and this is a piece of good faith that I happen to think is true, regardless of whether we're talking about software or restaurants—if you look at the very large players and do what they do, you're likely to fail in a startup. In fact, your best recipe is to look at the very large players and do the opposite of what they do.

Bob: Just because you're not them, and by imitating them you are setting yourself up to fail?

Eric: That's right.

Being the Guy Who Signs the Checks

Bob: Let's turn to management for a second, because while you may have been a project manager in a large corporation, now you're the guy writing the paychecks. What does that feel like, and how is that different?

Eric: Well, it's been very different. I think what helps me quite a bit is that I don't think I was a very good project manager in a large corporation. [laughs] I was just a lot more suited to being an entrepreneur. I didn't know that until I tried it. But when I sort of got on my own, I realized I'm a little bit of a jack-of-all-trades. I like to tell people sometimes that I'm a little bit good at everything and not really, really good at anything. And that's just the way I'm wired, and it makes me a pretty decent entrepreneur.

But I don't think a lot of people that worked with me as a project manager in my prior life would say that I was the best project manager they ever had.

Bob: Well, how about the CEO now of SourceGear? In other words, what sort of lessons have you learned as the executive, as the guy in charge, that you just didn't even suspect existed when you started this out?

Eric: I would say the number one lesson I've learned, or the number one thing that has prevented me from destroying my own company, is that you have to be self-aware about your limitations. You've got to know what you're not good at and make sure that there are people around you who are good at those things so that they can get them done. A lot of CEOs that I see are such control freaks that they can't allow somebody who complements them, who basically helps with their weaknesses, they can't allow that person to grow and gain influence in the company because they feel threatened by it. That's the guaranteed way to make sure your company never grows and, in fact, probably shrinks. You've got to make sure things get done well, even if you can't do them.

Bob: We're talking about very common human failings or insecurities or whatever. How do you get over that fear? How did you get over that fear?

Eric: That's a really good question. I think by the time I went out on my own I had lost it. If I had gone out earlier, I might have self-destructed in that way. This is a fear that you probably get over by learning from a mentor. I'll say it that way. That's one of the biggest problems with entrepreneurship, that you lost your mentor. You don't have anybody any more.

Bob: Class adjourned?

Eric: Well, kind of. I mean, I spent five years at Spyglass working with a manager who taught me so much. I can't imagine that I would have succeeded without those lessons.

Bob: So there is a place in the career path of a startup for doing the corporate thing.

Eric: Oh, yeah. I don't know if it's the corporate thing. The way I think of it is like this. I live and work here in Champaign, Illinois, where the University of Illinois is nearby. A lot of the students these days are going straight out on their own, starting a company right out of college. I did the five or six years working for somebody else first. And when I look at those students, I think, they're going to screw something up. Because I did, I just happened to screw stuff up as an employee instead of as a boss.

I have a strange path as an entrepreneur: I've never run a company that's gone out of business, because I've only run one.

Bob: OK.

Eric: I mean, most serial entrepreneurs fail three times before they succeed. I don't know Jim Clark's background. He's a legend in Silicon Valley for his successes, but I bet you there are three failures back there somewhere. And these students that are starting right out of college? They're going to fail, they're going to screw something up. I would have if I'd started out of college. You've got to learn this stuff. But what I wonder about these kids is, will they learn better lessons than I did by failing on their own? Or would they be better off working for a great mentor for five years and then going out? I don't know. It's a tough call.

Who Do You Hire?

Bob: Probably one of those case-by-case ones. But let me ask you about part of that. One is, what do you look for from your new hires? And two, being in Champaign, Illinois—which is not exactly Silicon Valley—how do you attract people out to the flyover country there?

Eric: [laughs] Flyover country, that's great. OK, the first question, what do I look for in new hires? Hiring developers, to me, is getting simpler and simpler all the time. I don't know why. I care about a lot of things, looking at a résumé. But one of the things that I care about most is, I think almost every coder that we ever hired that did well was somebody who at some point in his life has written code as a hobby. It's one of the first things I look at.

Bob: Really? That's sort of counterintuitive. What's the angle there?

Eric: The angle is that people who are good at writing code love doing it, so much so that they do it whether they get paid or not. Everyone wants to talk about the internship they did at Intel between their sophomore and junior years. I'm like, fine, that's impressive. But at the same time, when I see a résumé that has all that kind of stuff, but they never wrote a game during college, they never worked on an Open Source project, all they did is they went to classes, they did their machine problems, and then they got an internship. That kind of spooks me. Not a lot of really great developers follow that path.

Bob: So they really have to love coding. They really have to love the activity of designing software.

Eric: I don't know if I'd phrase it as they *have* to, but I'll just say it this way: I look at those two résumés as very, very different. There's always exceptions, but most of the time the résumé of the guy who loves coding so much that he or she does it on their own, that résumé attracts me more.

Bob: OK. How about noncoders? I presume out of 27 employees you've got now, there's probably some salespeople.

Eric: Yep.

Bob: Does this mean you're looking for the same attribute in them, or is it a different set of attributes when you're talking about nonprogrammers?

Eric: Oh, it's all different. This is another lesson I've learned, that hiring noncoders is very different from hiring coders. I came out of my previous work experience with pretty decent skills at hiring coders, but not such good skills at hiring and working with noncoders. I've had to learn that along the way. I don't know, I suppose my staff could tell you if you if I've ever learned anything at all, but I think I've gotten better at this over the years. But, yeah, it's very different. And if you approach it the same way you do as when you're hiring geeks, things go bad.

Bob: OK. Any suggestions when hiring noncoders?

Eric: The main suggestion would be, first of all, your noncoders will not succeed unless all the geeks in the company respect what they do, including you. It's real easy for a software company, especially a company that was founded by a geek like me, it's really easy for that to turn into a developer-centric company. And that's not a bad thing. But if that takes the next step, and now it's so developer-centric and anybody who's not a developer can't be recognized for making valuable contributions to the company, then that's a really bad thing. That's the first thing you've got to get past if you're going to hire, especially, sales and marketing workers. Most developers think most sales and marketing people are idiots. That doesn't work.

Bob: One of the things that traditional business management obsesses about is leadership, with a capital "L."

Eric: Right.

Bob: How do you lead your company? How do you get people to do things when you tell them to do them? Is it the way you tell them? Is it just that they know that they're supposed to do it, you've picked someone that works that way? That's like the day-to-day level. But then way above that is how do you lead your company when you're the guy that's got to be thinking about "Where do we go in three years?"

Eric: First of all, I'm going to quibble a little bit with you, because that's part of my answer. You asked, "How do you lead?" And then you said, "How you get people to do things?" And I think getting people to do things is the opposite of leadership. [laughter] I think that's management.

Bob: OK. Explain that. I don't get that.

Eric: I'm quibbling a little bit. I think of it this way: Somebody very early on taught me that the only true test of leadership is to look behind you and see if anybody is following. That's it. There really isn't anything else to leadership. Management is about keeping an eye on what people are doing and making sure they're doing the right things and things like that. I've never really believed that I'm a good manager; I'm probably not. But when it comes to leadership, leadership is relatively simple. You said, "How do I make sure that people are going the right place over three years?" I go there first. And if I'm going the right place, people follow me. That's leadership.

Bob: OK, so one thing I should learn and other people who want to be startups need to learn is that there is a difference between management and leadership. And your model for leadership is: you go there first, other people follow if you are doing the right thing. How about management? I guess I'm used to the typical hierarchies you see in large companies, which probably most developers are used to. It all flows up to the top and flows down from the top and it's hierarchical. How do you manage, then, a small group of people like those involved in a startup?

Eric: Well, I'm not saying there is no management. I mean there has got to be a certain amount of structure but, in many companies, far less structure than you think. So, I mean my approach to running a company would never work if SourceGear got to 250 people or, more to the point, if and when SourceGear gets to 250 people, I'll have been fired and that's fine. [laughs] I'm OK with that. But at 25 people, managing a company is great. What you do is you start with the assumption that most people will make the right decisions if they have all the information they need. So you give people lots of freedom, you give people lots of information, and all the right things happen.

Along the way, what you will find is that you picked up some people from big companies who don't like working that way. They want more structure. They want the comfort of knowing that nobody is going to step on their job description. And they have a little fence around their area and they don't go outside it and they don't want anybody coming inside it. And you just get rid of all those people.

And Who Do You Fire?

Bob: [laughs] OK, we solve the problem by shooting the people with the problem. Hey, that works.

Eric: It's callous, but there is a certain truth to that.

Bob: Let me ask you about callous for a second. I mean, OK, you've got 27 people right now. You must have fired at least some people during your career. First off, how hard is it? Second, do you get over it? Because you've just shown somebody the door, and, having been shown the door enough times, I know it's not a pleasant experience.

Eric: [laughs] Certainly, for me, parting ways with an employee under almost any circumstances is one of the worst parts of the job. I speak sort of jokingly about it, but the fact is, when it's happening, I'm nowhere near as heartless as I like to joke about. It's really hard and there have been very few cases that weren't, but every case is unique. I'm actually not sure that I have ever fired somebody for the joke I just made, because we tend to filter out those people before they ever get hired. But at the same time, yeah, a company that's 12 years old has had to let some people go.

And you asked: Do I ever get over it? Well, yeah, mostly. But I know some guys that can be a little colder and more methodical about this kind of thing, and I've always sort of envied them for that. But at the same time, it is who I am, so I don't want to change that.

Lessons Learned

Bob: OK. Let's wrap up here with the big lessons learned that you would like to pass on to other people who are founding startups. Let's start with product development. People get very, very focused on getting that 1.0 out the door. What would you advise them in general about the development of their product?

Eric: About the development of their products?

Bob: Past 1.0.

Eric: I would actually have to start with pre-1.0 because the biggest thing determining the success of your product is, first of all, to make sure you are building the right thing. There is a lot I can say about that, but you said we are wrapping up so I will just say this.

Bob: No, go ahead, please.

Eric: Well, people get so hung up on competition pre-1.0. When they decide what product to build, most entrepreneurs go about the competition discussion all wrong. What you need to do is, you have to find something that has competition, which is exactly what entrepreneurs tend to avoid. They think, "Oh, I can't do that, there is a competitor." You have to find something where you will have competition, and you have to find something where you have the right size of competition. So, I mean a classic mistake here is going after this huge market, but I know one entrepreneur who will not go after any market above a certain size. And I think that's incredibly smart. He targets niche markets that are too small for the big players to go after and more than big enough to buy himself a Ferrari. So it's a wonderful approach to competition, and I think most entrepreneurs don't do that.

And then you said post-1.0: Once the product is shipping, the number one mistake is not sticking with it, because the fact is if you pick the right market and you build your product and you ship your 1.0, it is almost certainly going to disappoint you in sales. 1.0 products don't sell very well. You've got to stick with it.

And unless you get new information, once you've picked your product and you know it is right, stick with it until 3.0 before you start thinking about bailing out on that. I have made that mistake too.

Bob: How about lessons learned in terms of people. Just working with and having people work for you and just the people aspect of the startup process?

Eric: Oh, man, everything I know about managing people won't take very real long I guess. Lessons learned from people: I think that working with people is one of the toughest parts of the whole game, because I think people naturally tend to have conflict, different people handle conflict in different ways, some people avoid it by nature, some people thrive on it. All I can say, I suppose, is that this is an area that requires a ton of attention, and I think it's one of the easiest ways to fail. I actually am a big believer in taking the time to understand how to work in relationships just as well as you understand how to work on code.

So if for you that means getting some consulting, that means—it is radical to suggest it—but maybe it means that you and your business partner need to see a therapist together so that you can communicate together. I don't know. But these things are just of critical importance. And, whatever it means for you, figure out how to work with the people around you effectively and that will pay off some pretty big dividends.

Bob: OK. Any final advice for an experienced developer who is thinking about going out there and making a startup?

Eric: Final advice for an experienced developer thinking about a startup? I have said this before, so it may be repetition, but ask yourself lots of questions about whether you are the right kind of person to be an entrepreneur. Being an experienced developer is probably not enough, and I don't want to tell anybody don't go after your dreams, it's not my place. But at the same time, I don't want to see anybody fail either. So ask yourself and ask the people around you to what extent am I sort of a jack-of-all-trades, because I really do think that's one of the critical things for startup success. When you go out on your own, you are going to be wearing—well, Bob, I think you even say this—you are going to be wearing, what, 47 hats?

Bob: There you go.

Eric: And you're going to be doing so many different things. You may look at it and think—Wow! I'm a coder, I can do this. But you've got 46 other things you are going to be doing besides being a software developer. And those things and your ability to do them competently, if not well, are really going to be the things that determine your success. So make sure that you go into that with your eyes open.

Joel Spolsky, CEO and Cofounder, Fog Creek Software

What do you say about Joel Spolsky (Figure 9-4), a guy who's, on one hand, the founder of a very successful software company and, on the other, probably the most read programmer on the net today. Simple: he's smart—really smart.

He's smart enough, as a Microsoft program manager, to write the spec for Excel's Visual Basic for Applications, he's smart enough to build a developer-centric company that continues to grow market share against far larger competitors, and he's smart enough to write about 1,100 articles for his blog, Joel on Software (http://www.joelonsoftware.com), that are so awesomely good they've become four excellent books you should read, and to speak at numerous tech conferences and cohost the Business of Software Conference (http://www.businessofsoftware.org).

Figure 9-4. Joel Spolsky

First and foremost, Joel's a developer who believes very strongly that developing great software is what a software company like Fog Creek Software (http://fogcreek.com) is all about and what a startup like yours should be about.

The CEO Mindset

Bob: I'm interested in the distance between being a really good developer and being the founder of a "going, actually making money" type of startup and in what happens after that. Maybe the place to start is the "CEO mindset" for a small software company. What do you think that mindset should be?

Joel: Oh, that's a good question, the "'CEO mindset." There are so many things. First of all, you need to have an entrepreneurial, businesslike approach to things. You know what I mean? And by that I mean that at some point the goal has to be to make money, if only to survive.

And no matter how much you've told yourself that you're going to be a cool, enlightened company and you're going to be Open Source, and you've got this long list of Not Evil plans that you plan to do—if ultimately you're not concentrating on the goal of making as much money as possible, then the business is not really going to be viable for very long.

Bob: OK. So one is keeping an eye on the bottom line?

Joel: Yeah, and that's actually hard for developers, because a lot of times developers launch a startup because they were sick and tired of the bean-counter accountants at their previous company, who were always doing things that appeared evil from a developer perspective, like rushing out buggy software or promising customers things that didn't exist or whatever evil things they may have done.

And maybe they've gone out as a reaction against that and they say, "We're not going to do that. We're going to be cool. We're going to be honest. We're going to be ethical. We're going to be blah, blah, blah. And we're going to have the finest-quality code without regard to how much it costs to get there, or whatever." And that's a great place to start from. On the other hand, if your mindset is not one of making money and paying attention to the bottom line, then you're not really going to be successful. You can't be successful.

Bob: So if job #1 is paying attention to the bottom line because you're the CEO, was job #2 the people that you hire?

Joel: Yeah—well, that's another thing. They're all job #1, aren't they? It depends on where you're at. If you're just starting with a couple of friends, hiring people is probably not yet a concern. You probably don't have that concern until you've gotten to the point at which you can pay people.

Most people start with a couple of friends. Unless you've actually either raised venture capital or have gotten to $30,000 to $40,000 in revenue a month, you're probably not hiring people yet; that's probably not your issue. But when you do get to that point, then your number one concern does become, of course, hiring people and creating talent and creating the team that's going to be able to create the great software.

Rock-Star Hires

Bob: Well, when you hire that first person, what should a startup be looking for in terms of programming talent? I think there is a difference between programmers and nonprogrammers. But just on the programmer side, what should you be looking for?

Joel: You're looking for the programmers that are 10 times as productive as the average programmer. You're looking for very, very high productivity. The only cost-efficient way to hire programmers as a startup is to get the ones that really accomplish massive amounts of stuff.

And there are, obviously, some other issues. Many of the people reading this will say: "Oh, well, you just want them to rush and write bad code? You know, the kind that just spews out fast and sloppy code." I never said that. I said there are programmers who create good-quality, debugged code at 10 times the rate of other programmers. In fact, the fast ones usually do better code than the slow ones and usually produce better code. So I'm not saying that.

Another thing, I sometimes use the expression *rock-star developers* to refer to these very, very special, highly talented developers who work so far above and beyond the average.

Bob: Sure.

Joel: They're just so much better than the run-of-the-mill developer that they seem like rock stars. And I often get the criticism: "You don't want rock stars because they're egotistical, self-centered, non-team players." And I've never said any of that.

Bob: I would have said "expensive" as the first comment.

Joel: No. I haven't found that you pay extra—a little bit, but not much—maybe 20% more expensive. But you're getting 10 times as much code out of them. So it's really the only economical way to hire programmers, if you ask me.

Bob: OK. How about that first nonprogrammer hire?

Joel: It depends. Our first nonprogrammer hire at Fog Creek was somebody who did customer service. And we carved out a position for this person as everything from customer service to sales to tech support. And we even said system administration, office management, why don't you do all kinds of fun stuff? And it turned out the person we hired was more inclined to customer service and inside sales, and so that's what he did, and a little bit of coding actually.

I guess it depends on who you start with, but we started with two developers. To me, the choice was: I'm a pretty good developer, and Michael's a really good developer, and we can write great code. And to find someone with our skills is a lot harder than finding somebody who can take all the nonprogramming tasks off our plate so that we have more time to program.

Bob: So really, when you're starting as two developers who are the founders, what you're looking for is somebody to complement that in nonprogramming areas.

Joel: Yeah.

Bob: Hiring another developer isn't what you necessarily need at that point.

Joel: Right. And once we had all of the nondevelopment tasks basically taken care of, then we started hiring additional developers. Now, not every company is going to be in the same position. You might have a company that's in the position where it was created by salespeople and they've somehow outsourced the creation of the first version of the software. I've actually seen a lot of that, where a startup is a couple of business guys that have no idea and don't know anything about technology.

They just have an idea. They put it up on one of these web sites where you get people to bid on it, and they've got some first version of the code that they're now selling. They're pretty good at the sales cycle, but they need a second version, and they need to develop their own in-house development team or they're not going anywhere. And so, at that point, they start looking for the more senior developers; maybe that would be a good first hire for that kind of company.

Course Adjustments and Major Releases

Bob: OK. Let's talk a minute about product development, and I guess product outcomes are part of that. Fog Creek's first product was CityDesk.

Joel: Yes.

Bob: And it met with some success, but not anything like what FogBugz has met with, which is really your flagship product.

Joel: Right.

Bob: I guess there are two questions here: One, is it just something that founders should expect to happen, that their first product is not going to be the one that makes the company?

Joel: Technically speaking, we did launch FogBugz first, although CityDesk came shortly thereafter. But we really did expect CityDesk to be the main product. I can give you a good analysis about why certain things failed and certain things succeeded in the market. But the truth is that you can't know in advance exactly which products are going to be successful and which products are going to fail. You could try to predict that, but sometimes you just get surprised. And so I think that you have to go in with the assumption you're going to tweak and adjust course a couple of times.

Bob: OK.

Joel: A lot of the biggest successful companies became successful with their second or third product. Sometimes they never even managed to launch the first product. Blogger was the product of Evan Williams and his friends at a company called Pyra Labs. They were doing some kind of project management thing—I don't know what it was they were trying to build. Blogger was an internal tool that they built for—I don't know what. Then they suddenly made that available, and that obviously became the gigantic hit that Blogger was.

Bob: How do you direct the growth of the product? FogBugz is now on version 6.0.

Joel: Yep.

Bob: How do you decide, "OK, we're going to work on this for this next major release, then we're going to hold on that until maybe two releases down." Or do you think that way?

Joel: When we're ready to start a new release, we first come up with sort of a vision for the release that describes what we want to be able to demo when we go out to visit our customers to demo the new version and explain what they're going to get.

The idea for a vision may vary from release to release. So in previous releases, one of our visions was to use AJAX to make the interface faster. That turned out to be useful but did not increase our sales, because I guess it was not a differentiating factor in the sales process. But anyway that was the FogBugz 5.0 vision. FogBugz 6.0 had a whole list of things.

FogBugz 7.0, for example, which is coming up [as of April 2009] also has a vision that states the kinds of things that we want to be in there and explicitly the kind of things that won't be in there, that won't be in that release. Once you have that vision, which can be something fairly simple, it can be just a list.

I remember at Microsoft, the Windows 95 vision was a list of five things that Windows 95 was going to have, that Windows 3.x did not have. It was long file names, it was the ability to put files on the desktop, they were really just plug-and-play. There was just a list of about five specific things.

When you look at it, that's really all that it was in Windows 95, and yet it was a gigantic upgrade. Once you have that vision statement, then you go through the list of everything everybody has ever imagined that they wanted to do and you decide whether it's in or out. And you get your initial list and you go through and prioritize and you decide what the highest-priority features are that you're going to do, that you can get done within a reasonable amount of time.

Bob: What's the process for seeing this vision? Do you go off by yourself, or do you have a company retreat? How does collaborative versus, I guess you call it, leadership works for you? What's the style there?

Joel: It strikes me as kind of a weird question, because we're talking about this in the abstract. In the abstract, I can give you a good abstract answer. For anybody that is actually product managing a product, meaning they have a product in the marketplace, they're responsible for figuring out how the product has to change to make more money in the marketplace.

I call them a product manager, and for anybody who is shepherding a product in the marketplace that way it is almost inconceivable that he wouldn't already have a pretty clear consensus in the head about what they really need to do next. It's those things that everybody raises their hands in those demos and says, "Can you do this?" And you have to say, "No."

You know what those things are, and everybody does for their product, everybody knows. It would be very surprising if there was somebody that was responsible for products that didn't have a clear idea as to what was causing you to lose sales. I've always known what those things are.

I'm sure that when you have a very mature product, like, let's say, the Microsoft Office team at Microsoft. There is nothing; they already have every possible feature. I'm sure that they have a lot of trouble figuring out whether they're going to put in the dancing paper clip or take out the dancing paper clip or rearrange all the toolbars to have different-sized tools or what they're going to do today. They've just got to make stuff up. I don't know what they should do. Maybe they should stop spending so much money on developing a product that already has 100% market share.

The other possibility is that the product is so immature or so nonexistent and has so few customers that you can't even decide what to build. That's an earlier-stage problem. But as to the problem of to how to get the product from version *n*.0 to version *n*.1 or *n* + 1, the answer is something that will be obvious to you when you've had 10 conversations with customers. There will be two things that came up with every single one of those customers who decided not to buy your product. You'll implement those two things, and then you'll discover another 10 things that you keep hearing from customers.

Bob: So is the person in charge of the startup supposed to be, more than anything else, the person who listens to the customers, or is that something that everybody is doing?

Joel: Everybody can do that; it depends on the size of the company. Here at Fog Creek it's the program manager's job to do that. There's a particular title of the person who is responsible for actually doing that. It's OK on a larger team for there to be a bunch of developers.

If you have a developer who's a really good coder and does not particularly care to talk to customer service and is perfectly happy to do what he's told, then it's OK to let him be a heads-down coder and let other people be in charge of making sure that what the coder is doing is appropriate to what the customer's needs are.

But they do have to be a bunch of people that have a pretty clear awareness, and it may be customer service people, it may be salespeople, it may be management, pretty much anybody that has outside customer contact. It's kind of odd to me, if you were to go right now and do a Twitter search for the keyword "FogBugz" and look at the cases where people are actually complaining or they're saying, "I don't want FogBugz because . . ." you'll discover that the things that are most repeated in that search, the things that come up the most frequently, are going to be in FogBugz 7.

Speaking of Twitter

Bob: Speaking of Twitter, I can remember not so long ago when you were pretty dismissive about the whole idea of Twitter, because it's a time waster, people talking about what they had for breakfast. Yet now you've got 8,000 followers. What happened there, Joel?

Joel: I'm perfectly willing to try things out; I don't have to be closed-minded. I understand the value of Twitter as a customer service tool, for example. I'm actually kind of tempted to go take that FogBugz search that I talked about and put it up on a big 50-inch plasma screen TV in the middle of the office so that everybody can see what people are saying about FogBugz. Not that they couldn't see it on their desk, anyway, but just to show that what people are saying about FogBugz is important to management and therefore we put up on the big screen so that you can walk by and see it.

That said, despite the usefulness of Twitter as a technique for listening to and reaching customers, I think the medium in general is a version of CB radio without conversations. It's like CB radio that's broadcast only. It drives me crazy. I can't stand it. [laughter]

Bob: Bottom line is you use it but you can't stand it.

Joel: I use it to a limited extent. Obviously lots of people use Twitter in different ways. But such a large part of it is this strange feeling that we are getting closer and closer to a world . . . we're asymptotically approaching a world in which people are continually expressing their opinions and their judgments about everything they see, do, eat, smell, and excrete—continually, all day long—and nobody has to listen.

It's a write-only medium, where everybody is just blathering about "I saw this movie and I liked it. I saw this movie and I didn't like it. I had a waiter and he was an idiot. I had a waiter and he was bad. I had this waiter and he was good. I had this experience." You're just in a constant state of being in judgment on the world around you and the sort of sense of self. Because you've got to squeeze everything into 140 characters, you're not allowed to justify any of these opinions.

Because you're allowed to talk to people that you're not listening to, you're in this funny state of just kind of spewing these not-backed-up opinions. I recognize that other things happen on Twitter besides this, but the general feel of just hanging out on Twitter and listening and broadcasting for a while is—at some point it feels to me like an atomizing, socially destructive service.

Bob: Well, OK. Since you don't have much of an opinion about Twitter . . . [laughter] Let me ask you what you think of the rest of the social media out there? I'm just going to lump them together. There's everything from Friend-Feed to Facebook to Ning Networks to all that.

Joel: Yeah.

Bob: Some people look at this stuff and say, "This is the new way that markets get found and talk to and conversed with." Do you buy into that, or do you not think that's what actually works, when you look at your sales numbers?

Joel: Are people on FriendFeed discussing products that they wish they could buy, and then suddenly a new product erupts? I don't get it. It actually strikes me that very few of the people on social networks are consumers. They're not using them to consume more stuff. Right? They're not on Twitter because they want to buy something or have something sold to them or sell something to other people. And if they are on Twitter because they're trying to sell something to other people, they're going to be . . .

Bob: . . . shot very fast.

Joel: Not very successful. Twitter is used for people to express their opinion about everything, endlessly, continually, and perpetually, without any kind of feedback. It happens to be a fairly useful way to find customers who have issues that you can fix, so there's a specific customer service role you can do.

Bob: OK.

Joel: And it's not a terrible way to find out about what features people want. But that whole 140-character limitation, to me . . .

Do you remember that short story? I wish I could remember who wrote it . . . was it Ray Bradbury? It wasn't Ray Bradbury. It's a science fiction story about a future world in which everybody is handicapped to the point of equality that the people who happen to be good at athletics have weights put on their legs so that they can't compete, and the people who are particularly smart or good at math have to wear these headphones that play loud noises that distract them from concentrating. It's *Harrison Bergeron*, by Kurt Vonnegut.

How Fog Creek Markets

Bob: How does Fog Creek sell—or maybe *market* is actually the word—FogBugz? What does the driving there? If it's not social media, what works for you guys?

Joel: Right. There's a bunch of stuff that works. We obviously started through my own blog, Joel on Software, and a part of that was establishing credibility among our exact target audience. My own personal authority is being somebody who writes things that make sense about the software development process, which made people think: "You know, it is worth checking out FogBugz, at least because Joel has the authority that it's worth seeing if, maybe, that is a valid . . . if the product that he's come up with in this space can solve our problems." And, indeed, since the product is good, we can then sell to them. So the first part, I would say, is almost the appeal to authority, whereas the authority was established completely innocently, and independently, through Joel on Software.

Once we had that initial base of audience, there's always natural growth, as the companies that buy FogBugz get larger and the people on teams that use FogBugz move around to a new job. And if they ever get to a job that's not using FogBugz—it's using some other, lesser bug tracker or no bug tracker at all—they tend to be our evangelists. And therefore there's a certain amount of spreading, throughout the history of our product, as people move from job to job.

And the other marketing thing that we've done that was extremely successful was that world tour. We actually went to 30 different cities and gave a demo of the new version, FogBugz 6.0, which we did a couple of years ago. That was unbelievably cost effective. It was absolutely remarkable, the number of sales that that generated for a given cost—very, very, worth doing, something we'll do again. I think that making the world tour work is predicated on having something that people are going to want to come hear. You can't just go to 30 cities and expect people to show up. But they did, since I promoted the world tour through my blog, through Joel on Software, and to existing FogBugz customers.

Bob: OK.

Joel: So we had enough people come to that that made it pay off.

Bob: So was it a situation where you evangelize to your existing customer base and they actually started bringing other people that weren't customers?

Joel: Yeah. That's always going to happen, there's always a lot of that.

But part of it, really, is that we were—I don't want to say we were really lucky, but it wasn't really by design. But the fact that the web site, Joel on Software, had a very large audience meant that we had somebody to sell to and somebody that would check out our products.

Now, I'm always very hesitant to give this as advice to other people launching startups, in whatever area, because the number of people that are able to establish a large audience through blogging, as large an audience as I did, is very limited. For every blog the size of Joel on Software, there are a million blogs that don't achieve anything like that kind of critical mass.

Bob: You mentioned earlier the idea of establishing your authority, separate from the product. That could be a blog. But that could also be—maybe you become the go-to person for a part of the technology that's related to your product, but not directly your product.

Joel: Yeah, and there's certainly examples of that. But I don't think it's the most common way in which a company successfully achieves mind share.

It definitely worked for us at Fog Creek, there's no question. On the other hand, I don't know if I recommend it, because I've seen a lot of people try to do it and just never really build up a big enough audience or enough authority in their field to do it, except maybe in very, very narrow niches.

I guess you have the Gary Vaynerchuk model or something.

Bob: Sure.

Joel: And then there's even the authority translating in a funny way. So you've got the Donald Trump model, where you're Donald Trump and you become this big celebrity business dude, and you've got a big enough audience that you can sell them expensive, overpriced condos on the Upper West Side, even though that's unrelated, in a sense.

Bob: Well, you're trading on the name, if nothing else.

Joel: Right, right. But that's a very limited approach.

If you look at the successful startups, a lot of them succeed because they create something—I don't know if you'd call it successful yet—but Facebook or Twitter or something like that. Create an incredibly viral product that happens to hit it out of the park. Sometimes it's just providing a service that is so useful, and so easy to communicate as to why it's useful, that it's going to take off almost no matter what happens.

And then there are companies that go in there with a product that just needs to be forcefully marketed in traditional ways: lots of advertising and about a million sales calls.

Bob: So you're basically of the mind that traditional marketing works today, and sometimes that's what the company should be doing?

Joel: It doesn't work as much as having a good product that meets needs in the marketplace. [laughs] But look Jet Blue, for example. They didn't have a blog. They didn't have a hot air balloon that everybody talked about. They had a service that was a little bit unique, so there was a little bit of conversation around them as a better kind of airline. They had a better product, which got people to talk about it. And I think that's a great shortcut to traditional marketing. But they also ran advertisements all over the place.

Developers and Methodologies

Bob: All right. Let's talk about how you get that great product. If you've got two or three developers today, what should be their guiding software development practices to get the job done well? I mean, there are so many different methodologies out there and many, many people talk about Agile in many different ways, for example. But for a startup, what makes the most sense in terms of software development?

Joel: Doing what works. When you say that there all those methodologies out there, up to and including the most extreme of the Agile Scrum-like methodologies, all of them are designed to get a team of random assorted bad programmers up to a minimum level of not-horrible incompetence. That's what methodologies are designed to work with. For the most part they are designed as a way of getting consistent performance, albeit horrid performance, out of a large group of people. So it is sort of the same way as Starbucks is designed to get at least a consistently bad cup of coffee, which is not ever horrible but is never good. That is what these methodologies are designed to do: take a whole bunch of political science majors that have gone into computer programming because it's the hot thing to do.

Bob: Hey, I was a political science major! [laughs] But seriously . . . OK, I get that. But . . .

Joel: A methodology for a startup is just to be avoided. If you have developers who can't figure out for themselves what the right thing to do is or do the right thing without being told "We must follow the following methodology, and we must have meetings in which we stand, and we must have new code released to customers every week," or every two weeks or every month, whatever the methodology dictates that you do instead of just doing what makes sense, then you're already in trouble. You really need very bright, self-driven developers who can figure out what to do.

Sometimes the methodology may inspire them to try some techniques that may be effective. But to slavishly follow a particular methodology or to even think "Hey, we are an extreme programming shop" just means you are making decisions about how to do things. You are outsourcing the making of decisions to somebody who has written a book in order to sell consulting gigs about programming methodologies.

Bob: So the bottom line is not the quality of the methodology at all, it's the quality of the programmers. The better the programmers are—and they'd better be good programmers—the less you need to be told how to do what you are doing. Does that make sense?

Joel: Right, right.

Stack Overflow

Bob: In a way, you have just launched, a little while ago, another startup. And that's Stack Overflow (http://stackoverflow.com). Two questions: (a) Why did you do it? And (b) what did you learn from doing it?

Joel: Well, I haven't learned anything yet. [laughs]

Bob: OK.

Joel: I did Stack Overflow because my philosophy for launching a business is that when you see an obvious need in the marketplace—something that you need and would pay money for—and the need is not being met, then you should launch it. That's a great business opportunity. Thus one reason why it's good to do a startup and be in business is that you discover these needs that are not being met in the marketplace.

In the case of Stack Overflow, it was just bizarre to me that you could type programming questions into Google, which is otherwise such a great search engine, and find such terrible results. It was obvious to me that there was a better way of doing this. Maybe there was a certain amount of hubris there, but I think we've proven it to be the case that there is a better way to do this. So that was the motivation in starting it, just knowing there is something out there that I would pay for. It doesn't exist. It turns out you don't even have to pay for it. So it's even better.

Bob: Well, first off, as far as I know, Stack Overflow is advertising supported.

Joel: Yeah.

Bob: Is it making money?

Joel: Yeah. It's in what I would call the first-stepping-stone path toward revenue. That is sort of basic advertising that goes on there. We have a long-term plan for something that hasn't launched yet, which we think will also bring in more revenue in a way. That is . . . well, it is hard for me to say since we are not announcing what it is.

Bob: How many programmers are using Stack Overflow on a day-to-day basis now?

Joel: I think we are at about 600,000 page views a day, 250,000 visitors a day, on a daily basis.

Bob: OK. That's pretty substantial. It's working. That's the bottom line.

Joel: Yeah, it's somewhere like 2 million unique visitors a month. And that is a very substantial percentage of the working programmers in the world. Somewhere I remember a statistic that there are about 4 million working programmers in the world. I don't remember where I heard that. But I feel like we are pretty close to getting that kind of thing—it's only a matter of time. The growth rate is ridiculous. It's doubling every four months.

So we're only a year off from being something that literally every working developer who uses the Internet will at some point encounter, just because we come up in searches. It is not because they know about Stack Overflow.

Final Advice?

Bob: OK. I guess the final question would be: What advice would you give to a couple of developers who want to start up a company today?

Joel: Boy, I've got so many things. I guess my number one piece of advice right now—well, I've got a lot of things. I can talk about this endlessly. First of all, charge more; make your prices higher. People are always afraid to charge enough, and this is a problem because they don't make as much money as they could. They always underestimate how much businesses are willing to pay for things. If you have been a consumer, it's easy to understand what consumers would pay for things because those are the decisions you've been making all your life when you decide whether to buy things.

But if you ever start selling to businesses, which is actually where the money is, businesses have a very different opinion about what is a reasonable amount of money to spend on things.

Bob: OK.

Joel: So that's probably my number one advice: You are probably not charging enough. I think equally important is to focus on making the product better at all times. Don't waste time with weird marketing deals trying to make some kind of affiliate-link programming thing with coupon codes and direct mail, trying to figure out basically tricks to try to goose a little bit more revenue out of your product. This is not nearly as valuable and not nearly as good a use of time as just writing more code to make your product better and to make it meet the needs of more people. We've always found that the best use of our time here is releasing new versions of FogBugz that have more features and are more capable.

So far we've been talking with software developers who've gone down the road toward startup-dom, the same road you want to travel. But there are other, less obvious challenges on the Underground Railroad that leads past your manager's office and on to freedom. The next interview introduces a non–software developer with important advice to offer you about launching your startup.

Pamela Slim, Author and Coach

Pamela Slim, a coach, mentor, and blogger, has helped hundreds successfully make the jump to a self-designed destiny. Her blog, Escape From Cubicle Nation (http://www.escapefromcubiclenation.com; Figure 9-5), and her book, Escape from Cubicle Nation: From Corporate Prisoner to Thriving Entrepreneur (Portfolio Hardcover, 2009), are major information sources for anyone planning to make a break with the corporate workplace.

Figure 9-5. Escape from Cubicle Nation

Why Leave Your Cozy Cubicle?

Bob: Why should people leave the warm, cozy cubicle they've been living in their entire professional career to launch a startup?

Pamela Slim: In my experience working with a lot of clients, it has to be a place where there really is a significant defining moment and a really strong feeling that it truly is the right move for them, because of who they are. It sounds a little bit "the big picture" or philosophical, but it's really true that a lot of people do want to do a lot more with their life. They have dreams. They have aspirations. You probably find a lot of people you run across in your daily life, as I do, people who have just kind of fallen into jobs. They do work, and they do a decent job at it, and get a salary, and so forth. But they don't necessarily feel like they're doing something that really has meaning. They don't enjoy it while they are doing it. They might enjoy the outcome, like getting a nice paycheck. There's nothing at all wrong with that, feeling good about earning a living and taking care of yourself or your family.

But I find that for people who actually make that choice to leave, they have some kind of defining moment. For some, it's a health issue, where they realize that they are pushing themselves so hard, to stay in a life that's really not meant for them, that their body just rebels. They get really, really sick, and they realize they have to make a change.

For other people, they see the benefit of a future life that's really different. Maybe they meet a friend. Maybe they meet somebody. Maybe they read a book. All of a sudden, they get motivated, thinking, "You know what? I think I could actually accomplish that."

The reason, to me, why it needs to be a defining moment is that it is really a lot of hard work and effort and energy. All of that. It's not something you can just casually fall into.

That said, that idea of having a safe job in a cube these days is one that's a bit of an oxymoron. Because jobs that all of us thought were a bit untouchable, in companies that were untouchable, it's just been amazing to see what has happened.

So I think people have been shaken into a new level of awareness that if nothing is safe, then how could they maybe realign their work, maybe in steps, to eventually be something that really feels good while they're doing it and also gives them a sense of purpose and meaning.

Bob: Well, a couple of things strike me. First off, yes, life is more than a paycheck, or at least it ought to be. There's a difference between living and existing. I think you're striking at the point that, for some people, creating a startup means that they can go, in their own personal development, from the existing plane to the living plane, if you will.

Pamela: That's right, and that's why, for some people, it really does come in many forms. It's interesting, to me, always to note what that moment is, but some people really do get that flash of it. Maybe a friend of theirs that's at a similar age passes away. Or a parent passes away, or, again, it can be a whole different variety of things that have that moment happen. It sounds so cliché, but it is true that there really is only one life. And when you're sitting every day and spending all of your energy doing something that you truly don't care about, that takes a lot of life energy just to keep you going, just to force yourself to stay motivated and keep a smile on your face. Boy, I think there's a lot more to life than that.

Bob: This may sound trite, but as I've gotten older I've noticed that my regrets are stronger about the things that I've *not* done than any memory or concern over the things that I *have* tried at which I didn't succeed. You have to go out there and do more than just occupy space.

Pamela: I think so. I think an interesting flip side of that, though, is that some people might actually be perfectly happy and content with what they're doing, and yet they might feel that they should be doing something else. So they think they should explore it. That's the case where they might try something and have it not work out. Then they gain new appreciation for what it is that they had.

I think that can be an interesting outcome. It's not for everybody, the entre-preneurial lifestyle. Startup life, starting a company, is not for everybody, and that's totally OK. It's more about finding a work situation that really works for you.

To Be or Not to Be . . . an Entrepreneur

Bob: Let's talk about that for a moment, maybe discerning whether or not you should launch a startup. What's the litmus test that you think exists out there to decide whether or not someone is able to handle being an entre-preneur?

Pamela: I wish there were that test, Bob, and I wish I administered it, because I would be a rich woman. [laughter]

It's everybody's question. It's totally valid. People look at profiles of successful entrepreneurs and characteristics. I would say, in terms of what can have more probability of having somebody be successful, certainly a strong sense of being very self-directed.

Confidence, I would say. Sometimes entrepreneurs can be very unconfident and have all kinds of fears, but the key with them is that they actually do push through that fear. They do things anyway, even if it doesn't always feel good or, as you said, even if they fail.

In terms of the actual testing of the viability of an idea, I believe so much in having the experience of really testing and trying things out to make sure that there is a real market, that you have real people who are purchasing, before you actually make any decision to leap.

That probably is the distinguishing factor. Somebody on paper could have all of the right characteristics. Their personality profile could be perfect, if they're sitting back and planning for three years, versus somebody who might not look perfect on paper but who actually tests and tries and gets things going.

I've seen all kinds of different personality profiles succeed. Usually those who do are those who recognize their limitations and surround themselves with complementary skill sets.

Bob: Let me put that in a somewhat different way, because I think you're hitting an important point there. If you're going to be a startup, you have to be a son of a bitch. I mean this in a positive way. I don't mean that you're a nasty person or that you torture animals or anything like that.

I mean that you're the type of person who, when you set your mind to doing something, you're going to put everything into making that thing happen. You're not easily dissuaded by what other people think. You're not going to take failure as a judgment, from whomever, that you're unworthy of ever trying this and that it's time to crawl back to your cube.

You really have to push to be able to be an entrepreneur. I've yet to find any entrepreneur or startup who's managed to have really noticeable success without first meeting failure along the way.

Pamela: It is a totally crucial part. I completely agree with you. It is not an easy thing, and I really have had to look at myself in the mirror many, many times and really ask myself, "What are you made of? How much do you want it? What is the meaning behind what you're doing?" It goes to our earlier conversation, that if you do not feel strongly that there is a purpose and a meaning for what you're doing. I usually get a visual in my mind of somebody who is sitting in that cube who might be really miserable, whose health is failing, who doesn't feel like she has any joy in her life.

When I run into a brick wall, when I create a program that nobody buys, or a whole myriad of different things that can happen as I'm pushing along in my business, I step back and I just try to look at that person, and say, "How much do I care about this? How much do I care about moving forward?"

The more that I can be human, allow myself sometimes to feel a little crappy for having failed, but then pick up, take the learning from it, and move on, and not let myself be defined by that—that really is the key difference. Because it is not easy and there definitely will be failures. Because when you're testing and trying something totally new, it's impossible that it's always going to work out the way that you think it is. Life doesn't work that way.

Packing for Your Escape

Bob: What sorts of things should you pack before you start out from your corporate home, assuming that you're still in it?

Pamela: Meaning Post-It notes and pencils? [laughs]

Bob: Raid the office supplies. That's always a good one.

Pamela: Not very ethical. No, I'm teasing you. In terms of what you should really have in line, before you decide to make the leap?

Bob: Everyone obviously gets the idea of having some savings put aside, because there's inevitably costs to building a startup, even today. What other things would be good to have for the journey, maybe emotional and social and psychological things?

Pamela: I think there are a number of things. It definitely makes sense to have your finances in order, even for people who might not be naturally inclined to look at their finances in detail, because everybody's different about that. I think this is a case where you might need to get a little bit of help, just to really get a clear sense about where you are. You need to know what's coming in, what's going out.

Trim as much as you can so that you have as much of a cushion as possible. The finance experts that I talked to when I did my book would say anything from six months to a year of having money set aside, as a cushion.

This is not just savings that you have. But it really is money that will be there specifically in order to help fund you if your plans don't go as you think they will. Or if you're still in the development phase, it will give you the necessary money in order to develop your business idea.

I think that's a really critical piece. It's really important to have a circle of people around you, where you already have begun to build up. Just given the way the world works today, it could be a virtual circle of a lot of people who might be in your corner, who are peers and mentors and friends, who can really be encouraging of your moving in your new direction.

For a lot of corporate employees, who have always grown up around other employees, it can feel very lonely to take this path. People that you talk to might think you are totally crazy, because they don't know anybody who's actually done it before, successfully.

So before you even begin to step out on your own, I encourage you to do things like join the Business of Software forum, so that you can begin to build up a network. Through a broad network like that, you're really going to find the people who you relate to.

I always like to have people in my circle who are what I call my *peer mentors*, who push me. I know that we have similar background and experience, but they're the kind of people who are really going to go that extra mile. That makes me think, "You know what? I have to hustle. I see what Bob's doing. He's on his third book. I just made it through one. I better really be moving forward." You want to have that in place, as well.

The other thing is that you definitely want to have as clear a picture as you can about the nature and framework of your business. You want to have a good understanding of how marketing works in your arena.

You should have already begun to build up your list—the people that you want to serve, your target customers. It has some kind of regular, predictable way in which you are beginning to build relationships with people, on the marketing side. Because, as you know, people buy from people they know, like, and trust, which, on the marketing side, can take a year, 18 months, two years. It's not that everybody who's just going to stumble across your site is going to buy immediately.

But somebody who's been enjoying you and getting great feedback and information from you over time, in different social environments, is going to feel, like, "Wow, if Bob is going to sell something, I really want to buy it."

Bob: It sounds like one of the ways of doing that would be through a blog.

Pamela: It's been great for me, definitely. I've realized that I have had so much personal success with my blog in terms of pleasure, for one. But also on the marketing side and also in how it's brought me clients and a book deal and many more things. I, definitely, am biased that way. I realize that not everybody is a writer, not everybody is going to have that as the chosen form of their core marketing activity.

But there are so many benefits to it, that where all things are pretty much equal, I just see so many benefits to writing a blog. Because it can be the source of your core intellectual property, about what you know, about your field of expertise, whether it be a service business or a product.

The information that you're sharing can become a repurposable source of so much great stuff. You can create an e-book, an audio program, a workshop. Use it for your marketing materials. Use it for an actual, physical book.

So I'm a huge fan. If you don't have a total aversion to writing, if you can be clear, and if you learn how to write, keeping your audience in mind and providing useful information to them, that's definitely a great start.

From Layoff to Bootstrap

Bob: What about the situation where you've been pushed? In other words, you've just been laid off from your job. Maybe you saw it coming, maybe you didn't. How do you, first, cope with the bereavement of your work situation and then be able to go off and launch a startup?

Pamela: That's a really good term with which to talk about it, *bereavement*, because it can be a very traumatic thing. I find, even if people are expecting it, that it really does put you in a whole state of grief. You need to allow yourself to go through it and not feel crazy for being very sad or sometimes being very angry or going through all the traditional stages of grief. If they can, I really encourage people to just take the time in order to work through it and get the kind of support that they need, because it is not an easy thing to go through.

That said, I've actually talked to a lot of people recently who have been in that situation, not surprisingly. This is one distinction, one way that might be helpful to think about how you actually get back on your feet and get working again. And that is when you're talking about building something that is a full-fledged startup, a company that would be your sole source of income where you could make the equivalent amount that you made as an employee.

If you have not already, then do a lot of work on the side to make that actually happen so that when you get laid off all of a sudden, you can just step into that company full time and basically just do more of what you have been already doing, which is selling products or services, and make it full time.

For a lot of people, they actually could be so much earlier in the process, where for some they don't even really know what kind of business they want to start. Or, they had not put anything in place. They haven't tested anything, they have no product or any kind of service defined.

So in this case I would recommend having more of an interim strategy. And that can be looking at making a very clear assessment of your own skills and competencies that are salable. So if you've written code before, if you've been a project manager or software developer, whatever it is, you can make an assessment of all the different skills that you have, inside of work and outside.

Maybe you're a great landscaper. Maybe you know how to organize garages. Really take nothing off the table at all. Just think about all the different ways in which you can generate income. Think about a shorter-term strategy where you can just begin to monetize some of the stuff that you know really well in order to bring in some income.

And don't be shy about that. And I hope that people feel really good about doing that, because it's very, very hard to be thinking about the long-term, bigger picture when you're totally worried and you have no plan for how you're going to bring in money.

Bob: So you have to deal with the fear first. I guess you have to deal with the fear and the worry and the grief and the hurt. And maybe there needs to be a transition stage between yesterday's pink slip and tomorrow's master of the universe?

Pamela: I think so, because, yes, when you are afraid . . . Fear actually is a great teacher. You can really think about what are you afraid of, if you're totally panicked because you don't know where your next source of income's going to come from, and that's because you do not have anything defined. You have no idea how you will make money. Then that's probably why you have that fear. It's a different kind of fear than, as I said, if you have been working very specifically on a side project for a long time and you have some normal anxiety and fear about getting customers and so forth. That could mean pointing you in a different direction where maybe you really do need to beef up on your sales and marketing skills.

But pay attention to what that fear is saying. We can often have a really strong reaction that's very extreme. I call it the *lizard fear*. It's related to that fight-or-flight mentality that we have, which nowadays is fueled by the news about everybody's being worried that there's not enough, there's not enough—even though there are some great opportunities for those who can feel strong and move forward. So when you feel that, I think the first thing, as you said, is to listen to the fear, figure out what is it trying to tell you.

And then, yes, don't be shy about getting some interim things in place, which for some people could be getting another job in order then to be able to go further down the road and work on the longer-term plans.

One of my clients actually did exactly that thing, and he found that when he was trying to work on the long term or worried about the short-term cash flow, it just didn't work at all. And he got another job, and now he's feeling so much better. Now he's aware, and his eyes are open that he's not going to sit back and not do the work like he did before—you know, when he was employed and he kept putting off creating his plans—because now he knows that nothing is stable, since he got laid off before. But the difference is that he realized for himself that he needed to have more of a predictable income coming in, in order to work on the longer term.

Bob: That makes sense. What lessons would you'd like to point out from your new book for startups that's just coming out?

Pamela: One of the biggest lines that I tried to walk in the book is to be very encouraging to people who were sitting back feeling like they were crazy for not being happy in their corporate job and encouraging them to really take some time to figure out what it is that they do want to do. There are a lot of wonderful opportunities, today more than ever, to do things a different way and potentially either to make some income on the side or to work fully for yourself.

That said, the second main point in the book is that it's not always a fairy tale. And I caution people against thinking that it's going to be easy. One of the themes from the book that seems to be resonating with a lot of people is that hating your job intensely is not a business plan. A lot of people feel that the biggest decision is "Oh, I hate my job. I'm going to do it: I'm going to quit." And then they really are just quitting and jumping into a big pit of nothingness because they really haven't done the work to plan and prepare.

So I try to lay out a very specific, what I hope is realistic, process of what actually are the things that you need to have in place. And it's not just having your finances in order or then defining ideas in a business plan, but it's also getting things straight on the home front: really working out a very good open communication with your spouse and your family members so that you're all in alignment in terms of the new direction in which you're going.

It's also important to really focus on building up this extended network of people who can be friends and peers and mentors, even the High Council of Jedi Knights, which is the term I use for people who you truly, truly admire, who you really want to aspire to be like and also really follow and learn from, as mentors.

So there are a lot of things, I think, on that path, where the key is not to be overwhelmed but to really break it down in stages and give each stage the time that it needs.

So if you are really early in the process and you have no idea what you're actually passionate about and what you want to do, don't put pressure on yourself to have to get a whole business up and running quickly. You might be much better served to just do things that actually engage your creative self. Take a tango class and cook and wander through a new neighborhood. Do things that are really going to wake you up so that you get a sense of what you really care about.

Once you get through that place, that's where, then, all of the sudden it's like the fog clears and you can see what the next step is. I think people just want to jump in and get everything done at the same time, and that's really what feels overwhelming.

Bob: Let me recap what we've got here. First off, there are things that you have to do to make something real. And one of the biggest things is to see the steps involved that actually need to be done. You have to get it down to what David Allen would call the *action level,* where you actually are doing physical things about it.

The other part that I see here if you're going to succeed is that you need to do things that have absolutely nothing to do with technology, especially if you're coming from "corporate land," where you've been living in a way that has a whole set of rules and you've internalized all those rules because you've been a good corporate team player. And now you have to go through the process of picking and choosing which of those values will still serve you in this wholly different role that you're going to take on.

As you mentioned a moment ago, you've also got to get your house in order. Part of that is financial, but by *house* I mean more like your home, the people or persons in it, and your extended family and friends. You're going to need their support. You may ask them for money. You want their buy-in and their encouragement. And you need all these things before you just go flail at the idea of being a startup.

Pamela: Right.

Lou Carbone, Founder and Chief Experience Officer, Experience Engineering

Now I'd like to introduce you to fellow ex-UPI reporter Lou Carbone (Figure 9-6). Lou has both made a name for himself and built a thriving consulting firm focusing his talents on the art and science of experience management. What's that? That's the next business idea after *branding.* It's the kind of experience a company—such as your startup—creates for its customers. Is it going to be a living hell of endless voicemail trees, the whiff of smug arrogance, and a base of customers desperately seeking an alternative that most "real" companies now pass off as serving their customers? Or is it going to be the sleek, above expectation, respectful with-it-ness of, say, Apple? And how do you as founder control this outcome?

Figure 9-6. Lou Carbone

It's not the size or nature of the company that determines customer experience. Both small and large companies can get it wrong. But for startups, the results of ignoring the kind of experience you're creating for your customers can stop your company dead.

Lou's book *Clued In: How to Keep Customers Coming Back Again and Again* (Financial Times Prentice Hall, 2004) lays out a framework for understanding what customers need and desire and how to manage those needs and desires.

In this interview, Lou helps me—and you, I hope—understand what goes into what a customer experiences, starting with the Edsel[1] of operating systems, brought forth by a company that prided itself on understanding the customer: Microsoft Vista.

---

[1] *"The Edsel was a marque of the Ford Motor Company during the 1958, 1959, and 1960 model years. The brand is known best as one of the biggest commercial failures in the history of American business."—from* http://en.wikipedia.org/wiki/Edsel

Customer Experience, Vista, and the iPhone

Bob: What is customer experience?

Lou: I think one of the critical factors, and especially in IT applications, is to begin to think of the effect that software has on individuals, on their lives, and how they feel about themselves using the software, versus the functionality. And I think that when you begin to look at some of the experiences that we've had, what is amazing to me is, at what point do you reach the law of, I guess, diminishing returns, in terms of effect on a customer? And I think some of the greatest examples of those particular applications are certainly Microsoft, in terms of all of the functionality that I'm not even aware of that exists in my PowerPoint program.

And I think what happened with Vista is the interesting piece of what's there: You not only had difficulty doing what you always did with it, but you didn't understand what the effect was. Why did they do what they did? It didn't make me feel any different. It was just rearranging some things.

Bob: So, if I wanted to put in sort of IT shorthand: to get an idea of what happens when customer experience goes wrong, look at Vista.

Lou: Exactly! Exactly! Look at Vista. And also, ultimately, when we begin to look at cloud computing, if you will, what's so beautiful about that is the feeling, the effect that it has on people and that people will be willing to give up certain functionality for its effect on their lives and how it causes them to feel, versus dealing with software that has all of this hidden resource that you almost feel like you've paid for but don't get to use. So when we look at the percent of what I'm using in Microsoft Word, there's part of me that feels very enabled and very powerful. I'm able to write a book that I would have never been able to write with a typewriter, perhaps.

Bob: OK.

Lou: Yet there's a whole aspect, unconsciously in Word, that deals with margins and all of these other aspects that . . .

Bob: Ad infinitum.

Lou: Yeah, that I don't have the time to invest. So, consequently, I feel somewhat inadequate, not fully vested in the power that the software can bring to me. And when you look at it, where was the saturation point when they reached the law of diminishing returns on what was there? And then I begin to look at cloud computing and some of that, at the feeling of efficiency, the feeling of what's there and what it does in my life.

If we look at the iPhone and the power of what it puts at my fingertips, from a functionality perspective, it has all of these things that I can master and use. I think it's brilliant, the way that they provide you with a basic framework on the iPhone, and then you can begin to customize it and make it as complex or as simple as you want. Being an early adapter, I overloaded my iPhone with every possible piece of software . . .

Bob: [laughs] Yeah.

Lou: . . . determine compass directions, wind, et cetera, et cetera. And consequently, I'm now feeling, boy, maybe what I need to do is really understand what I need, rather than being overwhelmed thumbing through all of these icons and so on. I think it would have been great if there was a way for the software store to think about itself, in a sense, in respond mode, versus make and sell, where I would tell a piece of software or tell the store if you will, "This is what I need. I need time management. I need what's important to me—a to-do list."

Bob: It sounds like you'd like to see concierge shopping at the iTunes Store.

Lou: Exactly. That would have been more powerful for me. And then, if it recommended, maybe you might want to leave one spot open that you put stuff in and out of to test, almost a sample area. But then they're thinking about its effect on me as an experience, versus putting software in a store and selling it as product. So then I would have seen the iStore, the Apple Store, where you get the software, as a partner in my life, which I see the phone as to a great degree. But have they really fully leveraged what that feeling is like? And, to me, the iPhone has been one of the most unbelievable experiences.

Why Care About What Your Customers Feel?

Bob: Let's back up a moment here. It sounds like I should care, as a startup company, about how my users feel? All I want is their money. Why do I care about what they feel?

Lou: Because what they feel is what will shape their attitude. Unconsciously, how we feel about ourselves in an experience really begins to affect our framing of the attitude that we have toward that. Take a relationship with the cell phone companies, for example.

Bob: Yeah, I know how I feel about my cell phone company. So let's take that.

Lou: Yeah. And what they don't understand is that they could have all of these great products. They could have extraordinary coverage. But every time I've been through my carrier, I realize that they could give a crap about how I feel and how their whole experience causes me to feel.

I think the greatest example of that was when the iPhone 3G actually came out and I went to the iStore. I had a first-generation iPhone and the 3G comes out. I go to the store. They said, "Well, you can't walk out of the store like you did last year and activate it on your own. It has to be activated here in the store." So we go to activate it, and for some reason I was on a discount plan. And on that particular discount plan, AT&T wouldn't offer the promotional price, which was actually $299, and the phone was going to cost me $499. And that's because of AT&T.

And so I had this huge, four-person conversation, four different levels, at the AT&T call center. And they said, "Nope, these are the rules. This is the way it's been done. This is what we've created." And I was very, very disappointed and a little upset, because I had waited in line at the Apple Store for God knows how long.

Bob: It sounds like this customer experience stuck in your mind.

Lou: It was horrible, absolutely. It left a lasting impression that reinforced my feeling about AT&T.

Bob: And that typically happens with customer experiences.

Lou: Exactly. So it lived up to its reputation. And what does the person do at the Apple Store? He calls his manager over and explains what happened. The manager apologizes and says, "You know, I'm really sorry, but AT&T and what they're doing is out of our control. But why don't I just give you a $200 gift card to put toward the phone, and that will bring it down to the price that you should be getting it for."

Bob: And how do you feel about Apple?

Lou: Fantastic! One treated me with incredible respect, incredible understanding of how I felt and how I would feel leaving. I felt unimportant. I felt insignificant. I felt unappreciated, after being with AT&T for 13 or 14 years. And when I left the Apple Store with what they did, I felt special. I felt closer to them. I felt empowered. I felt stronger. I felt much more confident in the decision that I made.

Bob: I had a similar experience with the same two companies when I bought my 3G. I went to an AT&T Store to buy it, because that's who my carrier was. They treated me like dirt. And I literally just said, "Forget it," and walked out. I just didn't want to be near those people. I stood in line for three hours at an Apple Store, and I haven't stood in that long a line for a long time. But when I got in there, they couldn't have been nicer. They moved me right through, they did what I needed to do, and I was out the door in 10 minutes.

Lou: Yeah.

Bob: And I felt so good, because here is this person helping me do what I want to do. I can still remember that I had also planned to buy a new mouse for my MacBook Pro, because I had literally worn out the other one. And they said, "Oh, you've got an extended warranty. Here you go." And he just hands me a new mouse. I'm going, "Oh!" I didn't have to fill out a form to get this. I didn't have to jump through hoops.

I think it's something that a lot of people underestimate—well, let me ask it this way. Is it true, do you think, that most people come up with reasons to do things, in terms of rationalizations, based on their feelings rather than on, necessarily, the facts of the matter?

Lou: Absolutely, without a doubt. I mean, we see this over and over, in terms of human behavior, that we will create an intellectual alibi and create rational reasons for the emotional feelings and decisions that are in our unconscious thoughts.

Engineering Customer Experience

Bob: Well, then, let me ask it this way. To take a pun off of your company name, how do you engineer experience?

Lou: It's a set of clues and signals that we send in experiences that we have. And it's a careful orchestration of the experience, according to a plan, so that they don't happen at random. Now, the plan is built on sensing and responding. And it's not a product plan, the way that we would build a product, because experiences are considerably more dynamic. Again, let's cite Apple. I think that the thing that's interesting is that I hear everyone, from design folks to whomever, all citing Apple in terms of what the magic of Apple is.

And over the years—I'll probably date myself a little bit—we heard the very same thing about Disney, for years and years and years. What I can't believe is that, rather than looking for next practices and understanding what is embedded in these experiences that bond people in a certain way, we tend to search for best practices. And in searching for best practices, we become very superficial and never understand the infrastructure underneath the experience.

So let's look at Apple a little deeper than most people do. Let's look at the experience of the Genius Bar.

Bob: OK. For our Windows readers, that's where you walk up, after having made an appointment prior to that, with your laptop and you say, "I've got this problem, and I want you to help me."

Lou: Exactly. And let's take an example, again, a real, live example. And I'm going to contrast this to the Geek Squad at Best Buy.

Bob: OK.

Lou: I go to the Apple Store. I have my Sony computer, which is a Windows PC. And I walk in, and I have a problem with the iTunes software.

Bob: OK.

Lou: Now, the first question that one would normally have is "Are they going to tell me it's a software problem [laughs] and, therefore, we have nothing to do with it?" And no. I come in, and they put my computer on the workbench. They look at it. They spend almost an hour and a half with me, reload the software, do this, do that. And all of a sudden, my music is syncing up again on my iPhone. And I'm expecting to pay something. And by the way, I was able to make an appointment online, show up, and within five minutes of the time I was supposed to be waited on, I was waited on. And at the end, I'm, like, "OK," and they said, "No charge." And I was like, "You're kidding me." They said, "No." They said, "No, no charge. We really got it taken care of, and that's all that matters."

Now, I have been there probably seven or eight times and have had only three incidents where we've paid something. There was a little thing that happened with my daughter in replacing a hard drive recently on an Apple computer. The Genius Bar looked at it and said, "Oh, my gosh." And she was almost three weeks out of warranty. And they said, "You know what?

It needs a new hard drive. The hard drive is gone. This happens. And let us order one. They're usually 200 and some-odd dollars. But what we'll do is take $100 off for you."

So there's this tremendous sense of reciprocity that's built, that they do something for me, I owe them something. And it really invoked this spirit of generosity. And my understanding is it's like a slot machine. Sometimes they charge, sometimes they don't, depending upon how busy they are, and it's at the discretion of the individual.

Now, Robert Stephens, the founder of the Geek Squad, sold it to . . .

Bob: . . . Best Buy.

Lou: Best Buy. Best Buy has taken that concept and, prior to Best Buy's taking the company and the concept, you would be able to go in and get advice, and these geeks were phenomenal. You really trusted them.

Bob: They were actual geeks.

Lou: They were real geeks, and there was real passion. And all of a sudden, Best Buy takes the company and starts instituting some elements of its culture into the company. Suddenly, it's almost like greed and avarice in terms of who's in charge. So I bring to the Geek Squad a computer that's still under warranty.

Bob: OK.

Lou: A Sony VAIO. They look at the computer. And the first thing they hit me with is, "There is no diagnostic charge because it's under warranty. But we would recommend that you back everything up, and that's going to cost $120."

Bob: [laughs] Yeah.

Lou: "Let's proceed." Then they take it and they look at it, and it's going to have to be there for a week and a half. And I get a phone call, after about four days, asking me for my code number or my password. I give them the password. Another week passes. They call and they say, "We can't really recreate the problem you're having and think it's a software problem." And I said, "It's saying that it doesn't see that the device," which is a phone device on the phone. It's like a cellular link.

It's showing that there's no device. And I said, "The device is either not working or there's something wrong. And I've got this warranty that I've paid for, an additional $300 on top of the cost of the computer. I expect you to figure out what's wrong." So they look at it, and they say, "Well, we just recommend reinstalling everything . . . "

Bob: Oh, yeah. I've heard that one before, too.

Lou: "And we'll start all over again." And they send it to Geek City, down in Memphis or wherever, and it's there for however long. And it comes back, and they couldn't get it fixed, and they said it was a software problem.

Bob: [laughs] Yeah. That's been the type of experience that I think everybody in this business has had. And as I'm listening to you . . .

Lou: How does one cause me to feel, versus how the other one causes me to feel?

Bob: Yeah. One makes you feel great. The other makes you feel like something you should wipe off the bottom of your shoe.

Lou: Exactly. They made me feel like crap, like I was like gum. They wanted to get rid of me. They wanted to make money off of me. And I know that Robert Stephens, the founder of the company; these are not the founding principles that he started the company on. But I know that it's basically corporate stuff that causes, "Oh, my God! We can get bigger margins! Look at what it's costing us to do this and that!" Because they are looking at the experience in parts rather than looking at it holistically, whereas what you have at Apple is a holistic view of the customer experience.

Customer Experience, Step by Step

Bob: Walk me through the steps. I realize that this may be a case of describing music to someone who can't hear, but walk me through the steps of how a startup CEO should look at their offering and try and understand what people feel about it.

Lou: I think that it comes down to a very simple premise, which is really listening for what is buried in conversation. And often, when we do market research or usability studies, we tend to look for customers' opinions. And opinions are the intellectual alibis and rationalizations and justifications that we create for deeper feelings that we have. So what we end up doing is committing one of two mistakes. We either take everything at face value, or we have a set of prescribed questions that we want to ask because we think that they're important questions.

And what I would encourage someone to do that's starting a company is to have someone experience their experience and then just ask them, "Well, how does the experience feel to you?" And you listen for the next hour to hour and a half, just pressing down, asking, and following them where they go in the storytelling, where they go in the discussion, and asking them why. It's almost like conducting a psychological . . . [laughs] I don't like the color red. "Oh, really? That's interesting. Tell me more about that." Well, red represents . . .

Bob: . . . makes me angry. [laughs]

Lou: Yeah, makes me angry and makes me see flames. "Well, tell me more about flames. What do flames do?" Oh, flames destroy things. Flames release energy. "Tell me more about releasing energy." [laughs]

Bob: Just to follow up on that metaphor for a moment: If you're doing research, one of the things you want to try and do is get some sort of consensus on what people think. That stuff seems pretty touchy-feely, pretty hard to quantify. If you do that with one person, that person may hate red. If you do it with another person, that individual may love red. How do you deal with that issue of human nature?

Lou: You actually transcribe all of the interviews. And then you begin to look for patterns and doing phrase searches. There's actually a technique that we've used quite a bit, called ZMET, which is examining metaphors that appear in the language that people use to understand how they frame their thoughts and feelings. So I think that as we've evolved into a whole new world, the need to look at different ways of creating value than we have in the past, and especially in the development of software, we need to go beyond looking at usability and functionality, to the effect that it has on people. That's where the ultimate value is created, in the effect that it has on us. That resides deep in our unconscious thoughts, shapes our attitudes, and drives our behaviors.

Let's look at Intuit, for example. And I used Intuit many, many years ago and kind of outgrew Intuit over the years. And I don't know what Intuit does any longer. I lost interest, because what it represented to me was a move beyond . . . I think the first PC I had was the most expensive check register I ever owned.

Bob: Yeah.

Lou: And I'd moved from that to Intuit, which moved me to a new place. And then somehow they lost me. And I think that the reason that they lost me was they really didn't understand the bigger picture. They understood the functionality of what I had to do but not the emotional pressure that's created around when I need to sit down and do bills. It's the motivation to sit down and do them, and get it out of the way, and how I feel after it's out of the way, versus how easy it is. Ease and functionality are important. But they never relieved my largest pressure. So suddenly, my online banking sends me a reminder and actually gives me my balance. And I'm like, "Oh, gosh. I've got *x* amount in there. I should sit down and do bills tonight."

Bob: It's interesting, because one of the startups that I interviewed for this book is the guy who started mint.com, which is an online alternative to Intuit's basic consumer offerings. And he talked a lot about exactly what you're talking about and how he decided that he was just going to create something that didn't make people feel that way anymore.

Lou: Exactly. That I have a feeling of inadequacy that Intuit doesn't help me with. And it's the inadequacy built around the discipline of sitting down, because I don't like parting with cash. [laughs] No one does.

Being Your Customer's Protector

Bob: Any final advice for startups?

Lou: Someone has to be the vanguard and protector of alignment around the experience that we want to create. So we need to determine (a) what it is that the customer desires feeling and (b) our commitment to creating that feeling and then the alignment of every element of the experience, to reinforce that feeling. And, to me, that's what Steve Jobs does. That's why, so often, companies like that, they're companies that are referred to in a book called *Firms of Endearment*, which are companies that, if they went away tomorrow, we as customers would mourn their loss.

And what he has done is really managed to be that protector, that guardian. Now, in the absence of a Steve Jobs, you need to set up a system that creates that discipline. And that's what we talk about when we talk about experience engineering. It's an experience management system in the absence of or to augment a very, very visionary, very demanding leader, which Steve Jobs is and Walt Disney was.

But it's that thread that I studied in my initial work, many, many years ago in looking at Disney. And I see huge parallels at Apple, and it's why people are worried about Steve Jobs' health. And I would say that for any person who is gifted in this regard or a person who tries to create a system that is in the startup company, the big thing is to create a system that does that—whether it's through a strong leader, whether it's through an experienced management system that's built, that operates even in the absence of the strong leader, which is what happened at Disney, where that legacy that he created went on for many, many, many, many years, because the system he built was so strong. It wasn't driven by a person.

And what that system is built around is understanding the deep emotional needs of customers, committing to meeting those deep, emotional needs, and then aligning everything with that. And that, to me, is the ultimate in terms of winning customers' hearts and souls. How they feel about themselves and that experience, they then associate with the brand, which drives loyalty.

Bob: OK, I think that's going to do it.

Guy Kawasaki, Author and Founder, Alltop

Guy Kawasaki (Figure 9-7) is nothing short of a living legend in the software industry. Twenty-five years ago Guy brought the concept of evangelism to the software industry, convincing several hundred new and existing software companies to roll the dice on an untested, radically different computer: the Apple Macintosh. Since then, Guy's been funding, inspiring, and building startups while writing nine books and one of the top 100 blogs (http://blog.guykawasaki.com/) on topics near and dear to hearts of software startups.

Photograph by Bryn Colton / Assignments

Figure 9-7. Guy Kawasaki

His latest book, *Reality Check: The Irreverent Guide to Outsmarting, Outmanaging, and Outmarketing Your Competition* (Portfolio Hardcover, 2008), is must reading for any startup founder. His latest startup, Alltop (`http://alltop.com`), is fast becoming a major Internet destination.

Bob: How has Alltop been able to go from 200,000 unique visits a month to 500,000 unique visits in just 14 month?

Guy: Well, first of all, you could make the case that 14 months is a long time. [laughing] It's not a short time! To answer your question, really what I did is I just used Twitter. I used Twitter to get ideas for Alltop, which topics, what feeds to put into Alltop, and then to promote Alltop. So I don't know how I would have done it without Twitter, frankly.

Bob: That's one hell of a recommendation for a startup that doesn't yet have a revenue model. Would it have been possible to start Alltop before Twitter or without Twitter?

Guy: Started? Yes. Make it successful? Probably not! [laughs] Let's just say it was very fortunate timing that Twitter existed, because prior to Twitter— let's say if I did an Alltop, the best case would be I would just have to keep trying to get bloggers to write about it. Bloggers need some kind of reason to write about something, not that you simply exist. That may be the first story, but never again. So Alltop is a very unusual service, in the sense that we have 600 topics and we release more every day. So we have a constant flow of announcements.

Whereas, if you're writing a spreadsheet, you announce version 1 and then a year later you announce version 2. So you had two press announcements, big press conference, big press release, big press event, et cetera, et cetera.

But Alltop is unlike any other thing. In that 14 months we could have had 600 press kits for 600 different topics, and obviously that wouldn't have worked. So how else could I have got the news out about 600 mini-introductions other than Twitter?

Bob: Has Twitter changed the game as far as startups?

Guy: Yeah, absolutely. Now, obviously if you're a life sciences company and you're making a new kind of stent or if you have a cure for cancer, you're not going to do the marketing on Twitter. But if you have most kinds of consumer-facing products, whether it's a gadget or software or a service, I think you can market it on Twitter. Twitter is basically fast, free, and ubiquitous. What's wrong with this picture? Nothing is wrong with this picture!

Bob: How about the rest of the social media networks out there like Facebook, private networks, and all the other tools. Are they . . . ?

Guy: The only reason I don't mention those things is because I don't know how to use Facebook well. Facebook is sort of focused on more of—it's more of bringing friends to you, whereas Twitter is purely broadcasting and pushing. So it's a different perspective.

Bob: Do you use Twitter to listen to prospective people talking about Alltop?

Guy: Yes. I have 160,000 followers, so I can't just watch the public timeline of my followers. What I do is I have dedicated searches for my name and Alltop. That's the only thing I watch.

Bob: And I take it that would be one of the things you would recommend to a startup as well.

Guy: Yes, absolutely. Yes.

Bob: By the way, what do you think of microISVs, one-person software companies that are self-funded?

Guy: There's nothing wrong with that. We're pretty close to that!

Bob: Well, let me ask you another general question about startups. How do you pick a partner for your startup? How many partners should you think about having?

Guy: Well, I think the ideal number is three. Basically you need someone who can create the thing, someone who can market the thing, and someone who can be the adult and pay the bills and make sure you're not going nuts with expenses and that kind of thing and collect the money.

What's Changed?

Bob: That makes sense as a combination. Let me move on to some of the other aspects of what you do. You have written extensively about what founders need to do to get funding, especially in *Reality Check*, your latest book. Has anything changed, given the global recession we're in right now, forecasted for the next couple of years here?

Guy: Yeah. As a matter of fact, I think a lot has changed. Not just because of the recession, but because of Open Source also. I think before, people had to raise millions of dollars in order to get to version 1. I no longer think that is true. I think because of the relative cheapness of everything in the recession plus Open Source, the expectation is that you show up with a working prototype.

Bob: So that's the first raising of the bar: They have to have more than just an idea or a team. They need a prototype.

Guy: Yes.

Bob: How about revenue?

Guy: You mean for seeking first funding?

Bob: Yeah. Has the bar gone up that high?

Guy: Well, of course it would be nice to be showing revenue already. But probably as important, maybe even more important, is to show that the dogs are eating the food.

Bob: By that you mean . . . ?

Guy: That people are using it, that people are registering, that people are showing up.

Bob: Besides Open Source, besides global recession, what other big changes do you see here?

Guy: That's it. Isn't that enough?

Bob: It probably is. As a founder, when is the right time to sell your startup? And as an investor, when is it the right time to sell? You've been both, first with Truemors and now with Alltop.

Guy: That's a very hard question to answer. I think most people, they sell too late. You of course hear the story that Twitter has been offered X hundreds of millions of dollars, but they're holding out. I think when you come to a point where you're about to make more money than you ever dreamed, you should just sell rather than just try to take every penny off the table.

Bob: Greed is not a good idea?

Guy: I don't know if it's greed. It is maximization.

Bob: OK. About getting that funding: When you're out there as a first-time founder, you have not done this before and you don't have the track record, how important is it to build a network with angel investors and VCs? In other words, is that a must-do, a nice-to-have, or somewhere in between?

Guy: Well, only if you need money. [laughs]

Bob: OK. So I guess that's a yes, it's something you have to do.

Guy: Yeah.

Bob: How do you go about getting the interest of angel investors such as yourself?

Guy: First of all, it's just man-on-man networking. It's also targeting angel investors that make sense. If someone made all of his money in semiconductors, he's probably not going to invest in the next online music site, and vice versa. So some of that is just targeting. And a lot of it is just appealing to the angel investor as a fun person, maybe even a daughter or son substitute. None of that comes into play with venture capital.

I think a lot of angels have the perspective of wanting to pay back society by helping the next generation. And that certainly doesn't exist in the venture capital business!

Bob: So there really is a big difference between angels and even very small investments in VC money.

Guy: Yes. There is a huge difference. Now, it's not always easier, because the angel is also investing his or her after-tax money, whereas a venture capitalist is investing some pension fund's money. It's not really his money, right?

Bob: But the motivations are different, I think, per se.

Guy: Yes. And having said that, I don't think you should think of an angel investor as an easy mark that you can fool and get money from faster and cheaper, et cetera. You should have the same standard of presentation to a VC as to an angel.

Bob: What other mistakes do first-time founders make when it comes to angels?

Guy: Isn't that enough? [laughs]

Bob: It probably is, but I'm curious: Is there a magic formula for a startup to get angel investment?

Guy: Only what we just discussed already.

Recap

So what have we learned in this chapter? And I say *we* because these people have been kind enough to mentor me a bit in my startup efforts as well as sharing with you here.

- From **Dharmesh Shah** we learned two things: First, we had a crash course in what VCs and angel investors want, in case you skipped Chapter 5. Second, and more important, whether you're talking about finding a cofounder or making your first hire, "Just find those practical people that have a passion for building something and pull them in."

- From **Eric Sink** we learned, besides that most of the revenue of a product comes after the developers have lost interest, that "the number one lesson I've learned or the number one thing that has prevented me from destroying my own company is that you have to be self-aware about your limitations." You are not going to be able to do everything. And in terms of your own maturity you need to be at a point in your life when you've learned this, when you aren't threatened into inaction by people who can outdo or outthink you in a given area.

- Two things that **Joel Spolsky** shared with us are especially worth mulling over, besides his withering opinion of Twitter. The single most important thing you must focus on is how to make your software great. All other considerations are side issues. One way to get there is to be the kind of programmer who makes the rest of us look lame and to hire programmers of that same high caliber. Because software development is still more art than science, one programmer can be—and should aspire to be—10 times better than average.

- **Pamela Slim** brought into focus three things. First, if escaping working for someone else isn't a life-changing, life-improving dream in your heart, maybe it's not the right thing for you at this point in your life. Second, the time to begin creating your startup is before, not after, you get laid off or quit your corporate job. And finally, getting your emotional, financial, and human relational house in order is pretty much a prerequisite for the kind of whole-life change that starting a company entails.

- **Lou Carbone** reminded us that the software business, like all businesses, is about people. Your job, as the leader of your company, is to think long and hard about the effect your product and your company has on people. Done right, you build something people care about deeply. Done wrong, and your company will win the contempt and scorn of your customers, not their hearts and minds.

- **Guy Kawasaki** pointed out this is a business that changes constantly. Twitter has gone from online oddity to startup necessity in months, not years; by the time you read this book, something else might have already taken it's place as the latest disruptive technology or at least be waiting in the wings to do so. Your job as a founder is to track, know about, and take advantage of these shifts. And, as Guy pointed out, it's up to you to get out there and do some "man-on-man networking." You've got to get out from behind your computer if your startup is going to succeed.

Now that we've heard from six really smart people, you're nearing the finish line, at least as far as this book is concerned. Next up, a few last bits of advice before you roll up your sleeves and build your startup.

What's Next?

Intro to the Outro

Writing a conclusion for a book like this is both artifice and necessity. It's artifice in that *you* are the one who's going to write the ending of this particular effort; your hard work from here on out will determine the success of your startup. Writing this concluding chapter is a necessity because it's good to finish things. It lets you reflect on what's just happened, what's next, and whether you are still on course.

Let me summarize what I think this book's big takeaways are for startup founders. Then I shall wish you good luck in your startup endeavors before I give you a healthy push out of the nest.

There Have Never Been More Opportunities for a Startup to Succeed

I won't bore you with stories of the bad old days of, say, two years ago, but the fact remains: This is the most favorable period for a startup since this industry began some 40-odd years ago. Some of the reasons are obvious, others less so.

- **The cost barrier to entering the global software market is now a speed bump.** Between cloud platforms, virtualized servers, and instant access to a global market and a world of people who now look to the Internet first for solutions and answers, your startup's cost structure is very different than what necessity demanded even a few years ago.

- **Silicon Valley has spread out.** Gone are the days when would-be startups packed their bags and headed to Silicon Valley like hopeful starlets on their way to Hollywood. You don't need to come to Silicon Valley to be discovered; if you've got something good, the world will come to you. Nor do you need to be in the Valley to find talented programmers and designers; they, too, are a click away.

- **Startups are a market too, and that's a very good thing.** The growth of startups from the dark days of the dot-com bust at the beginning of this century has, among other things, created a market, and other startups and companies are happily making money selling to that market the tools and services that startups require. Need another dozen servers? Amazon E2C is a click away. Want to use social networking to get the word out? Take your pick from hundreds of consultants who know their stuff. Need to staff up? Take your pick of Web 2.0 apps designed to make it easy for a startup to do just that.

- **Small is trustworthy.** The thrashing that the global economy has taken has also proven to be a trashing of the reputations of big institutions. Big is about as fashionable now as a Hummer 3 bought via a credit card backed by a home equity loan. Part of this is the next phase of moving from an industrial world of big to a postindustrial world of small; part of it is a series of economic events that have shown over and over that large isn't necessarily smart. SaaS and mobile startups in particular have benefited from this change in attitude on the part of the buying business and consumer public.

- **Crisis is opportunity, scary as hell opportunity, but opportunity nonetheless.** Stability may make it easier to sleep at night, but it makes for few opportunities for entrepreneurs. Between the still-accelerating rate of change and a global economic system that's anything but stable, there are huge classes of new problems, needs, and wants looking for startups to address.

The Quality of the Idea Behind Your Startup's Product or Service Is Paramount

One theme you've heard over and over in this book—from startups up the road from you to industry veterans to the money guys—it all ignites with a really good idea. You can go through all the motions of creating a startup, but if a really good idea is not at its core, you're not going to get the attention, effort, or money it takes to succeed.

The days of (relatively) easy money for "me too!" startups ended in the fourth quarter of 2008. The core proposition of your startup has to got to have real intrinsic value, whether it's SaaS enterprise software or a new fitness iPhone app. Doing what everyone else has done isn't enough in a world where everyone knows the available solutions to a problem—or can within a few minutes via Google.

You don't have to discover antigravity—although that would be nice—but you do have to envision and then execute the delivery of real value to real people, not hypothetical "everyone who uses a PC" markets, which brings us to our next point.

Your Idea Has to Hold Real Appeal to at Least One Specific Market Segment

If you look at the startups in this book, you'll notice that one of the things they have in common is a crystal-clear idea of exactly who their market is: none of this "everyone with a mobile phone," "all Mac users," "small, medium, and enterprise businesses" stuff.

More often than not, the startups that succeed are the ones that obsess over who their customers are and what those customers want. Whether it's Aaron Patzer of mint.com understanding that people are tired of acting like bookkeepers or Adam Wiggins of Heroku focusing on Rails developers tired of acting like system administrators, these people base their coding and business decisions on what their intended customers want, and everything else is secondary.

And it's not enough to "be in the mobile game space" or to "address the CMS market"; that's double-talk. The market segment you need to do the work and spend the time to find—ideally before you write your first line of code—is going to be defined by a combination of who they are, how they see the world, what problems they face, and what they struggle with when they get up and go to work each day. They are going to represent a tiny sliver of a market or industry that is really going to love your new app.

I think Tony Wright of RescueTime put it best: "The idea there is that once you find the heart of people who are madly in love with what you are doing, to get bigger and more successful as a startup, all you need to do is find more people like that or move laterally to serve a slightly different type of audience." That's doable. Making something that a lot of people are only mildly interested in is a dead end.

Serious Value + Great Customer Experience Means You Get Taken Seriously

So you find your starter market segment. What's next? Next you deliver some serious value. That means you create a tool, a service, or an app that has some significant worth to that market segment. The more value you deliver to your customers, be it the quality of the ideas and design that go into the product or how well your startup executes the entire customer experience, the more your startup is going to be worth.

Note that proviso—having a great product with lousy customer support means you've missed the point. As Lou Carbone talked about in Chapter 9, delivering a great product is the start of the process; as the founder of your company, you (even if you are the company) need to be thinking about what your customers are experiencing from the moment they step through your online door.

If You Play by Everyone Else's Rules, You Lose

Let's step back a minute. What advantage do you have over all the established companies who are after the same customers you want? Besides looks, charm, and obvious keen intellect (you bought this book, after all), as a startup you have the decided advantage that you can pick the platform or combination of platforms on which to build your startup, and your established competitors can't.

Disruption is the name of the game you want to play, because then you get to write the rules, and the rules say you win and they lose. Let me pick on Aaron Patzer and mint.com one last time, because they're a shining example of how to rewrite the rules of the game.

It's no secret that Intuit has owned the consumer financial software market for the past decade. Despite Microsoft's best efforts—including even trying to buy Intuit outright—Intuit has maintained a huge market share. For example, QuickBooks small business accounting application had an overwhelming 74% market share at retail and 3 million customers as of 2005.[1] Now, Aaron could have gone toe to toe on Intuit's home platform—the desktop—and joined countless other startups who've tried

---

[1] http://www.businessweek.com/technology/content/aug2005/
tc20050825_8432_tc024.htm?chan=sb

that and failed. Instead, he went after a new generation of young Internet-centric users, a market and a platform Intuit does not dominate.

Has this strategy paid off? Well, in February 2009, "Intuit . . . can't believe how well its competitor Mint is doing. In fact, they were so bewildered by Mint's claims of gaining 3,000 new users a day and jumping from 600,000 to 850,000 users in a matter of months that they decided to send a threatening letter demanding an explanation for this apparently inconceivable feat" (*TechCrunch*, "Quicken Online Can't Believe Mint Is Doing So Well; Sends Threatening Letter"). Does that sound like a disconcerted competitor to you? It does to me.

A whole generation of client-server, barely webified vertical market applications are out there—literally tens of thousands—that are going to be equally disconcerted, as today's crop of startups offer SaaS, PaaS, mobile, cross-platform solutions that run rings around formerly successful software. Taking the time and doing the hard mental work of understanding what platform or platforms you're going to use in your startup is a key step to rearranging the rules in your favor.

Social Networks Are Key to Your Success

Now, for some of you this is so "Duh!" that you might wonder why I'm stressing it in these final pages. It's because not everybody's gotten the message. Again, you see people in this business taking one side or the other: "Twitter and Facebook and the rest are just noise factories" vs. "We've got 3,000 followers on Twitter—woot!"

In Chapter 6 we covered how this idea of groups of people actually interacting with each other electronically went from geek plaything to groups of people the size of countries all connecting and conversing, but let me rehash just a few stats here:

- Of all U.S. broadband users (105 million), 76% are active contributors to the web via social media (including uploading photos, blogging, rating products, and other Web 2.0 activities).[2]

- Moreover, approximately 29%, or 40 million broadband users, are regular contributors to the Web specifically through social networking sites and are spending increasing amounts of their online time communicating with each other, both one-to-one and one-to-many.[3]

---

[2] *http://www.netpopresearch.com/node/26554*

[3] [3] *http://www.netpopresearch.com/node/26554*

- Facebook in early 2009 had 150 million users, about half of whom use Facebook every day.

- Hi5 has 60 million users.

- MySpace has 76 million users.[4]

Let's leave aside that social network attention is like oxygen to startups, or how buzz on Twitter about a startup, magnified via the online trade press, opens funding doors undreamed of. Let's just talk numbers here. Social networks have become too big for any sane company, especially a startup, to ignore. For startups in particular, finding the right ways, venues, and approach to being part of the online conversation is now as important as developing the solution, and this is edging out/replacing/morphing "marketing."

So what's your social network plan? Are you or one of your partners wearing the hat of community manager? These are key questions to ask—and answer—if you're going to succeed.

Have a Plan to Get Through the Bootstrap Valley of Death

Speaking of plans, if you're creating your first startup while you're consulting on the side or working for a living, you'd better have a plan for making it through what I call the Bootstrap Valley of Death. We touched on this in Chapter 5 and especially in Chapter 8, but it bares repeating as we wrap up: You need a plan to bootstrap successfully.

Again, this is not the traditional "business plan" for drumming up VC funding; it's how on earth *you* are going to manage *you* to get out the smallest acceptable selling app or service in a survivable length of time. Yes, you need to think about money. But money is not the only resource you have to manage and plan; everyone has a limit to how long he or she can push to turn a vision into reality. Upfront planning means you're going to be dead serious about how to get this job done. Not planning means your fate is at best in the lap of the gods.

---

[4] *A Collection of Social Network Stats for 2009—Jeremiah Owyang, Senior Analyst at Forrester Research: Social Computing.*

Money Is the Lifeblood of Startups— Manage It Well

OK, so you've mapped out your startup plan, and you know you're going to have to spend or offset X amount to get to a prototype, Y to get to your first sale, and Z to grow like crazy. How do you get that money? As covered in Chapter 5, you'll need to start with the person you see every day in the mirror.

As we learned from the angel investors and venture capitalists in Chapter 5 and elsewhere, gone are the days when "give us money and we'll build the next Google" worked. If you're going to pry money from people other than family, friends, and fools, you're going to have to demonstrate at the least a hell of a good prototype with all those nasty technical issues solved.

Moreover, if you would still like to have some control over the fate of your startup after you go for equity funding, you'd better be well read in, not just the coverage given that world in this book, but how the game is being played and by whom as of right now. It's more than knowing what a term sheet is; it's doing the research, reaching out to other startups who've played the game, finding mentors, and knowing exactly what the stakes are.

Good startups will attract and find investors, in even the toughest of economic times. But you'd better know the rules of the game, today, and those rules get made by the people with the money.

One Final Bit of Advice

So here we are. If I've done my job right, you should now have a much better idea of what it takes to go from being a developer to being a founder. Here, then, is one last bit of advice from me—and, I'd like to believe, from just about every other developer who has taken the road you want to walk.

It's fine to change your product, adjust your market position, restate your message, adapt to what your market tells you—odds are good you'll do all those things and more as you work you're butt off finding the right combination of moving parts that, like a superconductor magnet, attract attention, money, and value to your startup. Flexibility is the middle name of every successful startup in this business. Just as long as you never, never, never, never give up. **If you don't give up, you're going to succeed. It's just that simple.**

Thanks for reading my book. Please feel free to e-mail me at bob. walsh@47hats.com or to stop by StartupToDo.com and let me know how you're doing.

Index

You Need the Companion eBook

Your purchase of this book entitles you to buy the companion PDF-version eBook for only $10. Take the weightless companion with you anywhere.

We believe this Apress title will prove so indispensable that you'll want to carry it with you everywhere, which is why we are offering the companion eBook (in PDF format) for $10 to customers who purchase this book now. Convenient and fully searchable, the PDF version of any content-rich, page-heavy Apress book makes a valuable addition to your programming library. You can easily find and copy code—or perform examples by quickly toggling between instructions and the application. Even simultaneously tackling a donut, diet soda, and complex code becomes simplified with hands-free eBooks!

Once you purchase your book, getting the $10 companion eBook is simple:

❶ Visit **www.apress.com/promo/tendollars/**.

❷ Complete a basic registration form to receive a randomly generated question about this title.

❸ Answer the question correctly in 60 seconds, and you will receive a promotional code to redeem for the $10.00 eBook.

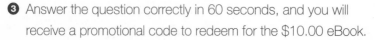

2855 TELEGRAPH AVENUE | SUITE 600 | BERKELEY, CA 94705

Offer valid through 11/09.